When Capitalists Collide

When Capitalists Collide

Business Conflict and the End of Empire in Egypt

Robert Vitalis

UNIVERSITY OF CALIFORNIA PRESS

Berkeley / Los Angeles / London

University of California Press
Berkeley and Los Angeles, California

University of California Press, Ltd.
London, England

© 1995 by
The Regents of the University of California

Library of Congress Cataloging-in-Publication Data

Vitalis, Robert, 1955
   When capitalists collide : business conflict and the end of empire in
Egypt / Robert Vitalis.
      p.   cm.
   Includes bibliographical references and index.

   ISBN: 978-0-520-30235-8 (pbk. : alk. paper)

   1. Investments—Egypt—History. 2. Industry and state—Egypt—
History. 3. Egypt—Economic conditions—1918- I. Title.
HG5836.A3V58   1995
332.6'0962—dc20   94-16550

for Betty and Tony

Contents

Tables

Preface

What do capitalists do and what should they do? These questions are critical to comparative political economy of development and, even more so, to the lives of millions in Asia, Africa, and Latin America. The answers to these questions are a window to the core assumptions and values that underpinned the insurgent movement in North American social sciences and to the currents—from *dependencia* to dependent development, from structural theories of the state to institutionalist analysis of bargaining, from class conflict to elite pacts—that are the legacy of the anti-imperialist intellectual project of the 1960s. The premise behind this book is that our answers need rethinking, as others in the field seem to recognize (Canack 1984; Block 1987; Evans and Stephens 1988; Haggard 1989; Hawes and Liu 1993). Yet, while the insurgent moment continues to fade into the past and a generation of radical intellectuals matures, ideas about capitalists seem particularly resistant to change.

The problem of national capitalists and capitalisms has never been simply a question for intellectuals to argue about, and adopting the conventional assumptions has at times spelled real disaster. In 1983, I had the opportunity to meet the Argentinean economist Carlos Vilas, who was then an adviser to Nicaragua's revolutionary government. Over dinner, Vilas described the thinking that led to the Sandinistas' land-reform project and, in particular, the idea that the expropriations served the objective interests of the country's industrial bourgeoisie. Vilas and many others believed that once the estates were confiscated, a patriotic national-capital fraction would be inspired to undertake new long term-investments in production. But Nicaraguan investors viewed matters differently from the revolution's theorists, and the outcome, familiar enough to those who know Nicaraguan history or for that matter the Egyptian case and the early history of the July 1952 Revolution, was a costly conflict between investors and the state and a takeover in stages of the economy's commanding heights (Vilas 1986; Colburn 1986).

When Capitalists Collide is a study of the politics of investment conflict. In the 1930s and 1940s, representatives of some of the world's largest and most powerful firms in industry's leading sectors were drawn to Egypt and, together with local investors, engaged in a long, protracted and costly competition for the contracting and concession rights to build power plants and develop the country's chemical industry. The massive archival record that exists of these projects, an artifact of Egypt's equally protracted process of decolonization, provides a rare, deep, sustained and detailed view of the objectives, capacities and political strategies of both the international firms and, even more valuably, of Egypt's local big-business rivals.

The archives supply the most striking confirmation to date of Evans's proposal in *Dependent Development* that, in focusing "on the power of the multinationals," we have ignored the "power, the bargaining leverage, alliances" and other strategies "of local capital" (1979: 41). I trace the leverage-enhancing alliance strategies of a "business group" headed by Ahmad 'Abbud, who in most Egyptian historians' eyes serves as the avatar of a collaborating comprador class fraction. I show how he and other "foreigners and their comprador allies," as Peruvian specialist David Becker (1983: 331) might well have described them, successfully merged their interests in foreign-backed ventures with their interest in local accumulation. And pushing the premises of the dependent-development debate, I argue that the politics of investment in Egypt was ultimately less a struggle between foreign and local capital than a conflict among local investors for access to resources and control over the rents represented by industry building.

A more thoroughly revisionist or "postcolonial" account of the political economy of investment conflict is long overdue. While I was living in Egypt in the early 1980s, there were few signs that the left had changed its ideas about the nature of the bourgeoisie in thirty years. Thus, the response to a new capitalist cohort's rise out of the shadows of Arab socialism was to tear a page from the historical tracts, updating the caricature of the comprador class as a parasitic bourgeoisie whose objectives were allegedly to shun productive investment, consort with the American mission and undermine the project of a mythical, patriotic national-capital fraction. One investor, 'Uthman Ahmad 'Uthman, a confidant of Sadat's whose construction firm's logo seemed to frame virtually every large-scale Egyptian skyscraper, roadway and factory site in the late 1970s, followed in the footsteps of 'Abbud to become the symbol of a new parasitic class (Waterbury 1983; Springborg 1989 and 1993; Sadowski 1991). More than once in my conversations with intellectuals they insisted that 'Uthman was acting as a front man for Israeli interests in Egypt!

By the late 1980s, the more zealous of the Reagan-era political appointees and a new generation of development technicians who arrived in Cairo with de Soto's *The Other Path* (1989) packed in their bags were drawing conclusions about 'Uthman and his cohort that betrayed a romanticism, in this case about entrepreneurs, that was hardly less misty-eyed than the left's saga of national capital. For Americans, the problem with 'Uthman was his too cozy relationship to the bloated Egyptian state and the rent seeking that ostensibly had come to stifle and replace the private initiative of an earlier free-enterprise era; for the left, the state and, in particular, the public-enterprise sector protected the nation from a collusive antinational alliance of foreign and local capital.

Yet, as this book details, it was local investors' access to these two forces—the state and foreign capital—that made possible in the first half of the twentieth century the creation of the private enterprises and national industries—airlines, shipping lines, chemical plants, agroindustries, spinning mills—that form the core of Egypt's embattled public sector today. And the patterns of collusion and conflict that characterize present-day relations between Egyptian capitalists and their ambivalent allies within the state and the international business community underlie each successive phase in the "discontinuous evolution" of capitalist institutions and production relations in Egypt (Bianchi 1985: 153).

The fears of foreign domination that retain so much power in contemporary Egyptian popular culture today are perhaps understandable given the relatively enduring consequences of an original massive transfer of resources engineered by British colonial officials in the late 1800s and delivered to the giants of European finance and their local, predominantly non-Egyptian partners.[1] But in the early decades of the twentieth century the resources of the state—subsidies, tax exemptions, property, law, coercive force—were increasingly captured by a new, rising cohort of Egyptian investors competing for control over production and distribution of goods and services.

For a generation prior to the national revolution of 1919, local foreign and ethnic-minority investors served as junior partners for dominant sectors in the advanced economies of Britain and, to a lesser extent, France and Belgium. These joint ventures were one of the main sources of accumulation for domestic business interests, permitting them gradually to expand their field of activities. A limited industrialization program advocated by leading business elites in Egypt at the end of World War I rested on a new round of collaboration between local and foreign interests. Who would finance infrastructure development, including electrification? How would Egyptians obtain machinery and other capital goods? Where would the local capitalists find the engineering services and technology for ventures like the proposed chemical industry?

Industrial policy in the "liberal era" (1922–1952) was synonymous with power politics. The state played a specific role in the expansion of the country's capitalist sectors. Britain's unilateral grant of Egyptian "independence" in 1922 and introduction of a constitution in 1923 resulted in the fracturing of the state executive. In the place of a single agency ruling Egypt three executive agencies—the British residency, the palace and the cabinet—contested for control and reduced the state's capacity to coordinate policy. At the same time the administrative agencies of the state began a new period of growth marked by the hastened pace of Egyptianization of the bureaucracy.

Egyptianization had two facets. As is commonly recognized, the bureaucracy was rapidly politicized. For the first time, party politics intruded on the civil service, producing great turnovers of personnel with every change in government. Perhaps less recognized, the bureaucracy was also rapidly "colonized" by family and other networks that had established ties to investors or sought to forge them. This particular route from government office to company boardroom was well marked. British officials charged with the public trust in the 1870s and 1880s pioneered this route to private wealth in Egypt's corporate sector. With independence, the circles of public-private collusion were widened to include Egyptians.

These are important factors in understanding the politics behind the competition for electrification contracts and related business in state building and infrastructure and industrial development that engaged local investors and foreign capital in Egypt in the 1920s and beyond. These industrial schemes were at the intersection of changes taking place in society as well as in the state. In particular, the years immediately after independence coincided with the efforts of Egyptian nationals to join the ranks of the business community, often through privileged access to the politicians in control of contracts or other subsidies. Conflicts in this period reflected the emergence of new and competing Egyptian business interests.

This early phase in the country's ongoing effort to develop adequate energy resources likewise stood at the intersection of changes taking place in both the domestic and the international economy. The aggressive promotion of projects like the Aswan power scheme reflected the dawning recognition that Egypt had entered the industrial era. Electricity was needed to power cities and industries. At the same time, the promotion of Egyptian development reflected the increasing competition for markets among the world's major heavy-electrical-equipment manufacturers. Complicated intraindustry arrangements had closed off the producers' home markets to one another and drove them to redouble their efforts to sell abroad. In this case selling abroad meant developing Egypt's power resources. Battles were waged by the international firms and their local business allies for state sanction and resources to electrify Egypt.

Structural political and economic changes combined to create conditions that permitted local Egyptian business interests to extend their activities into the creation of local industry. These conditions included an increasingly competitive international market; the emergence of new, leading industrial sectors in the advanced industrial nations; and the relatively rapid decline of Britain's hold on the levers of the Egyptian state. The bargaining that took place between 1922 and 1952 resulted in new national ventures in shipping, aviation, chemicals, mining, food processing, agroindustry, pharmaceuticals, textiles and electrical goods, among other enterprises.

Until now, the politics underlying this formative era in Egypt's industrialization have been understood primarily as a conflict between local and foreign capital for dominance in the country's expanding industrial sectors. I argue that they are better understood as Egyptian investor coalitions competing for leading positions in new ventures and new sectors. Investors viewed the market in zero-sum terms, leaving little room for concord and coordination. Competition for the resources necessary to build industry proved fierce.

This study will explore the intimate connection between rent seeking and politics in colonial and postcolonial Egypt. Part I argues for a new approach to understanding how capitalists organized and acted in the local political economy. In Chapter 1 I develop a critique of conventional views of the dilemmas facing Egypt's so-called emerging national bourgeoisie and begin to outline an alternative view of the capacities, objectives and political strategies of Egyptian investors. In Chapter 2, I trace the development of investor coalitions or business groups, a basic institution of the private market-oriented economy created under colonialism, focusing in particular on the Egyptian capitalists who adopted this form of organization in the 1920s. The discussion centers on the 'Abbud Pasha group, which eventually spanned construction, trade, banking, shipping, urban transport, real estate, textiles, agroindustry, tourism and chemical manufacturing.

Part Two of the study argues for a new understanding of the political economy in the decades after World War I, which has come to be seen as a period in which British power was used to construct a neocolonial economic regime. I argue instead that this effort failed, and I analyze the circumstances that permitted Egyptian capitalists to undermine the neocolonial project. Chapter 3 recounts the strategies employed by rival Egyptian investor coalitions in the electrification schemes of the 1920s and 1930s. Chapter 4 focuses on the 'Abbud group's attempt during World War II to become the key force in Egypt's industrial sector as a whole.

Part Three argues for a new conceptualization of Egyptian capitalists and their relations to the postcolonial state. In Chapter 5, I analyze the strategies employed by capitalists to blunt new state regulatory agencies and rationales. The vehicle for doing so was the country's main political party, the Wafd, which was dominated by a bloc of landlord-industrialists. In Chapter 6, I look at the response of competing investors to the escalating political crisis of the postwar years, the coup d'état of July 1952 and the consolidation of military authoritarian rule. The origins of etatism in Egypt are found in the years 1954–1955 as Nasser and his allies began to engineer the downfall of the business oligarchs who governed the economy and the takeover of the investment groups that they had built over the previous three decades.

There were only limited places for the old capitalists in the new order. In the 1960s, the regime built a statue to honor one Egyptian businessman: Tal'at Harb, the founder of the Misr group who had died in World War II after driving his bank holding company into receivership. The more successful of Harb's competitors have not been accorded similar honors. The Misr group's main rival, the investment complex headed by Ahmad 'Abbud, is unknown by most, still reviled by a few. One of the only signs of his impact on the twentieth-century Egyptian political economy is a set of dusty, hard-to-read plaques listing the names of his various holdings in sugar, shipping, construction, hotels and chemicals. These are fastened to the wall of an office bloc in downtown Cairo named the Immobilia Building. The city's largest commercial real estate venture of the 1930s is now a slowly decaying monument to 'Abbud's business empire.

This book completes a research project started in the summer of 1984, when I first looked at U.S. State Department records on Egyptian industrialization projects. The prominence accorded 'Abbud and his role in the key political events of the 1930s was jarring to someone who had absorbed the growing collection of histories and specialized monographs on Egypt's political economy, in terms both of the conventional view of 'Abbud as a comprador and of Egyptian capitalists generally as a class or class segment allegedly incapable of promoting its interests. My investment of time in the archives led me eventually to turn away from these ideas and concentrate on what capitalists were doing in Egypt rather than explaining what they ostensibly had failed to do.

Analysts conventionally exercise the privilege of erasing themselves from the genealogies of historiography and theory that are called into question by a new interpretation, formulation, argument or narrative. But, in this case, writing *When Capitalists Collide* has been an exercise in trying to understand my own intellectual relationship to third worldism (Harris 1987). As such, this book documents one North American student's turn away from political economy conceived primarily as anti-imperialist theory and history written from a point balanced unsteadily between objective laws of material development and solidarity with the nationalist project. Worse, perhaps, here is another foreigner, and a Greek(-American) no less, exploiting Egypt's historical resources for his own interests—in this case, investment in an academic enterprise whose product is contained here. The gains remains to be determined.

Readers skeptical of my conclusions will still find the most detailed account to date of economic intervention and interest conflict in the decades after independence: how British officials pursued their neocolonial project, how foreign investors organized, and how 'Abbud, Harb and other Egyptian capitalists managed to extract maximum advantage from the political, material and ideological resources at their disposal.

Those who take the arguments seriously will have to revise, alter and sharpen their critiques of locally domiciled minority (e.g., Greek, Jewish, Syrian, British) investors who saw their own industrialization project and strategies adapted by a cohort of Egyptian business oligarchs who then eclipsed the "Levantines" as a leading force in the rent seeking that underpinned industry building in Egypt—if not rapidly or thoroughly enough for some. And those who understand the objectives, bargaining strategies and capacities of state builders like Nasser in dealing with foreign firms will appreciate the similar dilemmas and opportunities in the path of local Egyptian investors, then and now.

A few may, like myself, conclude that the existing canon unreasonably denigrates the prodigious abilities of these pioneer Egyptian capitalists who theorists such as Frantz Fanon likened to brothel owners when comparing the national bourgeoisie of the South to its (mythical) Western counterpart. Other critics of capitalism should find that there is no longer a need to indict local investors in particular for exercising the privileges that are inherent in capitalist production relations. At the same time, I have begun to appreciate anew the capacities of other Egyptians to challenge these effects. After all, the organization of production and distribution of power and privilege in Egypt today bear faint resemblance to the political-economic order sought by Harb, 'Abbud and the other business oligarchs.

Numerous people and institutions are implicated in the writing of *When Capitalists Collide*. First and foremost, I need to thank those who facilitated my rent seeking: the American Research Center in Egypt, the Friends of Carrol Wilson at the Massachusetts Institute of Technology, the Truman Library, the Department of Government and the Center for Middle East Studies at the University of Texas at Austin, the LBJ School of Public Policy, the Social Science Research Council and Clark University. Numerous organizations in Cairo generously allowed me access to their records, including the National Library, the National Archives, the American University in Cairo, the *al-Ahram* Center and *al-Ahram al-Iqtisadi*, the *al-Akhbar* newspaper, the Center for Political Economy, the Engineering Society and the Ministries of Irrigation

(Water Research Center) and Public Works. At the Middle East Centre of St. Antony's College in Oxford, Sir Miles Lampson's unpublished diaries were a gold mine on the political economy that I plundered for days.

Second, the intellectual powers of a long list of colleagues, comrades and critics were exploited even more shamelessly. I am happy to acknowledge the contributions of Lisa Anderson, L. Carl Brown, Nathan Brown, Kiren Chaudhry, Joshua Cohen, David Gibbs, Joel Gordon, Deborah Harrold, Clem Henry, Jim Henson, Steve Heydemann, Caglar Keyder, Issam al-Khafaji, Philip Khoury, Atul Kohli, Vickie Langohr, Afaf Marsot, Joel Migdal, Tim Mitchell, Roger Owen, Sevket Pamuk, Marsha Posusney, Gretchen Ritter, Samer Shehata, Marc Steinberg, Bob Tignor, Peter Trubowitz, David Waldner, Gabriel Warburg and John Waterbury. Bob Bianchi and Walid Kazziha started me on this project, and Tom Ferguson admonished me to get the documents. At the end of it, Joel Beinin and Ellis Goldberg were instantly available by the Internet to help see a better book through to completion.

Third, my debt to Catherine Boone and Zachary Lockman grew intractable long ago, and yet they allow it to keep multiplying. They remain the most tolerant critics of and unceasing influences on virtually every page of every draft of this study. The only way I can think to repay Zach in particular is to try to be as generous in the future as he has been with me and the dozens of others of students with whom he has shared his passion for Egyptian history.

Fourth, Maggie Browning has had nothing to do with the writing of this book, nor is she likely to read it, but she is nonetheless vital to a larger project of which the book is one small part, and I am forever grateful.

Finally, without Chet Baker, Juliana Hatfield, J Mascis, Lou Reed, Lucinda Williams and Neil Young to listen to, writing *When Capitalists Collide* would not have been as much fun.

Note on Sources, Citations and Transliterations

I have adopted a composite system for citing sources in this book. Archival sources, which are mainly declassified files from U.S. and British government agencies, private papers, together with interview transcripts, are cited in full in all notes, following standard practice by historians. All other sources are cited both in the text and in the notes in the abbreviated author-date format now common in the social sciences. Arabic works are cited according to the author's full name, as normally found in Arabic references (e.g., 'Abd al-'Azim Ramadan rather than Ramadan). The References includes a general description of the archives consulted and the full citations of all secondary works.

All Arabic sources are transliterated following the *International Journal of Middle East Studies* but omitting most diacritics, ayn (') and hamza (') excepted. Place names and names of persons commonly referenced in English language texts are not transliterated (e.g., Cairo and not al-Kahira, Gamal Abdel Nasser rather than Jamal 'Abd al-Nasir).

PART ONE

Capitalists and Politics
in Egypt

CHAPTER ONE

Divided Rule

*The Politics of Business-Group Conflict
and Collaboration*

> *For all the talk and all the public curiosity about the
> relations between business and politics, there is a
> remarkable dearth of studies on the subject. . . . One
> would suppose that the role of business, particularly big
> business, in the political system would be a matter of
> central concern to political scientists.*
>
> Robert Dahl (1959: 3)

> *Nor does anyone write a book on the making of the
> bourgeoisie; rather they write books on* "les bourgeois
> conquérants". *It is as though the bourgeoisie were
> a given, and therefore acted upon others: upon the
> aristocracy, upon the state, upon the workers. It seems
> not to have origins, but to emerge full grown out
> of the head of Zeus. . . . An analysis of the historical
> formation of this bourgeoisie would inevitably place
> in doubt the explanatory coherence of the myth. And
> so it has not been done, or not been done very much.*
>
> Immanuel Wallerstein (1988: 99)

This book attempts to widen the inquiry into business
and politics in newly industrializing countries beyond the question of
why capitalists there failed to "capture the state" and beyond the rote

responses that are grounded in idealized views of collective action and class formation. The first way this book attempts to widen the inquiry is by focusing more closely than is common in comparative politics or political economy on investors as economic and political agents and, in this case, on the specific institutions or arenas in post–World War I Egypt that shaped investors' strategies.

The period between 1922 and 1952 was a key era in the "discontinuous evolution" (Bianchi 1985) of Egypt's capitalist class, yet little is known about the role capitalists played in the Egyptian party system. There are no studies of sectoral conflict for these years, and while the event is referenced in virtually every discussion of the period, there is still no study of the making of the famous 1930 tariff law, to cite just one possible example. In sum, there is much to learn about how and why investors in Egypt organized, colluded and clashed in the market, the boardroom and the prime minister's chambers.

The gains, in turn, are precious because others both inside and outside the field of Middle East studies have had limited success so far in investigating the actual politics of investment for any non-Western case. Certainly it is rare, even in studies of the United States, to find the kind of documentation that permits the detailed account of competitive conflicts that forms the core of this case study of Egypt's power and manufacturing sectors. And, crucially in this case, conventions about and models of collective interest and agency that often fill in for detailed knowledge of investment-related political processes turn out to bear little relation to the institutional universe of investors, firms and sectors.

The second way in which this book attempts to expand debate, therefore, is by proposing an alternative to "political class analysis" (Evans and Stephens 1988: 728) of interest conflict and industry building in the developing world. Those who write on Egypt or other cases often make it seem that the paradigmatic macrohistorical account of a native bourgeoisie in an invariably losing confrontation with imperialism and its allies in the primary export sector has a more or less faithful correspondence to the world of capitalists in the periphery, but that world is a different and perhaps more complex one than we have imagined.

The model of interest aggregation and conflict that I develop centers on rival coalitions of local investors, or what are often called business groups. These are families or other communally linked investors, typically, with holdings that span primary, secondary and tertiary economic sectors—that is, they are combination big landlords, bankers and manufacturers. And these groups are typically tied by bonds of mutual dependence, consensus and shared advantage with foreign investors and governing factions. Given the relatively small number of capitalists involved, the concentrated market power represented by their holdings, their sector-spanning leadership positions and their privileged access to state power, I refer to these organized groups collectively as a *business oligarchy*. But it is the conflict among oligarchs that is central to understanding Egypt's early industrial development.

Rival groups of investors and their intensely entrepreneurial leaders competed for the rights and other state resources necessary for the creation and protection of rents in the highly oligopolistic "private market" economy built by the colonial authorities. Decolonization was in turn crucial for the Egyptians' ability to gain control of these rent circuits and, thus, for the initiation of a series of fierce and protracted distributional conflicts that rocked the country's main industrial sectors over the ensuing decades.

As a result, the dynamics of industrialization at a key juncture in Egypt's recent history are more usefully and convincingly understood as the outcome of the war of position among these rival investor coalitions than as a representation of enduring structural features of agrarian society and the dominant hierarchies of the international capitalist system. Put even more plainly, the politics of business and industry building in Egypt can no longer be reduced to the idea of an overarching struggle between imperialism and the nation, and I believe this must be true for other cases of late industrialization as well.

Certainly, from the perspective of a small number of real, rent-seeking oligarchs pursuing a strategy of market avoidance, the industrial polices of interwar Egyptian governments were more successful than others portray them to be. And, in retrospect, capitalist institution building and the expansion of local industries during the eras of effective British sovereignty (1882–1922) and protracted decolonization (1922–1954) look impressive when compared with development in other parts of the former Ottoman Empire or in non–Middle Eastern territories that were then under some form of colonial or semicolonial rule (e.g. Cuba, the Philippines, Indonesia). For instance, local capital in Egypt appears to have evinced a greater degree of internal social and economic differentiation than did the business community in Anatolia/ Turkey during the same period (Pamuk 1988; Kasaba 1988; Keyder 1987 and 1988). Those features of social and economic transformation critical to identification of emerging capitalist sectors in the 1960s and 1970s in parts of postcolonial Africa as well as in neocolonial Central

America and South Asia were unquestionably evident in Egypt decades earlier (Aubey 1969; Swainson 1980; Robison 1986; Lubeck 1987).

As with these other cases, the analysis of capitalist development in Egypt is not generally rooted in such comparisons. Instead, it is based on a historical-comparative paradigm that is in essence a highly stylized account of *the* capitalist development path. Much of what we ostensibly know about capitalists and politics in Egypt is mediated by a set of implicit and generally unexamined beliefs about the bourgeoisie "as a corporate political actor with a collective class interest" (Blackbourn and Eley 1984: 56) and how it somehow forged stable hegemonic systems rule while creating the advanced industrial economies of the United States and Western Europe. Adapting an argument developed by Blackbourn and Eley, I describe the more rigorously analytical (or less triumphantly nationalist) approach to Egyptian political economy analysis as a kind of "colonial exceptionalism."

Colonial Exceptionalism and the National Bourgeoisie

As in other exceptionalist accounts, the story of the emergence of the capitalist mode of production, the formation of classes, the creation of domestic industries and the institutionalization of democratic political arrangements in Egypt is told in terms of, and is measured against, a "classic" course through which capitalism emerged and the bourgeoisie triumphed in Great Britain and France. In Marx and Engel's (1888) evocative account, the bourgeoisie, "wherever it has got the upper hand, has put an end to all feudal, patriarchal, idyllic relations. . . . In one word, it creates a world after its own image." The crucial difference, as formulated in one discussion of the Egyptian case, is that "the Egyptian industrial bourgeoisie never gained an upper hand in the Egyptian political economy" (Tignor 1984: 246). A moment's reflection should lead one to see that the identical claim has been put forward about every country undergoing late industrialization in the twentieth century.

The equally classic accounts of German exceptionalism provide both the idea of the relatively weak bourgeoisie and the narrative of bourgeois failure at the heart of much work in historical-comparative political economy. The incorporation of imperialism into the basic framework coincided with its widespread dissemination and use by historians from Algeria to Zaire in explaining how newly independent or postcolonial societies (should) move through time. A rich series of variations on this basic narrative was invented, debated and reformulated between the 1960s and 1980s as theories of underdevelopment, dependency and dependent development (Evans and Stephens 1988).

The marriage of imperialism theory to exceptionalism—hence, colonial exceptionalism—produced what are essentially historiographies of national-class formation (the rise of the national bourgeoisie in Egypt, Kenya, the Philippines, etc.), including the now familiar reformulations of the relatively-weak-class problem. Thus, in addition to the classic exceptionalist constraint posed by feudalism or feudalization, the national-bourgeois project faced additional obstacles in those instances where imperialism did not simply destroy or somehow act to inhibit the evolution of indigenous capitalist strata (Phillips 1989; Boone 1992).

Explanations for why a relatively weak bourgeoisie in a particular country failed to carry out thoroughgoing liberal and industrial revolutions are varied, but in the Egyptian case it is common to focus on so-called divisions within the bourgeoisie itself, conceived variously in terms of identity ("foreign"), outlook ("compradors"), function ("middlemen") or sectoral location ("agroexport," the "commercial bourgeoisie"). More generally, as in other exceptionalist cases, the analytic terrain of class and politics in Egypt is littered with research results ostensibly showing how and why the national industrial bourgeoisie could or would not act in its own best collective interests or why its economic and political power was never great. But many of these assumptions have to be rethought. In the daily arenas of capitalist collective action—markets, government agencies, party headquarters, cabinet offices—the Egyptian case provides scant evidence to support these pessimistic views.

The centerpiece of both triumphalist (nationalist) and exceptionalist (neomarxist) accounts of Egyptian economic history is the story of Bank Misr and the industrial investment group led by its outspokenly nationalist chairman, Tal'at Harb. As historians of the Egyptian labor movement Beinin and Lockman (1987: 10–11) summarize the story, the Bank Misr group "symbolized the organizational consolidation of an aspiring Egyptian industrial bourgeoisie," which allegedly "took on itself the task of creating a purely Egyptian-owned industrial sector."[1] In broad outline, therefore, analyses of the Egyptian case reflect the general terms of debate in the 1960s and 1970s about local so-called indigenous capital and whether it could develop industry without recourse to foreign collaboration. What is unique about Egypt is that the size of this seemingly national-oriented stratum was so small.

The conundrum for most historians is that the Misr group, like other, less well-regarded investor coalitions, also collaborated with foreign capital in developing Egyptian industries. This investment strategy is interpreted as a failure, ultimately, to carry through with the independent, or national, industrialization project. This failure is in turn conventionally—and, as I argue, incredulously—explained as a series of forced compromises with foreign capital and its local allies, a reluctant capitulation to the superior power of this reactionary capital coalition. These compromises culminate in the Misr group's "entry into joint ventures with British corporations in the later 1930s," at which point "the Misr group ceased to be 'national' in character" (Beinin and Lockman 1987: 10–11).

The origins of the basic narrative can be traced to the radical oppositional currents and discourses of the late 1940s and early 1950s, including the writings of Rashid al-Barrawi and Muhammad Maza 'Ulaysh (1945) and Shudi 'Atiya al-Shafi'i (1957), among others. By the early 1960s, during the era of Arab socialism if not before, concepts such as imperialism, feudalism, comprador and national bourgeoisie had become ruling ideas in governing and intellectual circles inside Egypt. In this period of prolific cultural production and debate, historians such as Ra'uf 'Abbas, 'Abd al-'Azim Ramadan and their followers elaborated and refined what remains until today the basic organizing framework for the history of the Egyptian political economy in the twentieth century.[2] Consciously or not, turn-of-the-century capitalists were constructed as a set of protoetatists who ostensibly prefigure and, by having failed, legitimate what is variously described as Egypt's state socialist or state capitalist-accumulation model under Nasser.

The specific arguments about the rapid rise and fall of national capital in the guise of the Bank Misr group were revisited in the 1970s and 1980s by North American scholars who, in tandem with insurgent intellectuals in other parts of history and the social sciences, pioneered a political-economy approach to Middle Eastern social history. Davis's (1977) Ph.D. dissertation, "Bank Misr and the Political Economy of Industrialization in Egypt, 1920–1941," which was published under the title *Challenging Colonialism* (1983), framed the study of the Misr group as a critique of "simple dependency models"—that is, the rise and alleged decline of Bank Misr attested to the possibility of an indigenous or national industrialization project under certain conditions, even if in this case Bank Misr failed to free Egypt from foreign economic control.

Again, consciously or not, the contribution by a small group of American scholars to Egyptian social history at this juncture was nothing less than a defense of the Nasserist accumulation model, which by the 1970s was under challenge, or so it seemed, from a resurgent comprador coalition of merchants and multinationals, supported now by U.S. rather than British power. Thus, the idea of an earlier, fleeting moment for national capital in Egypt received new intellectual buttressing even as the same kinds of arguments had come under decisive criticism in the latest round of neomarxist political-economy studies of Africa and Latin America. In successive iterations of the dependency debate, prospects in at least some countries and regions for realizing key parts of the national-bourgeois project (e.g., sustaining the process of capitalist accumulation, expanding a national manufacturing base) without recourse to widespread nationalization of capital were revised steadily upward, and analysis focused on the factors that made dependent development possible (e.g., a relatively-autonomous state). To make the revisionist case starkly, local if dependent capital and its allies often evinced distinct capacities to domesticate foreign investment and otherwise counterbalance the structural advantages accruing to foreign capital within the existing global distribution of productive forces.

Nonetheless, the continued influence of and normative assumptions underpinning the most recent wave of exceptionalist accounts of Bank Misr can be gauged by the reaction to the research of the liberal historian of Egyptian colonialism Robert Tignor. In a series of articles that he began to publish in the mid-1970s, Tignor (1976, 1977a, 1980a and 1980b) sought to document the specific contribution of ethnic-minority and resident-foreign entrepreneurs—that is, non-Egyptians—along with the Egyptians who founded the Misr group to the creation of the country's local manufacturing sector. He, too, framed his work as a critique of dependency theory though he was arguing what in essence had been recognized by writers such as Fernando Henrique Cardoso and in countries such as Argentina and Chile: that so-called foreigners can also act like national capitalists (Cammack 1988; Evans and Stephens 1988). Yet, the results of his research were received coldly by a younger cohort working explicitly within a marxist framework.[3]

The thrust of Tignor's argument was nonetheless correct, and I rely heavily on his ongoing research, particularly in Chapter 2, where I show both how local minority investors evinced an independent interest in accumulation, even if in alliance with international investors, and how after 1922 Egyptian capitalists made rapid inroads into local finance, trade, manufacturing and services by this same route. Since the 1950s, however, analysts have evaluated the capacities of these early Egyptian capitalists more as history makers than as investors. Here, Tignor is ultimately no more nuanced in his judgment than his marxist-oriented critics. He sees the history of the political economy after 1918 as an attempt by "a dynamic and farsighted" group of industrialists to "create a vibrant and autonomous Egyptian capitalism."[4] Davis argues along slightly more traditional lines, emphasizing the subset of self-identified Egyptian (national) capitalists. Nonetheless, the lasting insight of Davis's path-breaking archival study into the social origins of the Misr group's founders and of their failure, ultimately, "to challenge fundamentally foreign capital's domination of the Egyptian economy" is found in the conclusion, where he acknowledges, in parentheses, that *"Harb and his colleagues probably never thought in those terms anyway"* (Davis 1983: 199, emphasis mine).

The story of Bank Misr is the colonial-exceptionalist narrative in miniature. It is the account of an alleged failure of a single institution representing a class ("the organizational consolidation of an aspiring Egyptian industrial bourgeoisie") and rests on a set of unexamined assumptions about objectives that, Davis admits, the capitalists themselves did not hold. The rise and fall of Bank Misr nevertheless is the core myth around which historians in the 1950s first began to weave usable if now fraying accounts of neocolonialism in Egypt.

Class Power and the Postcolonial State in Egypt

If Harb and the other interwar Egyptian investors did not think precisely like later anti-imperialist theorists, then what terms did guide their actions? Is there a better way to conceptualize basic features of capitalist collective action at a particular juncture in Egypt's recent past? To answer these questions, we need to map the universe of investors and political action, beginning with basic institutions like the firm (Ferguson 1983; Bowman 1989; Plotke 1992).

Conflicts over markets and over the public resources that sustained local investors' market power were pervasive in the interwar and post–World War II Egyptian political economy, but these distributive conflicts are little known and little understood, despite their central importance both to where, when and how industry was built in Egypt and to the nature of party and elite political cleavages more generally. Local or Egypt-based capitalists were organized in rival investor coalitions or business groups, and these organizations were among the most powerful private institutions governing the Egyptian political economy during the first half of the twentieth century.

In retrospect, what is most noteworthy about the colonial enterprise in the Egyptian case is its having facilitated the creation of archetypal, large-scale, privately owned and controlled capitalist institutions. The medium of accumulation was the booming cotton export economy. Locally based merchants and landlords (investors) together with representatives of European banks and investment trusts steered the economy and began a project of investing in early import-substitution industries (food processing, textiles, building materials).

BUSINESS PRIVILEGE

Until the military coup of 1952, British and Egyptian governing authorities together with the country's leading local investors shared and reproduced a common view of the institutional hierarchies ostensibly underpinning "all private enterprise market-oriented societies" or what Lindblom describes as "the privileged position of business. In the eyes of government officials, therefore, businessmen do not appear simply as the representatives of a special interest, as representatives of interest groups do. . . . When a government official asks himself whether business needs a tax reduction, he knows he is asking a question about the welfare of the whole society and not simply about a favor to a segment of the population" (1977: 170, 175).

In other words, the power of capitalists as a class in the decades before the 1952 Revolution had little to do with a bourgeoisie's (in)ability to act cohesively in order to "capture the state."[5] Yet, Lindblom's argument about business privilege, like those explications of Antonio Gramsci's concept of hegemony, which it resembles, is centrally concerned with the contemporary functioning of advanced capitalist democracies, systems where a stable, highly nondemocratic relationship of shared authority between corporate capitalists and government officials is not an issue around which political forces struggle.[6] Egypt, in contrast, witnessed a conflict after 1952 precisely around the issue of business privilege, or the distribution of "major leadership roles in the politico-economic order. . . . At least hypothetically, government always has the option, if dissatisfied with business performance, of refusing further privilege and simply terminating private enterprise in a firm, industry or the entire system. Short of taking that course, however, government has to meet business needs as a condition of inducing performance" (Lindblom 1977: 179).

This "hypothetical" case is a fair précis of the actual direction taken by the Nasser regime, beginning in 1954–1955, when the new governing elites began to challenge the central institutions of the private market-based economy. Put another way, the post-1952 state was either unwilling or unable to supply the necessary incentives that investors had come to require if they were to act as capitalists: concessions, subsidies, protection, self-regulation, monopoly rents, a tightly controlled if not completely hostile environment for workers, and regular access to the top leadership of the state.

LOCAL CAPITAL

The idea of business privilege helps us to make sense of the marked disparities in the capacities of different social groups and institutions in Egypt to affect outcomes in various arenas of the political economy. Certainly, the pattern of access to those who governed in the decades after 1882 was not random, and the distribution of these capacities bore more than a chance resemblance to other, relatively more entrenched market-capitalist systems. Those who governed the market were privileged.

There remains the question of how to make sense of the institutions that governed the market, or, as it is sometimes posed, who controlled the Egyptian political economy in the decades prior to the 1952 Revolution? Waterbury (1983) usefully summarizes current thinking on this matter as follows: "The largely unregulated economy was in the hands of European bankers, insurance companies, and utility concerns with a Levanto-Jewish bourgeoisie that handled internal commerce and some foreign trade. . . . Harb and his allies [i.e., the "indigenous wing" of the bourgeoisie] could scarcely make a dent in this *exogenous capitalist monolith,* and Egypt's landowners had little desire to do so" (1983: 232–233, emphasis mine).[7]

Since my own argument can be understood as turning this familiar picture on its head, arguing that by 1952 Harb's "allies" (that is, local Egyptian and non-Egyptian capitalists) were more or less effectively in control of the day-to-day administration of most key sectors of the economy (with finance and petroleum the most important exceptions), it is necessary to clarify at the outset some basic analytical categories and assumptions.

First, there are no convincing analytical grounds for conceiving of the structure of ownership and control in the Egyptian economy (or any other existing market-based economy for that matter) as a monolith. Second, and again for the purpose of understanding the locus of control in particular firms and sectors as well as judging the potential for expanded domestic accumulation (two of the most basic concerns in the study of peripheral capitalist political economies), use of the term *exogenous* in generalizing about both the individual identities of capitalists and the corporate identities of firms in Egypt is extremely misleading. And though analysts often distinguish between indigenous and foreign wings of the bourgeoisie (e.g., 'Abd al-'Azim Ramadan 1971; Waterbury 1983; Tignor 1984), it is important to keep in mind that throughout the entire period studied here investors themselves never seemed to have organized in Egypt along these lines.[8]

Drawing on generally accepted usage in the international political-economy literature, I use the term *foreign capital* to refer exclusively to investment originating outside Egypt's borders by investors whose relevant horizons are not primarily the Egyptian market (e.g., Sir Ernest Cassel or the London-based directors of Imperial Chemical Industries). *Local capital* by contrast refers to investment originating inside Egypt by investors whose relevant horizons are primarily the Egyptian market. The conception of an exogenous capitalist monolith obscures even this elemental distinction in analyzing the locus of control in a particular economic sector.

As in Argentina and Brazil among other countries, local capitalists in Egypt carried many different kinds of passports (or equivalents) and, as individuals, claimed a variety of national identities. Thus, the founders, top shareholders and managers of various ginning factories, export agencies, construction firms, land-reclamation companies and spinning mills, circa 1930, included European nationals and their descendants or other so-called foreigners (e.g., Armenians, Syrians) who had settled in the Egyptian region of the Ottoman Empire in the mid-1800s along with more recent and shorter-term residents; even older, Egypt-born Jewish families whose members nonetheless held British or other European passports; and those whose identity and world-view were basically Egyptian. The sociology is made only more complex by the fact that both the narrowly legal and the more broadly cultural bases of Egyptian national identity were changing during the first half of the twentieth century (Krämer 1983; Shamir 1987).

The grounds for distinguishing analytically between foreign and local capital are well known. Arguments about the distinct capacity of foreign (or multinational or transnational) capital to shape, distort, block the process of domestic accumulation and escape effective regulation by local political authorities are central to the influential, largely marxist-inspired research projects on imperialism (world systems theory, underdevelopment theory, etc.). A central thesis underpinning the various revisionist, late imperialism or postimperialism positions of the 1970s and 1980s (e.g., Evans 1979; Becker et al. 1987) is that the particular and, from the point of view of national industry-building efforts, negative effects of foreign capital are better understood as variable and contingent rather than as uniform and necessary across eras, regions and localities.

In the Egyptian case, many of the pioneering foreign-owned enterprises of the late 1800s and early 1900s (e.g., the sugar monopoly) were gradually domesticated in the decades after World War I through a combination of market pressures and political action, though the process was an uneven one whose impact varied across economic sectors. On the one hand, as Tignor (1989) shows, the activities of the two Manchester-based textile producers operating in Egypt between the 1930s and the 1950s bore little resemblance to the activities of such sovereignty-flaunting market giants as Doheny in pre–World War I Mexico, the Guggenheims in interwar Chile or, from a later period in Chilean history, ITT. On the other hand, the multinational-dominated Egyptian petroleum sector seems to have proved much less vulnerable to regulation by government agencies or to the rent-seeking strategies of local investors. In Chapters 3–5, I look specifically at the electric-power and chemicals (nitrate) industries.

Local capital was a key factor in pushing for and shaping the course of what, borrowing from Richard Sklar (in Becker et al. 1987), I call the *domiciling* of the political economy, by which I mean a shift in the locus of control of specific enterprises, of economic policymaking generally and of the economic surplus to those whose lives, fortunes and families depended on calculations about the future of the Egyptian economy. The issue of the national and ethnic identities of domestic investors was largely irrelevant in this regard; leading members of the so-called Levanto-Jewish bourgeois faction and key parts of the Greek settler colony (among others) had no less interest in pursuing, and maximizing control over, the rents from industry building than their more indigenous Egyptian cohorts.

In making this claim, I do not want to be read as defending colonialism, privileging foreigners' contributions or, most crucially, dismissing the many real and pernicious effects of an era in which Greek and other immigrant capitalists flourished. For instance, entrenched patterns of discrimination in favor of one's own communal groups (e.g., Greeks hiring Greeks) no doubt limited opportunities for Egyptian technical and managerial cadres, a point that was underscored by the Misr group's celebrated policy of hiring Egyptians wherever possible. Many Egyptian men and women experienced in their encounters with foreigners other forms of indignity and injustice that may seem to be erased in the course of the following analysis. I hope that readers will recall the different ways that power was made material inside the textile mills and on the streets of Cairo even as I develop a revisionist argument here about those who came to run the factories and to profit from building the city.

STATE POWER

The largest agricultural and industrial ventures undertaken by private investors in Egypt in the late nineteenth century and early twentieth century all relied on direct and indirect state support, including the transfer of state resources. Local coalitions of investors or business groups played a role in such ventures from the start, and, as will be shown in detail in the chapters that follow, they steadily extended their influence and control, often through privileged access to state power. In other words, the Egyptian case conforms to a familiar pattern of political intervention in support of private accumulation, profit and productive investment. Private investors followed an equally familiar path in pursuit of these objectives. Competitors promoted their particular interests through reasoned appeal to authority, patient cultivation of influence and, on more than one occasion, by audacious political maneuver.

Yet the reduction of broad class interests to particularistic demands is frequently portrayed as part of a strategy of political domination imposed on society by autonomous state officials and designed to divert or contain class forces. Informal modes of politics persist because the state successfully neutralizes formal political associations and channels of interest articulation. Importantly, some also see deep cultural roots in the exceedingly elaborate network of patron-client ties extending from the shadowy corridors of executive power to the sun-drenched villages along the Nile. The costs of unchecked authority stifling weakly articulated economic interests and initiatives were seen in the past and are seen in the present as underdevelopment and the cultivation of a nonproductive, "parasitic" capitalist class.

In private market systems, however, patronage is neither easily nor convincingly reduced to an instrument used by governing officials to control capitalist clients. Patronage is in many instances and respects a market relationship, a synonym for literally doing business with the state. The state is an immense economic consumer, even where its role in direct production is limited. In market systems, government agencies purchase goods and services (for instance, construction services) through contracts and concessions. In a similar way, conventional views of clientelism as a structured, vertical and unequal hierarchy between state and society fail to account for the privileged position of investors in the political economy.

In a brilliant account of the colonial and postcolonial political economy of Senegal, Boone (1992) describes how the Senegalese state used clientelist mechanisms to stem the rise of an indigenous capitalist accumulating class. Robison (1986 and 1988) shows how apparently similar clientelist arrangements fostered the growth of a privileged local manufacturing sector in Indonesia.[9] These cases seem to suggest broader forces shaping relations between bureaucrats and business interests, however one chooses to describe the channels through which businessmen articulate demands and bureaucrats dispense largesse.

One important and obvious distinction is in the type of development strategy underpinning business-government relations (Haggard 1986). At the risk of oversimplifying, is the leadership of the state committed to strengthening capital or undermining it? If it is committed to strengthening capital, then however conflict-ridden and uneven the process, state officials, however reluctantly, find themselves surrendering exclusive authority over broad stretches of the political-economic terrain (Hamilton 1982).

The general commitment of Egypt's core governing institutions and agencies—the monarchy, the cabinet, the ministerial officials and the British residency/embassy—to private enterprise and a market system is hardly disputable. The already-existing social coalition on which such a system was built—a merged class of landlord-capitalists—steered a virtually unregulated commercial, agroexport economy through the last decades of the nineteenth century. In the decade after the crash of 1907, British and Egyptian governing officials cooperated with the leadership of the business community in outlining a strategy for economic diversification, including development of a domestic manufacturing sector subordinate to the dominant export sector.

A project of limited local industry building in cooperation with foreign capital remained the basic development model for approximately the next four decades, until the mid-1950s, when the Nasser regime began to undermine both the privately steered and state-supported, limited IS (Import Substitution) model and, more fundamentally, the local capitalists that governed the economy. Thus the many conflicts about industrial development that engaged state officials, foreign capitalists and domestic investors in the 1920s, 1930s and 1940s must be understood in light of the underlying basic consensus about means and ends.

Local Business Groups and the Politics of Competition

Though the ownership structure of the domestic economy may have appeared at times both as exogenous and as a monolith—and intellectuals in the 1950s and 1960s in particular made it appear so in a series of influential texts on the political economy—Egyptian investors viewed capital—that is, themselves, their allies and their competitors—differently. For instance, the divisions among the various London-, Paris-, Brussels- and Berlin-based banking houses and investment consortia competing for profitable outlets or new markets outside Europe were of crucial importance to Cairo- and Alexandria-based firms. Local Jewish and Greek capitalists evolved specific institutions to offset the bargaining power of, for example, Crédit Lyonnais.[10] In the 1920s and 1930s Egyptian nationals followed variants of this same strategy, resulting in a rapid and steady indigenization of possibilities for profit and accumulation.

My account of how Egyptian investors emerged by 1950 as the most powerful members of the local business community begins with the assumption that investors are divided on the policies that most directly concern them. Political outcomes more often than not reflect the persistence of conflict among competitors rather than some vast concert by a class or its so-called fractions. I am stating this point starkly to distinguish it from alternative views of a bourgeoisie pursuing (and, in the most unrealistic accounts, attaining) power or domination through institutions that represent the general interests of the class as a whole or its collective interests.

I agree with Bertramsen, Thomsen and Torfing (1991: 113) that the well-worn distinction between the general and the particular interests of capital is a myth. Certainly, students of Egypt have never defined exactly the frequently invoked collective interests that all capitalists are or should be pursuing through their classlike institutions. As for the equally well-worn ideas of class fractions defined in terms of (that is, with their interests read off of) their structural location, "the structural location of agents does not reveal anything about their interest, identity and character as a political and social force because classes as well as interests are constructed via particular conjunctural strategies. In this way strategy rather than interests or structural location of agents becomes the central explanatory concept, since we cannot talk about interests or agents in the abstract" (Bertramsen, Thomsen and Torfing 1991: 113). Whether one agrees with the general thrust of this claim, there can be little doubt that the Egyptian exceptionalist historiography misstates the extent to which political strategies among investors reflected their "relatively distinct locations" in production and distribution.

In Egypt, as in a number of other countries undergoing a process of late capitalist development, the leaders of the business community were a set of individuals, families and groups of families whose interests in virtually all cases encompassed both industry and trade among other economic sectors. No wonder, therefore, that the French social historian Jacques Berque once described Egypt's rising business stars as "would-be industrialists [who] still only expressed themselves as tradesmen" (1972: 338). More important, as Markovits (1985) discovered about the business community in India, circa 1930, it was impossible to differentiate between a commercial class linked to imperialism and an industrial class opposed to it. Nor was it possible to make a clear distinction between traders, financiers and industrialists, with "most big capitalists at least being the three at the same time" (Markovits 1985: 24). Similar arguments are made in the cases of Chile (Zeitlin and Ratcliff 1988), Brazil (Topik 1987) and Mexico (Saragoza 1988), among others. In the Egyptian case, at least until the 1950s, there is a blurring if not an obliteration of distinctive class-structural identities or interests among those who owned the country's largest firms and farms and who simultaneously sat as heads of the country's main industrial, agricultural and commercial interest associations.

INVESTMENT COALITIONS AND COLLECTIVE ACTION

From the 1890s until the 1950s, the families whose fortunes funded Egypt's industries were simultaneously the country's biggest bankers, merchants and landowners. The sociology of this core segment of the country's aristocracy, which I refer to as the business oligarchy, was reproduced institutionally in a set of centrally controlled firms in different economic sectors. Following convention across many national settings, including Egypt, I will refer to this form of capitalist coalition as a *business group*.[11] It is an exceedingly common institution in late-developing capitalist economies. Leff in fact considers it "the dominant form of private, domestically-owned capitalism in the LDCs" (1979b: 723).

The defining characteristics of a business group are relatively straightforward: (1) the group encompasses a diversity of firms across different economic sectors; (2) the ownership-management coalition includes several businessmen or notable families, though a single individual is often identified as the group's leader; (3) the group's core leadership is bound by personal, family, ethnic or other communal ties that provide the basis for coordinating its operations.[12] These features are routinely emphasized in the various existing descriptions of business groups in Egypt, though there has been little concern to develop a political analysis of the group as a capitalist institution.[13]

The groups were a chief means by which local capitalists came to define, and to organize collectively in pursuit of, their frequently conflicting interests. The various constellations of local investors—e.g., the Misr group, the 'Abbud group—were probably the most important institutions within the business community. As I will show, they possessed advantages and pressed them over other social sectors to obtain financial resources, access to decision makers, and information that made it possible to reduce the costs of collective action.

Most discussions of Egyptian businessmen misconstrue what is, in reality, one of the most important features of interest articulation in capitalist systems: so-called individual capitalist firms may regularly and effectively act on their own, essentially bypassing the problems inherent in collective action (Olson 1971; Ferguson 1983). Nonetheless, large firms (e.g., corporations) or, in the case of groups, combinations of firms will tend to represent capitalists, not a capitalist. In Egypt, as in other private market-oriented systems, representatives of these institutions obtained regular access to governing officials, invested resources in elections as well as in alternatives to them and shaped public discourse.

Two features of the business group will prove particularly important in developing an account of the politics of local investor coalitions. The first is the marked concentration of economic power, or oligopoly, that is virtually synonymous with this form of capitalist enterprise, and the second is the conspicuousness of the ties between groups and particular state agencies, governing officials or factions.[14] Like capitalists elsewhere, Egypt's investor coalitions recognized that their survival in the market depended on the capacity to reduce, avert or eliminate competition. Entrepreneurs attempt to secure this objective by two often related routes: by concentrating resources or by securing favorable government policies. Egyptian business groups successfully pursued both strategies at once.

Markets in Egypt were highly noncompetitive (el-Gritly 1947). Government-sanctioned oligopolies in particular sectors resolved a particular kind of collective-action problem. "To an extent, the coordination of business strategies through interest associations or through economic concentration seems to be functionally equivalent" (Schmitter and Streeck n.d.: 17). This concentration of resources was generally sanctioned by the state and buttressed by the political alliances that businessmen forged with bureaucrats and politicians. Additionally, the multisectoral investment strategies devised by Egyptian groups led to coordinated and centralized decisions for holdings in different economic sectors. In other words, the locus of power and decision was not the various firms but the group itself.

The central arenas of interest conflict and of capitalist collective action were neither limited to nor, in the Egyptian case, dominated by organizations such as the Federation of Industries, where, among other sites, analysts have tended to situate their arguments about an industrial bourgeoisie's failed designs to capture the state. I do not mean to suggest that peak associations played no role in policymaking in the period.

Rather, until now, analysts have generally failed to pay enough attention to the particular institutional domain of the business group; they have defined the associational universe of investors in an overly restrictive way.[15]

In effect, both the nature of post-1920 Egyptian industrial policy and the arenas most centrally concerned with industrial policymaking have been misidentified. Rival coalitions of landlord-capitalists fought over credits, subsidies, licenses, joint-venture deals, consultancies, contracts, subcontracts and, through such instruments, control over markets, industries and entire economic sectors—that is, investors organized to capture shares of the state's resources. Expansion of local manufacturing capacity was one consequence of these efforts.[16]

MONOPOLY RENTS AND RENT SEEKING

The most basic resource perhaps was the direct transfer of public funds into the coffers of private capitalists, but investors often seek much more than subsidies from the state (Stigler 1986). This process had a loose relationship at best to the working of any invisible hand and yet was intrinsic to the development of capitalism in Egypt. Investors did indeed compete with each other for rights to these transfers, and the resources devoted to doing so provide a rough measure of their perceived revenue- or profit-enhancing value in comparison with, say, expanding production or improving efficiency. The returns to such political investments are now conventionally described as rent.

In classical economic texts rent is a return to a factor of production in scarce or inelastic supply (Tollison 1982). Samuels and Mercuro offer a more contemporary and broader understanding of the concept "as income received over and above the amount that would be received under a different institutional, or rights, arrangement" (1984: 55). By this definition, rent (or quasi-rent or monopoly rent) can also encompass a return to investment in price-fixing arrangements or other measures that restrict competition or market entry.

Rent seeking is thereby the attempt by investors to escape competition, an activity that is often described in other terms (e.g., cartelization and monopolization) (Colander 1984; Wallerstein 1988). Politics is a main means by which investors seek rents. By politics I mean strategic action taken outside of the production site or process in order to shape the market or the behavior of competitors. This action may or may not entail appeal to authorities (Bowles and Gintis 1990; Bowman 1989).

Cartels can be formed without government intervention. Competitors can be persuaded to merge their operations. But in practice investors turn to the state to create monopoly rents.

From the point of view of nineteenth-century investors, colonialism in Egypt was a rent-seeking project on a vast scale, beginning with the building of the Suez Canal and eclipsing the wildest dreams of Egyptian entrepreneurs today. The series of commercial conventions and treaties that Great Britain and other European powers enforced in the Arab provinces of the Ottoman Empire, known as the Capitulations, were nothing less than barriers to entry into the trading sector. Lord Cromer, who governed Egypt after the occupation in 1882, oversaw the transfer of thousands of acres of Egyptian farmland to his brother's business partner, Sir Ernest Cassel.

Little wonder, then, that the French state protested Britain's grip over Egyptian finances in the 1890s or that British trading firms and contractors feared the consequences of Egyptian independence in the 1920s. And the neocolonial strategy that post–World War I British governments began to pursue in Egypt and selected other parts of the empire in support of local manufacturing industry meant nothing less than millions in new rents for the largest and, in global terms, the increasingly uncompetitive textile, cable, steel, chemical and turbine manufacturers in London, Manchester and Birmingham (Hubbard 1935, Shimizu 1986, Cain and Hopkins 1993).

Following independence in 1922, a pioneering cohort of Egyptian investors engaged in a single-minded pursuit of the rents that had drawn foreign capital and foreigners to Egypt. The electric-power industry is a case in point. While mainstream economic theory views the production and distribution of power as a natural monopoly, the problem of who collects the rents—private owners or the national treasury—turns on politics, as Egyptian investors were well aware.[17] In similar fashion, investors competed for the windfalls that would accrue to owners of a new national monopoly like the proposed fertilizer-manufacturing industry, which was underwritten by the farmers who were to be "protected" from chronic overproduction and declining prices in the world market.

OLIGARCHIC DEMOCRACY

The basic institutional arenas for much of this rent seeking were the Egyptian monarchy, the cabinet and the parliament—that is, the formal governing institutions in the liberal regime established by the 1923 constitution. The constitution in turn demarcated a fundamental change in the terms of the protracted conflict between the imperial power and representatives of the cross-class national movement (*al-haraka al-wataniyya*) that erupted at the end of World War I. In 1914, the British state had finally formalized its thirty-year occupation of the Ottoman province by declaring Egypt a protectorate. But a countrywide revolt in 1919 tipped the scales against ultraimperialist currents in the British state and society, and paved the way for the formal grant of independence to Egypt in 1922.

The mechanisms by which the British state sought to preserve its privileges in a nominally independent territory are familiar from the history of U.S. imperialism in Central America and the Caribbean during this same era. First among these mechanisms was the specification of domains where local authority was simply not recognized. In Egypt's case these included external defense, policies that affected the European resident minority community, authority over the private Suez Canal Company and the Canal Zone in general (imperial communications), and policies in the Sudan (officially an Anglo-Egyptian condominium). Second, British power was buttressed by institutions that had been established in earlier decades, including a wealth of legislation, the set of extensive extraterritorial privileges embodied in the judicial regime and administrative oversight of the army and most parts of the civilian bureaucracy. Third, the structure of democracy itself was a further check on the country's leading electoral force, the Wafd party. Under the constitution, the new king, from the Turkish-speaking dynasty that had governed Egypt in the name of the Ottoman sovereign, possessed extensive powers over the parliament and cabinet. Finally, British authorities at times intervened directly in the formation of various postindependence governments.

Unsurprisingly, the most militant and indeed some of the most popular of the national movement's leaders at times derided independence and the constitution as little more than colonialism under a new guise, and much subsequent nationalist and materialist analysis has likewise tended to emphasize continuity over change in Egypt's relationship to empire (hence "neocolonialism"). The argument in this book by contrast is that, however constrained, independence and the constitutional regime were important to Egyptian politicians and investors.

Certainly, the contest to wrest effective control of the agencies and prerogatives of state power was drawn out over decades—from the reformation of the customs regime (1930), the treaty negotiations that gained Egypt a seat at the League of Nations (1936), the ending of the Capitulations (1937), the transfer of the British military base in Cairo (1947) and the closing of the Mixed Courts (1949) to the final evacuation of foreign troops from the Suez Canal Zone (1954–1956). And success was obviously uneven across these different domains. By the time the last British soldier left Egyptian soil, the monarchy, the constitution and Egypt's extremely "thin" (Held 1992) version of democratic rule had all been dismantled. But disenchantment with democracy in Egypt was in no small part due to the successful, virtually single-minded focus on the part of Egyptian oligarchs with the state as a fiscal institution and with the rents to be obtained via privileged access to state power.

The fragility of this particular "liberal experiment" (Marsot 1977; Maghraoui 1991) was made immediately apparent in the most significant early challenge to the consolidation of democracy: the resignation of the country's first popularly elected government in November 1924 after only eleven months in office—a resignation that was forced by British officials (Gordon 1992: 16). Thereafter, periods of at least formally democratic rule under the 1923 constitution alternated with periods of more-nearly authoritarian rule. During the next twenty years the Wafd party held office only after elections in 1936–1937 and by appointment in 1942–1944, when the British state found it necessary to trade the benefits of rule by palace-based "minority-party" coalitions for an Egyptian government that could legitimately claim a measure of mass support.

The enduring basis of the Wafd party's appeal among those citizens who could be mobilized to cast their ballots or, at other moments, to take to the streets was its origins as a "delegation" of nationalist politicians and factions (*wafd* means delegation in Arabic) that had hoped to press the case for Egyptian independence at the Paris peace conference in 1919 (Vatikiotis [1969] 1991: 262–272). Led by the delegation's original chairman, nationalist hero and popularly proclaimed "father of the nation," Sa'd Zaghlul, the Wafd (or Zaghlulists as the party members were sometimes called) swept the 1924 parliamentary elections, and Zaghlul was named prime minister. The original campaign platform was a simple one: those Egyptian political factions that cooperated in the transition to independence (and, by implication, the king) had compromised the principal of an immediate and complete dismantling of the occupation.

In 1924 and in all subsequent contests through the last elections in 1950, the "official" (that is, legally recognized and electorally oriented) opposition to the Wafd comprised either pre–World War I nationalist factions-turned-parties that Zaghlul had included in the original Wafd delegation or else factions that subsequently formed inside and then split with the party in the 1920s and 1930s. These rival parties ranged from an individual and his followers to larger patronage networks to formal, dues-paying political organizations with branches in cities and the countryside. However, the Wafd's close identification with the independence struggle, the apparently vast reservoir of support that could be mobilized by its superior organization and, in particular, its ties to the emerging trade-union movement, student groups, and other organizations made it unbeatable at the polls.[18] As a result, the Wafd's rivals were drawn both to allying with the palace and to tampering with election laws and ultimately the constitution as means to gaining power (Deeb 1979).

A recurring problem in analyses of this electoral regime is that accounts do not stray far from the terms that Wafd ideologues were likely to use themselves to mobilize the faithful. Against the party's own supposedly uncompromising nationalist commitments, its opponents, however impeccable their own credentials may have seemed in the events leading to independence, are portrayed as too eager to trade away the nation's sovereign rights for the trappings of rule. In this specific sense the palace and minority-party leaders are often depicted as ultimately serving foreign interests or representing those social forces most closely tied to the status quo.

I do not mean to denigrate the specific political and organizational skills that at a particular juncture permitted the Zaghlulists rather than some other faction to harness the force of popular protest against colonialism, but we have no good reason to believe that the basic perspective and objectives of the Wafd's leaders differed from those of their electoral rivals. More to the point, it is difficult to distinguish the behavior of the Wafd in office from that of non-Wafdist elites (or from that of postcolonial regimes more generally). To give one example, Isma'il Sidqi, a participant in the original Wafd delegation and a rival of Zaghlul's who joined the transitional (non-Wafd) government in 1922 as finance minister, began pressing for Egyptianization of the commanding heights of the state administration and private economy, a project that he advanced much more effectively in the 1930s, when he governed Egypt as a virtual dictator (Goldberg 1986: 73). But Zaghlul and his allies pursued the exact same course during their brief time in power in the 1920s, enriching some investors in the process and leading others to invest in alternatives to the Wafd, as I will document.

Recognition of this mundane but critical facet of postcolonial governance is to be found in the idea that the Wafd's nationalist *bona fides* were compromised when, after restoration of the constitution in 1935, the party took power only to sign a treaty of alliance with Britain in 1936. Judged against the party's most militant public oratory and especially the idea of full, complete, and real independence, Zaghlul's successors are often condemned today as having presided over the Wafd's decay and the consolidation of a neocolonial regime in Egypt. I will spend much time in succeeding chapters challenging this particular view of the trajectory of the political economy. It is important to note here, however, that through its actions the Wafd was more nearly finally fulfilling its destiny and satisfying the pent-up demands of party leaders and allied investors for control of and access to administrative appointments and resources.

The dimension of emerging postcolonial politics that I am primarily concerned with here is given passing and wholly inadequate recognition at best in the anecdotal references to patronage and corruption in post–World War I Egypt. As we will see, though, the mode of governance (Boone 1992) was quite logically linked to what has long been a central concern of political economy: where, when and how industry is built in the periphery.

Summary

The various components of the argument can be brought together. Previous analyses of these formative decades in the development of Egypt have misinterpreted the basic issues that confronted and divided those who governed the economy. Would-be industrialists did not wage pitched battles against two thousand big landowning families. Nor did a national bourgeoisie ever champion a heroic but doomed struggle against foreign capital and the foreigners' powerful and numerous domestic allies. A project of economic diversification via investment in manufacturing industry was hardly an enduring or deeply divisive issue at the end of World War I; it had already been hammered out relatively easily by Egypt's largest landowners, bankers, colonial officials and representatives of foreign capital.

The most basic and enduring conflict within the business community after 1920 grew out of the fierce struggle of competing coalitions for dominance over these new, albeit limited opportunities for profit and accumulation. State support was critical in gaining access to and (often) assuring the success of these ventures. All the coalitions or groups therefore relied on, were linked to, collaborated with and came into conflict with different political-bureaucratic principals, institutions and factions. Yet, these conflicts, however acute or hostile, were constrained by a development model that privileged markets and private enterprise. The most powerful governing officials accepted this model or at least accommodated themselves to it. Business had uninterrupted access to state officials. Relations between class and state were, indeed, marked by "an extreme degree of mutual adjustment and political pluralism" (Lindblom 1977: 179).

The central business-state conflict centered on which business groups tied to which bureaucratic factions would gain control of (would privatize) public resources in building Egyptian oligarchic capitalism. The various local coalitions of Greek, Jewish and other minority investors may have imagined a continued expansion of their holdings under the protection of a colonial administration, but in the decades after 1919, as an Egyptian political elite gradually but steadily wrested control of the administration of the state, Egyptian nationals rapidly came to monopolize access to these resources.

The Egyptian development model was predicated on cooperation between foreign capital and local investors in owning and managing Egypt's privately controlled infrastructure and early import-substitution sectors, a pattern common to numerous developing capitalist economies in this period, including those of Brazil, Chile, South Korea and India. From the point of view of Egyptian business groups, joint ventures were sources of profit and accumulation at least partially outside the state, which strengthened their bargaining power and reduced the risk of bureaucratic manipulation. Collaboration with foreign capital was also a basic means for local capitalists to strengthen their position against their local market rivals as well as their political antagonists.

In other words, business and politics in this key period in Egyptian history prove to have been more complicated than capitalists lining up in a tug-of-war over economic development, one side pulling the economy toward independent industrialization, the other straining to keep the economy locked in the grips of foreign capital. Kitching (1985) argues forcefully for a similar view in the midst of the "Kenyan debate" over the nature and impact of collaboration between foreign and local capital. His argument is worth reproducing at length (1985: 31, emphasis in original):

The point, then, is that on *both* sides in the Kenya debate a great deal of dubious inference from highly partial information is being dignified as theory (ies) of the state and made to stand in place of the sort of knowledge of political processes and struggle which academics do not have *and cannot get.* My own guess, for what it is worth, is that every businessman in Kenya and every state official from a lower-middle level upward could be categorized as a "national bourgeois" from some points of view, and with reference to some of his/her activities and aspirations, and as a "comprador" from others. They enter into conjunctural alliances around particular struggles and issues which could be categorized as in the interests of transnational capital sometimes in some respects, and as hostile to those interests and nationalist in thrust at other times and in other respects. Such alliances at times give parts of the state apparatus . . . one coloration and at times another. Similarly "transnational capital" (or particular representatives of particular parts of it) is in there too, making alliances, trying to use people who are trying to use it, at times succeeding, at times failing wholly or partly.

In short, it is all very complex and shifting, and a great deal of it social scientists never see and can not see.

His "guess" in fact is an uncannily accurate description of the investment strategies of Egyptian business groups and the struggles over the development of industry in interwar Egypt. Using declassified diplomatic archives and other primary sources, I have reconstructed the private politics behind the major public projects of the pre-1952 era. The remaining chapters of this book analyze the development of Egyptian business groups, the arenas in which they competed and their impact on the political economy. Kitching's pessimism about information gathering, therefore, requires some tempering. There are methods that permit social scientists to overcome, at least in some places and at some points, obstacles that hide the "complex and shifting" patterns of collusion and conflict among capitalists.

CHAPTER TWO

The Origins of the 'Abbud
Group and Its Rivals

*[P]olitical parties as such have no decisive influence,
since all authority is in fact vested in a small group
of families. . . . There are, furthermore, wealthy persons
like Ahmad Abboud Pasha who though unaffiliated
with any party exercise a considerable influence on
Egyptian policy.*

U.S. Office of Strategic Services (1945)

There is no single path which local investors have followed in building capitalist industry in late-colonial and postcolonial
societies. Certain paths seem well worn however. In pioneering new
ventures and charting new industrial sectors, domestic businessmen often have joined forces with foreign capitalists—international financiers,
banks, manufacturing corporations, and engineering firms—as well as
with local competitors. Similarly, they have looked to the agencies of
the state for resources, subsidies, protection and related means of un-
derwriting risk and guaranteeing profit. In this chapter, I highlight
some of the basic landmarks of this particular development path in
Egypt by analyzing those who traveled it in the decades after World
War I.

The economic dislocation of the war years—shortages, acreage restrictions, the loss of export markets—revealed weaknesses in the
agroexport-based economy and reinforced those members of the busi-

ness community calling for diversification (Berque 1972; Tignor 1976, 1980a and 1984; Deeb 1976 and 1979). At the same time, the war fueled resentment against the British occupation and catalyzed a broad-based movement of resistance. Many Egyptians recall the revolution of March 1919 as the nation's finest hour. In its wake, Great Britain retreated from its plan to incorporate Egypt into the empire and, by granting a form of limited independence in 1922, took the first tentative step toward ceding state power to Egyptian institutions and officials.

The full impact of these years on the evolution of the political economy must be assessed both in terms of the development of new ventures and sectors and also in terms of the rise of new centers of power within the domestic business community. Egyptians sought to join the ranks of the country's capitalists. The political changes ushered in by the war proved immensely helpful to Egyptian capitalists who could finally begin to overcome the significant entry barriers erected in the mid-1800s. From the perspective of these aspiring economic elites, manufacturing was one potential area of investment. The dominant sectors of the economy, such as finance, cotton export, transport and construction, were equally inviting avenues for the pursuit of profit and power.

The rise of the banking group around Tal'at Harb, the commercial complex steered by the Yahya family and the construction empire built by Ahmad 'Abbud signified a shift both in the weight of local economic forces and in the sectoral composition of investment activity by local business groups. Politics played an important role in the unfolding of these twinned processes, but little is known about the strategies employed by Egyptian investors or about the conflicts that engaged these new key interests along with the rest of the local business community. Certainly these issues have never been reducible to some unequivocal antagonism toward foreign capital on the part of local investors or, the opposite, a compulsion to serve these same foreign firms.

The activities of the 'Abbud group, a closely controlled but disparate set of enterprises steered by an Egyptian contractor, Muhammad Ahmad 'Abbud, afford a unique vantage point for studying business and politics in post–World War I Egypt. 'Abbud's legacy is both fascinating and controversial. Unlike the other Egyptian capitalists who attained great wealth and power in this era, 'Abbud launched his Egyptian business career relatively late, having obtained his first contracts around 1924. By comparison, the Yahya group dates back to the 1860s. Harb, who would go on to found Bank Misr, joined one of the first Egyptian business groups in 1905. In other words, it was 'Abbud's star that rose swiftest.

The conflicts that accompanied this meteoric ascent in Egyptian business and politics are undoubtedly factors in the conventional portrayals of 'Abbud in much of the colonial-exceptionalist historiography as the bête noire of the bourgeoisie. He is represented as a core part of the reactionary social coalition that allegedly brought about the end of an autonomous industrialization project begun with the founding of the Misr group in 1920. In this way, the economy itself is seen as the second face of a fatefully compromised project on the part of the national political elite to secure complete independence for the country. These two nationalist projects are portrayed as rising and falling (and rising again after 1952) in tandem.

This chapter argues for a somewhat different trajectory for the political economy. Coalitions of local investors and allied interests—business groups—had emerged in Egypt decades before the founding of Bank Misr. The investment activities of Egypt's first business groups included manufacturing and nonmanufacturing industrial ventures. Many of these efforts involved cooperative links with international interests. The Misr group, the 'Abbud group and other coalitions emerging after 1922 continued this pattern of selective collaboration with foreign capital. At the same time, they created new industries in Egypt and advanced local control (the Egyptianization) of existing sectors. They competed with one another for control of these ventures.

The chapter begins by analyzing the origins of Egypt's first local business groups and the role that these businessmen envisioned for foreign capital and for manufacturing industry in the evolving political economy. Through their plans for limited diversification, these investors charted a course for new sets of Egyptian competitors. The continuities are plainly evident in the record of the 'Abbud group. The discussion thus turns to the rise of 'Abbud Pasha and the 'Abbud group of companies. I review the origins of his business career in the Egyptian construction sector and the diversification of his holdings during the interwar period, 1924–1939. During this period of sharp competition for limited public resources 'Abbud consolidated his position as a major new force in the local political economy. The chapter concludes with a discussion of the institutional bases of power of the 'Abbud group and its competitors in the interwar market.

The main argument can be summarized as follows. Until now, our

views of 'Abbud and his rivals have had little basis in the actual institutions, interests and activities of these local investors. In particular, the
tendency to discount investors as a political force stems from a false and
indefensible assumption: that these interwar capitalists or some subset
of them tried to industrialize and transform Egypt but failed. Analysts
differ mainly in identifying who (or what class segments) pursued these
objectives and who (or what social forces) stood in their way. The conclusion is nonetheless the same. Capitalists did not have the political
resources necessary to promote their interests. This conclusion is not
surprising, given how boundless we imagine those interests to have
been.

Replanting Egyptian Industry: The Cotton-Export Economy and the Emergence of Domestic Business Groups

Following the collapse of Muhammad 'Ali's system of
state monopolies and manufacturing ventures in the 1840s, the weight
of economic activity in Egypt shifted toward commercial agriculture,
where the local dynastic state-in-formation (Egypt was still officially a
province of the Ottoman Empire) had overseen innovations in support
of production of a high-value export crop—cotton. From the mid-
1800s on, fortunes rose and fell in Egypt on the strength of the prices
commanded by its prized, long-staple fiber in the world market.[1] The
British occupation in 1882 led to a series of administrative, economic
and fiscal reforms that deepened commercialization of land, cotton-
export production and capital accumulation.

Two points need to be stressed about the sociology of those who
appropriated the surplus in this economy. First, it is conventional to
stress the dominance of "foreign" capital in this period by concentrating on the national origins or communal identities of individual owners,
company directors and managers operating in various sectors. But when
foreign capital is defined in this way, the French-based commercial giant, Crédit Lyonnais, is indistinguishable from the locally organized
J. N. Mosseri Fils et Compagnie, a commercial bank founded by a family resident in Egypt since the mid-1700s. The Mosseri firm and its
owners are an institutional expression of local capital in nineteenth-
century Egypt.[2]

The identities of these local investors were undoubtedly complex. For example, the Mosseris were legally foreigners rather than Egyptian subjects. Though born and raised in Egypt, at some point in the nineteenth century members of this family obtained Italian passports, which gained them competitive advantages under the terms of the international commercial regime in force in Egypt and other parts of the Ottoman Empire (the Capitulations). Their communal identity, meanwhile, was Jewish. The vice-presidency of the organized Cairo Jewish community was a hereditary position held by the Mosseris for decades. (Shamir 1987; Krämer 1989: 41–43) The emphasis on nationality or communal identity has tended to obscure the role played by these local capitalists in the development of industry as a subsidiary sector of the agroexport economy.

The second and related point concerns the usefulness in distinguishing between a class of large landowners, on the one hand, and an urban bourgeoisie, on the other, in narrating the history of the country's local manufacturing sector. There are, of course, well-established grounds for doing so in the Egyptian case, whether these grounds are marxist ideas about modes of production or the collective sociological profile of Egypt's early-twentieth-century national governing elite. Nonetheless, virtually all large-scale industries of local origin were steered by families with vested interests in the agrarian structure. Fortunes accumulated during the boom of the 1860s were used to buy land. Rural rents funded commerce and, later, industry. In other words, it was a merged set of leading landlord-capitalists that supported import-substitution manufacturing investment.

At least two distinct coalitions of local investors emerged in the prosperous postoccupation decade of the 1890s. The first included local Jewish families, Suarès, Cattaoui, Menasce and Rolo, closely linked by marriage and by investment activity.[3] I will refer to this coalition as the Suarès group because Raphael Suarès (1846–1902) fronted for these families in a series of spectacular, turn-of-the-century joint ventures with French and British financial syndicates. The holdings of these families included massive private agricultural estates, rural land-development ventures, urban real estate, numerous private and joint-stock banks, public transport, urban services, and textiles.

A second group involved leading members of Alexandria's large Greek community, the Salvagos, Sinadino, Zervoudakis, Choremis and Benakis families.[4] The diverse activities of the Salvago group, as it was referred to in the Egyptian press, came to encompass cotton export and finance, private estates, rural-development companies, urban real estate and commercial ventures (e.g., warehouses), public utilities, transport, insurance, textile manufacturing, petroleum marketing, and, eventually, chemicals and metallurgy (*Akhbar al-Yawm,* 13 November 1948). Their economic roles proved no less complex than the other components of these local investors' identities.

Tignor (1984: 72–73) includes Mikés Salvagos among Egypt's "foreign industrialists" and highlights his role as a founder of the Association of Industries in 1922. At the time, Salvagos served as chairman of the boards of Filature Nationale d'Egypte, then the country's largest textile enterprise, the Alexandria and Ramleh Railway Company and the Alexandria Water Company. At the same time, however, Salvagos sat on the steering committee of the Alexandria General Produce Association, an institution comprising "large export houses, bankers and merchants" that privately regulated the cotton trade (Tignor 1984: 58; Papasian 1926: 300; Pilavachi, 1932). Kitroeff argues that it is misleading to label bankers and exporters like Salvagos "industrialists" (1989: 82–83, 122). Meanwhile, the Salvagos family owned an estate totaling 2,000 faddans, which qualifies them for inclusion in the lists of Egypt's top landowners. Local capitalists like Salvagos, Suarès and their allies cooperated closely with foreign capitalists in many of the biggest ventures of the period. The Suarès group built their Egyptian commercial empire through alliances with competing European financial powers. These alliances can be seen in the period of expansion of the group's holdings between 1880 and 1907. In the first major joint venture, the Suarès group and a consortium of French banks founded the Crédit Foncier Egyptien (1880), which proceeded to dominate mortgage banking in Egypt (Crouchley 1936: 34; Owen 1969: 277; Collins 1984: 43–45; Tignor 1989: 86). The power exercised by Raphael Suarès and his allies on the local board proved a central concern of the French embassy, increasingly so as local investors gradually gained control of a majority of the internationally traded shares (Tignor 1989: 86–87).

"PRIVATIZATION"

The Suarès group benefited enormously from a massive transfer of ownership rights carried out by the Cromer regime (1883–1907), which paved the way for these investors' expansion into new economic sectors. For instance, in 1888 they received a concession from the government that ceded to them the state-owned Tura-Helwan railway, south of Cairo, and granted them permission to extend the line north into the city center at Bab al-Luq (Krämer 1989: 41; Kalkas 1979: 230; Wright and Cartwright 1909: 183). This venture led to a series of further transport enterprises, including the private financing in 1895 of the last segments of the railway line running from Cairo to Aswan in cooperation with the German joint-stock bank, Berlin Handels Gesellschaft. Once it was built, the Suarès group leased the line back to the Egyptian State Railways (Krämer 1989: 41; Kalkas 1979: 231; Platt and Hefny 1958: 338)!

In the late 1890s, investors scrambled to obtain the rights to run light railway lines in the Delta. The Suarès group won the concession for the three eastern governorates of Sharqiyya, Dhakhaliyya and Qalubiyya. Competitors included a British financial syndicate and a Belgian holding company known as the Empain group, which built and managed railways and tramways across Europe, Asia and Africa. In 1900 the Suarès group sold their concession to the British interests and joined the board of the competing, London-based Egyptian Delta Light Railways Ltd. (Wright and Cartwright 1909: 183–186; Krämer 1989: 41; Kalkas 1979: 174). The transport markets of Cairo and the Delta were thus effectively divided between two forces. The Suarès-British joint venture ran light rail lines in most of the Delta as well as the Cairo-Helwan line. Independently, the Suarès group ran the donkey carts that crossed the Musqi quarter and that were known colloquially as "siwaris." The Empain group operated a light railway in the eastern Delta connecting Mansura to the coastal towns of Dumyat, east of Alexandria, and al-Manzala, near Port Said. More significantly, the Belgians also built and operated electric tramway lines in Cairo.

These transport ventures were only one component of larger, privately directed urban-development schemes that changed the contours of Cairo. The Suarès group and their British partners created a second firm, the Egyptian Delta Land and Investment Company (1904), which developed the suburb of Ma'adi along its Cairo-Helwan line. While building the rail lines, the Suarès group also developed public-utility companies in Tanta, the third largest city in Egypt, and Mansura, another market city serviced by the Delta rail system. They eventually took over the Cairo waterworks as well. These various urban real estate ventures paled, however, beside the development scheme promoted by Empain and allied European financiers.

The Brussels-based investors constructed an entire new community in the desert northeast of Cairo—Heliopolis—linked by the new tramway line. The population reached 24,000 by 1928, and Empain's various companies controlled transport, power, utilities, and eighteen thousand faddans worth of commercial and private real estate by mid-century. In 1906 the Empain group set up a holding company, the Cairo Electric Railways and Heliopolis Oasis Company, which, in turn, held controlling shares in various related companies—for instance, the Société Egyptienne d'Electricité (1929), which built and operated the original Shubra power station (Levi 1952: 314).

The close control exercised by the Belgian administration left little room for local capital to operate, in contrast to the situation in foreign-financed development projects associated with the Suarès group. In the interwar period, the Belgians would fight hard to prevent Egyptian investors from breaking the monopoly on the Cairo transportation and power markets. At best, local capital acted on the periphery of the Empain group's urban fiefdom, at least until the end of World War II. The prime example is the set of construction, urban real estate and land-development ventures involving the local (Belgian) contractor Leon Rolin and two Syrian business families—the Eids, who were Belgian protégés, and the Shakours (Tignor 1980a: 423, 429; Wright and Cartwright 1909: 115–16, 312–13, 397; Philipp 1985; Papasian 1926). Their interlocking firms included the Egyptian Enterprise and Development Company (1904), the Cairo Suburban Building Land Company (1906), the Koubbeh Gardens Building Land Company (1907), the Gharbieh Land Company (1905) and La Société Agricole de Kafr al Dawwar (1907).

The tremendous expansion of Alexandria in the 1880s and 1890s proceeded in similar directions: the bankers and exporters financed urban transport, land development and, lastly, manufacturing industry. Development took place in an unregulated environment overseen by a business-dominated municipal government whose autonomy was sanctioned by statute (el Saaty and Hirabayashi 1959: 218). The Salvagos and allied families played prominent roles, together with European-based capitalists, in many new ventures, including the Egyptian Salt and Soda Company (1899), which was a state-sanctioned monopoly, and the Filature Nationale d'Egypte (1899, reorganized 1911), the first textile firm to obtain even minimal government support (Owen 1966 and 1969: 222–223; Tignor 1989) Salvagos also held a large stake in the locally controlled Société Anonyme du Béhéra (1880, reconstituted 1894), which, supported by government dredging contracts, grew into one of the largest companies developing the farm land of the Delta (Baer 1962: 68–69, 124–127; Owen 1969: 212, 281; Kitroeff 1989: 82).

THE CASSEL–SUARÈS GROUP
JOINT VENTURES

While the ruling authorities thus encouraged and facilitated capital investment and private control of urban development, this new division of labor received its fullest expression in the sale to Suarès and various partners of prime agricultural lands in the Delta and Upper Egypt, along with the state-owned sugar mills. The Suarès group, which in the 1880s operated the refinery in al-Hawamdiyya, joined with French investors in a second enterprise in Upper Egypt (Owen 1969: 277; Kalkas 1979: 169; Tignor 1984: 34). The Suarès group originally held the controlling (66.6 percent) share in the joint venture, but consolidation and expansion of these various sugar-manufacturing operations involved new capital shares traded on the Paris bourse. The merger in 1897 led to the creation of the Société Générale des Sucreries et de la Raffinerie d'Egypte, the largest industrial firm in Egypt. The giant refinery operation absorbed all of the state's own manufacturing facilities by 1902 (Crouchley 1936: 114; Owen 1969: 296; Collins 1984: 70; Tignor 1989: 87–88; Krämer 1989: 40).

Not surprisingly, the Suarès group devoted considerable time, energy and capital to land development in Upper Egypt, where most of the cane was grown. Once again, they joined forces with foreign financial capital in a venture sanctioned by the governing authorities and resting basically on the subsidized transfer of three hundred thousand faddans of state-owned lands. The unprecedented giveaway amounted to a quid pro quo for the assistance that Ernest Cassel, one of the most powerful international financiers of the era, provided the government (i.e., Lord Cromer) in the construction of the Aswan Dam (1898–1902). Cromer, who backed the dam project as a chief means to develop Egypt's irrigation system, could not obtain the release of the funds from the multinational commission in charge of the Egyptian treasury. Cassel, whose closest business associate was Cromer's brother, Lord Revelstoke, the director of Baring Brothers, arranged private financing for the dam. He was amply rewarded.[5]

In 1898, Cassel, the Suarès group and the French partners in the sugar-manufacturing venture formed the Daira Sanieh Company. The state sold them what remained of the former Khedive Isma'il's properties, much of it in Middle and Upper Egypt. As Collins notes, "The false claim was made that the Daira Saniyya was losing money and should therefore be sold off as the best means of stemming a fiscal hemorrhage that might eventually drain the Egyptian government treasury" (1984: 351). The company purchased the land for £E 6.4 million and between 1900 and 1906 sold three hundred thousand faddans for £E 13 million. The investors' share in the profits totaled, minimally, £E 3 million (Baer 1962; Owen 1969: 268–269; Collins 1984: 347–353). The board of this lucrative venture comprised a remarkable alliance, including Cassel's business partner, Carl Meyer; Paris bankers; the recently retired financial adviser to the Egyptian government, Elwin Palmer; members of the Suarès group; and one of the most powerful Egyptian landowners of Minya province, 'Ali Sha'rawi (British Chamber of Commerce 1905: 11, 50).

The lines of competition and cooperation grew increasingly dense and complex. Cassel and his partners gained an important interest in the Société Générale des Sucreries et de la Raffinerie d'Egypte in 1902 by financing the firm's purchase of the state's refineries, and they played a major role in the reorganization of the company when bankruptcy threatened in 1905. The new management team included the Belgian expert, Henri Naus, who in later decades became a leading spokesperson for local industry. In addition, Victor Harari, a Finance Ministry official, went to work for Cassel and his allies in 1905 in the sugar company and the closely linked Société Anonyme du Wadi Kom Ombo (est. 1904), an enormous agricultural company in Aswan province. At the same time, a French-Suarès joint venture, the Crédit Foncier Egyptien, took over the Daira Sanieh Company, in a move apparently intended to preempt Cassel's entry into Egyptian mortgage banking (Owen 1969: 291; Tignor 1984: 34 and 1966: 369–373; Berque 1972: 246–247; Thane 1986). Existing studies only hint, in a frustratingly vague way, at the conflicts which underlay this tremendous extension of private wealth and power.

Through such familiar institutions as officially sanctioned private monopoly over public service, subsidies, appropriation of state resources, and direct pathways from government ministry to company board, investors built capitalist enterprises in Egypt. Local investor coalitions like the Suarès group played central roles in virtually every major financial, commercial and industrial enterprise of the era. They all but obliterated the lines distinguishing public and private, foreign and local, through such operations as the National Bank of Egypt, founded in 1898 by Cassel, Suarès and the Alexandria-based Salvago group (Crouchley 1936: 32; British Chamber of Commerce 1905: 24; Kalkas 1979: 276). Tignor tellingly summarizes developments in this post-1882 period by noting "a marked forging of interests between the administration and the financial community" (1966: 369).

BUSINESS GROUPS AND INDUSTRY

The developments mapped here are important for three reasons. First, they highlight basic institutional features of the business community in Egypt, including mechanisms underpinning its privileged position. Whatever the motivations of individual British administrators, or the power of the London and Paris bondholders, or Cromer's expectations about the pressures that might be exerted by the Lancashire textile lobby, the post-1882 governments needed the cooperation of the business community to realize all their basic economic objectives. Cromer, the ruler of Egypt from 1883 to 1907, transferred assets and authority in many domains from public to private hands. The business community enjoyed minimal state interference: the construction industry was unregulated, the cotton exporters supervised their own affairs, while the private Khedivial Agricultural Society served in place of a governmental ministry of agriculture until 1910—this in a country where export agriculture was the basis of national wealth.

The business group—individuals and families organized as coherent coalitions of investors—emerged as an important form of autonomous capitalist organization during the period 1880–1900, coinciding with the consolidation of local capital generally as a political-economic force in Egypt. My basic portrait and periodization depart from conventional accounts, which have been concerned above all with the foreign communal or ethnic identities of these early investors and company directors. These accounts either collapse the distinction between local and foreign capital in this period or else portray these local capitalists as compradors, serving the interests of foreign capital.

The second reason for mapping these early, pre-World War I institutional developments is to clarify the specific role played by these business groups in various economic sectors, especially their early investment activity in industry. Cromer's infamous refusal to accord protection to the first two modern textile ventures started in Egypt in 1899 is generally seen as an expression of the strength of the social forces opposing local industrial development, articulated and led by the top administration of the state. The local business community had supposedly not yet shown meaningful signs of an ability to express common interests and to act in defense of the national economy. Local ("national") capital, equated narrowly with industrial interests, only begins to emerge in 1917, 1922, 1936 or even 1952, according to various interpretations.

The depth of opposition to Cromer's policies belies the arguments about the delayed birth of local capital. As Owen pointedly notes about Cromer's actions against the textile firms, they were "criticized by almost all sections of Egyptian [sic] opinion," attacked by the main newspaper of the business community, *La Bourse Égyptienne,* and initially struck down by the Mixed Courts. Once Cromer orchestrated the reversal of the judiciary's decision, the action "was attacked as detrimental to the country's interests even by the *Egyptian Gazette,* normally the most staunch supporter of the Occupation." It would seem that, in fact, the organized voice of local (though overwhelmingly non-Egyptian) business could be plainly and loudly discerned. Criticism of the British attitude to the development of local industry continued unabated for the remainder of the period up to 1914. Crucially, by the end of his rule, Cromer found it necessary to push aside his own cherished principles of free trade long enough to intervene on behalf of the tottering sugar-refineries joint venture (Owen 1969: 343–344). Cromer's successors continued in this same direction.

The crash of the Egyptian market in 1907 catalyzed a number of important developments as government officials, landowners and leading local businessmen responded to the crisis. The Suarès group gained vital exemptions for their nascent textile-manufacturing joint venture, while the government created the Ministry of Agriculture between 1910 and 1912 in response to plummeting export prices and a disastrous cotton harvest. Businessmen engaged in new forms of collective action, founding at least two new interest associations in this period: the Property Owners Association (1911) and the Egyptian Chamber of Commerce in Cairo (1913). Members of the Suarès group played prominent roles in both (Owen 1969: 223, 346–348; Berque 1972: 243; Deeb 1978: 17–18; Tignor 1984: 60–61). Finally, the economic crisis gave impetus to a more forceful and sustained articulation of the need for economic diversification, including the expansion of local industry.

The most powerful constituents of the nascent industrial lobby in

Egypt were simultaneously the country's richest bankers, largest exporters of cotton, main investors and directors in numerous foreign-
backed ventures and, through the extensive network of interlocking
transport, irrigation, and land-development companies, some of the
largest landowners as well. They successfully integrated these diverse
interests, and, not surprisingly, the subsidiary role envisioned for industry in Egypt complemented rather than undermined their investments
in the agroexport economy. The multisectoral investment model that
they pioneered remained the basic institutional form of the largest
Egyptian capitalists for at least the next half century. These powerful
coalitions, and thus the business community as a whole, even had the
capacity to weather the storm of Egyptian nationalism which swept the
country in the years leading up to the 1919 revolution.

The third reason for mapping these investor coalitions carefully is to
clarify the role they played in cultivating or accommodating Egyptian-
Muslim economic elites and promoting the fortunes of rising new
Egyptian business stars. One example is the ascent of the Yahya family,
landowners and merchants prominent both in Alexandrian private
(business) and public (municipal-council) spheres, as well as in the
emerging Egyptian nationalist movement.[6] Amin Yahya sat on the
landmark 1916 Commission on Commerce and Industry (the Sidqi
commission). So did Harb, the fastest rising of the Egyptian businessmen and landowners associated with the Suarès group from 1905 on.[7]
Others included families like Sultan, Sha'rawi, Siyufi and Lutfi.[8] All had
ties to local or foreign capital and, with the exception of Lutfi, would
join with Harb, as well as with key members of the Suarès group, in the
historic founding of Bank Misr in 1920. Harb was throughout the
1910s and 1920s probably the most effective publicist among Egyptians of the industry-building strategy advocated by "foreigners" like
Suarès, Cattaoui, Salvagos, Naus, Rolo and Barker, the backbone of the
local business community.

Manufacturing: The Nonrevolution

Before turning to the post-1922 period and the rise of
the 'Abbud group, we must be clear about the nature and timing of the
industry-building project associated, perhaps too prominently, with the
political and economic ferment of the years surrounding Egyptian inde-

pendence. These limited initiatives at economic diversification were steered by businessmen who remained thoroughly integrated into international circuits of capital. Yet, they are routinely described as a strategy aimed "at stimulating industrial growth *independent* of European capital and intervention" (Krämer 1989: 94, emphasis mine). Historians use three key events to anchor this interpretation and to pinpoint the birth of a national industrial bourgeoisie. The first is the creation of the Commission on Commerce and Industry, which issued its public report in 1918. The second event is the creation of Bank Misr in 1920, a commercial bank owned exclusively by Egyptian citizens. The third landmark is the formation of the Association of Industries in 1922 (Issawi [1967] 1975: 452–460).

The basic problem with this projection back into the past of post-1952 anticapitalist discourses is that no one has convincingly shown that businessmen ever organized and acted on the basis of the goal of autonomous industrialization. This was certainly not the project articulated by the Sidqi commission. It was not the investment model pursued by the local capitalists and landowners who steered Bank Misr (or any other business groups for that matter). And it was never advocated by the leadership of the Association of Industries. It is worthwhile looking briefly at these three important institutions, then, to see how investors actually defined the place of industry and foreign capital in the evolving political economy and operationalized this project.

THE SIDQI COMMISSION ON COMMERCE AND INDUSTRY

In 1916, the Egyptian cabinet assembled a nine-person mixed committee of businessmen and government officials to assess the impact of the war on the domestic political economy and to make policy recommendations for the postwar era. The committee was chaired by Isma'il Sidqi, a rising star in the administration whose career had been momentarily stalled by public scandal. The appointment helped to assure him a long and lucrative public life as the single most closely business-identified Egyptian politician of the 1920s and 1930s. Five leading businessmen served with Sidqi: Yusuf Cattaoui and his protégé, Tal'at Harb; Amin Yahya, the Alexandrian cotton exporter; Henri Naus, the Belgian engineer who rescued the Cassel-Suarès group sugar-processing joint venture; and F. Bourgeois, a representative of the French international investment trust that owned the gas concessions for

Egypt. Two British technicians working for the Egyptian government and the French commercial attaché rounded out the commission (Tignor 1977a: 162 and 1984: 56).

Their recommendations, included in the commission's lengthy (1918) report, reflected many of the prevailing critical views on the economy and arguments about diversification, and can be read as a virtual précis of the investment strategies and political initiatives pursued by leading local capitalists in the next two decades.[9] The commission outlined three basic objectives: (1) the *gradual* expansion of the roles of Egyptian labor, managerial staff and capital in the local economy; (2) the cooperation of foreign and local capital in a *limited* import-substitution diversification effort tied to processing of agricultural raw materials; and (3) a *coordinated* response to signs of social unrest during a period marked by an upsurge in labor militancy. They urged that capital be channeled into factories for paper goods, textiles, bricks, glass, processed foods and leather goods, as a way to absorb a part of the growing population. The commission meanwhile omitted any discussion of starting heavy-goods industries—machinery, agricultural equipment, etc. These industries were not part of the agenda. In the one case where creation of a technologically advanced manufacturing venture was advocated—namely, the call to set up a domestic nitrate plant—the initiative came from governing officials. Kitchener was already involved in direct negotiations with German manufacturing and engineering firms in 1912.[10]

There was nothing ambiguous or mysterious about the call for foreign capital to participate in expanding Egypt's manufacturing sector. First, foreign capitalists and representatives of foreign industrial powers served on the commission. Second, local business groups were already pursuing this strategy. Third, even the limited industrial diversification envisioned by the commission required increased involvement with metropolitan interests—for instance, in developing the necessary power resources, obtaining machinery and technology, and securing financing for the most ambitious projects. If a "common theme" of this report and related initiatives was "the loosening of the bonds of control exercised by metropolitan interests" (Tignor 1984: 55), then it is important to remember that local capitalists sought to do so even as they increased their involvement with foreign capital.

The program articulated by the Sidqi commission reflected the outcome of some three decades of change in the domestic and international market, as well as the investment opportunities made possible by these changes. In particular, the growth of engineering and heavy-manufacturing industry in the advanced industrial economies of Britain, France, Germany and the United States afforded opportunities for complementary expansion of manufacturing and nonmanufacturing industrial investments in countries like Egypt.

Local business groups, through their multisectoral investment strategies and strong international connections, narrowed the scope of conflict over competing sectoral priorities. Despite the claims in exceptionalist accounts, this limited industrialization project posed little threat to what is often envisioned as a formidable opposing bloc of foreign merchants and manufacturers. Many foreign commercial interests would profit handsomely from a limited degree of local industry building, namely those representing advanced manufacturing and engineering sectors, heavy-equipment producers, contractors, electrical-supply firms and those banking interests allied to heavy industry. And no one has yet provided evidence that the Sidqi commission and the early investment initiatives that followed faced any kind of serious, sustained and systematic opposition by either domestic or foreign rivals. Mostly these efforts were ignored or else treated patronizingly. This benign neglect would only change with the gradual realization that British firms were losing their longstanding comparative advantage—political and economic—in the Egyptian market.

THE BANK MISR GROUP

All the points made above are reflected and reinforced in the investment activities of the Misr group, the set of businessmen and landlords led by Harb who founded Bank Misr in 1920. This new business group linked its fortunes to the conservative wing of the national movement, gained privileged access to the post-1922 Egyptian state, and used its political influence to establish the group as a serious competitor in various economic sectors. The bank's managing director and vice-chairman were authors of the 1918 commission report, and, not surprisingly, they adhered closely to the agenda set by the Sidqi commission. For instance, in his public pronouncements, Harb rightly extolled the bank's preferential hiring policy and its principle of selling the bank's shares only to Egyptian nationals. In the privacy of the boardroom, Harb and his allies mapped an orthodox multisectoral investment strategy that included selective cooperation with foreign capital.

The history of Harb and the bank constitute the core of the Egyptian colonial-exceptionalist narrative. Beinin and Lockman (1987) capture the essence of this narrative in their description of the investors' attempt to create a "completely independent national industrial bourgeoisie." What ostensibly most distinguishes them from other investors is their opposition "to collaboration with foreign and *mutamassir* [literally, Egyptianized] capital" (1987: 11). Nonetheless, empirical problems abound in this view. After all, Yusuf Cattaoui, Harb's employer, mentor and the original vice-chairman of the bank, along with another member of the ten-person board of directors, Joseph Cicurel, were themselves two of the most prominent "Egyptianized" leaders of the business community.

As I showed above, Harb and the other key figures in the Misr group had longstanding ties with foreign capitalists and firms that they never abandoned. Instead, Harb expanded his foreign connections. By 1924, he had joined the board of the Crédit Foncier Egyptien, the joint venture with French finance which was the earliest and most important symbol of foreign involvement of the agroexport economy. Harb and his partners in the Misr group would join the boards of other firms as well as explore and initiate their first institutionalized cooperative ventures with foreign capital in the period 1924–1929. Unfortunately, analysts have continued to employ a naive and sentimental model of Bank Misr, elaborating the factors that ultimately led the Misr group to collaborate with foreign capital, while mourning the loss of the bank's independence and the "purity of the ethos with which it was born."[11]

The objectives that Harb and other business leaders publicly articulated before, during and after the 1919 revolution—expansion of industry, diversification of the economy and enhanced local control— were at best broad, abstract and partially conflicting ideals that capitalists continuously had to reconcile and operationalize through their private investment strategies. Local businessmen understood this, and the versions of nationalism that different Egyptian investors championed proved flexible enough to accommodate shifting and pragmatic assessments of interest.

The public expressions of economic nationalism associated so prominently with the Misr group's chairman, Harb, proved equally useful to Harb's local Egyptian rivals, especially in trying to obtain political support for their various enterprises. There were no obvious penalties involved in doing so as long as economic nationalism was the discursive monopoly of capitalists or intellectuals who did not challenge the legitimacy of the prevailing private enterprise–oriented economic order. Harb, along with Yahya, 'Abbud and others, remained free to pursue strategies of selective cooperation with foreign capital. Business nationalism strengthened the competitive positions of local capital—Egyptian and non-Egyptian both—vis-à-vis potential foreign partners, even while Egyptian nationals could use it to advantage in neutralizing some of the well-known competitive advantages that had accrued to local foreigners. In sum, Harb's public-relations campaigns benefited, if unequally, a diverse range of local investors (Owen 1981b).

THE ASSOCIATION OF INDUSTRIES

Local investors founded the Association of Industries in 1922, I would argue, in order to better monitor sectorwide developments and to continue to secure a degree of cooperation among a growing number of competing firms. Other institutions also played a role in controlling the level of business conflict. The cross-sectoral holdings by groups was one. The quasi-public National Bank of Egypt, on whose board sat representatives of the main business groups, was another. All other things being equal, however, diversification made it difficult to continue to rely exclusively on these narrowly based institutional forms of cooperation.

The forms of economic nationalist discourse favored by some of the founders and spokesmen of the association have been reproduced too unreflectively in those accounts that describe its purpose "primarily to represent the foreign residential business community . . . threatened by a renewed influx of European manufacturers" (Tignor 1984: 72–73). If true, then what would have compelled nonmanufacturing firms such as the Empain group's giant power and transport company to join such an organization? Many if not most of the association's original members were not manufacturers. The sectors with the largest number of firms and the first to organize their own sections within the association were shippers and contractors, neither of which gained from reducing the volume or increasing the costs of imports.

Shipping and contracting firms were, however, affected as much as textile manufacturers and the tramways by a steep rise in labor militancy. Workers who had been mobilized in the nationwide demonstrations in the spring of 1919 remained active in the streets and on the shop floors. Industrial firms in fact faced an unprecedented level of strike activity between 1918–1921, a "mushrooming" of union organizing, the birth of a precocious labor federation and the creation of the country's first socialist party (Deeb 1976: 74; Beinin and Lockman 1987: 83–158; Bianchi 1989: 68–69). Yet this most basic dimension of industrial policy has been given little weight in explaining the origins of an association (renamed the Federation of Industries in 1930) that aided employers in the strong front they maintained for twenty years against union and welfare legislation.

Since most of the original members of the association carried foreign passports, analysts have found it important to stress that the interests of the Misr group's founders only partially overlapped those of the association as a whole. This is equally true for every other member firm in the association. Without clarifying when and how this mattered in the specific arenas in which the association acted, this claim conveys no useful information. It is asserted only because Harb's rise by 1925 to a leadership position within the association itself so clearly contradicts core beliefs about the Misr group's alleged original raison d'être or the deep gulf between Egyptian and non-Egyptian identities that is fundamental to exceptionalist accounts of capitalists and politics.

There is little solid information behind discussions of the Association of Industries in the secondary literature. The standard description of this institution as a powerful and effective pressure group tends to rest more on repeated assertion than rigorous demonstration. While collective representation to the state in the name of the association's membership was one of its functions and doubtless took place, this function should not be exaggerated. A multisector association had little need to lobby in an unregulated economy, though it could serve as a mechanism for self-regulation by investors. Assume that business leaders wanted to preserve the oligopolistic structure of the local market that British rule had helped to institutionalize. The association could help in reducing the information and enforcement costs associated with the oligarchs' preferences for price fixing, cartelization and labor control (Bianchi 1989: 69).

RETHINKING THE NATIONALIST MODEL OF THE EGYPTIAN BUSINESS COMMUNITY

These important initiatives between 1916 and 1922 reflect developments in the political economy dating back to the 1890s. A number of families linked together in investor coalitions or business groups emerged as central units of accumulation in the domestic political economy. These groups and their allies held leadership positions in every economic sector: agriculture, urban real estate, mortgage banking, cotton export, construction, power and transport. These same investors took the lead in promoting the development of local manufacturing as a subsidiary investment sector. The outlines of this limited diversification strategy emerged between 1907 and 1912, having weathered fitful opposition from the British authorities in control of the state and having received authoritative endorsement in the commission report of 1918. It remained the basic strategy underpinning public and private investment in manufacturing industry until the 1950s.

The above summary overturns all the key premises of the Egyptian exceptionalist narrative. Industrialization, as envisioned by the investors who steered the Egyptian economy, was not an outcome of the 1919 revolt. This limited industrialization project did not fail. Nor did landlords, "commercial capitalists," "metropolitan interests" and, in particular, business nationalists like Harb challenge it. To the contrary, Harb played a key role in articulating basic objectives of the business community in nationalist terms. It is therefore not surprising to find that, during his most outspokenly nationalist period, foreigners in Egypt continued to cultivate Harb, encouraged his investment activities and even joined him in his Bank Misr venture in 1920. Rather than Harb and the Misr group ceasing to pose a threat to dominant forces in the local economy in the 1930s as they increased their involvement with foreign investors, he and the other Egyptian business nationalists only began to pose a threat at that time, as these new groups demonstrated increasing influence over markets and politics.

The basic objective of the Misr group and all other post-1922 Egyptian investors was profit or, even more preferable, rent. "We are so accustomed to associate the beginnings of the Misr enterprises with the progress of nationalism, and indeed with the progress of the nation, that it is somewhat piquant to set them against their diminished context" (Berque 1972: 337). Rent seeking yields a far less exalted image than conventional portraits of bankers seeking to challenge European economic hegemony. It does, however, resolve many of the conventional paradoxes, including inexplicable complexities in the personalities of businessmen like Harb who, while "hostile" to foreign capital, served on the boards of the biggest foreign-owned firms in Egypt; as well as an "industrialization" drive that led industrialists to plow their profits into the cotton-export sector.

Since, as these investors realized, it is intensely difficult to mobilize public support for the objective of private enrichment, Egyptian business groups viewed and promoted all their ventures as contributions to strengthening the national economy. Nationalism was especially important when market competitors needed or were forced to take their private conflicts to the public. Attempts to build political coalitions in support of various commercial ventures could not, after all, be based on the narrow claims of profits that were to be amassed in the course of building dams, pumping stations, factories and power plants. Instead, investors appealed to the national interest, challenged the "Egyptianness" of particular competitors, protested the undue interference of the British residency, hinted at foreign conspiracies that threatened Egyptian sovereignty, etc.

Business nationalism strengthened the competitive positions of these new investors who were operating within a partially transformed domestic order and a changing international-sectoral division of labor. The new Egyptian investors adopted the multisectoral investment strategies of the earlier business groups and rapidly advanced to commanding positions within the evolving political economy. Egyptian coalitions like the 'Abbud, Misr and Yahya groups gained access to state resources, took over lucrative concessions, enterprises and markets, and expanded the local manufacturing sector of the economy. There is little mystery, variance or inconsistency in the actions of local investors before and after the 1919 uprising. Ongoing relations with foreign firms, state agents and local rivals were based on costs, benefits, risks and rates of return.

The Rise of the 'Abbud Group

In 1924, the Glasgow-trained Egyptian engineer Muhammad Ahmad 'Abbud started a private contracting company that in the space of two decades evolved into a sprawling business empire. By the 1940s, 'Abbud was regularly being referred to in the press and similar accounts as Egypt's most "successful" or most "powerful" businessman and the country's leading "industrialist." At its height, the 'Abbud group operated in construction, textiles, trade, fertilizer manufacture, sugar processing, urban and rural real estate, tourism, banking, transport, shipping and insurance. 'Abbud owned a vast estate in Armant, in Upper Egypt. In addition, he was the single largest shareholder in the giant Bank Misr conglomerate, and he successfully fought his way onto the board of the rival group's bank-holding company by 1950. At the same time, he became the first Egyptian businessman to gain a seat on the board of the Suez Canal Company. In the aftermath of the military coup d'état of July 1952, 'Abbud had made plans to extend his investments in import-substitution manufacturing sectors (chemicals, paper manufacture) and mining (oil); instead, the series of nationalizations between 1955 and 1963 ended 'Abbud's role in Egypt's economic life. His family had to flee the country.

The phenomenal rise in this upstart Egyptian capitalist's fortunes inevitably spawned antagonisms, not least among his local competitors, and for most of his career 'Abbud stood squarely outside of the business establishment. The composition of the steering committee of the Federation of Industries is a case in point. Despite 'Abbud's prominence in the largest affiliated body, the Chamber of Public Works Contractors, and his growing weight in industry generally, he was kept off the board until the 1950s. However, his Egyptian rivals, Harb and Yahya, as well as Sidqi, the politician and tireless spokesman for the private sector, were all prominently identified with the peak association soon after its founding.

For his part, 'Abbud did little to narrow the gap that divided him—socially and culturally—from Europeanized bourgeois circles, on the one hand, and from Egyptian-Islamic bourgeois networks, on the other hand. Instead, 'Abbud flaunted his success, publicized his wheeling and dealing, spent his profits liberally on mansions, speed boats, plantations, parties and sojourns to Europe. He regularly boasted of and exploited his power and influence with both the Egyptian palace and the British Parliament. He provided newspapers with good copy and an occasional scandal. Established Cairene and Alexandrian society either laughed or blanched at such blatant status seeking. At the same time, he was married to a Scottish national, had a highly Westernized life style and played little part in Egypt's Arab-Islamic cultural life. In the wake of the 1919 revolution, his many professional and personal connections with the British community in Egypt were hardly welcomed by the more uncompromising sections of the independence movement. His investment in business nationalism—evinced, for instance, by his support for Zaghlul, his denouncement of the Capitulations, his philanthropy and his involvement in the founding of the National (Ahli) Club—did little to enhance his reputation. Intellectuals today still speak

disparagingly of him as an Anglophile (Isma'il Sabri 'Abdallah, interview, Cairo, 4 June 1985).

While these factors contributed to the controversy surrounding 'Abbud, his success as a capitalist was the primary cause of his notoriety.
Behind his meteoric rise lay a ground deeply strewn with commercial
rivalries and divisive political-economic conflicts. Competition was
sharp for the contracts, concessions and subsidies upon which 'Abbud
and all other local investors depended. 'Abbud's accumulation strategy
straddled markets and politics. His pursuit of profits via public-works
projects led predictably to highly politicized forms of competition, including complex and shifting alliances with Egyptian politicians and
party factions, multinational managers and foreign powers.

"COMPRADOR" ACCUMULATION

The construction industry is a well-known career path for
many capitalists. Construction is a vital part of any national economy.
Public works and other large projects consume a large part of scarce
resources in developing countries, and the industry is a critical component of any development effort. At the same time, the characteristics
of production in the industry that set it apart from mass-production
manufacturing industry continue to assure relatively low costs for new
entrants.[12] In essence, a building or public-works contractor is an en-
trepreneur who organizes and assembles the various forces of production—capital, technology and the highly complex mix of labor skills—
needed for building a particular structure.

The construction sector is well known in Egypt historically as a
source for capital accumulation and, at a certain point, as the refuge for
an eviscerated class following the Nasser regime's assault on local capital
in the 1950s–1960s. The industry harbored remnants of Egypt's old
bourgeoisie while enriching a new cohort of capitalists in the building
boom that accompanied the liberalization of the economy in the
1970s–1980s. Waterbury describes the most recent cohort of Egyptian
contractors as "masters of the public/private symbiosis" (1983: 181–
183), though this characterization is hardly a peculiarity of the 1970s
or of Egyptian political culture generally. In analyzing the course of
Brazil's *arbatura* (opening), Evans found that the construction sector
was the single most important redoubt for local Brazilian capital during
a period of increased penetration by multinationals and significant de-

nationalization in manufacturing (1979: 143–158). The construction industry is a primary institution for a highly politicized form of accumulation in many late-developing capitalist economies, with examples ranging from the 'Uthman group in Egypt to the Sutowo group in Indonesia.

A key mechanism is the politically mediated market in which the firms and their investors operate. State agencies are major clients for the industry. In many cases, public-sector demand accounts for as much as 50 percent of the construction sector's output. Construction was probably Egypt's largest urban industry (Owen 1972, Hanna 1984). Until 1922, European capital and local entrepreneurs of foreign origin virtually monopolized the industry through their access to finance, their superior technical capacity and their close ties to colonial state elites. Ahmad 'Abbud represented one of the first Egyptians to compete successfully in this sector, beginning with contracts for canal dredging and, soon after, government orders for heavy machinery, industrial raw materials and electrical equipment from abroad. Until 'Abbud launched his canal-dredging venture, the Alexandria-based Salvagos group had monopolized the field. Similarly, in the market for government equipment contracts, he competed directly with local capitalists like the Suarès group and the merchandising subsidiaries of British corporations, most notably, the Association of British Manufacturers (Owen 1969: 277; al-Musawwar 18 July 1952; Time 10 August 1953).

Like other investors, 'Abbud needed political support in order to prosper. Great Britain's qualified grant of independence to Egypt in 1922 improved the prospects for would-be indigenous capitalists by enhancing their access to scarce state resources. In other words, the collusive public-private circles that steered the political economy since the British occupation in 1882 were widened to accommodate middle-class Egyptians.[13] In 1924, 'Abbud obtained his first contracts from officials in the Ministry of Public Works and the Egyptian State Railways.

The boost to his business career was provided by the Wafd party (al-Musawwar 18 July 1952). 'Abbud supported the party, and the party patrons, in turn, took care of supporters. 'Abbud ran as a Wafdist in the 1926 parliamentary elections and served as a deputy for al-Tafih. In the following year, he began publishing a short-lived daily newspaper, al-Kashaf, on behalf of the party and its head, Zaghlul. The newspaper venture was likely backed with funds from the British industrial financier Dudley Docker, who had begun to collaborate with 'Abbud in promoting an electrification scheme in Egypt (Davenport-Hines 1984b: 208).

THE LOGIC OF COLLABORATION

There is little mystery in why 'Abbud or any other aspiring Egyptian capitalist chose to cooperate with foreign firms in supplying the state with capital goods and services. Few endeavors offered better returns to a capital-poor investor. The interesting question is why would foreign firms choose to cooperate with an unknown like him? What resources did a businessman like 'Abbud bring to the bargaining table? A political connection of some type was essential, obviously, which explains 'Abbud's investment in the Wafd party. His value hinged initially on his ability to obtain contracts with attractive terms for his principals and, in the case of public-works projects, to organize the subcontracting. One of Docker's representatives was quite explicit in appraising 'Abbud's value to electrical-equipment, railroad-car and steel producers. In a January 1926 meeting at the Foreign Office, he described the failure to secure any Egyptian business until appointing the little-known agent, 'Abbud, who managed to obtain 1.2 million sterling in orders. 'Abbud's success, in turn, was attributed to the close links he had forged with the undersecretary at the Ministry of Communications.[14]

Analysts tend to focus on the more pedestrian elements of such arrangements. Undoubtedly, favors such as kickbacks to individual bureaucrats were common. Capitalists always seemed to have a directorship or two in their companies reserved for retired officials. British administrators (e.g., Auckland Colvin, Elwin Palmer, William Willcocks) pioneered this particular career path in Egypt in the 1890s. The Wafd bosses or patrons probably also secured a measure of institutional support and material aid for the party through their clients. Yet the relationship in this case went beyond rent seeking on the part of bureaucrats.

By arranging to cooperate with international manufacturing giants like Metropolitan Vickers, 'Abbud positioned himself strategically in multiple markets. He played an important intermediary role in the supply of physical goods, obviously. At the same time, he influenced the distribution of equally scarce, though less tangible, political resources. In the eyes of Egypt's governing authorities, 'Abbud's business connections were access points to British society and ruling circles independent of the British residency and the Foreign Office.[15] Such ties were clearly valued by Egyptian politicians. Their importance explains 'Abbud's participation in the delegation that accompanied the Egyptian prime minister, 'Abd al-Khalaq Tharwat, during the ill-fated round of treaty talks with Austen Chamberlain in August 1927 (Vitalis 1990). It was the first of his many missions in London during the interwar period on behalf of various Egyptian political factions.

'Abbud had quickly gained privileged access to the residency itself through his partnership with British capital. Given the central role which this institution continued to play in the domestic political economy, local businessmen and politicians naturally believed it to be another potentially useful point of leverage. The archives of the Foreign Office contain records of countless attempts by 'Abbud to shape policies on his own and his allies' behalf through the residency. In an early example, 'Abbud had one of his British partners make the case for reinstating an official at the Ministry of Communications and sacking the head of the Egyptian State Railways. The British corporate capitalist based his argument on the serious threat to his company's interests, which, in this case, neatly coincided with the preferences of the Wafd party's leadership.[16]

'Abbud's political investments supported his initial business endeavors as an intermediary in the delivery of goods and services to the state. His commercial success—measured by high returns and a rapidly expanding client list—strengthened his position with political authorities who, often grudgingly, found it necessary to deal with him. While his assimilation of British customs and tastes may have made relations with the residency easier, his business activities gained him access. The benefits that accrued through his initial collaboration with the export arm of British heavy industry included a rapidly and steadily increasing stock of resources—goods, money and information—valued by political leaders. The access and influence that he obtained in return strengthened his position in the local market. As the archival record makes clear, 'Abbud bargained steadily and hard to extend his independent control over the construction projects and other ventures with which he was associated.

Egyptian aristocrats may well have been contemptuous of 'Abbud's "opportunism." The British aristocrats rationalized the increasingly brazen political interventions and commercial coups of the Egyptian capitalist by resort to racism, paternalism and the consoling fiction that, above all, 'Abbud was a loyal ally. Viewed from behind the desk of the

Egyptian prime minister or the British high commissioner, 'Abbud and his business rivals no doubt looked to be dependent on the state's support and, hence, prone to its dictates. Nonetheless, the power of investors derived from their privileged position within the liberal market economy that the colonial state had built and post-1922 Egyptian governments preserved. To be sure, political authorities—from Lord Killearn to King Fu'ad—were vested with formidable prerogatives that capitalists, landlords and all other social sectors had to accommodate; but the limits to the reach of the state within the prevailing economic regime were clearly discernible. Thus, as I will detail in Chapter 3, "autonomous" British diplomats and Egyptian officials failed in their concerted efforts in the 1930s to sabotage 'Abbud's operations.

THE EXPANSION OF THE 'ABBUD GROUP

If 'Abbud's business benefited initially from his investments in the Wafd party and pluralism, his career skyrocketed after he shifted his investments in support of the monarchy and authoritarianism. The political realignment took place following the death of Zaghlul in August 1927. 'Abbud backed the losing faction in the contest for control of the party, weakening his position vis-à-vis rival business-political factions. He reaped huge windfalls from the switch in party tarbushes, however, landing lucrative orders for foreign manufacturers and fat commissions for himself. By the early 1930s, he was linked in one way or another with virtually every large public-works project sponsored by the Egyptian state. In less than a decade, 'Abbud had established himself as a major force in the interwar political economy.

The contracting ventures provided the capital for expansion into new sectors in the 1930s. He and his coinvestors received the concession for a bus service in Cairo and gained control of the Khedival Mail Line, the old London-registered steamship service which had thrived on concessions from the colonial authorities. In 1938, 'Abbud took over operations in another heavily state-subsidized sector, the sugar industry, which for decades had been the sinecure of the Suarès group and its French partners. At the same time, he and his own partners gained control of the Egyptian Commercial Bank and the Greek-owned alcohol distilleries in Tura. 'Abbud also invested heavily in the rival Egyptian-controlled Bank Misr and, for a brief period, in a petroleum-supply company which he needed for his fleet of buses. Despite his best efforts, however, he failed to push through the group's most ambitious industrial project: to electrify the Aswan Dam and use the energy to produce nitrate fertilizers, one of Egypt's chief imports.

CONFLICTS OVER INDUSTRY

In 1927, 'Abbud joined forces with an international consortium seeking new export markets in the intensely competitive, interwar heavy-electrical-goods industry. The group updated a plan first proposed on the eve of World War I to develop an indigenous nitrate industry by relying on cheap power from the Nile. They envisioned it as the first stage in a larger scheme for electrification of the entire country. 'Abbud worked tirelessly to build a domestic coalition in support of the Aswan project, vying with his rivals for the scarce public resources needed for the power plant and factory. The decade before World War II was torn by increasingly intense and prolonged conflicts of interest among competitors, both across and within sectors. The outcomes determined where and when local business groups built industry. When war erupted in 1939, Egypt still had neither a hydroelectric plant nor a fertilizer industry in Aswan.

I will take up the Aswan case in detail in Chapter 3 in order to analyze the political capacities and strategies of the rival coalitions that were locked in a battle for control of these new sources of subsidized profit. At the same time, the analysis will allow us to see some of the underlying weaknesses in the administrative capacities of the interwar Egyptian state. To put the problem bluntly, there were few mechanisms in place to resolve the conflicts that accompanied the development initiatives of 'Abbud, his allies and his rivals in the 1920s and 1930s. The diagnosis of the problem is confirmed by the efforts to restructure the relationship between public authorities and private interests, beginning in World War II, and the contests over the construction of a new regulatory regime.

Summary: Business Groups, Power, Industry and the State in Interwar Egypt

This chapter discussed some basic factors underlying the origins and rapid expansion of the multisectoral 'Abbud group. In particular, it showed how 'Abbud's strategy of selective cooperation with foreign capital followed along the lines of the project of limited industrial expansion articulated by the leadership of the local business community in the 1918 Sidqi commission report. The report was itself a formalization and extension of the multisectoral investment strategies pursued for at least a generation by local investors. Similarly, in his reliance on and appropriation of state resources, 'Abbud again continued along the best-known and least-risky route to private profit, power and privilege.

It should not be surprising, therefore, to find that other Egyptian capitalists among 'Abbud's cohort pursued similar strategies, most obviously, those like Amin Yahya and Harb who actually helped to formulate the Sidqi commission proposals. In other words, the investment strategy of the 'Abbud group was indistinguishable from its better-known Egyptian competitors along three dimensions: reliance on public resources; cooperation with foreign capital; and holdings in multiple economic sectors. These were the basic, defining features of local capitalist organization in Egypt between 1880 and 1960.

The best example is provided by 'Abbud's most relentless competitor, the Misr group, led by Harb. The Misr group's reliance on state business and subsidies in its initial 1920 commercial- banking venture and all subsequent enterprises is well documented. The group's largest sectoral investments during the first years of operation were in cotton trading and textile manufacture. Its commitment to expanding domestic industry was undeniable, but so was its commitment to strengthening Egypt's ties to the world cotton market. Thus the directors marked the bank's tenth anniversary in 1930 by joining with foreign capital in a major cotton-export venture. Any minimally objective reading of the archival record of the Misr group's activities during the 1920s would have to deal with the complexities immediately introduced to notions of the group's interests or objectives by this multisectoral investment strategy.

The essential features of the Misr group's strategy were firmly in place prior to its expansion, in the following decade, into insurance, shipping, construction, mining, chemicals, transportation and tourism. The strategy outlined in the group's heralded 200 page report, *The Creation of Domestic Industries*, issued in 1929, was essentially a restatement of the 1918 Sidqi report (Tignor 1977a: 170; Owen 1981b: 6). The bank endorsed the development of hydroelectric power, new transport enterprises, railway electrification and fertilizer manufacturing—all ventures that required the cooperation of foreign capital. The

Misr group and 'Abbud were competing to develop these new local industries.

This chapter revisited the idea that a particular section of the business community during this period was guided by ideas of a completely independent, national industrial economy or, just as vaguely, by the objective of industrialization.[17] The modest expansion in Egypt's manufacturing capacity obviously fell far short of such exalted ends. The political capacities and strategies of investors are often assumed to have played a basic role. But these are questionable assumptions. I have argued that the coalitions of local capitalists who owned (or, in the case of joint ventures, shared ownership in) most Egyptian industries treated manufacturing monopolies, at best, as one possible area of investment. Egypt's earliest business groups did not give up their holdings in the agroexport sector. Later coalitions of Egyptian capitalists—the Yahya, Misr and 'Abbud groups—obviously did not forego investments in these dominant sectors either. In 'Abbud's case—and I suspect the same is true in many other cases—he used his profits from industry to become a landlord.

The tendency to conceive of the interwar political economy, above all else, as a struggle for economic transformation makes it hard to understand the limited objectives actually sought by interwar Egyptian investors and the factors that helped to shape them. For instance, as Clawson (1981) proposes and as the empirical record bears out, the development of Egyptian industry reflected changes taking place in the industrial structures of advanced capitalist economies. "The growth of Egyptian industry, while aided by the local nationalist movement and by state assistance, depended primarily on foreign capital because only it could provide the extra foreign exchange necessary for the import of machinery required to establish industry" (Clawson 1981: 89). This argument tends to underestimate the capacity to domesticate these foreign joint ventures. Still, in exceptionalist histories, the bourgeoisie is invariably constructed as a group literally pursuing "a world after its own image," as Marx once put it, rather than as an inadvertent agency of change. In this latter sense, "the bourgeoisie" in post-1882 Egypt might more appropriately be rendered as the complex effects of a specific configuration of imperialism, the colonial and postcolonial state, and large fortunes amassed in land and cotton sales.

The bourgeoisie in Egypt is most often portrayed as a collective actor with an apparently limited capacity to act in pursuit of its virtually limitless objectives. But I have proposed that we reduce these objectives to human scale, taking as a guide the call in the 1918 Sidqi commission report for a limited expansion of local manufacturing capacity. This was hardly the opening broadside of a group of politically embattled visionaries. It was an accord among representatives of the most powerful economic interests in the country, and its terms continued to guide industrial policy throughout the interwar period.

The idea of an accord does not imply that outcomes were predetermined or that the interests of all parties were fully harmonized and accommodated or that conflicts were to be avoided. Tignor's short discussion of the negotiations leading up to the 1930 tariff reforms provides remarkable evidence of the mechanisms that underlay these accords. He recounts how the administrative head of the Federation of Industries attempted to achieve a consensus with agricultural interests on tariffs. More important, he quotes in passing the observation that the country's main agricultural-interest associations simply "had not organized around this issue" (Tignor 1984: 110–111).

Numerous conflicts of interest were played out in the course of building interwar industry; in particular, there were the recurring conflicts over control of state-subsidized ventures. And with the advent of the depression, sectoral conflicts clearly intensified over priorities and access to the state's meager stock of resources, as I will show. Nonetheless, conflicts were manageable even during the depression, and perhaps the best indication of the overall lack of discord is the resiliency of the liberal economic regime itself. Egypt weathered the depression at the hands of a dictatorial prime minister who steadfastly avoided any significant change in the regulatory instruments of the state or, more crucially, encroachments on the privileged preserves of private investors. This is noteworthy when compared with, for instance, the etatist course set by Turkish leaders in the same period (Keyder 1987). By the time of World War II, even British officials would find it remarkable that vast stretches of the economic terrain, like the electric-power industry and the resources it generated, continued to be in private hands.

The leaders of the local, predominantly foreign business community had articulated a project of limited expansion of Egypt's manufacturing capacity, and they pursued this goal as only one of many investment possibilities. The limited objectives accorded with their broad holdings across Egypt's agroexport economy. The same investment model and priorities were adopted by Egyptian investors like the Misr and 'Abbud groups in the 1920s. It is misleading to portray these important but nonetheless limited initiatives by 'Abbud, Harb, Naus or any other local capitalist in more exalted terms. In imagining that interwar Egyptian investors actually acted in pursuit of such goals as challenging colonialism or seeking autonomous Egyptian capitalism, there is the comfort in knowing what the outcome had to be.

PART TWO

The Rise and Fall of the Neocolonial Order

CHAPTER THREE

Shifting Lines of Power

*Egyptian Business Groups and the
Electrification Schemes of the 1920s and 1930s*

In 1927, the Egyptian contractor Ahmad 'Abbud and his rivals initiated a fierce contest for the right to develop Egypt's hydropower resources and the country's first import-substitution nitrate industry, in cooperation with some of the world's leading international manufacturing and engineering firms. The Aswan project was the most ambitious and costly industrial-development scheme proposed during the interwar period. For rent seekers both abroad and inside Egypt, the scheme represented a huge source of revenues in the form of sales of machines, equipment and engineering expertise; scores of contracts and subcontracts; spinoffs; and, of course, the creation of a new monopoly.

Investors therefore fought for the privilege of building the power project; alternative preferences were powerfully articulated and defended. Importers tried to protect their markets. Engineers argued about the project's design. Politicians mobilized constituencies around this issue. The intensity of the conflict reflected the relative immensity of the stakes. Expectation of the payoff may also explain the apparent willingness of investors to absorb the costs associated with the long delays in implementing the project. Development of an integrated power network was set back by decades. Because of this failure to develop a secure source of nitrates, farmers, the cotton sector and, thus, the economy as a whole paid dearly when fertilizer imports were cut off by the war between 1939 and 1945. And any linkage effects from early development of a basic industry important to agricultural production were foregone. In short, the case offers an extended view of institutions that shaped the Egyptian experiment with capitalism.

If the Aswan project exemplifies the kind of industrial policy articulated and pursued by Egyptian investors like Harb, 'Abbud, and Yahya (in fact, it seems to have defined the limit of what these local capitalists thought was achievable), then it is difficult to argue that the necessity or desirability of supporting such investment generated divisive and profound cleavages inside the circles that governed the interwar political economy. The leadership of every ruling faction—from the Wafd, to the Liberal Constitutionalist party, which is usually portrayed as the voice of Egypt's big landowners, to the palace's own "reactionary" Union party—championed one or another version of the Aswan project. Put another way, they generally backed the creation of new opportunities to enrich themselves, their business allies and related constituencies.

At the same time, Whitehall and its functionaries in Cairo also demonstrated in general a willingness to support the Aswan plan and other proposed new Egyptian industrial sinecures (textiles, transportation, power, chemicals). Others have noted as much, though they tend to interpret this emerging policy stance exclusively as a function of Egyptian nationalism. Instead, I broaden the focus, describing the Foreign Office's lagged response to shifts in the fortunes and investment strategies of core manufacturing sectors inside England (a phenomenon that had little if anything to do with Egyptian nationalism!). In other words, British policy in Egypt reflected a rising concern with Britain's steep domestic economic decline.

'Abbud and the local rival business groups were key intermediaries in the international competition to develop Egypt's electric-power industry. Without the participation of foreign investors, there was no possibility of electrifying the Aswan Dam in the 1920s–1930s (or apparently in the 1960s–1990s, for that matter). Yet, without the resources possessed by local groups—information, access, networks—foreign firms were unlikely to obtain the sales of their manufactured goods and expertise. Local business groups organized politically to secure these awards and, in doing so, attempted to advance their own positions within these ventures and sectors. While businessmen needed the government's sanction, post-1922 Egyptian governments needed local and foreign investors in order to fulfill—if not define—virtually any and all developmental initiatives—in this case, expansion of the country's power resources for irrigation, reclamation and building manufacturing industry.

The position of local investors in these international arrangements reflected a relationship rooted in the broad elite consensus about the naturalness of the market and the private-enterprise economic system. There was, of course, a great deal of bargaining and conflict among the partners. For instance, foreign investors generally sought to maximize their share of the returns in, and control of, any enterprise with which they were associated. At the same time, government agencies sought to overcome the resource disadvantages hindering their ability to monitor private economic activity and to enforce some minimal level of authority. These problems multiplied for any particular authority, whether it was a British ambassador or an Egyptian finance minister, as economic policymaking grew more fragmented after 1922 and the private pattern of production and distribution grew more complex.

The multiple and overlapping sectoral conflicts involved in this attempt to develop Egypt's power and chemical industries have not been adequately defined and analyzed in the existing, fragmentary accounts of the Aswan project. The orthodox nationalist interpretation, which dates to the 1950s, argues that foreign interests and the British state blocked Egyptian governments from carrying out the electrification scheme in keeping with their alleged longstanding opposition to any efforts at local industrialization ('Abd al-'Aziz Ahmad 1955). A revisionist view, emerging in the 1970s, challenges the claim that foreign capital was behind the failure. "The foreign business firms were prepared to carry out the program in the 1930s" (Tignor 1980a: 115). In this view, the delays were due to the instability of interwar Egyptian cabinets and the intense partisanship of the time (Waterbury 1979: 147). Any dispute about causality in this instance—why something did not happen—is unresolvable, but, this logic aside, neither version offers a satisfactory account of the objectives and actions of investors in these competitive conflicts.

Foreign sectors and firms in fact adopted a variety of positions toward the Aswan plan. Big engineering firms and electrical-equipment manufacturers generally supported the project. The degree of support evinced at any point by any competitor was, however, shaped by its representatives' views of the likelihood of actually gaining the contract. To simplify, as Associated Electric Industries' (AEI) competitive position grew stronger, English Electric Company (EEC) could conceivably try to underbid it. Alternatively, EEC's agents could promote a different project or a different decision-making coalition. They in fact tried both of these alternatives, actions that for at least some observers must have appeared very much like an attempt to undermine local industry-building efforts.

The positions taken by the various competing firms in the chemical sector (and their local agents or allies) were much more complex. To simplify them, I will describe three different orientations. At least one set of interests, headed by the Chilean Nitrate Export Association, actively and unambiguously opposed Egyptian attempts to build a domestic nitrate industry since it meant the loss of a critical market. A second set of manufacturing interests, headed by Imperial Chemical Industries, evinced equivocal support, as the second-best solution to the threat of losing the Egyptian market. And a third set of firms such as American Cyanamid that had no Egyptian market share to lose were relatively more open to cooperation in building Egyptian industry.

The impact of these conflicting sectoral forces cannot be assessed separately from local investors' attempts to forge coalitions in support of their rival claims over public resources. As the configuration of interests and their strategies in this particular arena began to take shape, circa 1927–1929, the local investor 'Abbud represented Egypt's best chance for developing an indigenous nitrate industry. His partners in the scheme included the engineering subsidiary of a U.S. firm that did not participate in the international cartel and whose basic objective was to capture the returns from the transfer of technology rather than protect an export position.

There appeared to be no effective mechanisms for, or governing agencies capable of, exercising broad supervisory control over the development project or mediating the many conflicts among competitors. British officials performed something resembling this function until 1919, using their prerogatives to restrict competition in the markets for public goods and services. Purchases by state agencies were for a generation the preserve of a handful of major British manufacturers. As late as the 1950s, British diplomats were still trying to find ways to recreate these kinds of arrangements. Nonetheless, after 1921 authority in economic matters tended to fracture, and policymaking was, not surprisingly, less coherent. British "reforms" had left Egyptian institutions with extremely enfeebled administrative and regulatory powers. As a result the competition for the Aswan project came to resemble a long, costly and unresolved spoils war.

The interwar years might be thought of as a period of protracted decolonization and fitful efforts at state building. Investment conflicts over opportunities to appropriate public resources and build local industry necessarily intersected with the decisive moments in the country's political development: the schisms within the Wafd, the struggles between palace and party, the infamous cycles of British intervention in domestic politics and, hence, the jagged course steered by governing elites.

The International Power Sector
after World War I

The international power industry comprised a relatively small set of manufacturing, financing and engineering-services firms that controlled the production of electric machinery and the generation of electric power in most of the markets of the world. Heavy-electrical-machinery manufacturers were the core of the industry, producing the turbines, generators and other equipment used in the production and transmission of electric power.

Virtually all the international power groups had interlocking engineering-services arms—the electricity-supply and tramway companies—that were the main sources of demand for the companies' products (Hannah 1978; Newfarmer 1980; Hughes 1983). For instance, the Empain family, whose role in Cairo's early power and transport sectors was discussed in Chapter 2, had welded together a massive Franco-Belgian trust. It produced steel, electromechanical equipment and other heavy machinery. By the 1920s, the group had interests in forty-two electric-railway and tramway operations in fourteen countries, along with twenty-five electricity-supply companies in four countries. Cairo was only one of its markets (BEAMA 1927).

Profit margins on heavy-equipment sales were small, yet these capital goods were the mainstay of the international power industry. Export markets in developing countries grew increasingly important to equipment manufacturers in the face of limited domestic demand and the combination of high tariffs and the privately negotiated agreements that closed off the home markets of rival producers. Producers vying for orders in international markets faced stiffening competition, particularly from U.S. manufacturers like the General Electric Company, which emerged as the most dynamic force in the international industry by the end of the First World War (Jones and Marriott 1970: 33, 143; Dummelow 1949: 82; Newfarmer 1980: 58–59; BEAMA 1927: 57, 65–66).

British investors were drawn to the Egyptian market in the 1920s by the need to revive a flagging national industry. 'Abbud's partner in the Aswan business, Dudley Docker, a founder of the British Federation of Industries, played a major role in reorganizing the country's power sector. By the early 1920s, he had decided that only international combinations could save British industry (and earn him sufficiently large commissions). Docker's new interest in international power projects led him to Egypt. 'Abbud represented the Egyptian side of a "multinational" network, fronted by Docker and comprising U.S., U.K. and Belgian-based investors (Davenport-Hines 1984b: 179–181, 201; Jones and Marriott 1970: 97–112; BEAMA 1927: 65–66). The group made use of a specific corporate identity: the Metropolitan Vickers Electrical Company (Metrovick), a firm that Docker secretly sold to U.S. General Electric in 1927.

The Docker group's main competitor for the electrification work was another U.K.-based manufacturer, the EEC. The EEC had been founded in 1919, with a capital of five million sterling. It was the largest firm in the industry, but it had little or no access to foreign technology, capital or management expertise. Heavy losses in 1927, the year it began bidding for electrification contracts in Egypt, portended serious problems. It was clear that the company's earning capacity could not meet its heavy fixed charges. EEC was on the verge of collapse by 1930, when American interests again stepped in to salvage a rival British giant. The American investors held a majority of the ordinary shares, but their control was not disclosed in part because of the controversy raised by G.E.'s takeover of AEI (Jones and Marriott 1970: 128–142; the *Times* 26 February 1930; Davenport-Hines 1984b: 209).

In Egypt, the overtaxed, understaffed administrative agencies of the state, such as the Buildings Department or the Mechanical and Electrical Department of the Ministry of Public Works, undertook a heroic effort to gain some overall coordinative control of developments in the power sector. They faced formidable odds however. British advisers in Egyptian ministries served as conduits directly to and from the residency. Many of the businessmen and politicians appointed to cabinet posts, legislative committees and consultative councils had personal stakes in the outcomes of these projects. Similarly, the outside consultants brought in at the state's expense were all linked to the various foreign competitors.

The Rival Proposals and Incipient Blocs

Though it is true that engineers had long been intrigued with harnessing the "foaming torrents roaring from the sluiceways" (Addison 1959: 106) of the Aswan Dam and British officials in World War I had made plans to use the power for producing artificial nitrates, what gave additional impetus to the revived interest in electrification and fertilizer manufacturing was a downturn in the economy in 1926 and a dramatically rising bill for fertilizers. Certainly these factors had helped focus the attention of legislators and cabinet ministers on the future of the economy (*Egyptian Gazette* 21 March 1927; the *Times* 20 April 1927; Daninos 1922; Department of Overseas Trade 1928: 40; Durrah 1939: 13; Chamber of Deputies 1948: 4). Engineering circles began to argue the relative merits of using the power locally in Aswan, where there was little existing demand, or transmitting the power north to Cairo and the Delta. Foreign investors never considered the latter idea feasible, and 'Uthman Muharram, the Wafd party official who was minister of public works between 1926 and 1928, quickly managed to quash it. His role provides some insight into the nature of the commercial rivalries generated by the electrification business.

Muharram worked with a set of foreign engineering consultants, bankers and manufacturing firms promoting a radically different set of proposals, centering on the electrification of the Egyptian Delta, the fan-shaped expanse stretching North from Cairo to the Mediterranean. Various plans for government-owned pumping stations, the electrification of the railways ringing Cairo and the development oɪ ɪɪew power sources for Egypt's two largest cities coalesced into a large-scale alternative to Aswan as the location for a power station. In its most expansive version, the rival Delta Scheme centered on construction of a large steam-driven plant to be constructed near Alexandria. Muharram and his allies were trying to shift the focus of debate from Aswan to the Delta.[1]

Both these alternatives represented a potential threat to the Empain group, the Belgian utility trust that supplied Cairo with much of its electric power. The Empain group and its local allies sought, therefore, to build a new a new "super" power station in Shubra, a northern quarter of Cairo. While arguing that it was needed to improve tramway service and meet the increasing consumer demand for power, these investors were trying to prevent other foreign firms from disrupting its monopoly position in the power sector and to constrain choices about the long-range course of electrification.

Table 1 summarizes the relationships between local capitalists and international firms and the projects with which they were primarily associated in the late 1920s. The general goal of international competitors seemed to be to capture as large a share as possible of the Egyptian market. The various projects were instruments toward this end.

The Aswan project was the most ambitious and, hence, the potentially most lucrative for manufacturers and service firms. But Docker and 'Abbud faced an uphill battle in gaining approval of the multimillion-pound project. A formidable set of sectoral rivals was arrayed against them.

The 1927–1932 Aswan Round:
Building Authoritarianism

In retrospect, the conflicts over these state-mediated opportunities for accumulation are unsurprising, given the familiar problems of, on the one hand, building support for postindependence parliamentary parties and governments and, on the other hand, the limited access to capital and related barriers that confronted would-be Egyptian investors. If the Wafd, a mass party closely identified with the nationalist movement, required patronage resources in order to govern, the problem was more acute for the various minority parties that vied with the Wafd since these small cliques of aristocrats, landlords and businessmen had no other possible basis for attracting backers or voters.

Berque captured a key aspect of the relation between investors and politics during the period: "It was no secret to anyone at the time that certain interests were opposed to the democratic prospects which the Wafd appeared to offer, and that the fate of governments was closely linked to that of big business undertakings. But these connections became more flagrant as Egyptians gained more understanding of their position and became more capable of assuming responsibility" (1972: 424).

Table 1 *Egyptian Electrification Schemes, 1929*

Project	Local Investors	Foreign Partners
Delta Scheme	Misr Group	Ganz Danubius
		Siemens
	V. B. Grey	English Electric Co.
Shubra Scheme	Misr group	Empain group
Aswan Scheme	'Abbud	Dudley Docker

The distributional conflicts grew increasingly ruthless with the onset of the depression in 1929. An authoritarian government took power to steer the political economy through the crisis. Led by Isma'il Sidqi, the single most closely business-identified politician of the interwar years, the regime was fatally weakened by disputes among competitors. Sidqi was forced from office in September 1933 as the outcome of a "corrupt struggle for the contracts of the Egyptian government" that historians have generally ignored.[2] The Aswan scheme and its indefatigable promoter, 'Abbud, played a central role.

The political arena was a logical place for market rivals to turn to in order to enhance their comparative advantage in the competition for the electrification business. In Chapter 2 I underscored 'Abbud's early association with the Wafd party, a political commitment that he deepened in 1927 by founding a new pro-Wafd weekly, *al-Kashaf*, just as public and private circles began seriously to debate the electrification issue. 'Abbud looks to have invested wisely. His friend and ally, 'Abd al-Khalaq Tharwat, took over in April 1927 as prime minister in the coalition government with the Wafd. Tharwat backed the 'Abbud-Docker group in the Aswan business, and in August his cabinet voted to proceed with the hydropower scheme. The same month 'Abbud joined Tharwat in London as a representative of the "Zaghlulist majority" for the round of treaty talks with the Chamberlain government. But Tharwat's hopes for a treaty and 'Abbud's for a contract were dashed following the news of Zaghlul's sudden death in late August.[3]

'Abbud opposed the choice of Mustafa al-Nahhas to succeed Zaghlul, and his relations with the Wafd quickly soured. In January 1928, the party disavowed 'Abbud's newspaper and denounced the British-identified, protreaty investor as "a stranger in the house and a spy in the camp." While 'Abbud continued to profess himself a Zaghlulist, control of the party had shifted in a manner threatening to him and led him to join forces with those seeking to undermine the Wafd.[4]

Catalyzed by the formation of the first Mustafa Nahhas-led govern-ment in March 1928, 'Abbud began investing in an alternative to the Wafd party and its firm hold over the electoral arena. The strategy, which he shared with the British residency, centered on forging a gov-erning coalition between supporters of the former premier Tharwat and a dissident faction of the Liberal Constitutionalist party led by Sidqi. The ambitious contractor campaigned against the Wafd at home and abroad, preparing the ground for a possible palace coup, a course which he counseled London business and political circles to support. For in-stance, in May 1928, members of the House of Commons hosted a dinner for 'Abbud. He took the opportunity to warn the policymakers of Nahhas's upcoming trip to London, which he said was planned in order to "intrigue" with British socialists. 'Abbud called for the down-fall of the Nahhas government as quickly as possible, in the interests of British trade and British goodwill. He assured his dining companions that the only thing needed was "an intimation to that effect conveyed to the King." It "would give secret satisfaction throughout Egypt."[5]

'Abbud clearly saw these efforts in support of Egypt's incipient au-thoritarian order as a means of advancing his economic objectives—in particular, the Aswan project. He made the linkage explicit when he and Docker, the head of the multinational Aswan consortium, attempted to buy the *Egyptian Gazette,* the largest English-language daily in the country, but British officials in London and Cairo quickly mobilized to block the sale in order to prevent control of the paper from falling into his hands or those of any other "native . . . with or without British backing."[6]

When the king installed the aristocratic Muhammad Mahmud as premier in June 1928, 'Abbud joined with other segments of the busi-ness community in celebrating the "movement against parliamentary decadence" sweeping "nearly all Mediterranean countries" (the *Times* 20 October 1928) and battled with Makram 'Ubayd, secretary general of the Wafd, on the letters page of the *Times* throughout October 1928. 'Abbud applauded the extraconstitutional change in govern-ment, denouncing Nahhas and his allies (chief among them, Makram) as a self-aggrandizing "clique." Makram reminded 'Abbud that the way to get rid of such a clique was through elections, not suspension of the constitution. The executive committee of the Wafd party ended the exchange by announcing the official expulsion of 'Abbud from the party (the *Times* 22 October, 1928).

In Egypt's case, the "movement against parliamentary decadence"

was a fluid alliance of palace stalwarts, dissident Wafdists, Liberal Con-
stitutionalists, and a set of political independents with close ties to
business (the *Times* 13 October and 6 November 1928; Berque 1972:
405–406; 'Abd al-'Azim Ramadan 1983: 9; 'Asim al-Disuqi 1976:
164–165). In return for their support, Mahmud offered an ambitious
program of infrastructure development, including irrigation works,
hospitals and other showcase schemes in the countryside, new roads
and bridges, a prototype workers' housing project, the expansion of the
harbor at Alexandria, the electrification of the state railways and, of
course, the construction of a power station at Aswan. Rival investors
positioned themselves to compete in and shape the outcome of this
highly publicized new round of state building.

THE ESCALATION OF THE POWER CONFLICT

The clash of competing interests and agendas in the
power sector is easy to trace through a series of political interventions
that took place during the Mahmud administration. Keep in mind that
the preferences of various factions for one or another of the proposed
electrification projects—Aswan, the Delta and Cairo—differed and that
the alternatives were seen in zero-sum terms; moving one program up
on the agenda moved the others down, or so it appeared to the business
interests and their cabinet and parliamentary allies.

The first of two stunning blows delivered to the Docker-'Abbud program came in the form of a decision by a special cabinet subcommittee
appointed in January 1929 to review the hydropower issue. The members voted to bury the power-plant proposal, arguing that it threatened
the structural integrity of the dam (the *Times* 7 December 1928 and 1
February 1929; *Engineering* 8 February 1928: 176–178; Chamber of
Deputies 1948; *Misr Sina'iya* January 1929). In doing so, however,
they were reinterpreting the finding of the government's own international advisory commission, which had examined the plan and developed proposals to improve the design of the hydropower plant. The
subcommittee was headed by 'Abd al-Hamid Sulayman, the minister
of communications and the government's staunchest advocate of the
Helwan electrification scheme. The second member, 'Ali Mahir, served
on Bank Misr's board of directors immediately before assuming the
finance post in the Mahmud government. The public-works minister,
Ibrahim Fahmi Korayyim, was 'Abbud's one ally on the committee.[7]

The action of the subcommittee successfully shifted the agenda away from Aswan to the Delta, and from the Ministry of Public Works to the Ministry of Communications, where a pet project for electrification of the Cairo-Helwan railway was being heavily promoted. Though the minister, Sulayman Pasha, was opposed to them, 'Abbud and Docker had bid for this work as well, hoping to link it to the larger and more lucrative Aswan electrification scheme. And they had at least one key ally in Sulayman's ministry. Though few seemed to realize it, the ministry's own chief consultant on the railway-electrification project was a British engineer and Conservative party MP whose firm had numerous business dealings with Docker (Davenport-Hines 1984b: 50–52, 110, 120–122, 209; Hannah 1978: 228–229). Unsurprisingly, the consultant passed over the lower bid tendered by the rival investors in the EEC (the *Times* 12 March 1929). And he could not be swayed by their clumsy attempt at a bribe. Instead, he recommended the higher bid submitted under 'Abbud's name.[8]

The competing investors were next forced to try to block the award of the contract to 'Abbud. They began with a press campaign accusing him of exerting undue influence on Egyptian officials. In response, 'Abbud sought to mobilize a sufficient counterweight to a bloc that included the Misr group, whose chairman, Harb, was busy dealing with both German engineering firms and representatives of the Belgian trust that monopolized Cairo's power industry.[9] 'Abbud's main weapon against this array of investors was his London partners and the influence that they in turn could mobilize within the Conservative party government. Lord Atholl, a member of the House of Lords and an investor in the Aswan scheme, lobbied both the Egyptian king and the British resident in Cairo on behalf of the railway contract, and 'Abbud pushed Docker to bring Whitehall into line.[10]

The next blow to 'Abbud et al. was delivered in the form of a new advisory council to the Ministry of Communication; its recommendation to cancel the adjudication of the railway contract and start the process over again was the precise course being urged on Mahmud by the Misr group and its foreign partners. In fact, allies of the main interested firms constituted the entire membership of the new council! The first appointee was Yusuf Aslan Cattaoui, Harb's mentor and a founding director of Bank Misr; the second was Muhammad Shafiq Pasha, the engineer and former minister who served as a director of Siemens Orient; the third member, Mahmud Shukri Pasha, a financier and confidant of the king, served on the board of the local Banque Belge et Internationale en Egypte.[11]

All the interested parties seemed to share a quite precise understanding of the short- and medium-term implications of this move, beginning with the elevation of the Belgian-backed Shubra power-station scheme to the top of the agenda and ending with the setback to 'Abbud and Docker's competitive position in the larger and more lucrative hydropower market. At this point the Misr group published its heralded, 200-page report on national industry building (Bank Misr 1929), endorsing the development of hydroelectric power and fertilizer manufacturing, markets in which their German partners were primarily interested (Tignor 1977a: 170; Owen 1981b: 6).

Proof of this claim is found in the tactics employed by 'Abbud, his partners and their allies to salvage the deal, with the British government, through Lord Lloyd, suddenly demanding that the Egyptian government postpone action on the Shubra project until the other electrification questions were settled. 'Abbud's main ally in the government, the minister of public works, supplied the prime minister with a convenient and possibly viable rationale, announcing late in May 1929 that the government intended to build a publicly owned power station at Shubra and would call for tenders sometime in the fall.[12]

This interpretation gains further credence from the decisions taken once Mahmud's government fell five months later, after it lost the support of the new Ramsay MacDonald (Labor party) government in London. MacDonald was insisting on a less blatantly neocolonial policy, beginning with the recall of the highly interventionist high commissioner, Lord Lloyd, and the holding of new elections in Egypt (the *Times* 31 December 1929; Marsot 1977: 129). Elections brought the Wafd party to power again, briefly, in January 1930. The Nahhas government quietly opened negotiations with the Belgian investors, abandoning the idea of public ownership, and Empain and the Misr group registered a new joint-venture construction company in March 1930 to build the Shubra power station.[13]

In 1927 'Abbud shifted his support from a populist-tinged party to an autocratic premier, hoping that the Mahmud government would award him the contract to build a power plant at Aswan. He found his objectives thwarted and his agenda for Aswan set back, however, by the concerted actions of a formidable set of rivals. With the help of the Misr group and other allies, Belgian investors protected their monopoly position in the urban power industry. There was little likelihood of 'Abbud's improving his position under the country's democratic interregnum between January and June 1930. His powerful patron in the British residency was gone, and his enemies in the Wafd party occupied key ministries.

'Abbud cast his vote for authoritarianism, lending his support to Sidqi, the dictatorial premier who took office in June 1930 at the king's behest. It had to have been a choice made warily. 'Abbud possessed documents from his Belgian competitors that acknowledged Sidqi's invaluable behind-the-scenes role in the Shubra business, confirmed by his furtive but decisive orchestration of a final agreement within weeks of his taking power. Though 'Abbud prospered during Sidqi's tenure, his successful expansion into new sectors depended on constant political maneuver. In the next section, I examine the conflicts of interest which underlay the business community's relations with the Sidqi regime, focusing particularly on the Aswan conflict and the regime change of the 1930s.

SIDQI'S BUSINESS COALITION

Segments of the domestic business community and foreign capital had been active in championing an alternative authoritarian coalition centering on the monarchy since at least the spring of 1928. Sidqi proceeded along lines similar to Mahmud's, appealing to the same social coalition. Through the 1920s, Sidqi had forged close ties to the business community, through both his leadership position in the new industrial peak association, the Egyptian Association of Industries (after 1930 the Federation of Industries), and his numerous company directorships. In the two years before assuming power, Sidqi had joined the boards of firms associated with the 'Abbud, Empain, Salvagos and Suarès groups.

Investors looked to Sidqi generally to deal with the country's deepening economic crisis. At the same time they anticipated more immediate and tangible benefits. The new prime minister began assembling an extensive patronage network, centered in his new People's party (*hizb al-sha'b*), which the British straightforwardly described as a means for Sidqi to distribute favors in return for support. One of Sidqi's cabinet ministers, 'Abd al-Fattah Yahya (the Yahya group), served as vice-president. 'Abbud's interests were represented conspicuously by Ahmad Rushdi, his employee and adviser, who served as the party's secretary general (Deeb 1979: 278–281; Davis 1983: 155; Tignor 1984: 136–137).

'Abbud's ties to British capitalists were a valuable political resource.

Perhaps the clearest example of their value is found in his interventions in London on Sidqi's behalf. The British Labor government initially hesitated to support Sidqi, in keeping with the liberal and so-called anti-interventionist line it had first articulated in 1929. 'Abbud's British business partners and their allies in the Conservative party had opposed this course from the outset. For instance, the Duke of Atholl, Docker's business partner, condemned the Labor party government in the House of Lords for the "incalculable harm" inflicted upon British economic interests, giving the loss of the Aswan hydropower contract as his example (*House of Lords Debates* 75, Column 1176, 11 December 1929). Lord Lloyd, another Docker ally, blamed Labor for the increase in communist activity "right up to the gates of the Levant," striking "hammer-blow after hammer-blow" against British interests and leading to "the betrayal of our great strategic and commercial position in Egypt" (the *Times* 4 February 1930).

Throughout the summer and fall of 1930, as the opposition pressured the MacDonald government, 'Abbud acted as Sidqi's representative in the negotiations to restructure the Egyptian political regime. Although Sidqi had been warned publicly in July against altering the electoral system, nonetheless by October he managed to unveil a new constitution "as reactionary in form as in substance" (Berque 1972: 442). 'Abbud had made clear that the goal was to prevent the Wafd's return to power, which would spell "the ruin of Egypt." His nemesis from the Wafd, Makram 'Ubayd, was in London at the same time, lobbying the Labor party to withhold support for Sidqi.[14]

'Abbud obtained instant windfalls from his personal investment in the new regime. For example, Sidqi's new minister of public works, Korayyim, the engineer who once worked for 'Abbud and had proved a loyal ally in earlier governments, engineered a switch in the contract for heightening the Aswan Dam and turned over the half-completed work to 'Abbud and his partners (Middlemas 1963: 305–306; *Egyptian Gazette* 22 September 1930; Davenport-Hines 1984a: 670). Under Korayyim, the ministry functioned as a regular source of contracts and, hence, capital for 'Abbud. This connection no doubt contributed to the meteoric rise of 'Abbud, who quickly came to be seen by the residency as one of the "most influential men in Egypt."[15]

Although Sidqi attended to the needs of agricultural and industrial investors as dutifully as he answered the persistent challenges of the opposition, nonetheless there were strict limits on the regime's capacity to accommodate competing demands, given the prevailing economic conditions, and conflicts over these scarce resources grew intense. For instance, in 1931, 'Abbud and his partners sought a government concession to begin a bus service in Cairo, which threatened the Empain group's monopoly over the urban transit market. With the help of Sidqi and allied cabinet ministers, the Belgians obtained a major interest in the venture and forced 'Abbud to pool the bus company's receipts with the tramway's (Vitalis 1990: 298–300). As Berque shrewdly observed, local investors "only withstood the difficulties of the time by an assiduous leverage of power" (1972: 448).

'Abbud's pursuit of the Aswan contract in 1932–1933 reveals the tensions and cross-pressures generated by Sidqi's appeal to the business community for support. 'Abbud backed Sidqi, expecting to obtain the multimillion-pound power project, but instead found his path blocked by his business rivals, abetted by the premier and his cabinet ministers. To remain competitive in the market for the state's resources, 'Abbud was driven to revise his political investment strategy once more. He abandoned Sidqi and next turned to the palace, backing the king in his efforts to debilitate and eventually bring down the Sidqi government.

THE SPLIT BETWEEN SIDQI AND 'ABBUD

The conflicts surrounding the power projects grew more intense as the Egyptian economy continued to deteriorate. This was hardly a coincidence. The depression produced its own set of cross-pressures on the state, most basically by multiplying and intensifying the rival claims on its resources. When the Sidqi regime decided in 1931 to press ahead with the development of a local nitrate industry, it was influenced by the need to cope with the deepening crisis in the agroexport sector. The support of cotton producers in this case did little to assure the project's completion or, of course, reconcile the competing capitalists.

The priority suddenly accorded the Aswan scheme created new difficulties for its indefatigable promoter, 'Abbud, and his allies. These investors banked on the government's awarding a concession to them to operate the power plant. The monopoly rents in supplying power would multiply the returns from the sale of turbines and generators. From the perspective of the rival power groups, building the nitrate plant was, at best, another, more round-about route to selling goods and services, one that required them to bring an additional set of interests into the negotiations. There was good reason to believe that chemical producers would prove to be difficult as partners.

The shift in the focus of negotiations also encouraged an emerging etatist current within the public-works administration and other agencies that pressed for public ownership of any undertaking at the dam site. Hydraulic works were, of course, already under strict government control, and since the construction and operation of the power plant would affect irrigation needs, strong institutional precedents and pressures were at work in this case. The etatist current was also fed by a strain of nationalist antimonopolism that had been pragmatically and, therefore, fitfully advanced by local capitalists, including Sidqi, for the previous two decades. Egyptian technocrats were empowered to revise the project's scope, and they apparently planned for government ownership of both the power plant and the nitrate factory, although they had to retreat on the second point.[16]

Through the good offices of cabinet members and other key political allies, the rival investors maneuvered to influence the outcome of the administrative process and, ultimately, gain the contracts to build and run the plants. The interministerial strife that came to plague Sidqi's administration reflected the intensifying wars for access to state resources. In early 1932, both U.S. and British diplomats predicted— wrongly, it turns out—that the Aswan contract would inevitably go to 'Abbud, though an updated dispatch from Cairo warned "to expect a dogfight." This prediction was right on target.[17]

There is no clearer example of the complexities underlying relations between Egyptian business groups and political authorities, and of the tensions that were engendered by these collaborative arrangements, than the effort by the Foreign Office and the Egyptian premier in 1932 to reverse 'Abbud's fortunes. British authorities had, in fact, taken the first tentative steps in this direction in 1931, following the Egyptian investor's latest foray to London on Sidqi's behalf.

The regime had been in the midst of a rigged election campaign, during May, which was accompanied by bloodshed. British business and political circles were alarmed by the intensifying agitation against the regime and its backers in London, including calls to boycott British goods. 'Abbud sought to reassure his influential business partners and thereby shore up support for Sidqi. Whitehall began objecting to 'Abbud's interventions and sought to counter them. To put it bluntly, the imperial authorities grew indignant when the Egyptian capitalist moved outside a carefully circumscribed orbit. Policymakers began making an illusory distinction between 'Abbud's commercial prowess, which they wanted to cultivate, and his political activities, which they wanted to rein in. They only reluctantly let go of the illusion that the two could be separated when 'Abbud defected from the Sidqi coalition.[18]

Foreign Office archives track the downward spiral of relations between Sidqi and 'Abbud through the summer and fall of 1932. For instance, London alleged that 'Abbud began to pay a *Daily Telegraph* reporter a regular subsidy in return for a stream of anti-Sidqi articles that began appearing in August, as Sidqi prepared for a round of treaty talks with the British foreign minister, John Simon. The businessman was also busy strengthening his ties to King Fu'ad and the king's main political go-between, Zaki al-'Ibrashi. And, as conventional accounts all agree, at about this time officials inside the palace launched an offensive designed to weaken Sidqi and his government.[19]

'Abbud's political activities, which increasingly incensed British bureaucrats in London, coincided with a renewed effort to push through the Aswan project. The Egyptian minister of public works, Korayyim, arrived in England in August for consultations with prospective engineering firms. 'Abbud and Korayyim conducted business together from a suite of rooms in a London hotel. Back in Cairo, the EEC's chief agent concerted with opposition Wafd party officials on a press campaign. From August 1932 on, it becomes progressively more difficult to disentangle the actions of investors from those maneuvering for control of the state or to discuss the fate of the Aswan project separately from the fate of the Sidqi regime.[20]

Key constituencies of the regime were troubled by, among other things, Sidqi's failure to restore political order, and they had begun to withdraw their support. Sidqi was pressing for the treaty talks with Simon, which were scheduled for September 1932 in Geneva, as a way of shoring up the regime. Business and political rivals alike were intent on exploiting Sidqi's new vulnerability. For instance, attacks on Sidqi's favoritism and allegations of corruption were common. In August opponents criticized the government for approving Korayyim's junket to London. While he publicly defended his minister's probity, in private Sidqi blasted Korayyim for colluding with 'Abbud. Korayyim countered by accusing Sidqi of scheming with 'Abbud's rivals. In September 1932, Sidqi escalated the campaign and deliberately began to sabotage 'Abbud's business ties to foreign engineering firms (*La Réforme* 7 and 16 March 1934; *al-Ahram* 14 March 1934; Vitalis 1994).

This widening rift between the premier and his one-time close ally was encouraged directly by Hafiz 'Afifi, the Egyptian ambassador in London, and indirectly by the Foreign Office, which probably produced the damning report on 'Abbud's contacts with the *Daily Telegraph*. 'Afifi acted at least partly out of personal hostility to 'Abbud, while Whitehall wanted to put a stop to his political activities.[21] For Sidqi and 'Abbud, by contrast, the dispute was basically about the price of cooperation. Nonetheless, the game yielded a set of uniformly undesirable payoffs. By the end of 1932, Sidqi faced a revolt in his cabinet, encouraged by palace-based politicians and triggered by the premier's efforts to keep 'Abbud from obtaining the contract for the power project.

THE FALL OF THE SIDQI GOVERNMENT

The ongoing disputes over distribution of resources were a significant and until now unknown dimension of the crises which overtook Sidqi's authoritarian administration in its last year in office. They help us to understand the reasons for the defection of key members of the regime's original coalition. In a showdown with palace circles, Sidqi, who apparently still had the backing of the former colonial power, reconstructed his cabinet on 4 January 1933, dropping three members while shifting Korayyim from his key post at public works. Nonetheless, it was a fatally weakened administration that ruled Egypt for the next nine months, as Sidqi's health deteriorated and the shaky foundation of his government finally collapsed.

This first cabinet crisis is conventionally traced to the "Badari affair," a story involving charges of torture by rural police forces that was given wide publicity in late December 1932 (Vatikiotis [1969] 1991: 284; the *Times* 27 and 31 December 1932). Nonetheless, British diplomatic dispatches from Cairo had disclosed the precise coordinates of the fault line in the cabinet weeks earlier, as Sidqi, who is usually recalled as an unceasing promoter of Egypt's industrial development, brazenly blocked his minister of public works from going ahead with the tenders for the Aswan power-fertilizer scheme. At the same time, Sidqi intervened personally to prevent 'Abbud from sharing in the contract for another massive project when the Egyptian government invited a handful of firms to tender for the Jabal Auliya' dam in northern Sudan. These interventions led to the virtual revolt of two of Sidqi's ministers, 'Abd al-Fattah Yahya (foreign affairs) and Korayyim (the *Times* 1 November 1932; *al-Ahram* 3 November 1932).[22]

In his report to London on the unfolding crisis, the British high commissioner Percy Loraine noted that the defection of Yahya was based on repeated charges of corruption leveled at both Sidqi and the minister of communication, though Yahya's loyalty to the monarch must obviously have played a part. Marsot cites the same Foreign Office document but assumes that it refers to "rumors . . . charging Sidqi and the members of his family with financial irregularities . . . mostly in connection with a project involving the Corniche at Alexandria" (1977: 161). The high economic and political stakes involved with the Aswan and Jabal Auliya' schemes dwarfed those of the relatively small-scale road-building project along the Alexandria coast line, and there is little evidence that what later became known publicly as the "Corniche scandal" was a significant issue in 1932 (*New York Times* 5 January 1933; Vitalis 1994).

Sidqi's deft administrative maneuver effectively sealed the fate of the Docker-'Abbud proposal to build and operate a power plant and fertilizer factory at Aswan, ending what I have called the 1927–1932 bargaining round. The new 1933 budget did not include provisions for the industrial project. As the *Daily Telegraph* viewed it, Aswan and other works such as the Alexandria harbor expansion and the strengthening of the Isna, Asyut and Delta barrages were being sacrificed to Jabal Auliya'. The Cairo opposition daily *al-Balagh* quoted the dispatch, while dismissing the importance of the hydroelectric project and focusing on Egypt's servitude to British interests (summary in *Egyptian Gazette* 3 February 1933).

The state's finances were of course terribly strained by the economic crisis (the *Times* 8 August 1932; *New York Times* 8 January 1933). Demands had continued to multiply while revenues stagnated. And, in the wake of Sidqi's maneuver, various opponents—among cultivators, the irrigation bureaucracy and competing sectoral interests—renewed their efforts to bury the scheme once and for all. Thus, when the finance ministry's chief British adviser stepped forward in December to criticize the proposed import-substitution venture, he argued that it was uneconomical, relying on data provided by I. G. FarbenIndustrie (IG Farben), the giant German producer that dominated world trade in nitrate fertilizers.[23]

'Abbud's prospects seemed no less dim than those of the power project. He held Sidqi responsible for interfering in his bus venture as well as in his bids for the Aswan and Jabal Auliya' business. The loss of a key ally in the Ministry of Public Works was another undeniable setback, one applauded by his competitors. At the same time, British diplomats in London began their own campaign against him. Insiders judged that the loss of political support spelled the end of 'Abbud's hold over the public-works market. Unsurprisingly, his political identification shifted once more, and in 1933 'Abbud emerged as the steadfast ally of King Fu'ad.

During the first six months of that year an ailing Sidqi fought tenaciously with a broad array of opposition forces, which by the spring had come to include the palace as represented by the king's shrewd attendant, Zaki al-'Ibrashi. Though it is less well known, 'Abbud cooperated with 'Ibrashi in his campaign to undermine the administration of the state—for instance, in seeking to block and then to overturn the Jabal Auliya' contract that Sidqi had steered to 'Abbud's competitors. British documents from the period record 'Abbud's earnest attempts to lay the groundwork for a "kingly autocracy" in Egypt, including, according to the interior ministry's chief British adviser, the farfetched idea that 'Abbud would replace Sidqi as prime minister![24] Although Sidqi expended vast resources in his effort to counter these intrigues and keep his regime alive—coming close to killing himself in the process—the embattled premier finally resigned on 21 September 1933 (the *Times* 1, 6, 7, 9 and 22 September 1933; 'Abd al-'Azim Ramadan 1983: 752–63; Deeb 1979: 249; Vitalis 1990: 307–312).

THE ROOTS OF EGYPT'S DEMOCRATIC TRANSITION

The fall of the Sidqi government both was hastened by and was a contributing factor in the gradual withdrawal of British support for Egyptian authoritarianism, or what officials at the time referred to as the policy of nonintervention under Loraine, the British high commissioner. Loraine's replacement, Miles Lampson (later, Lord Killearn), arrived in Cairo in May 1933, and for the next twelve years desperately sought to stem the loss of British imperial prerogatives by making and unmaking Egyptian governments. One long-time British official in Egypt later rationalized the interventionist episodes of the mid-1930s as simply part of a regular cycle in postindependence Egyptian politics (Warburg 1985: 151). In this view, Sidqi's downfall had tipped the (arbitrarily determined) balance of internal political power threateningly in the king's favor. Thus, between 1933 and 1935, Lampson would reluctantly come to support the Egyptian opposition's demand for restoration of the constitution, new national elections and the Wafd party's return to power in May 1936.

The ongoing conflicts over resources were crucial to the unfolding of the post-Sidqi "transition to democracy." Lampson and his staff viewed the conflict between Sidqi and the palace precisely as a war over contracts. They were also worried that 'Abbud's influence inside the new 'Abd al-Fattah Yahya government (September 1933–November 1934) would lead a new round of disputes over Jabal Auliya', Aswan and other projects. Indeed, within the month, 'Abbud and the minister of communications were promoting a new and controversial scheme to widen the harbor at Alexandria, where the contractor had invested in a shipping line and dockyard. Through the early part of 1934, in fact, 'Abbud repeatedly and brazenly clashed with the Misr group, influential segments of the state bureaucracy, major foreign firms and investors, and the Foreign Office itself, contributing to the decision by British policymakers to engineer the downfall of Yahya's government.[25]

As the Foreign Office archives make clear, a specific target of the 1934 intervention was the formidable power of the 'Ibrashi-'Abbud combination—a detail that has been obscured in the passing references to the excesses of palace rule and the Yahya government's intransigent nationalism. Concretely, these excesses consisted of the attempted hijacking of the state administration and, in particular, its vital distributive mechanisms—the contract and subsidy system, etc. (Marsot 1977: 171; Deeb 1979: 252.

At the same time, 'Abbud played a key and highly visible role once the Yahya government suddenly began to promote reform of the Mixed Courts ("obsolete international servitudes"), particularly in London, where he lobbied British businessmen and politicians on the regime's behalf throughout the summer (the *Times* 30 June 1934). When 'Abbud returned to London in the fall of 1934 to press his business allies to back the besieged Egyptian government, the Foreign Office blamed 'Abbud personally for forcing them to intervene, leading to Yahya's resignation on 6 November ('Abd al-'Azim Ramadan 1983: 767–768; Vitalis 1994).

THE BALANCE SHEET

'Abbud had invested heavily in Egyptian authoritarianism. In return, he obtained enormous orders for foreign partners, control of subcontracts and thus resources in the local political economy, as well as a fortune in commissions, which he used to buy the country's most famous shipping line and to launch a new bus company. Nonetheless, the twisting political path that he traveled between 1927 and 1934—from Wafd party MP to Sidqi's chief publicist in London and then to palace loyalist—exacted a heavy toll.

Perhaps the most costly aspect of this particular investment strategy was the escalating and seemingly unavoidable clash with the British residency and Foreign Office. Soon after the Muhammad Tawfiq Nasim government (November 1934–January 1936) took office, 'Ibrashi and 'Abbud resumed what the British called their intrigues, leading to another full-scale confrontation by the spring of 1935. 'Abbud's ties to British manufacturers and engineering firms simply did not insulate him sufficiently from political counter-pressures. Though he had obtained £E 855 thousand in orders for his British partners in 1934, the Department of Overseas Trade branded him a menace to British commerce and sought to undermine his operations. Thus the residency refused to assist his Liverpool-registered shipping venture, dismissed the "British" identity of his bus company accurately as more or less a façade and intervened with the Egyptian authorities against 'Abbud's company in a war over a new set of bus routes (Vitalis 1990: 298–300). Finally, 'Abbud found British and Egyptian officials cooperating to exclude him from negotiations over the Aswan power project when they were revived in 1935.

In the complex unfolding of the realignment in post-Sidqi Egyptian politics, the British eventually stood aside to permit the restoration of the constitution. Nasim's remarkably subservient and, not least for this reason, unpopular administration was replaced in January 1936 by a transitional government headed by another of the king's confidant's who ruled for five months while treaty negotiations with the British government began and Egyptian parties prepared for new elections.

Throughout, 'Abbud and other notables sought to forestall the return of democracy—or at least the return of the Wafd. Following the foreign exile of 'Abbud's close palace ally 'Ibrashi, 'Abbud invested heavily in a futile attempt by his erstwhile enemy Sidqi, of all people, to lead a new palace-minority party coalition government. But the king died in April, the authoritarian regime was buried by the avalanche of popular support for the Wafd party in the May 1936 elections, and the party's head, Nahhas, finally regained the prime minister's office.

In retrospect, it appears that 'Abbud Pasha's rise as a local economic force rested as much on his close association with the Sidqi regime as on his ties to British manufacturers and financiers. His own recognition of this basic factor behind his success can be gauged by the resources he invested in opposing the Wafd. As I have suggested, an equally basic factor guiding this fateful, proauthoritarian political turn was his interest in the massive Aswan power project, which he and a formidable array of competitors envisioned as the cornerstone of a burgeoning and potentially lucrative public commitment to the development of the Egyptian industrial sector. To put it simply, once the Nahhas faction took control of the party in 1927, 'Abbud believed that he stood a better chance of gaining the contract if the Wafd and its own business allies did not control the administration of the state.

Along with the Wafd, the British residency and Foreign Office emerged as a force that came to oppose 'Abbud at a critical juncture, as he turned to use the capital he had accumulated as a commission agent and public-works contractor to expand into new sectors of the economy. This conflict was due originally to the widening divergence in political preferences beginning in 1932, a problem that 'Abbud made threatening by his regular access to investors and, through them, the English press and Parliament. The decision to undermine a valued Egyptian partner of British business circles was doubtlessly made easier by the simultaneous, rapid expansion of investment ties to 'Abbud's main competitors, the Misr group.

A *Times* dispatch on 3 April 1935, reporting on an upcoming Egyptian trade mission to London, provides a concise summary of the unfolding realignment of political-economic blocs in interwar Egypt. As the Foreign Office made clear, the visit was designed to help cement Anglo-Egyptian economic ties, yet 'Abbud, the one Egyptian investor most closely identified with British capital, had been pointedly excluded. Instead, 'Afifi, one of his chief political enemies, led the delegation. The former ambassador to London had been appointed managing director of the Misr group's new insurance joint venture, and Harb, the Misr group's heralded chairman, joined his newest business partner in the highly symbolic pilgrimage to England.

The 1935–1939 Aswan Round: Failure of the EEC Bloc

In the second, protracted round of negotiations to obtain the Aswan project between 1935 and 1939, the relative positions of the rival investment blocs were basically reversed. The bloc originally built around Docker's multinational power consortium and associated locally with 'Abbud paid heavy political costs for its aggressive pursuit of the electrification business. Docker had finally withdrawn from the scheme, but his successors at the electrical-manufacturing conglomerate he helped to create, AEI, found themselves at a serious disadvantage in the changed political circumstances of the mid-1930s and driven to search for an alternative to the 'Abbud group.

In contrast, the competing EEC bloc reaped the political windfall. The company's local representative prepared the ground for a renewed push on the project virtually from the day the Nasim government took office. Significantly, the EEC bloc pressed for and eventually obtained the active involvement of the British Foreign Office and residency/embassy in the new bargaining round. By 1938, the intervention of the British state in support of the Aswan scheme had been recast in terms of securing a vital strategic interest, in anticipation of the production and supply problems that would invariably accompany a war with Germany.

THE DIPLOMACY OF NEOCOLONIALISM

Despite the threat to well-established competing sectoral interests, such as British shippers and investors in Chile's nitrate industry, by 1932 England's Department of Overseas Trade had unequivocally endorsed the proposed Egyptian import-substitution fertilizer industry. The British state framed its support as an allegedly long-held "general maxim" of the government not "to attempt to frustrate the development of local industries in foreign countries."[26] In doing so, policymakers were adjusting imperial policy in response to the fundamental shift underway in the structure of the global economy, as well as aligning with what, borrowing from Ferguson (1983), might be labeled Britain's own nascent internationally oriented manufacturing bloc, the heavy-electrical-machinery producers chief among them. The depression had hastened the decline in the fortunes of this hard-hit sector, and, as a result, executives of large and teetering firms like EEC and AEI redoubled their efforts to exploit new markets, from Egypt to the Soviet Union.

The depression undoubtedly intensified interest inside Egypt in building a domestic fertilizer industry in order to secure the supply of an increasingly vital agricultural input. Nitrate imports had started to grow enormously in the 1920s, as cultivators sought to counter the adverse impact of their cropping patterns and irrigation techniques on soil fertility. As an indicator of the importance of this fundamental change in agricultural production, Richards records a 400 percent rise in total fertilizer imports over the period 1920–1937 (1980: 66). Between 1929 and 1932, imports from Egypt's main suppliers fell by almost 40 percent, even while prices were dropping. The lack of foreign exchange drove Egyptian investors to conclude a series of complicated cotton-for-fertilizer barter arrangements with German chemical producers in 1931 and again in 1934.

Egypt had emerged as one of the most important new export markets for an international industry that entered the depression already suffering the effects of excess capacity, declining prices and rising tariffs (Stocking and Watkins 1946; U.S. Tariff Commission 1937: 12, 116; Monteón 1982; O'Brien 1989). Egypt was the seventh largest importer of chemical nitrogen (natural and synthetic) in 1929, ranking behind the United States, Spain, France, Japan, the Netherlands and Belgium. By 1934 it had climbed to fourth. It was the third largest customer for embattled, Chilean-based miners and exporters of natural sodium nitrate, whose-once dominant position in the world market had been eclipsed by synthetic producers, like the U.K.'s Imperial Chemical Industries (ICI) and the German giant IG Farben.

The collapse of agricultural markets in 1929 brought about a crisis for the industry and spurred the efforts by ICI and IG Farben to organize an international cartel for control of production, prices and markets. Thus, the prices which Egypt paid for fertilizers from 1929 until World War II were generally fixed by the cartel's members, though disputes with the Chilean producers led to breakdowns of the cartel and severe price wars between them and the synthetic producers in 1931–1932 and again in 1934 (Reader 1970, 2: 148–150; U.S. Tariff Commission 1937: 82–86). In addition, the cartel apportioned the Egyptian market among the various producers.

Examining Egypt's import figures for 1932, I found that the proportions of the synthetic market to German + Norwegian (IG Farben–controlled) + US importers equaled 80 percent, while UK + Dutch totals equaled 20 percent—that is, the exact quotas set by the cartel. While I do not have specific data linking ICI to the Dutch industry, British, Italian and Belgian capital accounted for 50 percent of the total capital of the major producing plants there. These plants included holdings by Banca Commerciale, Royal Dutch Shell, and Banque de Bruxelles, according to the U.S. Tariff Commission (1937: 169–170). U.S.

interests did not participate directly in the cartel, but the "grand alliance" between ICI and Dupont and a series of specific agreements negotiated with IG Farben undoubtedly secured the cooperation of major North American producers (Stocking and Watkins 1946: 149–154; Reader 1970, 2: 413–415, 428–443; Taylor and Sudnik 1984: 92–105, 166).

The cartel helped IG Farben and the other members of the German fertilizer syndicate improve their position in the Egyptian market at a critical time. Though Egypt did not rank as a major importer of German sodium nitrate before organization of the cartel, during 1930–1934 it ranked second after France. At the same time it became the single largest purchaser of nitrogen fertilizers from Germany. Similarly, it guaranteed (German-controlled) Norwegian producers their second largest market for calcium nitrate (U.S. Tariff Commission 1937: 141–142, 167).

Thus a second set of competing sectoral interests was gradually and unavoidably drawn into the Aswan business. The Chilean Nitrate Export Association had no choice but to oppose the plans for an import-substitution industry since Egypt was one of the only large markets left to this beleaguered mining industry. The large, technologically advanced chemical firms like ICI and IG Farben were better able to adapt to the underlying weaknesses in the nitrate market, leading them gradually to assume a more flexible position on the question of supporting local industry. Thus, according to a 1929 communication between ICI and IG Farben, written when the first cartel agreement was being negotiated: "It is certain that as soon as the empire markets show a demand sufficiently large to justify the creation of a home nitrogen industry, . . . [i]t will be created, if not by us then by others. It is to the joint interest of both parties that we should participate in such plants, rather that they should be put up by third parties" (Reader 1970, vol. 2: 114).

In broad terms, ICI, which represented another basic advanced industrial sector, was also shifting toward a more "internationally-oriented" investment strategy in the interwar period, though perhaps with less enthusiasm than the heavy-electrical-machinery producers. The record of the 1935–1939 Aswan bargaining round shows ICI's managers acting according to a distinct set of preferences: first, that the Egyptians not build a domestic industry, and a distant second, that ICI undertake the project (economical or not) rather than face the loss of the lucrative Egyptian market to a competing producer. The ambivalence underlying ICI's "cooperation" created an important complication for what I have labeled the dominant EEC bloc. Despite the significant momentum to see the project through before the outbreak of the war, ICI's managers were never compelled to adjust their preferences and to lobby on behalf of the scheme. To the contrary, they remained opposed to it and consistently counseled Egyptian officials to abandon the fertilizer-factory project.

Nationalism (British not Egyptian) was thus a factor shaping the Foreign Office's increasingly partisan support of the EEC bloc in the 1935–1939 Aswan round, but this defensive ideological posture was itself a reflection of the deepening problems in Britain's industrial economy. Not only had foreign and, in particular, U.S. capital been making deeper inroads into the empire's once vast economic preserves—oil, engineering, electric power, finance, communications, mining, etc.—but American investors were also buying up strategic British industries. The heavy-electric-equipment sector is a spectacular case in point. Docker's role in disguising American control of AEI had caused a political uproar in London.

Recall that AEI was an American-created and -controlled holding company (although G.E. executives reduced their majority holding to approximately 40 percent in 1935), which in turn controlled two separate (nonintegrated) manufacturing firms, Metrovick and British Thomson Houston Company (BTH). Both of these subsidiaries were competing for the Aswan contract. BTH supplied the engineering expertise and expected to build the turbines and generators for a consortium that was fronted by a smaller British electrical firm, Crompton Parkinson, which held shares in a newly founded company deliberately named "British" Nitrogen Engineering (BNE). BNE was a joint venture with Chemical Construction Corporation, which in turn was a U.S. subsidiary of American Cyanamid Corporation. BNE was to design and run the nitrate factory. Diplomatic support in Egypt seemed to hinge on the Foreign Office's assessment of the "real" national component in these new, large international ventures.[27]

The managers of the ailing British-based electrical-manufacturing firms were desperate to exploit any possible marginal advantage in the competition for the Aswan contract. Thus, in 1935, AEI's leadership scrambled to create a credible British façade for a consortium that had also come to include American Cyanamid Corporation, a major U.S. nitrate producer, and the corporation's British principals pressed the residency for support on the untrue and unconvincing grounds that it was free of any American "taint."[28] Their competitors were more successful, though no less scrupulous. The chairman of the board of EEC and its managing director, Lord Nelson, traveled to Egypt in January 1935, where he encouraged Nasim's cabinet to reject AEI's scheme as "American with an English veneer."[29] This claim was true but disingenuous, coming from a corporate executive hand-picked by American interests to head EEC following the secret bailout of the financially strapped electrical giant.

The EEC executives indeed appear to have secured what Jones and Marriott called the "fiction of British control" (1970: 134). Makers of foreign policy endorsed the EEC's bid on nationalist grounds and lent the group privileged support in Cairo; this support included close, quiet and effective coordination with the Egyptian state's remaining senior (British) ministerial advisers. The EEC directors praised the financial adviser, a one-time opponent of the project, who was kept officially apprised of "DOT attitudes." The chief irrigation official serving on 'Abd al-Wahhab's technical committee provided details of the committee's deliberations to the residency and, no doubt, to his friend, V. B. Grey, the EEC representative in Cairo. At one point Grey called him the "vital cog" in the negotiations.[30]

The records of the Foreign Office also confirm Jones and Marriott's conclusion that ICI had cooperated with American investors in the bailout of the EEC (1970: 128–143) and helped to supply the English "veneer" in this particular case. The problem, as EEC representatives frankly admitted, was that ICI belonged to "a syndicate which controlled the policy of the EEC," and ICI sought to "divert" the Egyptians "from their Aswan dam scheme."[31]

THE JUNE 1935 DECLARATION

The EEC's concerted, six-month-long campaign resulted in a favorable decision by Nasim's cabinet in June 1935, a date that conventionally serves as a benchmark in the history of the development project. Nasim's cabinet officially endorsed the building of the power plant–fertilizer factory complex, while deciding to bypass the usual system of open tender for the contract. Instead, the government ranked the competing project proposals and authorized the finance minister, 'Abd al-Wahhab, to begin negotiations with the EEC and ICI. This last point, which drew immediate protests from disgruntled competitors like 'Abbud, remained the subject of continuing political controversy for years. For instance, British policymakers abandoned all pretense of neutrality and insisted that the clause committed the Egyptians to sign with these specific firms. And the 1936–1937 Wafd administration used this same agreement in attempting to deflect criticism for its decision to resume negotiations with the EEC-ICI consortium.

The residency's files identify 'Abd al-Wahhab as the architect of the policy, and the actions of this highly regarded official in the finance ministry require some explication. Though he is now conventionally depicted as a nationalist and a technocrat, his opponents at the time attacked him for allowing the creation of a new private foreign concession rather than appointing Egyptian engineers to run the power plant (the *Times* 3 June 1935; Chamber of Deputies 1948: 5; 'Abd al-'Aziz Ahmad 1955: 59–62). Elsewhere, of course, public ownership of power resources was becoming increasingly common. Another, even more widespread criticism centered on the minister's remarkable decision to insulate the companies from the competitive pressures of an open tender, particularly when ICI's reluctance to carry out the project was well known.[32] The government temporarily forestalled a public vetting of the technical criticisms, but it would later provide powerful ammunition for the EEC/ICI's commercial rivals.

The Foreign Office explained these choices as the result largely of 'Abd al-Wahhab's determination to stop the 'Abbud group from obtaining the contract. The explanation was certainly plausible, given the depth of antagonism to 'Abbud and his palace allies, and it was an objective that British policymakers generally shared. For this reason, they encouraged the campaign and, unsurprisingly in this case, evinced little concern for the sudden and obvious departure from long-standing procedures in the award of a major contract. Nonetheless, 'Abd al-Wahhab and his British allies found it difficult to explain why the public interest would not be better served by judging the competing firms' proposals on their technical merits.

The promotion of the EEC's Aswan scheme sheds new light on 'Abd al-Wahhab's brand of business nationalism and must be viewed as part of a broader effort in support of a neo-Anglo-Egyptian private investment bloc. As an official at the finance ministry, 'Abd al-Wahhab had played a pivotal role, since at least 1932, in the joint ventures that the Misr group had formed with British investors, while as minister he sponsored the 1935 Misr group–led trade mission to London. The effort culminated in the massive textile joint venture that Bank Misr negotiated in 1937–1938, again with the close participation of 'Abd al-Wahhab, who resigned his government post in May 1936 and joined the boards of several of the group's enterprises (Davis 1983: 150–153; Tignor 1989: 40–41; Deeb 1979: 232).

The contents of his own growing investment portfolio may also help explain why ʿAbd al-Wahhab did not pressure ICI to undertake the nitrate venture. The technical commission that he headed in 1935 had also put forward the alternative for the first time of using electric power to mine and process the region's iron-ore deposits (*Egyptian Gazette* 11 November 1937; the *Times* 25 February 1938). He retired the following year to become the first chairman of a new Anglo-Egyptian joint venture holding the concession for mineral rights in Aswan.[33]

The EEC bloc's drive to gain the contract lost momentum with the change in government in January 1936. ʿAli Mahir, the palace loyalist appointed to oversee the May elections, is alleged to have used his power to sidetrack ʿAbd al-Wahhab's initiative. The foreign investors blamed the setback on the undue influence of ʿAbbud and his allies, although one of Mahir's own advisers was heavily criticizing the plan, and his objections hurt the EEC's cause. Even the high commissioner, Lampson, found the objections convincing and held back his support at a critical moment. ʿAbbud gained little by the delay, however, particularly when weighed against his own dim future prospects. His ostensible partners in the Aswan business increasingly viewed him as a liability. National elections returned the Wafd to power, and as ʿAbbud undoubtedly knew, one of the party's top leaders was a paid consultant to the EEC. At the same time, London policymakers were directing Lampson to see the incoming prime minister, Nahhas, as soon as possible and to press him for a favorable decision on the EEC scheme.[34]

THE 1936–1937 WAFD GOVERNMENT AND
THE ASWAN PROJECT

The popularly elected Wafd government unfortunately proved no more successful than its predecessors at resolving the conflicts that surrounded development plans for Aswan. To the contrary, these commercial tangles threatened to topple the government in March 1937 and contributed to another in the series of historic splits within the Wafd, leading to the formation of a dissident Saʿdist party (named for the Wafd's founder, Saʿd Zaghlul) by January 1938.

Despite the strong pressure by the supporters of the EEC-backed scheme, the EEC coalition failed to obtain the contract. This setback could well have been overdetermined by the circumstances surrounding the Wafd's return to power. The party leadership signed a historic treaty of alliance with Great Britain in August 1936, which burdened Egypt with increased defense-construction outlays while permitting British troops to remain on Egyptian territory. In the treaty's wake, the pro-EEC bloc would face stiffened resistance to public funding of the proposed project.[35] The political costs of the treaty were probably of even greater consequence however. Though the Nahhas government rallied parliament and the Wafd's hard core behind it, many Egyptians condemned the treaty, believing that the party had fatefully compromised the longstanding goal of complete independence. Nahhas faced growing divisions inside the party leadership and mounting losses in the party's once-solid popular base, which the opposition factions sought to exploit.

Sidqi, the former premier and 'Abbud's new business partner, emerged as leader of an opposition bloc that also included 'Abbud's palace ally, 'Ibrashi. Unsurprisingly, the businessman's name was prominently linked to the opposition, but 'Abbud, who had slowly begun to repair his relations with the British embassy, tried to deny a role in the anti-Wafd bloc. This denial was scarcely believable, judging from the accounts of British diplomats, particularly once the opposition began to focus its attack on the government's Aswan policy and the decision to resume exclusive negotiations with the EEC.[36] That opposition to the policy inside the Wafd's leadership was led by Ahmad Mahir, who the British sources identified as one of 'Abbud's closest friends and business partners (and ultimately the founder of the breakaway Sa'dist party), reinforced the perception of hopelessly entangled political and commercial factors at work in the government's eventual fall.

The circumstances were hardly auspicious for the EEC and its local allies. Although the Wafd leadership elected to resume negotiations with the consortium led by the EEC and favored by the British embassy, rather than holding an open tender, the electrical-manufacturing firm still had no sure way of securing the cooperation of the chemical industry in the project. The threat of competition was the one real possibility for influencing ICI to build a local nitrate plant in Egypt, yet the government, again with British backing, moved precisely in the opposite direction, marshaling its formidable powers to make sure that 'Abbud and allied competitors were excluded from this particular arena. And as the Wafd leadership must have expected, the new round of negotiations with the EEC left them vulnerable to attack from a broad array of opponents, all of whom could rally under the banner of nationalism (with some legitimate justification, it turns out) in assailing the government's policy.

Nahhas's own cabinet and party were both divided over the issue, and the attacks in the press and other public venues grew increasingly powerful through 1937, particularly once accounts of the internal splits began to appear, together with revelations of Minister 'Uthman Mu-harram's personal connections to the EEC. The most outspoken in this regard was *al-Balagh*, a long-time pro-Wafd organ whose editor, 'Abd al-Qadir Hamza, began writing against the Wafd following the August 1936 treaty. Both the British ambassador and the EEC's local represen-tatives saw the hand of 'Abbud and Sidqi behind the press campaign.[37]

In response to its critics, the government argued that it had little choice but to honor the commitment of its predecessors, set down in the June 1935 letter from the Egyptian government to the EEC, while pointing out that it had won new concessions from the companies that preserved vital Egyptian national interests. 'Abd al-'Azim Ramadan (1983) relies on the same arguments in defending the Wafd's policy, although both claims were disingenuous at best, and the government's public positions are clearly contradicted by the archival account. Nah-has's immediate predecessor as prime minister had already explained privately how the Egyptians were free to break off negotiations with the EEC at any point, a course which a successor, palace-backed adminis-tration publicly and unhesitatingly adopted a few years later.[38]

The Wafd government's feeble defense of its actions simply rein-forces my doubts about the coherence of its Aswan policy. Nahhas and his closest allies in the party and cabinet, in particular his minister of finance, Makram 'Ubayd, who played a commanding role in the Aswan business, were engaged in a complicated, multisided bargain. Unwilling either to open the door to 'Abbud or to close the door on the EEC, particularly given the insistent pressure of the British government's rep-resentatives, the Wafd's leadership simply let the Aswan negotiations hang. At the same time, they began to encourage the set of foreign and local investors promoting alternatives to the fertilizer-factory project. These alternatives included building a domestic steel industry at Aswan or, as a German consortium led by the notorious Otto Wolff group proposed, mining iron ore in the region for shipment back to Germany.

It turns out that a third local investor coalition, the Yahya group, reaped the greatest windfalls from the bargain, eventually emerging as a guiding force behind the promotion of this new industrial sector. At the same time, Yahya and his partners were about to start production at the country's first superphosphate plant at Kafr al-Zayat, outside of Cairo. In effect, these investors successfully checked the advance of the EEC in favor of their own rival claims to the state's resources. Within a year, the Yahya group began successfully to promote the idea of building a coal-powered nitrate factory in the Egyptian Delta. Meanwhile, the EEC's efforts to build a hydropower industry in Egypt ran out of steam (the *Times* 25 February 1938; *al-Balagh* 14 September 1937).

THE CABINET CRISIS OF MARCH 1937

The battle for the Aswan concession reached a climax in March 1937, when Prime Minister Nahhas narrowly averted—or, more accurately, delayed—a split in his cabinet and party over the privileged position seemingly being accorded the EEC and its allies. Nahhas's foes had chosen the eve of the prime minister's scheduled departure for the Montreux talks, where Egyptians were finally to negotiate the end of the foreign-imposed and bitterly resented Capitulations, to try and force the government to reopen the Aswan scheme to international tender.

Under orders from the U.K. Department of Overseas Trade, the British ambassador and his staff had joined with EEC executives and their local partners in a concerted campaign to pressure the Nahhas government to conclude a contract. In response, 'Abbud and his co-investors struck back in the press and other venues, seeking to mobilize opposition through time-tested appeals to Egyptian nationalism by charging the Wafd with failing to look after the country's precious resources. The Wafd's finance minister, Makram 'Ubayd, managed to outmaneuver the pro-'Abbud factions inside various advisory committees. Then, in a long and tense cabinet session on 31 March 1937, three of Nahhas's ministers, led by the outspoken Wafd party executive member and minister of communications, Mahmud Fahmi al-Nuqrashi, threatened to resign unless the Aswan project was opened to public adjudication. Nahhas finally diffused the crisis by agreeing to create yet two new international advisory committees to review the EEC-designed electrification scheme and determine whether it was feasible to open all or parts of it to public tender without compromising proprietary technology.[39]

There is little mystery in this bald power play inside the cabinet. Its purpose was to undermine the EEC's backers inside the cabinet, and the anti-EEC bloc chose a particularly strategic moment to push on this front. As Makram 'Ubayd confided to Lampson, Nahhas was forced to compromise rather than "precipitate an internal political crisis" on the eve of the Montreux talks (*Killearn Diaries* 1 April 1937). Given both the symbolic and material importance attached to abolishing the Capitulations, Nahhas simply could not afford to break up the government. For the same reason, few if any of the key figures in the diverse opposition bloc of business investors and Wafd dissidents (in the case of Ahmad Mahir, the majority leader in the Chamber of Deputies, the distinctiveness of the two categories collapses), former Wafdists and promonarchists, would have wanted the government to fall at that precise point.

This remarkable intrusion of competitive conflicts into the cabinet's chambers has gone unnoticed in most accounts, though it was directly responsible for the purge of the cabinet dissidents three months later, which in turn led to another of the historic splits within the leadership ranks of the Wafd. Nahhas had noted as much, assuring the British ambassador, Lampson, that he would purge the cabinet once he returned from Montreux, "with the Capitulations issue safely in his pocket" (*Killearn Diaries* 1 April 1937). Four months later, after consulting with British officials, Nahhas summarily fired four of his ministers, including Nuqrashi, and then attempted to withstand the backlash as the erstwhile officials turned to the pages of the opposition press for revenge. Meanwhile, Makram 'Ubayd and other party leaders continued to work closely with both the EEC executives and the British ambassador to try to stem the damage (*Killearn Diaries* 1 April, 31 May and 27 July 1937; *Egyptian Gazette* 4 , 13, 17–18 and 21 August 1937; *al-Ahram* 11–12, 14–15, 17–18 and 20 August 1937; *Ruz al-Yusuf* 495, 30 August 1937). Lampson and the company officials helped to write the letter that 'Ubayd Makram eventually sent to the companies! The British embassy helped the companies draft their reply. The intermediary in these exchanges was Amin 'Uthman, a rising star in the Wafd and a businessman who served as Lampson's unerring source on Wafd party politics.[40]

'Abbud and his coinvestors, whom Lampson and others blamed for orchestrating the campaign, in this case succeeded in shaping their commercial agenda to conform to Egyptian nationalist discourse, linking the EEC, the Wafd, foreign exploitation and corruption in a particularly compelling way. Nahhas and his closest colleagues found themselves increasingly on the defensive, forced to rationalize the public-works minister's personal business ties to the EEC as well as the government's continued refusal to consider competing bids for the work.

The embattled leadership of course also attempted to use the discourse of nationalism, though their appeals rang hollow. Thus, the staunchly pro-Wafd editors of *al-Misri* asked whether Makram 'Ubayd deserved "to be blamed because he did not leave the scheme in foreign hands, and the whole country at the mercy of foreign contractors?" (translated in *Egyptian Gazette* 17 August 1937; *al-Balagh* 6 September 1937; *Ruz al-Yusuf* 497, 12 September 1937). 'Abd al-'Azim Ramadan (1983: 73–120) used the same argument in his defense of the Wafd. For this reason, a rare attempt to deconstruct these conventional and rote nationalist appeals seems particularly compelling now.

As an unnamed minister in Nasim's 1934–36 cabinet analyzed the dispute, in an interview, "the discussion is merely the result of trade competition between the companies . . . and every line written on this subject, on the pretext of attacking the present government, is to make propaganda in favor of the companies competing against the company chosen" (*al-Muqattam* 21 September 1937).

I believe that the prime minister's inner circle finally came to see the commitment to the EEC scheme as a political handicap and tried, too late, to distance themselves from the Aswan project. The political controversy catalyzed by the dismissal of the cabinet ministers in August strengthened the opposition, which adopted an increasingly aggressive and confrontational stance against the government. The EEC's initiative abruptly ground to a halt.

In London, officials of the Department of Overseas Trade wanted the embassy to make new entreaties, but in an exceedingly pessimistic dispatch, in November 1937, Lampson advised against intervention since it was clear that the Wafd government was teetering. One month later, a newly empowered, eighteen-year-old King Faruq dismissed Nahhas's government on the pretext of bringing good government to Egypt. Faruq's advisers prepared for another round of rigged elections that ensured a parliamentary majority for a government of minority-party politicians.

The post-Wafd cabinets under Muhammad Mahmud (December 1937–August 1939) and 'Ali Mahir (August 1939–June 1940), which governed through the outbreak of the war in September 1939, opted politely but unmistakably to ignore further initiatives by the EEC and its allies.[41] Of course, this response was completely rational, particularly if these governments accorded some significant priority to the development of an Egyptian fertilizer industry, since the EEC team conspicuously lacked the capacity to deliver the goods. As the signs of war loomed on the horizon, and concerns for future supplies of nitrates grew more politically pressing, the Egyptian government turned to support the Yahya group's new, American- and Hungarian-backed venture to build a fertilizer factory in the Delta, and 'Abbud predictably sought to stop them.

Summary: Investment Groups and Sectors in the Interwar Political Economy

The record of protracted conflicts in the two nascent Egyptian industrial sectors has helped us see the emergence of the Egyptian wing of the industrial bourgeoisie in a strikingly new light. During the decade between 1927 and 1936, corresponding roughly to the two Aswan bargaining rounds, the investor coalition known as the Misr group consolidated its position as a pivotal force in the domestic political economy. In archetypal fashion, the investors' strategy focused on building a diversified set of state-subsidized enterprises. And the group's expansion turns out to have relied in important part on the cooperation of local political factions, foreign capitalists as well as British policymakers.

In excavating the record of the Aswan project, I obtained a fairly good cast of the contours of this broad, loose but nonetheless allied set of multinational firms, embassy officials, bureaucrats and party factions in what I labeled a neo-Anglo-Egyptian investment bloc (after the trade delegation led by Harb and 'Afifi). It is hardly speculative to suggest that this alliance contained the core of support for (if not the logic of) the controversial Anglo-Egyptian treaty of alliance signed by the Nahhas government in August 1936.

Harb and his coinvestors had, in a sense, replaced the Suarès group as a linchpin of the postcolonial political economy, a fact recognized and reinforced by the efforts of British officials (and former officials) to negotiate (and cash in on) successful joint-venture arrangements with British shippers, insurers and manufacturers. This process is documented quite carefully in Tignor (1989). The Misr group's success was fitting, and its willingness to assume the role perhaps less surprising than exceptionalist historiography has supposed, given that Harb entered business under the Suarès's wings and built his banking group based on blueprints drawn jointly with them. This chapter has helped us to appreciate the continuity underlying the accumulation model pursued by a new generation of interwar Egyptian investors. The key here of course remained the private appropriation of public resources in the form of concessions, subsidies, capital, etc., and the carving out (or redivision) of new and virtually unregulated "private" monopoly and oligopoly sectors.

This basic strand of continuity in business-group formation between roughly 1890–1910 and 1920–1940, which I underscored in Chapter 2, can be usefully extended and qualified here by considering one of the most salient discontinuities revealed in the interwar records. In the 1880s, British officials in Egypt literally took over exclusive control of the Egyptian state and reshaped basic institutions of the political economy to meet the needs of City money managers, Liverpool shippers and Manchester textile firms. Local capital served as junior partners in this classic late-colonial project. By the 1930s, however, British officials had been reduced to fighting a largely futile, rearguard action for a group of embattled firms and sectors. As the record of the Aswan negotiations makes clear, in the 1930s domestic Egyptian investors such as 'Abbud grew increasingly threatening to British interests, not least because they were deemed vital to preserving what remained of a dwindling set of colonial-like privileges. The two sides of the British state's relationship to Egyptian capitalists are illustrated in the intense campaign against 'Abbud and the equally intense courting of the Misr group.

The Misr group faced a concerted challenge for the privilege of building Egyptian industry. As the record of the Aswan project shows, during the key decade between 1927 and 1936 'Abbud formed the highly visible axis of a second, broad and loosely aligned political-investment bloc, comprising a generally different and identifiable set of foreign capitalists (Docker/AEI/G.E. as opposed to Nelson/EEC/Westinghouse), bureaucratic factions (Korayyim versus 'Abd al-Wahhab) and political factions (Sidqi, the palace and the Wafd dissidents as opposed to the Wafd leadership and 'Afifi); this bloc found itself increasingly on the defensive through the 1930s.

If investment blocs in Egypt competed for the power to create, shape and ultimately capture new state-mediated opportunities for private accumulation, by the close of the decade 'Abbud and his allies appear to have lost the contest. Not only had they failed to obtain the contract for electrifying the dam and building the country's first nitrate plant, but support for the Aswan project itself was eroded in the course of the two bargaining rounds. As I have shown, between 1937 and 1939, investors both introduced a competing agenda for hydropower development (mineral processing and steel manufacturing) and successfully promoted an alternative import-substitution nitrate project (the Delta Scheme).

'Abbud's investment in the authoritarian regime proved enormously costly. The close political identification with King Fu'ad provided his competitors with a powerful counterorganizing principle. Through the 1930s, the overlapping struggles over access to resources, accumulation of wealth and control of state power were often seen and pursued quite specifically as an attempt to weaken or undermine 'Abbud personally— an anti-'Abbud campaign. This attempt is well documented in private papers and archival records for a wide spectrum of organizations, agencies and factions, including rival investor groups, of course, and the British residency, but also the British expatriate community more generally, bureaucrats like 'Abd al-Wahhab and the Wafd's leadership. The costs for 'Abbud manifested themselves even more plainly, as many of these same forces tried to stop the 'Abbud group from expanding its economic holdings. The Aswan project is the most important case obviously, but similar struggles took place in other state-sanctioned oligopolies, including urban transport, shipping and the building of public works.

These local business rivals, their would-be foreign partners, their political allies as well as their political foes, all acted as if each new project or sectoral conflict of interest threatened to undermine a bloc's position or power. In other words, these competitive conflicts were viewed in something like zero-sum terms, with investors resorting to politics constantly in order to avoid or escape the market. There was nothing particularly Egyptian about this tendency toward market avoidance on the part of investors like Harb, 'Abbud and the rest of their interwar cohort. The foreign firms most directly involved in the multisector conflicts of interest engendered by the proposed Aswan project relied on precisely the same strategy. After all, both the nitrate and heavy-electrical-equipment producers participated in formal international cartels. If the Egyptians had actually signed a final contract with the EEC, the price of their Aswan turbines and generators would have been based on the decisions made at an annual meeting in Geneva.

More crucially, the nitrate producers' cartel existed in large part in order to prevent countries like Egypt from developing local industries of their own. The Chilean exporters (representing an American-dominated processing industry), who were the weakest party in the cartel, exerted extraordinary energy to dissuade the Egyptians from going through with the project (with shippers having a direct stake in the Santiago-Alexandria circuit enlisted in the effort as well). The continuous expansion of nitrate capacity in the postwar world economy suggests that Egyptians were hardly helpless in the face of this pressure however. The probability of implementing the nitrate project depended in important part on successfully exploiting the existing tensions within the cartel, as well as the cleavages between cartel members and nonmembers. Instead, the cartel leader, ICI, reaped the windfall from the deep and intensifying divisions among Egypt's leading business groups and their allies!

Those invested in the EEC's project, which rested tenuously on the possible cooperation of ICI, needed the threat of competition as a fulcrum to move the British chemical giant closer to its second-best preference—that is, to build the plant rather than have the cartel lose the market. Yet the war against the 'Abbud group recounted in this chapter hardly seemed the way to force ICI's hand. The blatant interventions by their representatives against the project in 1934–1935; the EEC's repeated admission that it had no influence on the chemical firm (the situation was, if anything, the reverse); the complete absence of ICI directors in the record of company-government-embassy negotiations from 1936 on; and the search for alternative rationales for producing electricity at Aswan in the latter part of the decade all suggest that the collective interest of ICI and the other members of the nitrate cartel were in the end well served by the competition among 'Abbud and his rivals.

Supposedly forward-looking state agents and agencies (or, in the most reductionist version, the state) are uniquely positioned to resolve precisely this kind of impasse. Evans (1979) worked out the logic most fully for the case of post-1964 Brazil, while others have confirmed how, in numerous settings, local capitalists gradually if sometimes reluctantly reconcile themselves to a enlarged regulatory regime (the relative autonomy of the state) as a trade-off for enhancing their bargaining capacity with foreign firms and sectors. The worldwide economic crisis of 1929–1933 is often pointed to as the catalyst for this partial reordering of class-state relations (e.g., Hamilton 1982).

This chapter raises basic questions about the generalizability of such arguments, particularly in light of the conventional and expansive claims of a "deep-rooted tradition of state autonomy in Egypt" and, thus, of a basic dilemma facing the group of Egyptian investors, "hemmed in by a state and regime it could never fully penetrate, no less control," as Waterbury (1983: 233) posed the dilemma. Conceptually, it is unclear what "state autonomy" refers to in a case and era marked by a largely unregulated economy in the hands of a business-landowning oligarchy, where a labor movement was barely given room to organize. Empirically, as I have tried to show, in the protracted bargaining rounds over the largest industrialization scheme of the era the highest public officials—British and Egyptian alike—showed little capacity or willingness to articulate a position separate from that of some set of investors, much less an ability to resolve these competitive conflicts of interest in line with their stated preferences. It might just as easily be claimed that in this case the interwar state or regime turned out to have been hemmed in by a diverse set of local and foreign investors it could never fully penetrate, no less control.

The conflicts among rival coalitions of investors (business groups) and among the broader configuration of allied political factions and foreign firms for which the groups served as an identifiable core (investment blocs) were a defining feature of the interwar Egyptian political economy. While investors evinced tendencies to cooperate in organizing particular sectors—for instance, via the formal cartelization of the market for finished textiles by the Yahya and Misr groups (and their foreign joint-venture partners)—such tendencies existed side by side with the powerful competitive cross-pressures described in this chapter.

In general, I have described this conflict as a competition to maximize access to public resources and control over state-mediated opportunities for private accumulation. In practice, it was a battle to carve out new sinecures (Misr Airworks, the would-be Aswan fertilizer and power industries) and, perhaps more frequently, to recarve existing ones (textiles, the bus and tram lines, shipping, the sugar-processing industry). The Egyptian investors with the deepest roots in the pre-1922 economy—Harb, the landowners who helped him to found the Misr group, and the Yahya family—were arguably the most successful and invested in securing places among, and in important instances wresting shares from, the economy's existing foreign and local capitalist factions (Empain, Suarès, Salvagos, etc.). It is therefore unsurprising that they would have fought so hard against the efforts of the upstart 'Abbud.

CHAPTER FOUR

War within "the War"

Business-Group Conflict in Egypt, 1939–1945

During World War II, Egypt's business oligarchs escalated their private war over markets, contracts, concessions, subsidies and related state-mediated opportunities for accumulation. This conflict among the Misr, Yahya and 'Abbud groups for dominance over Egypt's expanding industrial sector converged with the continuing constitutional struggle between King Faruq and the Wafd party, and with the Churchill government's attempts to redefine and secure the former colonial power's national interest in Egypt. Using the ongoing conflict over the Aswan project as an example, I will detail the role played by these local investors in the precipitous collapse of the British neocolonial project.

During the 1920s and 1930s, an Egyptian national political elite and closely linked groups of Egyptian landlords and capitalists came to exercise growing influence over the levers of state power and the private economy. As we have seen, they were the primary beneficiaries of a contested and protracted though nonetheless substantive transfer of power. This argument draws heavily on the more recent debate about the postcolonial state in Africa (Boone 1992 and 1994). The importance of this transfer of power can be judged by the British state's need to negotiate what amounted to a neocolonial pact with these forces, symbolized by the 1936 treaty. In this chapter, we will see how these same domestic elites used the war (or the war permitted them) to undermine these arrangements, in part, by turning to American capital.

British bureaucrats among others liked to draw a simple analogy between the two periods when they and the leaders of the Wafd party found grounds or necessity for cooperation—in 1936–1937 and again in 1942–1944. In the grand, Anglocentric accounts of Anglo-Egyptian relations these are two bright moments in the highly pragmatic diplomacy of a hegemony in decline, designed to help stem that decline. By contrast, in exceptionalist accounts these are two formative moments in a neocolonial project that allowed British statesmen and capitalists to maintain if not tighten their grip over Egypt until the mid-1950s. In both these versions of the wartime Anglo-Egyptian *problematique*, though, Egyptian investors play the same unchanging and supportive role in securing British economic objectives through the war and beyond.

In fact, British economic interests in Egypt were steadily undermined during World War II. British policymakers had realized as much, which I argue is a key to understanding both their abandonment of the Wafd again in late 1944 and their increasingly desperate search for institutions and doctrines that would preserve the postwar Egyptian market; their desperation led, for instance, to the sudden and remarkable portraits of King Faruq as a force for "serious social reform in Egypt" (Louis 1984: 232).

The analysis begins by trying to account for a basic and yet unfamiliar difference in the 1936–1937 and 1942–1944 Wafd governments: the identities of the investors who backed and benefited from them. Tal'at Harb and friends formed a core part of the bloc behind the Wafd government that in 1936 concluded a historic pact with the ex-colonial power, but at least two specific conflicts unfolded within this new order. The first involved factions within the bloc itself—namely, the Misr and Yahya groups—and is illustrated most powerfully in the overthrow of Harb as chairman of the bank in 1939.

The second conflict is equally implicated in the Yahya group's triumph, which was a further setback to the competitive position of 'Abbud, who was representative of a group of firms and investors that were aligned against the Anglo-Egyptian bloc and that since 1935 had been essentially excluded from feeding at the state's resource trough. Yet, by 1944 American intelligence agents were following the footsteps of the British in describing 'Abbud as one of the most powerful and influential men in Egypt. The key factor in explaining 'Abbud's renaissance is the pragmatic alliance he negotiated in 1942 with the leaders of the Wafd, fourteen years after they had expelled him from the party.

This political realignment, sanctioned and underwritten for equally pragmatic reasons by Churchill's war cabinet, buttressed the 'Abbud group in the war of position with rival investors for control of postwar markets, sectors and resources. As the details of the 1944 Aswan bargaining round reveal, these Egyptian investors had all come to see American capital as vital to their future—a shift that both foretold and assisted in the collapse of neocolonialism in Egypt.

We should not lose sight of the irony in the developments to be traced below. The original impetus for the Aswan nitrate project was provided by British colonial officials in World War I as a way to secure the strategic position of the empire. The resurrection of the project by local Egyptian capital during World War II reveals how tenuous the British position in postcolonial markets had grown.

The War of Position

At least three new and distinct coalitions of Egyptian investors had established themselves in and shaped the leading sectors of the economy by the mid-1930s. One of the most enduring and consequential form of business-interest conflict turns out to be what I have called the war for competitive position among these rivals. This war, which steadily intensified during the 1930s, is important in explaining 'Abbud's audacious play between 1942 and 1944 to become the country's self-styled industrial czar.

As can be seen in Table 2, the cross-industry investment strategies of the three main Egyptian business groups reproduced a pattern of direct rivalry for access to and control of virtually every one of the country's oligopolistic sectors. The only sectors not contested by at least two of these groups in the 1930s—tourism and insurance—became new arenas for competition soon after the war's end.

'Abbud's own efforts to enter or remain in many of these markets—the power-sector conflicts of the late 1920s and early 1930s, the bus-route wars of the mid-1930s, the scandals over shipping routes and subsidies in the late 1930s and, of course, the Aswan fertilizer scheme—were effectively undermined by the Misr and Yahya groups, together with their political allies. 'Abbud responded by seeking alternative investment possibilities, leading in 1938–1939 to his takeover of the Commercial Bank of Egypt as well as the Egyptian sugar company.

Table 2 *Egyptian Business-Group Holdings by Sector, circa 1939*

Sector	Group		
	Yahya	*Misr*	*ʿAbbud*
Mining	+ +	+	
Textiles	+ +	+ +	@
Chemicals	+	@	@
Construction	+ +	+ +	+ +
Cotton export	+	+ +	
Noncotton trade	+	+ +	+
Shipping	+ +	+ +	+ +
Urban transport		+ +	+ +
Banking		+	+
Insurance	+		
Real estate	+	+	+
Tourism		+	

KEY: + = exclusively group-owned; + + = joint venture with foreign capital; @ = attempting to enter sector

The opposition to ʿAbbud is itself evidence for what I am calling a bloc built around the business empires of the Cairo-based Misr group and the Alexandria-based Yahya group, rival investors who had nonetheless negotiated cooperative cartel-like arrangements in various economic sectors. Such arrangements did not, however, prevent the outbreak in 1939 of one of the most divisive conflicts of the wartime Egyptian political economy. At stake was the ownership and control of the Misr group's factories, information networks and rent circuits. Between 1939 and 1942, the Yahya group overthrew Harb, took control of Bank Misr and laid the ground for a new phase of economic expansion. During 1942–1944, ʿAbbud organized against his rivals with the help of the Wafd.

HAFIZ ʿAFIFI: THE PATH FROM DOCTOR TO PIRATE

A remarkable series of business-group conflicts unfolded in the months just prior to the outbreak of the war, in which it became clear, once the dust had settled, that the Yahya group had made enormous gains. One of the key figures in these interlocked affairs was Hafiz

'Afifi, who coldly helped engineer the overthrow of his original patron, Harb, to advance his own fortunes and those of an apparently more attractive patron, 'Ali Amin Yahya.

'Afifi was an ambitious doctor turned politician who had bolted from the Liberal Constitutionalist party to serve as the Sidqi government's representative in London. During this period, he took the side of Sidqi and the Foreign Office in the growing dispute with 'Abbud and his palace allies, a stance that the Foreign Office believed eventually cost 'Afifi his post. Upon his return to Cairo, 'Afifi embarked on a new career, thanks to Harb, who offered him the directorship of the Misr group's new Anglo-Egyptian insurance joint venture.

In his new guise as a corporate executive, 'Afifi quickly became a pivotal figure in the Anglo-Egyptian trade bloc that backed the Wafd's return to power in 1936–1937, and he was rewarded with an appointment as Egypt's first ambassador to London following the signing of the Treaty of Alliance in March 1937. According to Davis, Harb convinced 'Afifi to return to Cairo one year later, following the sudden death of Ahmad 'Abd al-Wahhab, the powerful former finance minister and close ally of the Misr group. In April 1938, 'Afifi rejoined the board of Misr Insurance, and took 'Abd al-Wahhab's place on the boards of four other Bank Misr subsidiaries as well (Davis 1983: 162). Harb and his coinvestors undoubtedly turned to the well-connected 'Afifi as a way of increasing their political support, given the group's perilous finances and an increasingly desperate need for funds to prevent a collapse of the bank.

The Misr group's uncertain future perhaps explains 'Afifi's apparent risk-adverse investment strategy because in the same period, 1938–1939, he extended his support to the Misr group's industrial competitor, the Yahya group. 'Ali Amin Yahya, the grandson of the family firm's founder, succeeded his father Amin Yahya (d. 1936) as head of a group that had ridden the crest of economic nationalism after 1919 to become a powerful force in cotton export, shipping, insurance, textiles (via Yahya's ties to Filature Nationale), mining, food and chemicals.

The Yahya group's involvement in mining, food and chemicals was through the Egyptian Salt and Soda Company, the London-registered firm that was created to operate the state's salt-mining operations at the turn of the century. Tignor (1989: 85) demonstrates that control of the company was nonetheless in the hands of local capital by the 1930s. The same group was the sole domestic producer of phosphate fertilizers and sulfuric acid until the 1940s, through a chemical plant at Kafr al-

Zayat, near Alexandria (est. 1937), held under a subsidiary, Société Financiere et Industrielle d'Egypte.

Yahya and the family's coinvestors, which included members of the resident foreign community like Alfred Lian, Silvio Pinto and Ladislas Pathy [Polnauer], enlisted 'Afifi in their proposed Aswan mining and Delta fertilizer joint ventures, which, as we have seen, emerged on the eve of the war at the top of the government's development agenda. In addition, they would cooperate in bringing Coca-Cola to Egypt.

LOOTING THE SHIPS

'Abbud gained first-hand knowledge of the potency of this partnership between a bitter personal adversary, 'Afifi, and two sets of competitors, when he lost his bid in 1939 to obtain a financial subsidy for his shipping joint venture: the old Inchcape subsidiary, the Khedival Mail Line. 'Abbud bought the ships from the Inchcape interests, but he had to raise the capital for their transfer by mortgaging them and was heavily in debt to the National Bank of Egypt. At the same time, the venture was running at a loss. He naturally turned to the state to bail him out, claiming that his ships deserved the same level of support as the heavily government-subsidized companies that the Yahya and Misr groups had launched with foreign capital in the early 1930s.[1]

Though Ahmad Mahir, the minister of finance and one of 'Abbud's closest allies, fought hard for the subsidy, Mahir's enemies in the Wafd joined with 'Abbud's business rivals in attacking both Mahir and the subsidy plan.[2] Saba Habashi, the minister of commerce and industry, spearheaded the opposition inside the cabinet, pitting himself against his fellow Sa'dist party member, Mahir. The attack focused mainly on the firm's historic links with Lord Inchcape, the long-dead British shipping baron. But in attempting to discredit the nationalist *bona fides* of 'Abbud's shipping company, the opposition's hand was strengthened by 'Abbud's penchant for indiscretion, which in this case linked Mahir's name too closely and prominently to the 'Abbud group. Mahir was finally forced to retreat in the conflict with Habashi, allowing his opponents to bury the subsidy question.[3]

'Abbud's sinking fortunes in the shipping business were salvaged only by the beginning of the war, when he successfully leased his fleet to the British state (after threatening to sell them to Italian buyers). Habashi meanwhile rather quickly overcame his objection to foreign investment (real and imagined) in the local economy. Immediately upon leaving office, he and two of his colleagues took up positions on the boards of a number of the Yahya group's joint ventures. Mahir, though, remained loyal to 'Abbud, a fact which may have cost him his position in the cabinet formed by his brother in August 1939. He and his undersecretary of finance, Amin 'Uthman, another partner in 'Abbud's expanding commercial empire, attempted a last-minute intervention on behalf of 'Abbud's Aswan scheme, though by this time the government had lined up solidly behind the rival project of the Yahya group.[4]

Once again, the business conflict in Egyptian political life that I have been highlighting tends to complicate conventional accounts of another key period in Egypt's history. As is usually noted, the new 'Ali Mahir government and the British authorities were involved in a series of escalating confrontations, which led both to Mahir's downfall by June 1940 and to the subsequent interpretations of his policy as one guided by an overarching and "long run" objective of weakening British "influence" (Morsy 1989: 66). The purges at the Finance Ministry are conventionally interpreted in this light. However, while "pro-British" figures like Ahmad Mahir, the former finance minister, and his deputies lost their positions, equally staunch pro-British figures were appointed to these same strategic sinecures. They included Husayn Sirri, who took over at Finance, where he helped the country's leading spokesman for Anglo-Egyptian commercial cooperation, 'Afifi, take over the country's most important national economic institution, Bank Misr.

THE HIJACKING OF BANK MISR

There is no more graphic example of the Yahya group's ascent to the commanding heights than its assault on Harb's massive, teetering monument to economic nationalism, Bank Misr. The management's questionable financial practices combined with a general economic downturn to weaken the commercial position of Bank Misr in the late 1930s. A run on the bank as the war broke out forced Harb to seek additional subsidies from 'Ali Mahir's government. The premier and his finance minister, Sirri, forced Harb off the board as the price for the government's support. 'Afifi took over as chairman of the bank in September 1939.

While nationalist historiography has tended to frame the Bank Misr crisis and Harb's overthrow as an example of foreign capital's continuing hostility to Egyptian industry, the explicitly revisionist accounts by Davis (1983) and Tignor (1984) have effectively undermined the view of the crisis as a British plot. Davis concludes that rival investors and their political allies had taken advantage of the bank's financial crisis. "At the center of the conspiracy to oust Tal'at Harb was Dr. Hafiz al-'Afifi" [sic]. In addition, both the premier, 'Ali Mahir, and his finance minister, Sirri, also sought Harb's dismissal, according to Davis, because "he was closely associated with Ahmad 'Abbud" (Davis 1983: 162, 166).

Though Sirri gradually moved closer to 'Abbud late in the 1940s, I have uncovered no evidence linking him to 'Abbud at the time of the Misr crisis. More tellingly, no act served 'Abbud less than appointment of his unswerving personal, political and commercial rival, 'Afifi. While Davis places 'Abbud in the thick of the multisided conspiracy, this interpretation is incorrect. 'Abbud's efforts to take control of the bank took place during 1942–1944, in response to the successful coup by 'Afifi and the Yahya group.

One of the most important results of the 1939 leadership change at Bank Misr has been overlooked. As the auditors were trying to make some sense of the bank's tangled finances, 'Afifi brought his partner and head of a major rival business group, 'Ali Amin Yahya, onto the bank's board. These investors in effect created a new institution for private regulation of markets through what at the time would have been called a combination, a form of common control over otherwise independent firms. At the same time, the original coalition of investors behind the founding of the bank and its subsidiaries was being forced to surrender its exclusive rights to appropriating and distributing the rents generated by Bank Misr's factories, firms and branches.

World War II and the Restructuring of the Postcolonial State and Economy

The intensifying conflict among these Egyptian investors is an unknown facet of the war years in Egypt. The details of economic policymaking and interest conflict generally have been ignored in the Anglocentric narratives of British efforts to secure loyal governments in a country vital to Allied defense plans, as well as in the nationalist counter-narratives of the war as a neocolonialist project and catalyst of the upheavals of the 1950s. The intersecting point of these alternative narratives is 4 February 1942, when, with the Germans pressing toward El Alamein, British armor surrounded the 'Abdin Palace and British ambassador Lampson forced King Faruq to appoint the Wafd party leader Nahhas as prime minister. With British backing, Nahhas and the Wafd remained in power until October 1944.

The exigencies of the war were undoubtedly the cause of the repeated British violations of Egyptian sovereignty, the explosive increase in the numbers of foreign soldiers on Egyptian soil and the burdensome administrative regulations imposed on the country; likewise, they obviously overrode concern for the inevitable backlash that would follow this resort to colonial-like forms of intervention and control. Egyptian nationalists are also correct in assuming that British policymakers hoped to exploit the position built up during the war in order to strengthen economic linkages between Great Britain and Egypt. But they erred, as did British policymakers like Lampson, in thinking that Egyptian capitalists shared these objectives.

My account of business and politics during the war years begins with the ad hoc creation of new forms of state intervention in the economy, a generally unremarked-upon side of the early years of the war, and the efforts by business rivals to shape the emergency regulatory regime in their interests. The analysis focuses in particular on the unfolding conflicts over fertilizers and the proposed import-substitution nitrate industry.

THE FERTILIZER CRISIS

Landlords, peasants and consumers paid heavy costs for the years of incessant private conflicts and incoherent public policies over the Aswan project, though some shippers and traders had reaped a handsome windfall. The shortage of fertilizers proved to be one of the most critical wartime problems faced by the predominantly agricultural economy. Egyptian producers required more fertilizers than in normal years in order to meet the increased demand for food and to counter the adverse effects on productivity caused by acreage and other war-related restrictions. Instead, fertilizer imports dropped precipitously below the prewar levels. In 1938, Egypt had imported 514 thousand tons of fertilizers. The figure for 1941 by contrast was only 5 thousand tons. Agricultural economist Alan Richards rightly labels this greater than

600 percent drop a "catastrophic decline" (1982: 168–173). Though deliveries began to increase in 1942, by the end of the war imports were still at less than half their pre-World War II levels.

The war had completely disrupted Egypt's normal channels of trade. Circuits between Egypt and Germany were completely cut off, and the Axis powers instituted a successful blockade of the Atlantic-Mediterranean shipping routes. At the same time, the Allied powers diverted the bulk of their supplies and relatively scarce shipping space to conducting the war, which meant in general a tremendous decrease in the volume of imports reaching Egypt.

From 1941 on, Egypt's access to foreign supplies was essentially controlled by the Allied economic authority in Egypt, the Middle East Supply Center (MESC), an institution designed to coordinate regionwide military and civilian supply requirements. MESC wielded tremendous power over the local political economy, according to one of its officials, primarily by its ability "to bring to bear just the right amount of pressure on the Egyptian government to induce it to forego what it wanted or to take action that it did not want to take, without provoking a political explosion." To an important extent, the drastic reduction and, at times, "the complete cessation of fertilizer imports" were "brought about"—that is, coordinated—by MESC (Lloyd 1956: 85, 87). The Allied authorities in particular exploited Egypt's dependence on fertilizer imports, holding back supplies until the Egyptian authorities turned over domestic food crops—wheat, barley, rice and millet—to the British army.

The steep rise in local fertilizer prices provided an early and obvious sign of the impending supply problem. Prominent landowners protested in parliament against what they claimed was a government-sanctioned jump in prices of over 70 percent between October 1939 and February 1940, and they accused the Mahir regime of helping the oligopoly distributors, the Royal Agricultural Society and the Agricultural Credit Bank, to cash in on the war (*Egyptian Gazette* 29 February 1940). The British embassy accounts report an even steeper price rise of 120 percent by January 1940.[5] Mahir's government found itself compelled by circumstances, as well as by the steady pressure of British ambassador Lampson, to reconsider the EEC's Aswan scheme as a solution to the fertilizer crisis. As it turns outs, however, the EEC's rivals applied pressure even more effectively than did Lampson, who found London suddenly deaf to his pleas on behalf of Egypt and the EEC.

CONTESTING NATIONAL INTERESTS

Though power, sovereignty and the national interest are three sacred concepts in realist conceptions of international political economy, the power of the investors and their allies who fought for control over development of Egypt's new fertilizer industry in World War II exposed both sovereignty and national interest as, at best, useful fictions.

The competition to build Egypt's first import-substitution nitrate factory had turned into a free-for-all on the eve of the war, a reflection of the tremendous uncertainty that gripped investors and decision makers alike. 'Ali Mahir's predecessor had ostensibly committed the Egyptian state (April 1939) to an agreement with Hungarian and American investors who were partners with the local Yahya group in the proposed Delta fertilizer scheme. Ambassador Lampson and his staff were intent on protecting what the British Foreign Office and the Department of Overseas Trade viewed as the EEC's prerogatives in this sector, insisting that the Egyptians sign a final agreement for the rival Aswan project.

Only days before the government fell, 'Abbud's ally, the finance minister Ahmad Mahir, intervened to hold up a possible agreement with the EEC. 'Abbud's long-time partners, the British Thomson Houston Company (BTH, part of the AEI combination), made a new, eleventh-hour offer that the Egyptians suddenly felt "duty bound" to examine.[6] Lampson and his staff sought to recover from this setback by beginning a new lobbying effort for the EEC—and their ostensible allies, the Egyptian peasantry—virtually from the day the new 'Ali Mahir government took office.

'Ali Mahir was an advocate of a proposed new Ministry of Social Affairs to improve the miserable conditions in the Egyptian countryside. One of Lampson's advisers sought to convince Mahir that if he really intended "to do something tangible for the fallah," he should instead let the EEC build the Aswan project! Of course, the EEC and its backers wisely chose not to rely on moral suasion alone. Thus, its bankers sought to block the Yahya group and its foreign partners in the Delta Scheme from access to capital in London, Paris and New York, a step which British officials both supported and believed ultimately to have succeeded.[7]

I believe that the 'Ali Mahir government looked futilely in the fall of

1939 for a way to salvage the fertilizer scheme for the Yahya group, the investors whose interests had been so well served by the recent palace-backed administrations, while trying to fend off the British pressure on behalf of the EEC. Thus, when Mahir appointed a new cabinet committee on Aswan, the EEC representatives found its members and, in particular, Sirri, who helped engineer the Yahya group's takeover of Bank Misr, "intolerable and difficult to deal with, always finding some fresh excuse to postpone a decision." [8]

The support for Yahya was constrained, however, as well as contingent on the Yahya group's being able to "deliver the goods," which was increasingly open to question. The group's Hungarian backers could not obtain financing, and the key U.S. firm, American Cyanamid, had prudently begun to revive its old association with the rival Aswan proposal promoted by 'Abbud and the AEI/BTH consortium (who were the heirs of Docker's original scheme). Two broader considerations affected the Mahir government's decision making in this case: the continued health of the agroexport sector and the fragile state of relations with the British authorities.

Both factors were critical ultimately to Mahir's survival in office and help to explain Mahir's decision, finally, to come to terms with the EEC in late December 1939 (Chamber of Deputies 1948: 7), a decision made less painful perhaps by a new package of financial concessions offered by these British investors along with a commitment to at least partial production at the plant within two years.[9] And the cabinet's insistence on implementing the scheme via a locally incorporated enterprise, for which the EEC would act as contractors rather than concessionaires, meant that some set of Egyptian investors would ultimately gain a share in the new state-created monopoly.

If Mahir found his particularistic agenda constrained by a broader set of institutional forces and relationships, than so did another local power holder, British ambassador Lampson, who had worked so hard over the years on behalf of the EEC. Following his meeting with the Egyptian premier on 20 December 1939, in which Mahir committed to a completed agreement within three weeks (Mahir still had to secure parliamentary approval), Lampson wired the following message to officials in London: "The Aswan scheme is now under the most urgent consideration of the government as a result of continuous pressure kept up by this Embassy. . . . The fact is that we are pledged to give financial support and I most urgently trust that further instructions will not cut across what has clearly been the policy of his majesty's government up til now. The Embassy is now unavoidably in daily contact with the Egyptian ministers on this subject."[10]

Dismayingly prescient, Lampson soon learned that directors of the rival electrical manufacturer, BTH, had intervened directly with the secretary of the treasury to block the "unfair support" given to the EEC. Within a week, Treasury had reviewed and reversed its position, announcing that the British government would not pay for the Egyptian fertilizer scheme nor allow the diversion of vital raw materials that were needed for the war. Though EEC executives tried to salvage their position in London, the effort failed.[11]

As Lampson's diaries reveal, he and the companies proposed to keep the news of this setback from the Egyptian government for as long as possible. Thus, while 'Ali Mahir and his colleagues negotiated with a parliamentary committee to secure approval for the expedited implementation of the fertilizer-factory project, the obviously desperate EEC and its allies in the British government looked for ways to obtain the Egyptians' signatures on a contract for a project that they knew would not be built in the foreseeable future (*Egyptian Gazette* 4 and 12 January 1940). Percy Horsfall, the Lazard Brothers banker, advocated outright lying to the Egyptians, but Lampson, to his credit, advised against it (*Killearn Diaries* 5, 11, 13, 16, 17 and 21 March 1940).

Mahir, whose government faced increasing domestic pressures on the economic front in the spring of 1940, risked his already-fragile relations with the British authorities over the fertilizer-factory issue. The prime minister apparently thought he could influence the EEC to deliver on at least part of the scheme—a factory capable of producing one hundred thousand tons of fertilizer, one-third of the original projected annual capacity—by threatening to turn to the competition. Thus Mahir made a show of inviting the EEC's rivals to Egypt and underscored the message by suddenly declaring the old 1935 commitment to exclusive negotiations with the EEC null and void (*al-Ahram* 17 March 1940). Lampson and the EEC answered by trying both to impose rigid conditions on contacts between the government and the competitors, and to force the Egyptians to uphold the old terms of the infamous 1935 agreement.[12]

When the Egyptians finally unveiled their reasoned compromise proposal in April, the British purposely ignored it, and in a tense confrontation Lampson instead demanded that they take back the legal adviser's "wretched letter" overturning the 1935 accord. At the same time, the ambassador privately advised the EEC to take a hard line with the Egyptians, advice which was undoubtedly influenced by the ambassador's own increasingly hard line toward Mahir. The British documentation on the 1940 Aswan negotiations abruptly ceases after April; these negotiations contributed to and were then overtaken by the crisis that led to Mahir's fall by June. As one British official later recalled, "Grave business was taking place in Egypt and this particular business [the nitrate scheme] had to be ignored for the time being."[13]

This summary of the aborted 1939–1940 bargaining round suggests that, in focusing almost exclusively on Mahir's alleged pro-Axis sympathies (and, thus, privileging Lampson's own obsessions), historians have possibly given us an overly narrow and ultimately misleading account of Anglo-Egyptian relations during this early and critical phase of the war. First, Mahir's government is often described as having complied fully with British authorities in various policy domains, yet this was clearly not the case with the proposed fertilizer factory. Mahir's government was brought around to support British preferences in this case—agreeing to deal with the EEC—only reluctantly, and under pressure. At the same time, the Mahir government obviously exercised its capacity to resist certain British demands—the burial of the 1935 agreement is a case in point.

Second, then, conventional accounts of wartime Anglo-Egyptian relations rest on an exceedingly narrow definition of intervention and the realm encompassed by politics. In continuing to focus almost obsessively on the details of such episodes as Mahir's removal from office in June 1940 or the even more (melo)dramatic encounter between Faruq and Lampson in February 1942, we lose sight of the fact that British administrators interfered daily in the political economy. Embassy and MESC officials oversaw an array of new controls over production, distribution channels and prices. Egyptian landowners and capitalists probably tended to discount the profits and inflate the losses resulting from what they (and most other sectors of society) viewed, quite accurately, as enhanced foreign manipulation, influence and control.

The brief resurrection of the nitrate-factory issue in early 1941 simply underscores the degree to which the local political economy was in fact a captive of the global conflict. On the one hand, local supplies of nitrates continued to decline. Egypt fertilizer stocks had fallen to eighty thousand tons by early 1941, while prices had nearly doubled again, to £E 21 per ton.[14] These conditions led the Sirri government to begin a centralized rationing and distribution scheme for supplies that were ultimately controlled by British businessmen and bureaucrats. On the other hand, a revived proposal for carrying out the Aswan project as an emergency war measure came directly from the MESC in Cairo.[15]

London's understandable reluctance to accord Egypt's needs for vital raw materials and machinery a top priority effectively ended negotiations over the Aswan project until the British victory over the Germans at El Alamein. The summer of 1942 was the most critical period of the war in Egypt. Rommel launched his first attack in the desert west of Alexandria, on 1 July, and while his advance had been stalled by 1 September, the decisive battle in the Egyptian campaign was fought on 2 November. Nine months earlier, the British had engineered the infamous return of a "loyal" Wafd government to power.

British officials in Cairo began fighting a different kind of war in Egypt in 1943, with tremendous implications for the Egyptian political economy and, ultimately, for British power. As the documents on the revived Aswan negotiations in 1943–1944 clearly attest, Ambassador Lampson led an ultimately futile effort to preserve the Egyptian market for British heavy industry. As a document from the Board of Trade's files defined the problem, "We shall need an outlet for our heavy industry after the war and Egypt will always need these nitrates. The situation in that country has changed beyond belief and I wonder if the time has not come to try and re-establish the position the group had built up for themselves by '35. ICI have said that they would have any amount of surplus plant on their hands after the war. It would be a blessing to get rid of it at a reasonable price."[16] Of course, one of the most visible kinds of change was the relative advance of a domestic manufacturing sector in tandem with the emergence of local investors like the 'Abbud, Yahya and Misr groups.

During the latter part of World War II, British state agents were drawn into the increasingly bitter battles among Egyptian business factions. Lampson and his colleagues sought to exploit their extraordinary political position to defend against what at the time was seen as the most potent threat to long-term British interests: U.S. capital. Thus, even with Rommel threatening Alexandria and Lampson facing a decisive political battle with pro-Axis Egyptian leaders, the Foreign Office was concerned that the ambassador not allow "Americans who might come in the disguise of British to step in" and take over the Aswan project.[17]

The 1942–1944 Wafd Government and 'Abbud's Bid to Become Egypt Inc.

A particular configuration of investors, state agents and political factions, which I called a neo-Anglo-Egyptian investment bloc, had secured what seemed by the mid-1930s to be a dominant position over the investment resources of the Egyptian state. The core of this bloc was the Misr group, the leadership of the Wafd party and the British residency. At the same time, the fortunes of an alternative authoritarian coalition linking King Fu'ad, the palace and 'Abbud gradually fell apart.

Between 1939 and 1941, a set of rival investors who were led by the Yahya family and who undoubtedly included associates of the new king (if not the king himself) successfully wrested control of Bank Misr and, thus, of the most important of the state-subsidized and state-protected rent circuits. The first two sections of this chapter have in effect recounted the power play by this bloc of palace politicians and Alexandrian investors who had backed the minority governments of 'Ali Mahir and Sirri. Between 1942 and 1944, this same loosely aligned set of businessmen and palace notables formed the core of the opposition to the British-backed Wafd government, and in some heroic-exceptionalist accounts they are identified—quite inappropriately—as representing the most progressive factions of the national industrial bourgeoisie.

The following section analyzes the steadily escalating economic conflicts that marked the second phase of the war, 1943–1945 and, in particular, the remarkable bid by 'Abbud to become, in the only slightly hyperbolic words of one British official, "the most powerful figure in Egypt, more powerful by far than the king or any group of Egyptians, whether political or financial."[18] The key to this effort was a set of three separate alliances that 'Abbud began to forge in 1942. The first was with the Wafd party, which had expelled the businessman in 1928. The second was with the British embassy, where he had been declared *persona non grata* for most of the 1930s. And the third was with American capital, much to the consternation of the British state.

'ABBUD BUYS THE WAFD

While the bargain that brought the Wafd back to power is well known, the accord between the party and the 'Abbud group requires some preliminary analysis. The British and the Wafd were pushed into each other's arms by the force of circumstance. The British confronted a growing threat to the Allied strategic position by the Nazi offensive across North Africa. The Wafd sought to return to power. The palace, spearhead of the anti-Wafdist and pro-Axis forces in Egypt during the war, was the common enemy. The British ambassador, Lampson, arranged for the Wafd's cooperation through his trusted intermediary (and 'Abbud's business partner), Amin 'Uthman, and carried out his coup with the help of British armored cars, which surrounded the palace on the evening of 4 February 1942. The ambassador offered King Faruq the choice between abdication or acquiescence to the appointment of Nahhas, whom the king detested, as premier.

For his part, 'Abbud had encouraged and benefited from the rise to influence within the party of an entrepreneurial cohort committed to adapting the Wafd to the standard model of postcolonial politics. Thus, according to Warburg, "favoritism, nepotism and politicization of the administration swept the countryside. The Wafd was 'digging in,' to use Lampson's words, and trying to make up for the five lean years it had spent in opposition" (1985: 138).

'Abbud established business ties with the premier's in-laws, the notoriously corrupt al-Wakil family, and other would-be investors, including Amin 'Uthman, the Abu al-Fath family, and the ambitious landowner Fu'ad Sirag al-Din, who seized de facto control of the party in 1942 and who remained at the head of the party more than fifty years later (Berque 1972: 544; Tignor 1984: 241; Warburg 1985: 137; Makram 'Ubayd [1943] 1984). As British embassy observers pointedly remarked at the time, there were "very few businessmen in Egypt with whom 'Abbud is wholly unassociated." [19]

What could 'Abbud offer the party in return for its support? Two things come to mind (apart from outright bribes). First, as was common in Egypt (and elsewhere of course), the businessman could offer ambitious politicians or their sons positions in his enterprises, lucrative subcontracting opportunities, etc. Second, though virtually nothing has been written on the subject, the party needed funds to function, and virtually all observers agree that as a party of "relatively poor men," the

Wafd was less able to fund its activities than "rich parties" such as the Liberals or Sa'dists.[20] From the time of their reconciliation in 1942 until the party was forced to disband in 1952, 'Abbud was widely recognized in fact as the Wafd's primary financier (Moore 1980: 124). Finally, and most important, the liberal economic model to which the Wafd remained committed empowered the private owners and managers of the means of production.

'Abbud gained handsome payoffs once what I call the business wing of the Wafd triumphed over the remnants of the party's old guard in an intraparty power struggle. The conflict pitted Sirag al-Din against 'Abbud's old nemesis, the lawyer Makram 'Ubayd, who was the finance minister and number two man in the Wafd until his abrupt dismissal from the cabinet in May 1942 and expulsion from the party itself two months later. Warburg (1985: 140) describes this last of the historic splits within the Wafd as the single most important factor in undermining the Nahhas government and helping the palace to recover the political initiative.

Makram 'Ubayd later portrayed the struggle with the Sirag al-Din faction as a battle against corruption inside the party, which he publicized (with the palace's help) in his infamous *Black Book* (1943). In fact, his dismissal came in the midst of a conflict with 'Abbud, who as the new chairman of Egypt's sugar monopoly opposed the finance minister's plan for widespread public distribution of the costly and increasingly scarce basic good. His fall cleared the way for what British diplomats called 'Abbud's "thief's bargain." The Wafd government virtually ceded sovereignty to 'Abbud, allowing him to trade "surplus" stocks of sugar for fertilizers, at a time when the domestic market was experiencing regular shortages of the commodity. After protracted negotiations, 'Abbud sold enormous quantities of Egyptian sugar to the British authorities, at an impressive profit, while completely circumventing the normally high export tax. At the same time, he obtained the release of fertilizer stocks for his sugar plantation at Armant, though these supplies were officially earmarked for use on other crops. He also received special shipments of machinery for his sugar factories as part of the deal.[21]

The Wafd-borne windfall was spread across 'Abbud's far-flung commercial empire. For instance, the Nahhas government awarded 'Abbud's shipping company the lucrative concession to transport pilgrims to Mecca, despite its having been an exclusive preserve of the Misr group during the 1930s.[22] The government also moved decisively to break the November 1942 strike by shipyard workers at 'Abbud's Khedival Mail Line, one of the first unions recognized under the Wafd's new probusiness labor law (Beinin 1982: 182; Bianchi 1986: 430–431, 433–434).

Another, even more remarkable aspect of this wartime political realignment entailed the rapid restoration of cooperative ties between 'Abbud and the British embassy, which included increasingly frequent, direct access to Lampson himself. 'Abbud's competitors among the resident British business community were understandably distraught over this shift in policy, particularly as 'Abbud sought to exploit this unique conjuncture and the unprecedented degree of political latitude that it conferred.

'Abbud's political maneuvering of the period is symbolized by the meeting he arranged at his Upper Egyptian estate in Armant in March of 1943, where Lampson was recuperating from a dangerously high fever. 'Abbud arranged for Lampson to see the king's representative and chief adviser, Hassanayn Pasha. As Lord Killearn (Lampson received his peerage on the New Year, 1943) wrote, 'Abbud "was obsessed with the idea that he had a mission to improve relations between the Embassy and king Farouk" (*Killearn Diaries*, entry dated 19 February to 30 March 1943). The meeting took place only ten days before the palace and Makram 'Ubayd launched the first of their attempts to bring down the Nahhas government (Warburg 1985: 140–143), and 'Abbud had obviously hoped to preempt such a challenge.[23] These efforts on behalf of the increasingly embattled Wafd government were linked to a plan whose scope and ambition gave even the British pause: by 1943 'Abbud had launched a bid to take over the Misr group's plants and factories and to use the resources of the state to create new nitrate and power industries under his exclusive private control.

'ABBUD BUYS A BANK: THE ASSAULT ON THE MISR GROUP

In late July 1943, 'Abbud called on the British ambassador to discuss two new confidential projects. First, he proposed to take over the Aswan negotiations by forming an Egyptian company that would own and operate the entire scheme. Second, he wanted to take over the Bank Misr group. He told Lampson that he already held a controlling interest in the bank and would seek to overthrow the present administration—i.e., his rival, 'Afifi. 'Abbud sought British backing of this naked power play, and to gain it he couched his scheme naturally in terms of encouraging Anglo-Egyptian postwar trade. The implications were clear however. His Aswan scheme meant that he and not the British companies (or the Egyptian government) would control the venture (*Killearn Diaries* 29 July 1943).

'Abbud claimed to hold 25 percent of Bank Misr's stock; British sources estimated that he held 20 percent at most; but at any rate, he was the single largest shareholder.[24] The chairman of the bank, 'Afifi, checked 'Abbud's first attempt to use his voting bloc by refusing to register a portion of his holdings and then by altering the voting rights. Davis (1983: 156) mistakenly dates this incident back to the mid-1930s, and he attaches to it an idiosyncratic interpretation: "Rather than waning, corruption in the Misr Group became even more pervasive as the struggle among members of the bourgeoisie for directorships increased" (168). Yet the "struggle for directorships" in this case was more accurately an attempt by the bank's largest shareholder to exercise his property rights!

The maneuver forced 'Abbud to revise his plan and instead seek to separate the bank from its industrial subsidiaries, with the intention of gaining effective control of those subsidiaries. 'Abbud concerted his plans with his close friend, the new minister of finance, Amin 'Uthman. He in turn consulted with Lampson, and, with the ambassador's approval, 'Abbud and the finance minister discussed the matter at length with Lampson's financial adviser. The ambassador gave their plan the go-ahead in a time-honored fashion:

> I caused both Amin Osman Pasha and Abboud Pasha to be informed . . . that the relations of either the government or Abboud Pasha with either the Misr Bank or Hafiz Afifi Pasha were far too delicate ground for me to have anything to do with. It was an entirely internal affair. I could not be drawn into any position where the Embassy could be rightly accused of having had any finger in the business. It followed that *it was for Amin Osman Pasha and for Abboud Pasha to decide entirely for themselves on the merits of the case.*[25]

Lampson's reasoning—that receiving full details of the plan was fully consonant with keeping the embassy's finger out of the business—is noteworthy. There is no sign in the diary entry or Foreign Office files that 'Abbud wanted anything from the embassy other than a green light, which he clearly received. The diplomatic dissimulation notwithstanding, Lampson fully supported 'Abbud, as revealed in numerous dispatches to London urging policymakers to approve 'Abbud's scheme for cooperation in Egypt's postwar industrialization. The embassy's financial counselor argued even more forcefully for joining with 'Abbud in the "postwar new order," pressing London to invite 'Abbud for talks at the ministerial level. Superiors at the Department of Overseas Trade were forced to remind Cairo that not even refugee governments in Britain were accorded the reception being advocated for 'Abbud.[26]

Amin 'Uthman's plan to launch an attack against the bank in parliament was delayed by yet another palace attempt to bring down the government in the summer of 1944 and a decisive intervention by Lampson to keep it in office. By the time he finally did move against the Misr group, the bank's chairman, 'Afifi, had enlisted palace support, the public face of which entailed a highly visible visit by King Faruq to the Misr mills at Mahalla al-Kubra and the bank's headquarters in Cairo. The outcome of the 'Abbud group's conflict with 'Afifi for control of the Misr group's manufacturing empire was ultimately determined by the successful palace coup against the Wafd in October 1944.[27]

As in the highly polarized arena of the mid-1930s, these fierce competitive conflicts tended increasingly to overlap with, and reinforce, the struggle for state power, thereby constraining the choices of businessmen and politicians alike. If in the spring of 1943 'Abbud had sought a reconciliation between Lampson and Faruq, by the fall he was warning direly that the "boy [i.e., Faruq] was a real danger to the country," a message he would repeat at regular intervals in the months ahead.[28]

'Afifi, the Bank Misr chairman who in the regime struggles of the 1930s sided with the British against 'Abbud and the palace, was forced by circumstances—'Abbud's massive stock purchases, the plot against his chairmanship and the rebuff by the British embassy—to turn to the palace to safeguard his position. Not only did the move help Bank Misr's directors thwart 'Abbud's attempted takeover, but 'Afifi and his new allies challenged 'Abbud on the fertilizer project, another battle that would be waged unceasingly through, and until, the Wafd party's defeat.

THE AMBIVALENT ALLIANCE BEHIND 'ABBUD'S BID FOR ASWAN

What emerges most clearly from the record of bargains and maneuvers to revive the Aswan scheme in 1943–1944 is the tenacity (or, in the British view, the audacity) of 'Abbud's efforts to take control of the proposed new industrial sector by positioning himself as the indispensable pivotal force in the multinational negotiations. Specifically, 'Abbud exploited the Wafd's short-term vulnerability and the British government's increasing concern with its long-term position inside Egypt to claim a controlling share in the venture.

The problem of fertilizer supplies plagued the Wafd government from the moment it took office in February 1942, the year in which nitrate imports fell to their lowest levels of the war. The Wafd government's first steps included a futile appeal by the finance minister Makram 'Ubayd for an immediate start on the Aswan project, though the exigencies of the war made obtaining the necessary raw materials (primarily steel and copper for the generators and other electric-plant equipment) impossible. The Egyptians periodically renewed their request, under increasing pressure from a variety of constituencies, as even Lampson recognized.[29]

From 1942 on, British strategy in Egypt consisted in disguising their own country's increasingly vulnerable economic position by exploiting the vestiges of colonial political privilege—in particular, the Wafd's dependence on British power. As the private correspondence on the Aswan scheme makes clear, British officials feared above all that U.S. companies would make a successful bid for the contract. Lampson thus regularly reassured Nahhas that the Aswan scheme remained a top priority, a point that he invariably coupled with a reminder of the EEC's historic right (eventually) to undertake the work. Among themselves, British company officials and government representatives admitted that U.K. firms probably would not be able to build the project until sometime after the war's end.[30]

'Abbud's intervention in the summer of 1943 to revive the Aswan project thus played on the vulnerabilities of Egyptian and British political authorities alike. He portrayed himself to Nahhas and Lampson both as the indispensable guarantor of the project and used this leverage to undercut the rival efforts of Bank Misr's new, hostile board of directors and its bureaucratic allies in such redoubts as the Ministries of Public Works and Supply. One measure of his own sense of increased agenda-setting capacity in this arena is his explicit redefinition of the project's terms: 'Abbud proposed to create a new, private Egyptian company to own and operate both the power station and the nitrate plant.

As I have indicated, Lord Killearn and his Cairo staff championed the strategic joint venture in the strongest terms, pressing Whitehall to arrange for 'Abbud's passage to London, which triggered a protracted policy debate inside the halls of the Foreign Office and the Department of Overseas Trade. Unsurprisingly, in light of the bitter conflicts of the 1930s, some officials counseled against cooperation with 'Abbud: "[T]he special pleading . . . does not impress me very much. It is surely evident that Abboud is aiming at becoming a kind of commercial dictator in Egypt and he thinks he may be allowed and helped in achieving this position if he is allowed to come over here and make contacts and affiliations which he can thrust down the throats of the people in Egypt when he gets back." [31]

The overarching concern for Britain's postwar manufacturing position and markets resolved the debate in 'Abbud's favor. In December 1943, both the president of the Board of Trade and the secretary of state for foreign affairs, Anthony Eden, endorsed 'Abbud's Aswan scheme as a move toward maintaining Britain's strategic position after the war.[32] Eden put it baldly: though "Abboud's first object is the furtherance of his own interests, our own look like being well served by the partnership." [33] In fact, the Churchill administration and its corporate allies seriously miscalculated the benefits of the "partnership" and spent much of 1944 trying to undo the damage; nonetheless, at this remarkable conjuncture, 'Abbud had successfully positioned himself and promoted himself to the politicians in London and Cairo alike as a vital element in Egypt's future.

During the Wafd's annual congress in November 1943, Amin 'Uthman unveiled his party's (and Egypt's) first "Five Year Plan," in which electrification and, specifically, the Aswan project featured prominently as part of the Wafd's agenda for developing new Egyptian industries. The Wafd's leaders were obviously groping for solutions to the country's multiplying economic problems—minimally, in order to stem the party's decline. Nonetheless, their views on Egypt's economic future coincided with those of planners and policymakers in both the United States and Great Britain who anticipated that industrialization would play a key role in the plans of postwar Egyptian governments (DeNovo 1977, Baram 1978, Bryson 1981).

Lampson's unwavering support for 'Abbud followed from what he correctly perceived to be an American policy of using the war to challenge Great Britain's domination of the Egyptian market. The Roosevelt administration had launched this new aggressive posture in Egypt by appointing the New Deal lawyer James Landis to the position of director of economic operations in the Middle East (and the ranking U.S. civilian representative at MESC) in August 1943 (Baram 1978: 164–165; Ritchie 1980: 115–127). Landis's single-minded devotion to challenging Britain's economic and political preeminence in fact contributed to a serious heightening of Anglo-American tensions. The British ambassador's defensiveness is captured in a long, exasperated dispatch complaining about Landis, whom he derided as a "super trade commissioner cum economic dictator," and in Lampson's pressing London to support the 'Abbud project "without waiting until the Americans have consolidated their position" inside Egypt.[34] Lampson's complaints, illustrative of emerging Anglo-Egyptian commercial rivalry, were among the subjects discussed with the businessman and Roosevelt confidant, Edward Stettinius, during his 1944 mission in London.

Lampson's defensiveness may help explain what turns out to have been a relatively uncritical, if not naive, policy of supporting 'Abbud and his various proposed investment projects, seemingly on the strength of 'Abbud's professed loyalty to the principle of Anglo-Egyptian postwar cooperation. Examples of this naivete abound, beginning with the question of 'Abbud's ability to secure the right to operate the Aswan power station itself as a private concession. The public-works bureaucracy and the Wafd party leadership had opposed this option back in the 1930s. V. B. Grey, the EEC representative in Cairo and a local British business-community leader, warned that the Egyptian government would never approve such a plan. Lampson lobbied hard, however, arguing that there were "strong grounds" to believe 'Abbud would win the new private concession, and, on the strong urging of the Foreign Office, the EEC directors reluctantly agreed to cooperate with him.[35] If only they knew how uninspired the ambassador's intelligence gathering had been, to judge from his unpublished diaries: "I did make it clear to Abbud that I presumed he felt reasonably sure that the Egypt government would be in favor of giving him the concession. He said he had made preliminary feelers and had no doubt on that score" (*Killearn Diaries* 3 December 1943).

What else would 'Abbud say? In fact, Nahhas's government insisted on public ownership and independent management of the power plant. 'Abbud tried contesting this condition but ultimately had to agree to it—at least on paper.

Between August and December 1943, 'Abbud had negotiated successfully to obtain British approval for moving forward on the power plant and fertilizer factory, Egypt's first large-scale industrial project since the mid-1930s and, as we have seen, a frustrated objective of every wartime administration since that of 'Ali Mahir. To do so, he depended heavily on the British ambassador, the war having facilitated the painstaking repair of their battered relationship. Lampson subsequently backed 'Abbud's attempted takeover of Bank Misr and various other business deals, though equally significant, from 'Abbud's point of view, throughout 1943–1944 the ambassador remained personally committed to the policy of propping up the Wafd against the palace, even as other British officials began wistfully to reimagine the night-clubbing King Faruq as a kind of frustrated, would-be reformer (Smith 1979: 477; Louis 1984: 232).

The details of the 1944 Aswan bargaining round, recounted below, are important both in tracing the tangled lines of political power and economic interest in Egypt at the war's end and in reconciling the apparently contradictory policies of British officials at a key juncture. After all, Eden and his staff had justified cooperation with 'Abbud on the ground that it served the British state's vital, long-term interests in inhibiting the penetration of U.S. capital. 'Abbud had repeatedly made it obvious that his plan depended on the Wafd party's remaining in power. And yet, almost immediately, the Foreign Office began to withdraw its support for the Wafd, again of course on the ground of protecting long-term vital interests. To what extent were these policies at cross-purposes, as Lampson himself seemed to think?

Senior policymakers in the Foreign Office and directors in the EEC distrusted 'Abbud and bridled at the conditions he had imposed on these arm's-length allies. More crucially, they realized that, his effusive celebrations of Anglo-Egyptian cooperation notwithstanding, 'Abbud's agenda directly conflicted with their twin objectives, which were reflected in an obsession with defining the Aswan project as British: (1) that the EEC would control the negotiations, and (2) that the involvement of American capital would be minimized, if not excluded all together. In response, his "partners" began secretly searching for a way out of the deal. The much-commented-on Anglo-Egyptian political realignment during 1944 coincided with, and in a sense depended on, these British capitalists' and policymakers' locating what they hoped would be a sturdier long-term redoubt against U.S. competition.

The Last Battle of the War: Aswan, 1944

There was a significant continuity in the *institutional* identities of the sectoral competitors, though almost two decades had passed since Docker first began promoting the Aswan scheme in the

Table 3 *Rival Coalitions in Egyptian Industrialization Projects, circa 1944*

Actors		Aswan	Delta
			Project
Foreign states	U.K.	Support	Equivocal
	U.S.	Equivocal	Support
Foreign capital	U.K.	EEC, ICI, (AEI)[a]	EEC
	U.S.	American Cyanamid[b]	American Cyanamid
Egyptian government		Wafd	Palace
Local capital		'Abbud group	Yahya/Misr group

[a]English Electric Company and American Cyanamid Company, with Associated Electrical Industries playing a subsidiary role in the "British" consortium. AEI had strong affiliations with U.S. General Electric.

[b]American Cyanamid often built such projects in conjunction with General Electric and had some understanding with G.E.'s British affiliate, AEI.

mid-1920s. A comparison of Table 1 (in Chapter 3) and Table 3 makes this clear. Of course, the EEC's interest in the scheme had grown steadily during the 1930s, aided by the Foreign Office and its representatives in Cairo, who served virtually as the EEC's exclusive private lobbying arm.

The EEC's "national" rival, AEI, Docker's old firm which had been secretly sold to and reorganized by G.E. in the 1920s, continued to compete for the business as well under the name of its two "independent" subsidiaries, British Thomson Houston (AEI-BTH) and Metrovick (AEI-MV). Though Docker was long gone, 'Abbud continued to cooperate with the AEI-MV interests and, through them, with the U.S. chemical producer American Cyanamid, whose engineers had drawn up the rival American-designed Aswan scheme.

Yet the role played by Egyptian capitalists had expanded enormously over time to the chagrin of British officials, such that by 1939 the sectoral conflict essentially had been recast as a conflict among Egyptian investors to develop an import-substitution fertilizer industry. In tandem with this change, the role of American Cyanamid and its engineering subsidiary, the Chemical Construction Corporation, grew as well since they were in effect the only available sources of the technology for both 'Abbud's and 'Afifi's rival projects.

This sudden and unprecedented prominence of American capital in plans for developing a new Egyptian industrial sector was an even more significant and alarming change in the eyes of British policymakers. To put it bluntly, the growing market power of U.S. producers in this case threatened to undermine the Foreign Office's policy of protecting the EEC's investment in the Aswan scheme and, by extension, of preserving the postwar Egyptian market for British heavy industry. This dilemma was made painfully evident by the discovery that every firm in the new, Foreign Office–backed consortium except the EEC had private arrangements with the Americans—including 'Abbud, AEI and the EEC's long-time affiliate in the scheme, ICI.

THE DESPERATE DIPLOMACY OF
ECONOMIC DECLINE

London's cable to Lampson on 3 February 1944, which provided the ambassador with his instructions on the Aswan project, reveal the twin fears that underlay the rapidly evolving positions of the British bureaucrats and their business allies. Though ready "in principle" to collaborate with 'Abbud, Lampson was to inform the Egyptian government that the EEC was also ready to carry out the scheme "without the intermediary of an Egyptian company"—in other words, without 'Abbud. When Lampson questioned the logic of this "loophole," London officials feebly justified it on the grounds of the high commission fee that 'Abbud was allegedly demanding.[36]

Letters exchanged between Grey, the EEC agent, and 'Abbud, along with entries in Lampson's own unpublished diaries (his information came from the censorship service), show that Grey originated the claim for "compensation for expenses incurred." Lampson sarcastically described the fee as "the paltry sum of £E 100 thousand," approximately one-half million dollars (*Killearn Diaries* 4 January and 21 June 1944). Grey had tried to disguise his role in the rent seeking.

Lampson's fear of loopholes was rational, given the second half of his brief: to keep Nahhas in the dark about the probable participation of U.S. firms in the project while approving negotiations only on the basis of the original EEC scheme. As the Foreign Office archives make clear, the British policymakers sought to control U.S. capital's direct involvement in the Egyptian industrial sector and thus dreaded the possibility that the Egyptians might begin direct negotiations with the Americans. Here lies the more compelling reason for the growing British reluctance to cooperate with 'Abbud, whose control of the project increased the likelihood that the rival, American-designed scheme would be adopted.

The U.S. investors showed little sign that they were about to accept a back seat in the project. To the contrary, American diplomats and businessmen coordinated an appeal to Nahhas in March 1944 to delay a decision until representatives of American Cyanamid could reach Cairo and present their own proposal. At the same time, these investors had opened a second "front" in the war for the Egyptian chemical sector by beginning negotiations with 'Abbud's local rival, 'Afifi, to revive the Delta Scheme, again with U.S. diplomatic support. In Cairo, New Dealers like Landis painted the opposition to the Delta Scheme as part of a British strategy to monopolize the postwar Middle Eastern market; and the Americans, who had recently expanded their diplomatic presence and appointed their first ambassador to Cairo, were thus eagerly drawn into the central arenas of Egyptian political and economic life for the first time.[37]

'AFIFI'S COUNTER-COALITION BUILDING AND THE DEFECTION OF THE EEC

'Afifi's tenacity in promoting the rival Delta Scheme should put to rest the canard that, unlike Bank Misr's original chairman, he showed no interest in developing Egypt's manufacturing sector. By gaining U.S. diplomatic support for their bid to enter the nitrate market, 'Afifi and his coinvestors had taken yet another decisive step to counter the formidable coalition of Wafd party leaders and British embassy officials that stood behind 'Abbud. Along the same lines, they offered shares in the deal to key notables, obtaining the capital and doubtless the political clout of, for example, Muhammad Badrawi-'Ashur, the wealthy landowner, Wafd party funder, and close relative of the number-two man in the party, Sirag al-Din. And as I have already noted, 'Afifi and his group were investing heavily in the fortunes of the opposition bloc.[38]

The group's most brilliant stroke was its attempt to disarm British opposition to the Delta Scheme by bringing locally resident British businessmen into the deal. 'Afifi began by offering a position on the board of the proposed new venture to Cecil Campbell, Cairo representative of the British multinational, Marconi, and one of the pillars of the British community. Importantly, Campbell was close to Grey, the EEC representative, and replaced Grey as chairman of the British Chamber of Commerce in Egypt. It is unclear that 'Afifi realized just how strategic a choice he made. The EEC had taken over Marconi during the period 1943–1944 and retained Campbell as its "political consultant" in Egypt (Jones and Marriott 1970: 178).

Campbell had likely been advising his clients to diversify their risk because the EEC quietly approved a plan of cooperation with 'Abbud's local rivals in the Delta Scheme. Campbell began by enlisting his friend Grey to draft a memo showing why the two projects were not competitive! Grey officially joined the board of 'Afifi's new company in June, a step that could hardly have been taken without the agreement of the EEC.[39] Of course, 'Abbud was outraged by the clear conflict of interest and would accuse Grey and Campbell of attempting to sabotage his project. Though the British ambassador joined him in protesting to London, the Foreign Office shifted its policy in line with the EEC's evolving interests and in the summer of 1944 ended its opposition to the Delta project.

The Foreign Office was also shifting its position on the fate of the Wafd at this time, though until now we have been given little understanding of the logic behind this move, save in the most general of terms. Thus, as in the political realignment in 1934–1935, analyzed in Chapter 3, the British once again began complaining of the corruption that had infected the Egyptian administration. Historians have preceded along similar lines, twinning the ad hoc argument about corruption with an equally unsatisfactory one about the inevitability of a shift in alignments sooner or later. And we find one more parallel between 1934 and 1944 as well. Once again, 'Abbud was lobbying fruitlessly in London to save an Egyptian government.

THE COLLAPSE OF 'ABBUD'S
ASWAN COALITION

In meetings in London between July and August 1944, American, British and Egyptian investors hammered together a final agreement on their joint Aswan venture, on the basis of 'Abbud's proposal to own and operate the factory. Technical plans for both the chemical and power plants were based on the scheme drawn up by American engineers in the 1930s. American Cyanamid would supply the key electrochemical technology. ICI would serve as management consultants to 'Abbud's Egyptian company, and ICI's Egyptian subsidiary, the country's largest sales and distribution agency, would market the fertilizer.[40]

The final plans for 'Abbud's new postwar industrial venture thus violated both conditions stipulated by the Foreign Office when it approved the project as an emergency priority. The major firms appeared either unwilling or unable to defend British national interests in this case. ICI had conceded the role of principal to American interests; it was represented in the negotiations by Frederick Pope, a director of American Cyanamid and a founder of its engineering arm, the Chemical Construction Corporation. And Pope rejected out of hand the British government's demand that the equipment orders be placed only with British firms.[41] The EEC's role was reduced to that of a subcontractor to 'Abbud and his American consultants, and they had to share the order for electrical equipment with a competitor, British Thomson Houston (which, despite the name, was substantially American-owned), which 'Abbud had long represented in the Egyptian market.

The key to 'Abbud's ability to influence the terms of the bargain rested most obviously on his influence with the Wafd administration. Various parties in the negotiation were explicit about this influence, though 'Abbud's tireless campaign in Cairo and London on the Nahhas government's behalf makes the same point even more unambiguously.[42] In turn, two key variables shaping the companies' decision about cooperating or not in 'Abbud's scheme (the opportunity costs) were the estimates of (1) the value of the expected return and (2) the likelihood of 'Abbud's actually securing the deal. The Foreign Office and State Department archives contain abundant evidence of the companies' continuously reestimating these variables and attempting where possible to influence them.

Following the conclusion of the negotiations in August 1944, I believe that the EEC began to reestimate radically the value of cooperating with 'Abbud on the terms imposed by him and his American partner, Pope, and to discount the risk in reviving negotiations with a post-Wafd Egyptian government. This had been precisely the advice tendered by their Cairo representative, Grey, who had argued against 'Abbud's project, claimed that Lampson and others exaggerated his influence, and pressed instead for direct negotiations with the Egyptian state.

The support for the Delta Scheme was in fact a way to protect and perhaps improve the EEC's position if the Wafd did fall from power. First, 'Afifi's group represented key figures in the opposition bloc. Second, by building the Delta plant, they would block 'Abbud's attempt to enter the chemical sector and ideally weaken his influence over the

power scheme. Certainly, it looks as if 'Abbud viewed the threat of the
Delta project exactly in this way because in September 1944 he and his
new American business partner decided to double the planned annual
capacity of the Aswan fertilizer factory, from three hundred thousand
to six hundred thousand tons, an output that would match Egypt's
entire annual demand and, importantly, make 'Afifi's project super-
fluous.

This was obviously a cut-throat business. American Cyanamid suddenly pulled the reins on the American embassy and the 'Afifi group,
informing them both that the Delta project would have to be "restud-
ied," while 'Abbud bragged that he had "torpedoed" 'Afifi's scheme.
But, by narrowing their options, he also drove key leaders and opinion
molders of the British expatriate community to promote the campaign
against corruption and to embrace the discourse of reform through
which a bloc of royalists, nationalists, oligarchs and capitalists sought
to pry loose the Wafd's grip on state power. Sidqi's plea in August on
the pages of *al-Ahram* to keep party politics out of the Aswan business
shows once more just how close in fact the two had become. And
Lampson's insistence on championing the side of the Wafd (and 'Abbud) during the summer left him increasingly isolated among British
elites in Cairo and London.[43]

There is nothing puzzling about the closely allied views of the EEC,
its Egyptian directors and the managers of Churchill's Middle East policy in this case. The objectives of regulating the role of American capital
and of securing millions of pounds sterling in orders for British manufacturers were linked to *the* central issues in postwar British political
economy and foreign policy, including Anglo-American relations, the
health of British heavy industry and management of the country's massive balance-of-payments deficits. As 'Abbud and his American partners
outmaneuvered their competitors, they also steadily undermined what
officials at the Foreign Office had defined as British national interests in
a strategic arena. The managers of Anglo-American diplomacy had even
come to see the Delta project as a possible bargaining chip in dealing
with U.S. investors and diplomats, to be traded to the Americans in
return for respecting British-company claims on Aswan.

The threat posed by 'Abbud's and Pope's designs on this key arena
made the costs of continuing to support their wartime allies, the Wafd,
remarkably concrete for London policymakers and contributed to the
well-known decision in the fall of 1944 to encourage a change of government in Egypt. In October, with Lampson on leave in South Africa,
the king received his green light to crush the Wafd. The fall of the

Nahhas government forced 'Abbud into a desperate and ultimately futile scramble to hold together the investor bloc that he had assembled
to support his Aswan scheme. The new government was riven by competing claims on these resources, and though one of 'Abbud's closest
friends and business partners, Ahmad Mahir, had been appointed prime
minister, Mahir's assassination in February 1945 proved to be a fatal
blow to the 'Abbud group's power project.

At the same time, however, 'Abbud defeated his local business rivals
in the competition to secure the cooperation of U.S. investors in
Egypt's postwar chemical industry. After returning from his first trip to
the United States, and in response to the government's May 1945 decision to open the Aswan project to international tender, 'Abbud and
his partner, Pope, laid the foundation of a new era in Egypt's political
economy. In August 1945, the last month of the war, 'Abbud founded
a new £E 4 million venture, the Chemicals Manufacturing Corporation
(*Akhbar al-Yawm* 1 February 1946). He then opened negotiations for
a U.S. government loan to build Egypt's first import-substitution nitrate factory at Suez, in the northeast corner of the Egyptian Delta.[44]

Summary: The Fall of the Neocolonial Project

Exceptionalist historiography rightly marks Harb's overthrow in 1939 as the end of an era in Egypt's political economy, though
for the wrong reasons. In the two decades since the 1919 revolution,
Egyptian investors like Harb, 'Abbud, Yahya and their cohorts had unquestionably emerged as the most dynamic segment of the country's
economic elite, successfully usurping as well as advancing what I have
described as the subordinate industrial-sector project originally charted
by local minority investors and international financiers like Ernest Cassel at the turn of the century. To put it as simply as possible, analysts
have clearly exaggerated the degree to which Greek, Jewish and other
"foreign" residents continued to command the heights of local large-
scale production and commerce in Egypt in the decades after independence.

The new Egyptian investors possessed enormous political advantages
that they used in promoting their competitive positions during the
1920s and 1930s. The renaming of the fashionable crossroads in downtown Cairo, long known as "Suarès Square" (*Midan al-Siwaris*), for
the family that was Cassel's partner and Harb's original sponsor is a

statement about the rise of a new national political and economic elite in Egypt. Of course, so is the fact that many of the ventures and sectors originally pioneered by the minority investors—the sugar company, the alcohol works at Tura, the textile industry, the Kom Ombo Company, etc.—were by the end of the 1940s effectively in the hands of Egyptian investors like 'Abbud.

This chapter too should finally put to rest the commonly repeated claim that Harb's overthrow in 1939 marked the end of attempts to build Egyptian national industries—that is, ventures in which foreigners did not hold shares—for which Harb is most often celebrated. Empirically, this is simply untrue, as I have documented. 'Abbud fought with Harb's successors (Yahya and 'Afifi) to build a wholly domestically and privately owned nitrate industry. Harb's removal as chairman of the Misr group more accurately marked an increased interest in building Egyptian industries, along with the beginning of a protracted struggle over the issue of industrial regulation.

Industrialism and related reform questions had gained increasingly wide currency by the eve of the war, evinced for instance in the spate of social provisions—rudimentary welfare and labor-relations bills—passed by the wartime Egyptian governments. At the same time, investors and undoubtedly others were clearly aware of the limits to the "easy" expansion of import-substitution industry under the liberal economic model in place since the 1880s. As Lord McGowan, the chairman of ICI, had reported confidentially in 1937, and as figures on domestic production levels at the time seem to indicate, there were increasingly fewer profitable investment possibilities in Egypt, barring either a significant transformation of the internal market or increased levels of government protection and other subsidies.[45]

One need look no further than the corridors of Whitehall for recognition of the growing importance of industry in Egypt and in other parts of the periphery, as British planners sought ways to protect postwar markets against American capital. But while explicitly articulated neocolonial projects may have been successful in parts of sub-Sahara Africa in the years after World War II, the strategy never stood a chance in Egypt. The privileged political position of local Egyptian investors and their clearly divergent economic preferences effectively checked British neocolonial ambitions at least a decade before the wave of national anticapitalism swept these investors from the Egyptian stage.

The role of investors like 'Afifi, Yahya and 'Abbud in this quiet, market- or interest-driven challenge to British power is all the more important given that, as Beinin and Lockman see it, these investors were "not particularly nationalist" (1987: 11). As we have seen, the war allowed 'Abbud to restore his relations with the British ambassador and, through his investment in the British-backed 1942–1944 Wafd government, to recover from the economic setbacks his competitors dealt him between 1935 and 1939. And in the war with his rivals for control of the proposed new nitrate industry, 'Abbud joined forces with American capitalists who were seeking access to the Egyptian market.

I believe that 'Abbud's celebration of Anglo-Egyptian cooperation during the war, along with his close ties to the "corrupt" (and, for many, "traitorous") Wafd government, originally earned him his enduring reputation as a comprador and an architect of the post–World War II neocolonial order among the influential wave of historians who began to publish in the 1950s and the 1960s. The irony of course is that, for the British imperial managers, 'Abbud was revealing precisely how hopeless the task had become.

The record of the 1944 Aswan bargaining round shows that the pace of change rapidly outstripped the ability of the Foreign Office to protect British interests in this sector, defined materially in terms of the size of the order to be given to the EEC, symbolically in terms of a British identity for the project, and politically in terms of a gate-keeping function to limit the role of U.S. capital. Needless to say, 'Abbud, like the other Egyptian investors, showed little interest in or commitment to any of these objectives. Certainly, from this point on, nationalists and others will have to base their criticisms of 'Abbud and his rivals on different ideological and empirical grounds. In light of the inevitable turn to American capital to build the nitrate project, perhaps they are destined to be recast as the spiritual fathers of the *Infitah*.

More critically, however, in this chapter we find the origins of a new view of the Egyptian political economy in the decade after 1945, during which the complicated and protracted struggle over the privilege of privatizing public resources and building Egyptian industries takes a decisive turn. We might conceptualize this struggle as being over the building of a new regulatory regime in Egypt, starting with the takeover of Bank Misr in 1939 and continuing with a host of other new forms of intervention introduced and administered by British officials during the war. The right of Egypt's investors to privatize resources would face increased challenges in the 1940s and 1950s, together with the other property rights that had secured business privilege in Egypt since the time of Cromer.

PART THREE

Business, the State and Industrialization 1945–1955

CHAPTER FIVE

Power and the
Postcolonial State

As in other countries undergoing the transition from colonial to postcolonial rule in the twentieth century, the elites who assumed power in Egypt following independence in 1922 faced challenges to their rule and, in this particular case, "failed . . . to consolidate
control, to govern, and to remain in power" (Boone 1992: 16). In July
1952, a military clique launched a successful coup d'état, overturning
the monarchy and, over the course of the next two years, the party
system. In the slightly longer term, 'Abbud and other leading local capitalists would be driven from the boardrooms and ultimately from
Egypt.

A defining feature of exceptionalist accounts is their locating the explanation for this outcome in the origins of the particular configuration
of capitalist production relations in the nineteenth century. Exceptionalist logics have generated conceptions of failure of a markedly different
order: the failure of capitalists to constitute themselves as a completely
independent national industrial bourgeoisie; the failure of the national
governing elite to achieve so-called true or complete political and economic independence. As accounts of imperialism, capitalism and party
politics in Egypt, they are no longer convincing. They remain important, however, as reminders of the discursive dimensions of the unfolding challenge to the established postcolonial order in the decade
after the war.

Though mobilization against the vestiges of colonialism was a key
part of the nationalist project after the war, it is clear that Great Britain

was not omnipotent, and in the arena under study here—the development of basic infrastructure and capital-goods industries—representatives of the new Atlee government lost virtually all capacity to dictate outcomes. This decline took place despite Egypt's importance as a potential market for British engineering firms and heavy-machinery producers, and the ample demonstrations by British officials of the importance they attached to preserving imperial prerogatives in this domain. As Waterbury correctly notes, "The British . . . tried in the 1930s and 1940s to make Import Substitution Industrialization (ISI) work in favor of British technology, expertise and supplies" (1983: 59–60). The critical point is that by World War II the effort had failed.

And though their compromises with colonialism and foreign capital would become central themes in oppositional discourses, the day-to-day administration of the Egyptian state was in the hands of an indigenous political elite, and, most certainly, local—and increasingly Egyptian—investors directed day-to-day decision making in various spheres of economic production and distribution. The thrust of this generalization holds even if the royal family is viewed as non-Egyptian. In tracing the outcomes of the competing plans for hydropower and nitrate industries in Egypt, I will provide further evidence for this deepening domicilization of the postcolonial state and economy, including the emergence of constituencies and cadres (and, implicitly, rationales) promoting industrial regulation.

The creation by the Nuqrashi administration of a public authority to build and operate the Aswan hydropower plant was the harbinger of a new era in the early postwar political economy. As such, this attempted extension of the state's regulatory and productive capacity was contested by private investors, and, under the Wafd government of 1950–1951, the initiative was blunted. When the military government took power in July 1952, its publicists would put the Aswan project forward as a symbol of a decisive break with the past, but the contracts for the project were actually signed and preliminary excavation work begun between 1947 and 1948. The related outcome of this key postwar bargaining round is that 'Abbud, whose efforts to capture the Aswan deal were undermined by a bloc of old political and economic rivals, went on to implement the first large, capital-intensive, import-substitution project of the postwar era, near Suez, where he founded a new Egyptian fertilizer industry between 1949 and 1951.

There is by now little need to explain the significance of the long-delayed Aswan scheme, which American intelligence agents identified as the "keystone" of postwar Egyptian development efforts and, thus not surprisingly, the focus of renewed controversy and conflict.[1] By the end of the war few still questioned the logic of developing a domestic nitrate-fertilizer industry. The arguments of the American and Chilean nitrate producers, exporters and their local allies lost much of their power, particularly as bottlenecks continued to hamper the recovery of postwar world trade. The strong consensus in support of this particular ISI scheme is perhaps best reflected in the decision taken in the Egyptian Senate in July 1947, where landowners approved funding for the Aswan project by a vote of seventy-eight to two, and where the lone opposing votes were cast by 'Abbud's allies, Sirag al-Din and Sirri.

While the significance of the opposition of landlords and merchants declined, in the aftermath of the war new factors emerged to influence the battle between 'Abbud and his rivals for control of the Aswan project and the course of postwar industrialization more generally. First, American businessmen and government officials began to widen their involvement in the Egyptian political economy, where they pursued the largely complementary goals of selling goods and services and undermining what remained of British imperial prerogative. Thus, at the end of the war, the Americans forced the dismantling of the Allied economic authority in Cairo (MESC), which the British had hoped to use to further their own postwar economic project.

A second factor was the unfolding of the postwar finance regime, or what was referred to at the time as the sterling question. Egypt built up massive sterling balances during the war as a result of heavy Allied spending. In 1945, Great Britain owed the Egyptian state and private creditors £400–440 million (or roughly $1.6–1.8 billion). The Atlee government clearly did not have the resources to repay any significant portion of this debt and rebuild its own domestic economy (Polk 1956). In response to the problem, the British state rigidly controlled Egypt's access to dollars, producing a serious foreign-exchange crisis between 1947 and 1949 and ultimately reinforcing ISI currents inside Egypt, even while creating significant obstacles in the short term to building new Egyptian industries. Most accounts of the postwar period inexplicably ignore the financial dimensions of the rapidly developing crisis in the political economy and in Anglo-Egyptian relations, in a sense adopting "imperial" views on the matter. Governing elites at the time clearly viewed things differently. For instance, Egyptian and other delegates to the July 1944 Bretton Woods conference pressed, futilely, to include the problem of blocked sterling assets on the agenda of the

International Monetary Fund and in discussions of the postwar international monetary order (Godfried 1987: 48).

Third, the renewed drive to develop national power resources and manufacturing industries was intertwined with efforts to build up the regulatory capacities of the state. This new postwar round of institution building extended to many arenas, including the partial nationalization of utility services (the tramways) in Alexandria, the incorporation of Cairo as a municipality, and the attempt to extend controls over the foreign-dominated petroleum sector. World War II had hastened the end of the laissez faire era in the Egyptian political economy, which posed new opportunities and new challenges for Egypt's business oligarchs. In the case of the electric-power sector, the creation in June 1945 of a new public Hydroelectric Power Commission to oversee the building of the Aswan project ended 'Abbud's bid to take over this resource. More generally, the contours of a new postwar regulatory regime began to emerge amidst, and as part of, the ongoing struggle over the distribution of resources.

The Political Economy of Development in Postwar Egypt

Under the guise of a revitalized national project of social reform and economic development, Prime Minister Mahmud al-Nuqrashi's cabinet decided in May 1945 to undertake the power-station project in the public interest. The project was to be funded by an internally floated loan, opened to international tender, and operated by the Egyptian state. The 'Abbud group tried what turned out to be one last time to salvage the competitive position that it had built during the period of wartime Wafd rule.

The composition of the fractured coalition government made predicting the ultimate fate of 'Abbud's project hazardous, though the odds seemed to be against him—or so the Cairo-based British investors Grey and Campbell argued in a torrent of dispatches to EEC headquarters in London. On the one hand, 'Abbud's closest confidant, Ahmad Mahir, had been named prime minister. 'Abbud clearly counted on Mahir's cooperation, and on this basis Lampson tried to make a credible case for continuing to back the 'Abbud plan in his own cables to

London. On the other hand, Mahir's position in the cabinet was weak. The finance minister and founder of the dissident Wafdist Bloc, Makram 'Ubayd, was arguably more popular, was more ruthless and, as he made clear to the embassy and to British company officials, intended to crush 'Abbud's scheme. The new minister of commerce and industry, Habashi, lined up solidly behind Makram 'Ubayd in this arena, not least because of his own connections to 'Abbud's competitors in the Misr group.

Whatever hopes 'Abbud still harbored for his Aswan scheme were sunk in the wake of Mahir's tragic murder in February 1945 and the elevation of Nuqrashi, cofounder with Mahir of the Sa'dist party, as the new prime minister. Nuqrashi, who in the old British personality reports had been dubbed an extremist and was once suspected of plotting the murder of a high British colonial official, was, like his own murdered colleague Mahir, now suspect in the eyes of young militants for collaborating with colonialism. The legacy of the past quarter century of nationalist politics and decolonization had emerged as part of the postwar contest for power in Egypt.

In the 1930s, Nuqrashi led the call to open the Aswan scheme to an international competition. His opposition to the EEC scheme had helped to fracture the Wafd party in 1937. Eight years later, Nuqrashi renewed his principled support for an open international tender, but now national interest coincided much more closely with those of his relatives, "intimate friends" and political allies who were organizing as a competing investor bloc in the power sector (*Egyptian Gazette* 26 September 1945; *al-Kutla* 2 May 1947). These included Tahir al-Lozi, Nuqrashi's brother-in-law, from a family whose members were themselves founding investors in the Misr group; U.S. Westinghouse, the newest multinational entrant in this crowded field; relatives of the king; and Mamduh Riyad, Nuqrashi's new minister of commerce and industry, who had propitiously closed a consulting deal with a U.S. engineering firm before taking office.[2]

The Misr group's investment in the opposition to the Wafd between 1942 and 1944 had obviously begun to pay dividends. Buoyed by the profits amassed during the war and steered by the politically astute and well-connected 'Afifi Pasha, these investors recovered from the financial crisis of the late 1930s and the hostile takeover bid by 'Abbud. In the power sector, 'Afifi and his allies had adopted a strategy much like 'Abbud's, building bridges simultaneously to the leadership of the British

Chamber of Commerce in Egypt in support of the proposed Delta Scheme while organizing a consortium to bid for the Aswan project. (See Table 4.)

Most crucially, 'Afifi and his partners again tried to attract American Cyanamid to their side, arguing with some justification that while the Misr group's political fortunes were waxing, 'Abbud's were clearly on the wane.[3] Examples abounded. The Misr group obtained government backing for its proposed new, American-supplied rayon factory. The Nuqrashi government had returned the state's Red Sea–Mecca pilgrimage concession to the Misr group's shipping line and the Egyptian Senate had opened a highly publicized investigation of 'Abbud's bus lines. The minister of finance, a relentless opponent since the 1920s, played the key role in this multifront attack on 'Abbud's firms, launching a drive to recover millions in alleged excess profits owed by 'Abbud's shipping and sugar companies (*Egyptian Gazette* 3 April 1945; Tignor 1989: 56–57). These claims would dog 'Abbud for the next decade.[4]

Governing officials and rival investor blocs were enmeshed in a protracted chicken game through the first half of 1945. 'Abbud's strategy entailed promoting himself as the key to a successful agreement with the international firms that controlled the necessary electrochemical technology. To put it simply, if the government wanted to see a domestic nitrate-fertilizer industry built in Egypt, they would have to reach an accord with 'Abbud.

No side blinked despite a quickly escalating mix of incentives and threats. Most crucially, Pope, the American Cyanamid director, showed little willingness to undercut his Egyptian partner, and he deferred, wisely or not, to 'Abbud's hard-ball strategy. Thus Pope refused all requests to submit details of the offer unless and until the Egyptian government decided to forego a public tender. In meetings with Prime Minister Nuqrashi, Pope pressured him on the grounds that scarce equipment earmarked for the Egyptian scheme was being bid for in India and other markets. More blatantly still, Pope tried to gain the support of the cabinet's technical adviser, 'Abd al-'Aziz Ahmad, a member of the Egyptian Senate, with a clumsy offer of a bribe! Pope's ethics were more fine-tuned than most. While admitting to having offered 'Abd al-'Aziz a job, he made a point to note that he never mentioned any specific salary.[5]

Nuqrashi did not blink. Instead, his cabinet voted in May 1945 to go to tender, a move that Lampson admitted might be logical from an economic point of view. Nonetheless, he deemed it reckless and

Table 4 *Competitive Conflicts over Projects and Partners, circa 1945*

	Project	
Group	*Delta Plan*	*Aswan Plan*
Misr group	EEC	Westinghouse
	American Cyanamid?	
	Power Gas Company	
'Abbud group		EEC/AEI
	American Cyanamid	American Cyanamid

irresponsible since it ignored the long-standing British claims in this arena. The ambassador also blamed the Misr group's chairman, 'Afifi, for playing a behind-the-scenes role. The cabinet, which had pointedly refused to commit to a specific end use for the electricity, elevated the long-time critic of the fertilizer factory idea, Ahmad, to head the newly created public Hydropower Commission.[6]

The vote met many constituencies' needs, most notably those of 'Abbud's rivals, Yahya and 'Afifi, who hoped, finally, to woo the Americans to their side. 'Abbud's response to the cabinet gambit demonstrates once more the zero-sum nature of the conflict as acted on by these Egyptian investors. The reversals at the hands of Nuqrashi drove him first to try to build new bridges to the palace, via both the king's adviser, Hassanayn Pasha, and Sirri, a wartime prime minister and a relative of the king's by marriage who 'Abbud had newly incorporated into his investment group. At the same time, though, he was urging Lampson to intervene to put his Wafd party cronies back in power.[7] And in tandem with these and undoubtedly similar political initiatives, he acted once again to end the Misr group's hopes of bringing American capital into their rival Anglo-Egyptian Delta nitrate-factory scheme.

'Abbud's U.S. partner, Pope, had warned that unless the cabinet acted quickly, he would advise 'Abbud to drop the Aswan scheme. Turning up the pressure, in August 1945, 'Abbud registered a new £E 4 million venture, the Chemicals Manufacturing Corporation, with Sirri and, if U.S. documents are to be believed, the crown prince of Egypt holding shares.[8] This company then became the vehicle through which 'Abbud and Pope eventually opened negotiations with the Export Import Bank of the United States (ExIm Bank) for a dollar loan to build a diesel-powered nitrate factory south of Suez, on the eastern edge of the Delta. Thus, the continued setbacks in his Aswan scheme and his partnership with U.S. investors led 'Abbud to take over the idea of the Delta Scheme from its original Egyptian promoters.

The outcomes of the play or plays in this arena accommodated some parties, reinforced the positions of others and turned disastrously against still others. It appeared that Egypt would finally have a domestic nitrate industry, though this outcome was not what 'Abbud's competitors intended. By January 1946, the Misr group chairman, 'Afifi, had admitted defeat, and toward the end of the year he began negotiating for a position on the board of 'Abbud's proposed new U.S.-backed venture.[9] There was little Lampson could do as he prepared to leave Cairo in March 1946 after more than a decade of promoting the EEC's hydropower project other than to construct a usable account of the failure. He blamed the Nuqrashi government's "negative attitude" and consoled himself with the lie that the Egyptians did not understand their own best interests.[10]

'Abbud's decision to found the Fertilizers and Chemical Industries of Egypt, Ltd., amounted to a double blow to the British investors with the longest-standing claims in these projects: the EEC and its Cairo-based affiliates, the Associated British Manufacturers in Cairo, V. B. Grey and Cecil Campbell. These foreign investors and their local representatives attempted to cooperate with both rival Egyptian business groups. Though the strategy was designed to minimize their risks in an unstable political environment, from 'Abbud's perspective it had contributed to the undermining of his own competitive position and ultimately led him to revise his objectives. As a result, not only was their potential share in the Delta factory scheme lost, but the obstacles in front of their one remaining hope—the Aswan scheme—grew steadily more formidable. As 'Abbud deepened his commitment to building the alternative Suez (ex-Delta) fertilizer plant between 1946 and 1948, his objectives in the Aswan arena began to shift against the Aswan fertilizer-factory proposal—the development project that he had been tirelessly promoting for almost two decades since 1927.

The Uphill Battle to Build a State

The decision in May 1945 to create the national Hydroelectric Power Commission (HEPC), which was charged with supervising the Aswan electrification project, should be seen as part of a broader process of institution building and reorganization that had been cata-lyzed by World War II. Wartime demands had exacted a tremendous toll on the country's crazy quilt of public and private power plants and had made the related issues of rationalization and expansion of the power sector a priority for postwar reform. The Aswan project was eventually integrated into the Public Works Ministry's expansive vision of a ten-year-long electrification program for all of upper Egypt.

The commission's chairman, Ahmad, a retired civil service official and Sa'dist party supporter who had developed the plan back in the 1930s to deliver power from Aswan to Cairo, reemerged as a key lobby-ist for public ownership of power resources and, unsurprisingly, for his own pet scheme of long-distance power transmission. His views were given extensive coverage in Cairo's main Arabic, English and French dailies as well as in the pages of *Majalla al-Muhandisin,* the journal of the engineers' professional association. Newly matriculated Egyptian engineers and other professionals, whose prospects for private employ-ment were limited by entrenched patterns of foreign and Egyptian mi-nority dominance in salaried positions, formed a supportive and increas-ingly visible social base for an expanded public sector (*Egyptian Gazette* 19 March, 20 April 1945; *Majalla al-Muhandisin* April 1945, May 1945; Bianchi 1989: 75–76; Moore 1980: 27–32, 41–44, 154–158). Ahmad's public campaign was also an open invitation for even more ambitious professional rivals to launch technical criticisms of his pet electrification plan.

More critically, however, Ahmad faced an uphill battle to secure the independence and authority of Egypt's would-be Tennessee Valley Au-thority against the competing claims and countervailing power of politi-cally influential blocs of domestic investors. Egyptian capitalists were intent on maximizing the flow of, and access to, distributive resources from the HEPC while minimizing the degree of regulatory interference with their own market-based privileges. For instance, 'Abbud and his rivals clearly did not want to surrender the gains accruing from their privileged bargaining position with foreign capital in this arena, in part because these local Egyptian capitalists saw the power-production and distribution sector itself as ripe for "indigenization" and absorption into their private empires. Similarly, Foreign Office documents from this period describe a proposed new private Egyptian venture to take over electrification of Cairo and the Egyptian Delta, with the govern-ment to be offered an unspecified number of seats on the board of directors.[11]

The justification for the Aswan project in the eyes of many of the country's business and landowning oligarchs hinged on the promise that it would subsidize a new, profitable manufacturing sinecure and fill the skyrocketing demand of food and cotton producers. Otherwise, the HEPC stood little chance of gaining the cabinet's support for the scheme, much less that of the pashas who headed the parliament's finance committees. Thus Ahmad's capacity to shape the agenda appeared limited, and he reconciled himself to the reconfiguration of the project as a development plan for the elites of Upper Egypt, where, incidentally, the Sa'dist coalition governments had the strongest regional base of support. The old engineer had his hands full in marshaling the political, economic and technical resources necessary to protect the HEPC from the withering attacks on its competence, institutional capacity and autonomy.

When the commission unveiled its in-house designs for the project in March 1946 and invited bids to supply the plant and equipment, the competing groups refused to tender, while blasting Ahmad and his prestigious British consulting engineers, the firm of Kennedy and Donkin, for their alleged inexpertise. The commission agreed to postpone the closing date of the competition while they rewrote the specifications. The companies then insisted on the right to submit their own proprietary designs, which seemed to cast further doubts on the qualifications of the HEPC and led to two additional postponements of the bidding deadline, until the end of January 1947.[12] Ahmad's retrospective account obscured the cause of this year-long delay, which he attributed simply to the companies' preoccupations with other concerns (1955: 63–65).

As the companies continued their maneuvers against the HEPC, a second front was opened in the war by Mahmud al-Shishini, an ambitious and prominent professional who headed the Electrical Engineering Department at Cairo University. Shishini emerged as the single most persistent and forceful new critic of Ahmad and the HEPC, whose design for the power plant, he charged, placed the fifty-year-old Aswan Dam in danger (*Majalla al-Muhandisin* March 1946: 5–9). The argument was an old one. The design, which was based on the work originally carried out by Ahmad and others on the staff of the Ministry of Public Works in the 1930s, was known as the penstock scheme. Penstocks were the steel pipes that were to be inserted into the dam's sluice gates to supply water to the turbines. Shishini argued that the pipes would transmit unacceptable levels of vibrations from the turbines, and he urged the HEPC to adopt his own alternative design, which, coincidentally, the U.S. Westinghouse-led consortium was proposing to implement.

Egyptian engineering circles commonly presented Shishini's interventions solely as a technical or professional matter, along the lines, for example, of the British irrigation engineer Willcocks's ill-fated dissent over hydraulic policy after World War I. Nonetheless, Shishini was a founding investor in the Electrical Development Company of Egypt, incorporated in 1946 to compete for the Aswan business and other anticipated electrification contracts. In essence, the new firm represented U.S. Westinghouse in the expanding Egyptian power-generation and -distribution market. Leading businessmen, *al-Misri* publishers and Wafd party allies, Mahmud and Husayn Abu al-Fath, were major financial backers of the venture who sided with Shishini when Shishini's overly confrontational approach with Ahmad, the HEPC and other government agencies finally led to an uprising among the directors and shareholders.[13]

The objectives of the two main competing blocs of investors converged on trying to stop the government from going through with a public tender. There is little mystery in the HEPC's choice of the tender strategy. Given a predictably optimistic assessment of their own abilities to monitor the process, the commissioners intended to obtain the most up-to-date technology at the most competitive price. Just as predictably, executives of American Cyanamid, EEC and other firms disparaged the Egyptians' technical capacities, though these capacities were not what had them worried.

Let us consider the case of the Aswan consortium then still nominally led by 'Abbud. For the two British machinery producers, EEC and AEI, to have to compete on price and delivery dates basically meant forfeiting the multi-million pound order. British officials admitted in private that these firms would be unable to supply any of the required electrical and chemical plant between 1947 and 1949, a "gloomy" forecast then, which in retrospect appears overly optimistic.

ICI continued to advise its Cairo office to string along Ahmad and the HEPC, while deprecating the government's attempt to regulate the industry and reiterating that it had no interest in running a factory in Egypt.[14] As for 'Abbud, the increasing time and resources that he devoted to the Delta project were as clear an indication as any of his own shifting objectives.[15] Tellingly, when the tenders for the Aswan project were finally opened in January 1947, 'Abbud had not even entered a bid (*Egyptian Gazette* 31 January 1947).

The Westinghouse consortium pursued a strategy similar to the EEC's, though the U.S. producers were presumably not concerned about their competitiveness per se. These investors also attacked the HEPC's competence while purposely holding back on their bid, with the ultimate objective of taking over the project. They were clearly well connected, as evidenced by the successful campaign mounted in the fall of 1946 by members of the Sidqi cabinet to delay the closing of the competition while Westinghouse ostensibly prepared an alternative plan for submission.[16] At the same time, the growing shortage of hard currency, and particularly dollars, toward the end of 1946 created a powerful disincentive to adopting the American designs unless and until Westinghouse could secure approximately $20–40 million in financing. The failure to do so led the firm and its allies both to mount a new campaign to discredit the HEPC and to propose to re-engineer the entire project (*Egyptian Gazette* 23 February 1947; *Akhbar al-Yawm* 26 April 1947). This delaying tactic came in the spring of 1947 as the parliament prepared to debate funding for the government's scheme.[17]

The focus of political action by the competitors gradually shifted to the parliament, where committees of the Chamber of Deputies and of the Senate began deliberations on the Aswan project and the Nuqrashi government's request for £E 10.5 million (approximately $43.4 million at the prevailing exchange rate). The deputies ultimately approved the project in June, and the Senate followed suit in July 1947. The details of the legislative maneuvers shed much light on the evolving interests of the 'Abbud group and its political allies.

Little evidence suggests that the commission or its own cabinet and bureaucratic allies (primarily within the Ministries of Public Works and Finance) expected the project to sail through the shoals of the legislature unassisted. Nuqrashi in fact tried to bypass the legislature (*Egyptian Gazette* 9, 11 February, 16 March, 29–30 April 1947). The course had to be well mapped in advance, beginning with the assembly in April 1947 of yet another international commission, the last in a long line of experts brought to Egypt to approve one or another version of the project.

The experts' endorsement of the government scheme was published at the end of April, strategically in view of the wave of publicity given to the criticisms of Westinghouse, Shishini and others, and the almost daily interventions in the pages of *al-Kutla*, the pro-Nuqrashi *al-Asas*, the Wafd's *al-Misri* and the Amin brothers' *Akhbar al-Yawm*. The government and its allies sought the high ground, defending the HEPC's decisions against alleged pressures from Great Britain, the "international monopolies" and their agents. They in fact succeeded in that these arguments have formed the core of the conventional narrative ever since. The opposition's defense of the national interest, by contrast, focused on the alleged threats to the dam and the irrigation system in general, the scheme's technical flaws, and the high and unnecessary costs that a hard-pressed population was being asked to absorb (*Akhbar al-Yawm* 26 April, 12 July 1947; *al-Kutla* 1–2, 13, 16, 21, 26, 29 May 1947; *al-Misri* 11 June 1947; *al-Asas* 17 June 1947; 'Abd al-'Aziz Ahmad 1955: 62; Waterbury 1979: 147).

The government appeared to clear one hurdle when a majority in the finance committee of the lower chamber endorsed the HEPC's project in its June 1947 report, but only after the minority succeeded in appending a report of its own, written by Shishini, condemning the project (Chamber of Deputies 1948: 24–25, 41; *Akhbar al-Yawm* 7 June 1947; *Egyptian Gazette* 12 June 1947). The debate in the full chamber was conducted along familiar lines: was the government successfully defending Egypt against "imperialist policy" or foolishly pursuing a technically and financially unsound investment scheme?

While the competitors continued to ply the legislators with reams of technical data, Nuqrashi fed the press key documents from the government's bulging archives; these documents were used to show how, for years, the British embassy had been promoting the interests of the EEC and opposing the principle of competition. The chamber, which was itself a product of rigged elections, voted overwhelmingly, 144 to 6, to support the allocation of funds (*al-Asas* 15 June 1947; *Egyptian Gazette* 15–17 June 1947; *Akhbar al-Yawm* 12 July 1947). One of the government's opponents on the subcommittee, 'Abd al-Qawi Ahmad, the minister of public works in Sidqi's 1946 cabinet, described the press campaign as extremely effective in convincing parliament to support the government's plan.

The president of the Senate, Muhammad Haykal, hoped to boost the government over the second hurdle, but the Senate's investigative committees protested the haste with which the issue had been discussed by the deputies and promised a more thorough review. The *Egyptian Gazette* (16 June 1947), which had long backed the EEC in this arena, raised the hope that leading engineers among the Senate's ranks might yet make the case for rejecting the government's plan. Nuqrashi was eventually forced to resolve the more glaring and costly inconsistencies between the blueprints of the HEPC, on the one hand, and the Ministry of Public Works' own, newly published ten-year plan for Egyptian electrification, on the other.

Under attack for his refusal to commit the government in advance to a particular end use for the power, Nuqrashi had to reject key parts of the HEPC plan as the price for a majority vote in the subcommittee, which finally passed the funding request by a vote of five to three. The HEPC proposal called for construction of a calcium nitrate-producing factory at Nag' Hammadi; the Ministry of Public Works proposed an ammonium nitrate factory and a steel factory in Aswan. The international commission that reviewed the HEPC scheme rejected the idea of a steel factory as uneconomical. Nuqrashi finally endorsed the Aswan ammonium nitrate project, obtaining the key support of Senate Vice-President Muhammad Shafiq in the process (al-Kutla 26, 29 May 1947; al-Misri 22 June 1947; Egyptian Gazette 23–26 June 1947).

The project's opponents in the subcommittee, led by the Wafd's ruthless boy wonder, Sirag al-Din, and 'Abbud's newest business partner, Sirri, redoubled the attack on government policy during the full Senate debate early in July 1947. Sirag al-Din blasted the government for its irregular procedures and contradictory objectives and for lying about the true costs of the project, including the cost of the fertilizers. Sirri seconded Sirag al-Din, arguing that it was crazy to build the project in stages. He wanted the power to be devoted to steel production (which, incidentally, would protect his new investment in 'Abbud's fertilizer project). Sirri called on the state to invite a competing set of tenders on the basis of the alternate design. The two failed to sway the solid pro-Nuqrashi bloc within the Senate, however, which defeated a last, desperate attempt to postpone the vote and approved funding for the scheme, seventy-eight to two (Madabit majlis al-shuyukh [Minutes of the Egyptian Senate] session 55, 7–9 July: 1412–1431, 1443–1462, 1480–1504, 1551–1556; Egyptian Gazette 10 July 1947).

The government's confidence was no doubt high in July 1947. Ahmad, the HEPC and, by extension, the Nuqrashi regime appeared to have moved the power project forward after years if not decades of setbacks and delays. At the same time, and following months of fruitless negotiations, Nuqrashi's Ministry of Finance had concluded an interim financial agreement with the British authorities. For a brief moment, Egypt looked to have surmounted its foreign exchange crisis.[18] Within days of the Senate vote, Ahmad announced the award of the contracts for turbines, generators and switchgear, with the bulk of the approximately £E 5 million in orders going to Swedish and Swiss firms (*Egyptian Gazette* 14 July 1947). Nuqrashi's cabinet quickly approved the decision.

Though Ahmad continued to press ahead with the project, the mood and motivation had changed dramatically by the fall of 1947. The biggest problem was London's decision in August to suspend convertibility of the pound, the effects of which reverberated quickly in Cairo and in the capitals of other creditor nations. For instance, though the Egyptian state had counted on the release of some $175 million equivalent of hard currency for the rest of 1947, after August they could count on no more than $6 million over what they earned on current transactions (roughly $30 million), according to American treasury officials. Egyptian negotiators spent the remainder of the year finalizing arrangements with manufacturers, central bankers and the contractors who bid for the preliminary excavation of the site. Ahmad was portrayed in British accounts as driven by the fear that the Nuqrashi administration's days were numbered.[19] The more accurate portrait would be of a government desperate to demonstrate to its own population some capacity to solve the country's mounting problems (Louis 1984: 257–264).

The declining power of the British state to shape outcomes in this sector left company officials protesting feebly in London and the career Middle East hands clucking self-righteously about Egyptian "national arrogance." Oliver Lyttelton, the wartime cabinet official who took over AEI, wanted the sterling negotiations to be used as a club to secure the contract. Yet the understandable view from Whitehall of the Aswan deal as one more case of "anti-British prejudice triumphant" needs to be interrogated.[20] First, British engineers served throughout as the main international consultants to the HEPC, and they oversaw the tender process (earning a hefty fee for their service). Geoffrey Kennedy, the head of Kennedy and Donkin, eventually received a decoration (the first order of merit) from Nasser for his firm's role in building the hydropower station.[21] Second, at least one major British manufacturing firm obtained $3 million in orders through the HEPC, roughly 15 percent of the award (*British Chamber of Commerce in Egypt* September 1947). Third, and much more pivotally, the conflict between the HEPC and the EEC consortium was at heart about investors' preferences for organizing and implementing the project—that is, with a minimum of state oversight and regulation—rather than the corporations' national identities. Thus, the rival U.S. Westinghouse consortium faced precisely the same kind of concerted and successful opposition to its own bid to take over the project from the HEPC. The relative tentativeness of this particular challenge in comparison with later rounds, or the fact that in other regulatory arenas (such as those encompassed by the company law of 1947) local capitalists presumably derived some benefit, would make little difference in the responses of 'Abbud and other investors to this claim of regulatory authority.

In the case of the 'Abbud group, the reaction included the founding of the new manufacturing subsidiary, Fertilizers and Chemical Industries of Egypt, Ltd., with a $5.6 million loan approved by the ExIm Bank board in Washington in July 1947. The founding of the company seems to have marked the beginning of a new phase of cooperation between 'Abbud and erstwhile rivals in the Misr group, which began with the offer of a seat on the board of the chemical firm to 'Afifi and culminated in 1950, when 'Abbud joined the board of Bank Misr, reportedly against 'Afifi's wishes. The significance of this rapprochement should not be underestimated, given the decades-long feud between these two personal antagonists and the history of relentless competitive conflicts between the rival groups that I excavated in Chapters 3 and 4.

This new and limited accord among rival investors was an organizational response through which the business oligarchs struck back at what must have appeared as related challenges to their privileged position by state-building elites, a new set of would-be competitors or both. Yet, by mid-1949, a government headed by Ibrahim 'Abd al-Hadi, who took over as Sa'dist party president and Egypt's prime minister after Nuqrashi's assassination, was pursuing a different, clearly less threatening and inclusive approach to regulation. It certainly must have appeared that way to businessmen such as 'Abbud, Sirri and 'Afifi, who were appointed to an entirely new commission to oversee the building of an iron and steel factory in Aswan that the government would underwrite and the oligarchs and their partners would operate. As for the proposed nitrate factory, this new administration deemed it somewhat less vital to the country's future development and filed the plan away.

Sirri, who would go on to engineer the return of the Wafd to power, was a main promoter of the iron and steel factory. 'Abbud joined the board of the new parastatal industrial development bank, founded by the 'Abd al-Hadi government in 1949. He also found the climate suddenly conducive to signing a new agreement covering the terms of the sugar-company monopoly after years of delay (*Egyptian Gazette* 20, 28 May, 14 June 1949; *al-Asas* 2 October 1949; Lemonias 1954: 34–35). These same investors successfully blunted the regulatory initiative by the Nuqrashi administration, though even British authorities admitted that creation of such a public authority was long overdue.

Once Sirri, who had an obvious and direct stake in these matters, took over the prime minister's duties in July 1949, the original head of the HEPC, Ahmad, was unceremoniously fired, and work on the hydropower scheme itself was suspended pending a thorough review by the new minister of public works: the Wafd's own Muharram. Thus, broad issues of party, interest and ideology were involved in this particular arena. At the same time, many of the criticisms leveled at Ahmad and his consultants during the 1946–1947 bargaining round over the alleged design flaws in the original scheme looked to have been sound. Ahmad was forced to admit that £E 5 million out of a total of £E 7 million in cost overruns since 1947 had been due to "modifications" in design and layout. These revelations, which were given ample space in the pages of the *Egyptian Gazette* (30 September, 6, 10 October, 29 December 1949, 21 February, 30 May, 6 July 1950) and the Wafd party's standard *al-Misri*, were welcomed by critics eager to dismantle the HEPC or at least dilute its authority (*al-Ahram* 3 April 1951, 6–7 January 1952; *Majalla al-Muhandisin* May 1952: 21–22; 'Abd al-Mu'ti 'Abd al-Wahab 'Amr 1960: 7–9).

Still, the Nuqrashi government's initiative was no illusion. On 19 March 1948, ground was broken south of the town of Aswan. King Faruq laid the cornerstone for the future industrial complex. And work—primarily excavation in the riverbed for the power station—finally began on the hydropower plant.

Reining the State Back In

Sirri's last and most important action as a transition prime minister in the winter of 1949–1950 was to prepare the ground for the return of the Wafd to power. I will take up the issue of the last 1950–1951 Wafd government in detail as part of a broader analysis of Egypt's business oligarchy and its relations with the governments that directly preceded and followed the July 1952 coup. Here, I am interested in the change in government mainly in terms of its impact on the course of the Aswan project. Since the electrification scheme was the centerpiece of Egyptian public industrial-development policy until at least 1954, when planning for the new massive Aswan High Dam and power project got off the ground, the institutional history helps in illuminating the evolution of state capacity in the industrial sector as well as the mythology of the early period of military rule.

When Sirri handed the reins of government to the Wafd in January 1950, Muharram remained at his old fiefdom in the public-works bureaucracy. He continued on the course plotted in October 1949, when he "temporarily postponed" the scheduled announcement of tenders for the second phase of civil-engineering construction at the dam site, to the chagrin of the British firms that were desperate to win the estimated £E 3 million contract. The main U.K. group suspected that a German competitor had engineered the delay, but the HEPC's internationally renowned senior consultant, Kennedy, confirmed that the delays were part of Muharram's project to discredit the commission chairman, Ahmad.[22] The venerable engineer was finally removed from his post just weeks before the general election (*Egyptian Gazette* 7, 10, 12 October, 29 December 1949).

The postponement of tenders remained in place for a year, until November 1950, while Muharram reorganized lines of authority over the project; retained his own favorite consulting engineer, Sir Murdoch MacDonald, whose firm was most prominently associated with Nile engineering works over the past half century; and recast the project's terms yet once more. Muharram created a new undersecretarial post within the ministry, which took over supervisory authority from the HEPC. More crucially, Muharram's new appointee followed the minister's (and MacDonald's) direction in returning to a comprehensive approach to power production and distribution, and he began to rewrite specifications for all remaining equipment and engineering services as a giant single tender.

Muharram's takeover and reconfiguration of the project survived the first hurdle in the spring of 1950, when yet another committee of foreign and local experts he had assembled approved the penstock design. A single dissenting vote was cast by representatives of a Swedish consulting firm, VBB, which had submitted a report criticizing it. This dissent would prove important to Muharram's opponents in 1952. But most noteworthy at this juncture was that U.S. Westinghouse and its local partners, notably Shishini, dropped their own longstanding public criticisms of the penstock plan. The reasons are now fairly plain.

These particular competitors had basically been shut out of the Egyptian heavy-electrical equipment market during the Nuqrashi years, not only in the case of Aswan but also in the competition in 1947–1948 to reoutfit the Cairo North power station. Indeed, Shishini blamed the old HEPC head (and Saʿdist party member), Ahmad, personally and brought suit against the Egyptian government after Ahmad allegedly influenced the outcome of this second competition.[23] The picture changed dramatically, however, once Muharram took over as minister of public works. In October 1949, he delivered an £E 5 million power-station contract to Westinghouse and, importantly, to party allies Shishini and the Abu al-Faths, who were investors in the joint venture. In March 1950, the contract was formally awarded with much fanfare, Shishini's suit against the government was dropped, and he was made a senator (*Egyptian Gazette* 30 October 1949, 30 January, 2, 21 February, 24 March, 4 April, 30 May 1950; ʿAbd al-Muʿti ʿAbd al-Wahab ʿAmr 1960: 7).

By the summer of 1950, Muharram and officials at Public Works were boasting expansively of a new and combined electrification and industrialization master plan for the Aswan region, to cost £E 100 million and to include both a steel factory and a fertilizer factory. When British embassy analysts attempted to reconcile this huge new public investment plan with the divergent preferences of the Wafd's private backers, notably ʿAbbud, they took note of Muharram's careful specification of the timetable for implementing the scheme. Work on the power plant, begun in 1948, was to continue as soon as possible—that is, once tenders for the new civil-engineering works were issued later in the year, the offers were evaluated, and final contracts were approved and signed. This phase was going to cost approximately £E 22–25 million (*Egyptian Gazette* 19 April 1949; *al-Ahram* 3 April 1951). Muharram insisted, however, that the most efficient way to proceed was to finish the power plant before starting the construction of the factories, and the new timetable envisioned completion of the power plant in stages between 1955 and 1957.[24]

An important obstacle in the way of Muharram's revised scheme was cleared as what some British officials called the Wafd's "Sirag al-Din–ʿAbbud wing" gradually extended its control over policymaking. This expansion of control took place in a series of conflicts with a so-called reform wing associated with Sirag al-Din's main rival inside the party, Najib al-Hilali. In November 1950, Prime Minister Nahhas fired his finance minister, Zaki ʿAbd al-Mutʿal, a fiscal conservative and Hilali's main protégé in the cabinet. Among other causes of this controversial cabinet purge, Mut'al resolutely opposed plans for financing the large-scale public-works project. 'Abbud and other critics of Hilali and company within the business oligarchy were then appointed to a newly created Higher Advisory Council (HAC) to assist in developing a coordinated government policy for the "national economy."[25] Though it is generally not recognized, this organization was essentially rechristened the National Production Council in the winter of 1952, when a new set of businessmen-advisers approved the Aswan project as the first "new" development scheme of the revolutionary regime.

Muharram's ministry and consultants completed design changes, called for new tenders, evaluated the offers and made the preliminary recommendations on the bids between November 1950 and mid-1951. As of that point, £E 4 million had been spent on consulting and preliminary construction. I have been unable to find detailed documentation on these deliberations, but Hamid al-Qaddah, then rising in the ranks of the engineering syndicate, close to its leadership (including Muharram) and an investor in the building materials and contracting sectors, claims that a consortium with which he and other local capitalists were involved had been tapped for the contract and involved in final negotiations late in 1951 (interviews with Hamid al-Qaddah, Cairo, 24 April, 14 July 1985; *al-Ahram* 3 April 1951). It is no wonder, therefore, that Qaddah used his column in *Majalla al-Muhandisin* (April 1952 p. 10; May 1952 pp. 21–22) to condemn the politicization of technical issues when the Wafd government's Aswan policy came under fresh attack in parliament in the winter of 1951–1952, just weeks before the explosion of fighting in the Canal Zone and riots in Cairo brought the last popularly elected Egyptian government to an end.

Political conditions in Egypt after October 1951 were hardly conducive to progress on any kind of development initiative. In place of administrative continuity, four governments rose and fell in quick succession in the months before the July 1952 military coup. Yet, for a post-Wafd prime minister like Hilali, who staked his claim to rule on the promise of substituting reform for Wafdist demagoguery and corruption, the Aswan project was an easy one to seize upon in order to legitimate his clique's rule. A revamped Higher Consultative Committee rubber-stamped the project, and, despite the invariable criticism of the technical design, Hilali apparently pushed through an authorization for credits by late spring 1952, while the new minister of public works prepared to complete negotiations with the prime contracting firms.

After July 1952, though, the earnest efforts of most of these particular *ancien régime* stalwarts no longer mattered (*al-Ahram* 16 April, 12 May 1952; 'Abd al-'Aziz Ahmad 1955: 66; 'Abd al-Mu'ti 'Abd al-Wahab 'Amr 1960: 9).

National Power and the Aswan Project, 1953–1960

Though Hilali did not remain in power long enough to reap the symbolic windfall, the power project paid off handsomely for Nasser and the other officers turned state builders. The rapid progress on the final-implementation phase of the Aswan scheme become emblematic of the new regime's ostensible technocratic and developmentalist ethos, while the turbines, generators and pylons were icons for the country's commitment to national industry and industrial power, at least until construction of the High Dam project in the 1960s.

Understandably enough, the new regime and its own key backers— for instance, U.S. Ambassador Jefferson Caffery, the CIA station chief and his staff, second-tier investors like the Amins and the journalists they sponsored such as Haykal, etc.—were invested in creating the appearance of a sharp, rapid and decisive break with the past. Nonetheless, O'Brien (1966: 63) pointed to possible tensions in such accounts:

During the early years when the officers remained very preoccupied with consolidating power and expelling the British from the canal zone, no very clear departure can be observed from the kind of economic policies pursued by the old regime. Men so overwhelmingly concerned with a struggle for political power naturally found little time to consider the long-term future of their country. Excluding land reform, up to the Tripartite Aggression [the 1956 War], continuity seems more evident than change.

This observation is indisputably true in the case of the Aswan power scheme, which was reapproved for implementation in November 1952 by a new Egyptian cabinet headed by General Muhammad Nagib, who also served as the junta's figurehead. His minister of finance, Galil al-'Imari, the bureaucrat-turned-businessman, held the same post six months earlier under Hilali. He was probably the single Egyptian most familiar with the financial aspects of the project, given his ubiquitous presence inside the corridors of the post–World War II Finance Ministry. More crucially, General Nagib's minister of public works was Murad Fahmi, the engineer who had served as the secretary general of the HEPC in the 1940s. No two figures were more capable and better placed for continuing this now even more crucial piece of development work.

Reports contemporary with these events could not easily narrate the past away, though when *al-Ahram* (15 February 1953) announced that Nagib's cabinet had approved award of the main civil-engineering contract to a French consortium, a distinction was made between those phases completed "in past ages" and those at hand "in the age of liberation." Thirty years later, a one-line account in the same paper reported simply that the original project "was started in 1953 . . . and finished in 1961" (*al-Ahram* 9 June 1985).

Viewed "on the ground" in the power department's offices and at the construction site outside of Aswan, rather than from the perspective of the Revolutionary Command Council (RCC), the history of the hydropower scheme would seem to reinforce O'Brien's point about the continuities marking economic policies. Nonetheless, certain new political factors likely facilitated the process of restarting work on the project. The most important was the closing of the channels—parties, print and parliament—exploited regularly by the shifting and diverse coalition of opponents in the past.

The significance of the authoritarian turn is immediately gauged by the remarkable turn by the new minister of public works, Fahmi. Long known as an opponent of the penstock scheme, he ignored the views of his own one-time superiors at the HEPC and the planeloads of international consultants who had flown in and out of Cairo after the war, and proceeded to build the power station using the alternative tunnel design. This particular feat of engineering was by all accounts impressive. Fahmi added the Swedish consultants, VBB, who back in 1950 recommended against the penstock scheme, to the payroll; he sent the revised specifications out to the 1950 short list of contractors in October; and he was reviewing the new offers by the end of December 1952.[26]

To the extent that they had to, Fahmi and his cohorts defended the case for the switch in design on two grounds. First, the decision to abandon the penstocks, which were essentially long metal pipes, and the new sluice gates into which they would be fitted meant a reduction in the price of the project (and a savings in hard currency). It also meant a larger share of the costs spent at home since local contractors and labor would be involved in digging the tunnels. Second, they argued that a new set of tests showed that altering the dam's sluice gates posed an unreasonable degree of risk to the dam's structure. In essence, this was a variant of the charge opponents had been using since the 1930s (interviews with Geoffrey Kennedy and Benjamin Croft, Thetford, England, August 1986: el-Kholy 1957).

A most significant difference in this arena compared with the earlier 1930s authoritarian interlude (or any period up to 1952) is that Fahmi and the rest of the cabinet were suddenly free of the need to vet these claims before a new "neutral" panel of experts. This freedom was likely to be judged a plus from the standpoint of national autonomy and defended inside the Ministry of Public Works on the related grounds of professional competence. Fahmi's situation was an Egyptian technocrat's dream come true. Parliament had been prorogued; the parties wrestled with the regime's orders to purge their ranks; and the most notorious of an earlier generation of "politicized" public-works ministers, the Wafd's Muharram, was in jail and awaiting trial in the regime's new Treason Court. The party presses had of course been shut down. Egyptian engineering circles, where debate on the project had been especially fierce, pointedly ignored the suggestion by the editor of *Majalla al-Muhandisin* in October 1952 for a new round of discussions on the power project (Moore 1980: 157). And, in a step that seems at once to stand for continuity and change in this arena, Ahmad, the first chairman of the HEPC, was restored to his old position by a cabinet minister who once served directly under him and who, more importantly, buried the design that Ahmad had been promoting for the past twenty years.

The new revolutionary leadership had little incentive, obviously, to emphasize its indebtedness to the institutions of the regime it had just overthrown, but if the pylons went up relatively quickly after 1952, it was due to the groundbreaking work, messy as it had been, carried out between 1945 and 1952. The contracts for the main electrical machinery had been signed in 1947–1948, and the same firms began delivery of the plant in 1956. The tenders for civil works submitted in 1951–1952 served as the basis for Fahmi's award of contracts, totaling £E 11 million and announced in February 1953, to a set of French and German heavy-engineering firms (*al-Ahram* 8, 10, 11 February 1953; 'Abd al-Mu'ti 'Abd al-Wahab 'Amr 1960). Work was finally resumed on site at the end of the annual flood season in the fall of 1953. I found no further sign of the kind of ubiquitous public interventions that had

surrounded this project for decades, with a single though hardly decisive exception that came, significantly, in the midst of the bitter power
struggle over the authoritarian regime's future in March 1954 (*al-Ahram* 15 March 1954).

Summary

        The years after World War II were ones of sharp and esca-
lating conflicts, of renewed political mobilization against the remaining
vestiges of colonial rule inside Egypt and, by 1947–1948, of war with
the Jewish settlers in Palestine and the new Israeli state. The decision
of the palace-backed Nuqrashi regime to fight in Palestine helped to
shape subsequent American views of Faruq and the "corrupt" Egyptian
landowning elite during the last years of the monarchy. But it was the
disastrous outcome of the war that shaped subsequent political developments inside Egypt, including the wave of assassinations in 1949, the
return of the Wafd in 1950 and the abrogation of the Anglo-Egyptian
treaty in October 1951.

        Though not usually seen this way, these familiar landmarks of the
postwar era highlight how the qualifications originally attached to "independence" in 1922 had generally ceased to constrain the political
leadership of the postwar Egyptian state. This is not a claim that Nuqrashi and his successors were free from outside interference, but neither
were those who governed after the July 1952 coup. And the opposition
to Nagib and Nasser in 1952–1954 rehearsed a theme familiar from the
demonstrations of the late 1940s and early 1950s: that the military, like
its civilian predecessors, was an agent of imperialism.

        Many have since come to adopt the revolutionary leadership's own
preferred narratives of this period, which naturally sought to put as
much distance as possible between it and the *ancien régime*. But the
symbolic distancing from the colonial roots of the state was no less part
of the project of the immediate postwar leaders and their cadres. In one
particularly relevant case, a high official contested a part of the history
that I have been excavating in this book, though "the facts" were literally carved in stone. When work on the original Aswan Dam was completed in 1902, a plaque was attached to commemorate what at the
time was regarded by some as "the greatest single work ever planned

and carried out by British contractors" (Middlemas 1963: 147). The plaque read as follows:

> This Dam Was Designed And Built By
> British Engineers
> Egyptians Assisted By Greeks Excavated
> To The Rock Foundations And
> Built The Rubble Masonry
> Skilled Italian Workmen Dressed And Built
> The Granite Ashlar
> (Addison 1959: 16)

Ahmad Khary, a civil engineer, one of the postwar government's main experts on dams and a member of the 1945 HEPC, had the plaque removed in 1947, on the grounds that it did "not shed a true light on things" (*Egyptian Gazette* 19 June 1947). To buttress his case he recalled his own role as resident engineer during the second heightening in the 1930s, though this was decades after the dam had been built. In essence, he was claiming the dam for the new Nuqrashi regime. The chairman of the commission, Ahmad, would do the same for the hydropower project in the late 1940s.

The site had been reinscribed with a radically new genealogy by the time Nasser traveled south for the official opening of the power station in 1960. This process began immediately after the military took power, as attested to by the following 1954 account:

No sooner did the Revolution take up the reins of office than it started to carry into effect Egypt's most important project which has engaged public attention for over a quarter of a century, namely the Aswan Hydro-Electric Scheme. The project which used to afford material for cheap political propaganda, has now become an accomplished fact. . . . Under the present regime, . . . and within the comparatively short period of six months, the project passed through all the preliminary stages, with the result that the country felt a new era of real development and progress has dawned. (Khadr and Hassoun 1954: 46–47)

It seems almost inevitable that the kind of stylized and triumphant text sampled above will appear contrived now. It was, after all, largely the previous progress that made it possible for Fahmi's ministry to shepherd the project "through all the preliminary [sic] stages" in 1952–1953. And after the timetable for completion was set back by the Suez crisis in 1956–1957, the new authorities perhaps considered earlier such "exogenous shocks"—World War II, the 1947–1948 Palestine

War and the 1951–1952 Canal Zone crisis—in a new light. Still, it seems reasonable to argue that the military brought something new and important to the equation after July 1952.

Analysts revisited the history of the Aswan project in the 1970s and 1980s primarily to refute the idea that British power had sought to hinder Egyptian industrialization. "It [the Aswan project], for instance, was not the victim of colonial hostility to Egypt's industrialization but rather of the clan infighting over award of contract, and the difficulties of financing" (Waterbury 1983: 60 and 1979: 47; see also Tignor 1977b and 1980a). As I have been arguing throughout, in its broad thrust, such a claim is surely correct: British policy generally supported the expansion of its country's own multinational-oriented engineering and heavy manufacturing firms in territories such as Egypt. But those in Egypt who pointed to foreign opposition to explain the project's delay were not all guilty of blind adherence to indefensible doctrinal positions.

Chapters 3 and 4 of this book provide numerous examples of efforts by foreign economic and political elites to block or otherwise interfere with decision making on the Aswan project. In the late 1940s, representatives of ICI, the largest supplier of fertilizers to the market, were still pursuing a strategy of diverting the Egyptians from the project for as long as possible. Emphasizing the retarding effects of foreign intervention is inherently no more or less plausible an explanation for why the Aswan project was not built before 1960. To make the point in slightly different terms, the list of factors that might explain the successive delays is in fact quite a bit longer: imperialism, war, bureaucratic infighting, Palestine, *shillal* (cliques), the composition of Egyptian cabinets, the timing of Egyptian elections, the technical capacity of public agencies, party rivalries, bribery, the competitive structure of international markets, the needs of Chilean fertilizer exporters, and so on. Explaining why the Aswan hydropower scheme was not built in Egypt (that is, why something did not happen) is logically equivalent to explaining why the bourgeoisie failed to transform Egypt.

The long history of successive bargaining rounds has nonetheless provided a unique vantage for studying the evolution of the bargaining capacity of local capitalists over time. 'Abbud had joined Docker's consortium in 1927, seeking, realistically, to obtain a share of the profits in return for securing the government's support for what, if their plan had been adopted, would have been a predominantly foreign-owned concession company. Nonetheless, by the 1940s, 'Abbud was promoting the project as his own, Egyptian-owned power-generating station and fertilizer factory, for which the foreign firms would supply the plant and expertise.

In the same way, the case underscores the basic, though often forgotten point that the scope and precise nature of state involvement in these two sectors was politically determined. As late as the 1940s, 'Abbud and his allies still envisioned the private appropriation of the Nile's power-generating resources as a plausible outcome. Public ownership of the hydropower plant was contested, and the contest appears to have been settled by 1945–1946, at which point 'Abbud and his allies apparently gave up their efforts to build and run the power plant as a private concession. In a similar way, local capital clearly demonstrated its preference and intent to run the various proposed chemical manufacturing plant as a private venture, but, in 1956, the state nonetheless emerged as majority owner in the new Aswan (Kima) fertilizer-factory joint venture. The political roots of the entire range of now naturalized views about what the private sector ostensibly could not or would not do, together with the claims about what the state ostensibly had to do after 1952, need to be rethought.

This unfolding contest over a new postwar regulatory regime reflected both the effects of the reorganization of economic administrative agencies during World War II and what analysts correctly point to as a postwar resurgence of "political and economic nationalism" (Tignor 1984: 175–176, 179–195, 213–214). But a contest was ongoing over the precise terms of economic nationalism or over competing nationalist projects. Investors viewed and promoted Egyptianization as a means to continue to privatize resources. In the Aswan case, this outcome was successfully avoided.

Finally, the details of the conflicts that I have been examining here, with their implications for understanding the factors that shaped the scope and pace of industrial investment after the war, are usually obscured in the conventional narratives of industrialization; these narratives are written generally as a parable of failed national-class formation and the seizure of power by army officers in July 1952 imagined as the logical culmination of a process of economic change steered unsteadily by the weak bourgeoisie.

Over the years, the disparate currents and historically contingent effects of a complex, overdetermined conjuncture (the "crisis" of 1950–1952) have been presented, somewhat too unreflectively, as a revolutionary situation, with the political economy made to appear spiraling downward, the elite establishment paralyzed, society "inflamed" and in ferment "from below," Egypt inexorably sliding "into chaos" (Baker 1978: 1, 10; Tignor 1984: 242; Beinin and Lockman 1987: 395–398; Botman 1988: 115).

I propose to look at the crisis or crises of 1950–1952 afresh, from the vantage of the end of World War II and the opening of a new phase in Egypt's postcolonial history when it was being steered by a cautiously confident, reactionary-capitalist elite that was trying to reconsolidate its authority while navigating the complexities of the unfolding postwar world order. The investors whose strategies and political choices I have been analyzing most certainly did not act as if the postwar years were harbingers of some latent, near-future upheaval, and they would be hardpressed to recognize themselves in the descriptions that typically follow from the familiar conceptualization of elite views at the height of the crisis: resigned and helpless to prevent the collapse of the old regime.

Certainly, the idea that after the war capitalists were too timid to undertake necessary investments or act forthrightly to implement the reforms that they knew were in their own best interests seems to be wrong. Accounts of the post-1945 political economy remain heavily tied to these particular premises among others in which the successor, revolutionary regime's own official histories were deeply invested. As I will try to show, the real problem for many in Egypt (and, keep in mind, the hope for many others) was that the Wafd and the investors who dominated the party seemed to offer a way out of the political impasse that followed the burning of downtown Cairo in January 1952.

CHAPTER SIX

Indigenous Roots of Egypt's Socialist Transformation

The Revolt against Business Privilege

It was in order to remove the obstacles to development by enacting basic reforms and allowing Egyptian capitalism to realize its full potential that the Free Officers seized power in July 1952.

Beinin and Lockman (1987: 12)

Then the revolution came in 1952 to impede the development of Egyptian capitalism even while permitting the establishment of a capitalist system in the technical sense.

'Asim al-Disuqi (1981: 56)

On 23 July 1952, a small group of junior army "free officers" launched a successful coup d'état in Egypt, and as they went on to consolidate their power and forge a social coalition to support their rule, they defended their actions in the name of "revolution" (Gordon 1992: 3). Many of the junta's earliest and most ardent supporters—for instance, the *Ruz al-Yusuf* columnist 'Ihsan 'Abd al-Qaddus and the American ambassador in Egypt, Jefferson Caffery—doubtless saw in the July 1952 Revolution confirmation of both the fatal shortsightedness of the *ancien régime* in the face of social unrest and the wisdom of the reform path that had been urged upon the king without success. As a result, Faruq was deposed within days of the coup, and by September

169

1952 the army passed the country's first comprehensive land-reform law. In the following months, parties were banned, and, thirty years after its birth, the 1923 constitution was buried.

The subsequent course of the Revolution—from a U.S.-supported, Peronist- or Cardenas-styled "national-popular" dictatorship (Maxfield 1990) under Nasser in the mid-1950s to a Soviet-backed "Arab-socialist" experiment in the 1960s and beyond—remains a defining focus of empirical investigation and theoretical debate among most subsequent analysts of the political economy (e.g., Issawi 1954, O'Brien 1966, Abdel-Malek 1968, Hussein 1977, Trimberger 1977, Cooper 1982, Waterbury 1983, Hinnebusch 1985, Zaalouk 1989). By contrast, neither the interpretation of surface events nor the deeper historical process underlying the July 1952 coup d'état and subsequent regime change are seen as significant analytical problems, with the single exception of defining the mode of production in the countryside ('Abd al-'Aziz Ramadan 1981, Owen 1981b, Richards, 1982). But this consensus itself needs some sharp questioning, beginning with what Gordon says is "too often taken for granted" (or at least taken too literally) by analysts, namely that "Egypt stood on the brink of a social revolution" when the army conspirators seized power (1992: 5).

The objective of this final chapter is to return to the idea of the Egyptian Revolution as the outcome of a failed national-bourgeois project launched in the 1920s. More accurately, it is to return to those foundational assumptions about class structure, interests and agency that are derived from colonial-exceptionalist narratives of political economy. As I first noted in Chapter 1, most claims about capitalists and politics until now are essentially about the Revolution, histories written backward to deduce Nasserism as an outcome of the exceptionalist circumstances of colonial capitalist development. For those whose reassessments of this narrative strategy will turn on empirical or internal-validity issues, it is important to show the ways in which the archival sources challenge basic claims about the alleged preferences and choices of Egyptian capitalist and party elites at a critical juncture.

The first section of this chapter offers a revisionist view of the 1950–1952 Wafd government, which in nationalist and exceptionalist historiography is portrayed by Revolution's eve as the instrument of the large landowners and led by an elite that was either unable or unwilling to implement the most crucial parts of the bourgeois project (agrarian reform, a more equitable distribution of wealth, and accelerated industrial development). And, from this particular conception of what allegedly constituted Egyptian investors' basic interests, Egyptian marxists argued that the postwar industrial bourgeoisie was "generally hostile to the Wafd" (Beinin and Lockman 1987: 10–11, 395–399).

I show that the Wafd party was more nearly the instrument of the entire business oligarchy—that is, the main Egyptian investment groups and thus the core of the country's industrial sector. These leading Egyptian capitalists quite rationally tended to ignore or oppose issues like land reform in the absence of positive inducements or credible threats. In other words, those most heavily invested in industry were least invested in ideas such as land reform and other forms of redistribution. Nor were such proposals more convincing when posed in terms of facilitating long-term growth, particularly when weighed against the party's strategy of enriching its business wing in the short term.

The second section of this chapter turns to the series of post-Wafd cabinets between January and July 1952, which are given little specific attention in the left's historiography and are instead absorbed into the larger narrative of incipient political-economic collapse. For instance, in Botman's history of the Egyptian communist movement, these events are background to an end already foretold: some counterestablishment force would have to take power. "A crisis of governing existed: no stable government could preside from above, . . . and from January to July 1952 four Cabinets succeeded one another." For the left, the basic concern has long been why the communists, as opposed to the military, did not "capture the moment" (1988: 115)

Since I am not as sure what these complex events foretold, my questions are different. Why did the Americans and British, who were centrally involved in these events, favor the Wafd's downfall in 1951? Who were the investors most centrally involved in this six-month-long crisis in 1952? What were the stakes? Was there no way out for the establishment? Working through the details of the successive and open-ended games among British, Egyptian and American elites is crucial because only by ignoring them can a structural account of the Revolution as an outcome of bourgeois failure or of a regime inevitably facing its final days be made to appear empirically plausible.

Finally, I no longer find it convincing to see the army conspirators as history's agent in this instance, acting so that capitalism could "realize its full potential" (Beinin and Lockman 1987: 12). In the third section, I turn to the rapidly unfolding confrontation with capitalist privilege and the challenge posed for the business oligarchy by U.S.-backed etatist and antimonopolist currents inside the new regime.

I can imagine two kinds of objections to my account and want to address them at the outset. First, the chapter is not intended nor should it be read as a new and comprehensive reading of the foreign-policy dimension of the unfolding Egyptian crisis of 1951–1952 as it is usually conceived. I am fully convinced of the priority that both London- and Washington-based elites accorded to military and strategic considerations at this critical juncture, even if I do not emphasize them here. But even the most sensitive diplomatic historians or others who use the diplomatic archives have tended to read these texts uncritically in discussing Egyptian domestic politics.

Second, though I concentrate here on Egyptian elite actions, I do not want to be read as implying that the mobilization of relatively large segments of workers and other parts of urban political society was unimportant to the way in which the Canal Zone crisis unfolded, or since I dispute conceptions of Egypt on the verge of revolution, that I am arguing that no crisis existed. Clearly, the Wafd party leaders faced a significant challenge to their rule. In 1951, contenders for power threatened to outflank them on the nationalist issue, leading to the decision to abrogate the Anglo-Egyptian treaty. Rather, I open up for question here the tendency to reduce the Wafd's decision making to a matter of a "wrong" choice on the basis of a misconceived idea about the collective needs and actions of capitalists.

The 1950–1952 Wafd Government: Big Business Finally Has Its Party

The 'Abbud group invested heavily in what Gordon (1989) has termed the Wafd's "last hurrah"—the remarkable election victory in January 1950 that secured for the business-backed, Sirag al-Din wing of the party two years of unrivaled and virtually unchecked control over state power and resources. The country's most powerful local Egyptian investors like 'Abbud, the Alexandria-based Yahya and Farghali groups, *al-Misri* owners Mahmud and Husayn Abu al-Fath, Muhammad al-Wakil and the Sirag al-Dins championed a conservative reform agenda that amounted to funding their own private engineering, trade and industrial ventures; reversing the mild etatist thrust of the previous three years; and conceding as little as possible to the redistributive project favored by the Wafd's left wing.

Clearly, those who championed and articulated various versions of etatism or the restructuring of property rights in the countryside reflected a variety of ideological orientations, but just as clearly the country's largest industrialists tended to see such a project as retarding rather than promoting Egyptian capitalism, and the explanation for this view cannot be reduced to the fact that they had holdings in land as well as industry. Barring a wholesale conversion of this property-owning class to the view that redistribution was a value in its own right, the highly dubious, future-oriented utilitarian rationale—the *fallahin* as a new consumer market—could hardly outweigh the concrete costs. From the perspective of the oligarchs, the national economy (and their pockets) could ill afford welfare measures at the expense of more immediately productive investment. Certainly, for many circa 1950 there seemed to be no compelling reason to alter this calculus. Instead, leading capitalist oligarchs like Sidqi, Sirri, Sirag al-Din, 'Abbud and 'Afifi preferred the time-honored mix of repression, religion and nationalism for containing counter-establishment currents.[1]

Ironically, the left's preferred interpretation of the Wafd's return to power in January 1950 seems as wildly off the mark as the predictions of various interested parties at the time, from the *Times* correspondent (and ardent Nuqrashi supporter) C. D. Quillam to U.S. Ambassador Caffery. It had been generally assumed that the king and his advisers would never let Nahhas and the Wafd return to power. The *Times*'s editors scoffed at charges that Sirri was favoring the Wafd, applauded his efforts to focus attention on "building, industrialization, development schemes and social legislation," and all but endorsed the rigging of the vote. Thus, the "main problem" was "how to conduct the election so that a balanced coalition will be returned without *unduly* interfering with the choice of the electors" (the *Times*, 17 October 1949, emphasis mine). Yet Sirri, though commonly identified as the "king's man," personally helped orchestrate the party's comeback, by choosing to run a fair election. His business partner, 'Abbud, poured cash into the Wafd's machine, the party went on to win an absolute majority in parliament and, though the king was reportedly stunned at the outcome, Nahhas was ultimately invited to form a new government.

The American officials in Cairo who were trying to puzzle out the turn of events assumed that the king must have miscalculated Sirri's "willingness to act in his own interest."[2] But the businessman who had brought Sirri into his expanding industrial empire and whose economic ventures had become synonymous in Sirri's mind with Egypt's future prosperity (not to mention his own) had made clear where his interest lay. By then, no *ancien régime* figure was more closely associated with the 'Abbud group. In the aftermath of the elections, Egypt witnessed an unprecedented degree of conciliation between party and palace (Gordon 1989, Tariq al-Bishri 1983). What has gone unnoticed until now, however, is the loose alliance of investors who served as the bridge—Sirri, Elias Andraos (another of the king's advisers who directed the Misr group–Bradford Dyers joint venture), the Sirag al-Dins and 'Abbud. And though the left sees in the Wafd's alleged deference to the monarchy unmistakable signs of both crisis and paralysis, again based on a questionable idea of what capitalists would have done if they were an independent and self-confident bourgeoisie, the flurry of activity in the months that followed suggests that investors at the time were viewing a different and far rosier horizon.

EGYPT INCORPORATED

The 1950 Wafd government's basic economic strategy emphasized publicly supported and privately guided infrastructure investment, rural public works, housing construction, "model villages," land reclamation and industry building, which, its proponents argued, would lift the standard of living for the population. One thing for certain is that the strategy increased employment in the public-works sector and augmented the ranks of the contractors registered with the Federation of Industries, as investors hoisted billboards in Cairo and the provinces advertising their new ventures: the Egyptian Engineering and Construction Company ('Abd al-Qawi Pasha's joint venture with George Wimpy and Company); Al-Shams (Sirri, 'Afifi, Mahmud Shukri and French investors); Al-Shark (newspaper owner Mahmud Abu al-Fath and locally resident foreigners); SOTRAC (the Shihata family and Hamid al-Qaddah, among others); L'Enterprise de la Maison Nouvelle (a new British construction venture that had the aging leader of the Nationalist Party, Hafiz Ramadan, as its president!); and HABECO (Mukhtar Ibrahim, the Rabbath group and the Shihatas).

While the Wafd pressed ahead with the infrastructure and industrial-investment schemes, it also introduced new and at the time unprecedented programs for universal, free primary, secondary and technical education; increased subsidies for basic foods; rudimentary health care in the countryside; and social-security and minimum-wage provisions in the cities (Tignor 1982; Gordon 1989). The administrators of some of these initiatives were identified as protégés of Najib al-Hilali, a member of the Wafd executive and Sirag al-Din's main rival inside the party. I want to consider the government's programs and investors' responses to them with some care because there has been a tendency to reduce the policy process to the issue of corrupt party insiders battling reform-minded outsiders—that is, in terms of the rise and fall of Hilali and "his men."

At least two different and conflicting policy initiatives are usually lumped together as reforms and identified with Hilali's protégés (ignoring those investment- and production-oriented policies discussed here and in Chapter 5 that after July 1952 were touted as reforms by the Free Officers). On the one hand, there were the new spending programs associated with the government's two most progressive appointees, Taha Husayn, the Egyptian author who headed the Ministry of Education, and Ahmad Husayn, son of a Wafd party notable and a future ambassador to the United States who skyrocketed to prominence at the Ministry of Social Affairs (*Akhbar al-Yawm,* 14 January 1950; *al-Ahram,* 30 November 1984). These ministers dreamed of building schools and health clinics across the country. On the other hand, there were the efforts by the new finance minister, Zaki 'Abd al-Mut'al, to curb spending and extend the regulatory authority of the state, essentially along the lines favored by Nuqrashi's government in 1947–1948. Clearly, these two impulses were in conflict.

Investors complained about the costs associated with the new welfare programs. The ultraconservative Sirri Pasha branded Taha Husayn an extremist, and 'Abbud, less viscerally, grumbled to the British about Sirag al-Din's failure to ride herd on the two young and idealistic ministers. Similarly, the opposition Sa'dist party head, 'Abd al-Hadi, protested to the Americans that Ahmad Husayn's social-security program was a waste of taxpayers' money and a diversion of scarce resources from industry (that is, from the pockets of 'Abd al-Hadi and allied businessmen).[3] Nonetheless, I would argue that business-group heads and their allies generally substituted talk for collective action in this arena, found ways to defray the costs and, at worst, resigned themselves to these programs.

For instance, when Hilali's protégé (and a favorite contact of U.S. Ambassador Caffery) Ahmad Husayn resigned, dramatically, in June

1951 after eighteen months in office, his defeat in an interministerial tug-of-war (along with, for obvious reasons, his preferred explanation for it) was absorbed into the general antireform brief then being assembled against the Wafd inside the U.S. embassy. But Husayn's programs themselves were simply not the target and certainly were not the target of the business interests most closely tied to the Wafd. The American embassy reported that 'Abbud himself had intervened to try to keep Husayn in the cabinet, no doubt in part for narrow reasons since 'Abbud's daughter was married to Husayn's brother, and such elite-family connections carried a premium. More broadly, though, party leaders appreciated the contribution that these programs made to holding together the Wafd's electoral coalition, though sometimes the cynicism was hard to disguise. Thus Sirag al-Din objected when an editor of *al-Ahram* (9 September 1951) described him as a capitalist. "I wish to affirm an undoubted fact that I am a convinced socialist, that the Wafd is a socialist party and that the present government is a socialist government."[4]

Segments of the American intelligence community at the time took Sirag al-Din's pronouncements seriously, if not literally, describing them as part of a "deliberate domestic political strategy" of controlled change to shore up the upper class of a "society [that] might well be characterized as reactionary capitalistic (in the opprobrious sense of the latter term)."[5] The writer pointed to personalities inside and outside the party—Sirag al-Din, 'Abbud, the independent 'Azzam Pasha (from a family of big landowners in Giza), as well as Ahmad Husayn—as lending support to this effort. I have identified others, like the Yahyas (generally not linked to Egyptian party politics) and Saba Habashi, prominently linked with U.S. oil companies and, until 1950, a member of the opposition Sa'dist party.[6]

The more vital concern of the party's "reactionary capitalists," Sirag al-Din chief among them, was the reforms championed by Hilali's ally at finance, Mut'al, whose antispending brief and attempted extension of regulatory powers brought him into conflict with an array of powerful investors. His ministry clashed directly with the party's business allies in at least three basic arenas, which led to his downfall before the year's end. I have already discussed one of these conflicts in Chapter 5: Mut'al's opposition to funding the country's biggest industrialization project at Aswan. In other words, Mut'al's reforms entailed a curb on the Wafd government's modest public spending levels.

The second conflict involved the regulation of the Alexandria cotton-futures market, which the wartime economic authorities had closed in 1940 and which Sirri's government reopened in September 1949. The ministry's attempt to control its operations during the height of the Korean boom put it on a collision course with the largest exporters, most notably the Yahyas and Farghali, whose influence in the cabinet and palace enabled them to counter Mut'al's ministerial authority. The irony is that many of these same investors welcomed the kinds of regulatory policies championed by Mut'al as the market began to collapse one year later, though by that time he had been forced from office.

The third conflict involved the decision by agencies of the Finance Ministry to proceed with the claim for some £E 10 million in back taxes from the Misr and 'Abbud groups. In a matter of months, the politically artless finance minister had managed to align the country's most powerful private institutions against him, but the details of this sectoral conflict were obscured as the Wafd's political opponents fed the rumor mills with a stream of lurid stories about collusion among the "cotton lords," rigged markets and speculative fortunes flowing to the bank accounts of Sirag al-Din, Nahhas's wife and her relatives (Gordon 1989: 204, 207). An alternative picture emerges in the reporting by the U.S. embassy's economic officers.[7] The Egyptian prime minister finally asked for Mut'al's resignation in November 1950.

The 1950–1952 Wafd government's approach to regulation was pre-eminently self-regulation by the country's (and party's) biggest industrial investors. In other words, the business oligarchs extended the process of rationalizing various sectoral holdings and transforming the Bank Misr offices into an executive coordinating committee of Egypt's leading firms and sectors. "Business investors have available a unique means for solving some collective action problems: mergers and acquisitions" (Devereux 1988: 29).

In Chapter 3, I noted the beginning of this process in the formal cartelization of the textile industry by the Misr and Yahya groups. In Chapter 4, I underscored the significance of 'Afifi's bringing the Yahya family—though they were ostensible competitors in textiles, shipping, cotton exporting and insurance—onto the Bank Misr board. By 1945, the Alexandria Navigation Company (Yahya) and Misr Maritime Navigation Company had merged their operations.[8] 'Abbud's shipping firm was linked via a formal consortium with the merged fleet by 1953. This process was further extended with the Wafd's support in early 1950. Under the auspices of the oligarchs, proposals first raised in 1947–1948 to nationalize tram and bus service in Cairo were reconstituted as a new private-monopoly joint venture of the Misr and remnants of the Empain (Belgian) groups—in others words, the consolidation of the entire Cairo transport industry under the auspices of Bank Misr (*Egyptian Gazette* 9 February, 22 July and 7 November 1949, 21 June 1950). Workers in the main transport union opposed this move and called instead for nationalization of the transport industry (Beinin and Lockman 1987: 407).

Along these same lines, the party leadership's distinctive approach to "commanding the heights" seems to be reflected in the unfolding organization of the new and controversial Ministry of National Economy, charged with administering what amounted to a rudimentary trickle-down strategy of development. Specifically, under a renewed mandate and with a reshuffled administration following its first rocky months of existence, the ministry appointed 'Abbud, 'Afifi, Andraos, Yahya and their cronies to its new, oligarch-dominated advisory council.[9]

But the Wafd's most significant contribution to oligarchic consolidation was the backing given to 'Abbud, who, in November 1950, despite the suddenly ineffectual opposition of the bank's chairman and his longtime foe, 'Afifi, was invited to join the board of Bank Misr. Recall that this was a goal that had long eluded 'Abbud, though he was one of the single largest stockholders in the bank by 1944 and apparently remained so until its nationalization in 1960. The ground was prepared for this new alliance with the Misr group ('Afifi notwithstanding) in 1949, when 'Abbud and Yahya agreed to serve as coinvestors in a joint venture with U.S. Monsanto to manufacture DDT. 'Abbud's political ties to the Wafd helped clinch the position, which he then occupied for the next seven years. Yahya and others within the bank's leadership presumably saw the logic in cooperating with 'Abbud, though Sirag al-Din made no secret of the government's capacity to influence appointments to the board.[10]

The core owners and directors of the country's largest enterprises lined up behind the Wafd, with industrialists like 'Abbud (using Sirri) and Andraos of the Misr group (one of the king's main advisers) working constantly to smooth relations between the cabinet and palace, and, again in 'Abbud's case, to manage the Wafd's relations with the British and American embassies. 'Abbud was essentially Sirag al-Din's main conduit to Caffery. In return, the leaders of the Wafd's unofficial big-business federation were showered with rewards and subsidies, including Senate appointments ('Abbud, Andraos, Farghali, Shishini); tax exemptions (the 'Abbud group's still unfinished fertilizer factory, the Misr Group's synthetic-silk factory); protection for their sinecures (the reorganized transport market, the sugar monopoly, the shippers' cartel); and Sirag al-Din's intervention on behalf of cotton exporters (Yahya and Farghali) and the petroleum sector (Habashi, a lawyer on retainer for ARAMCO and a "mediator" in the cartel's price dispute with the state).[11]

Most critically, these investors enjoyed regular, direct, effective—and, one is tempted to add, exclusive—access to governing officials, along with the flexibility to shift the costs associated with postwar price controls, job-security provisions and wage legislation. Thus, according to the account in Beinin and Lockman's *Workers on the Nile*, 'Abbud could rely on the "people's party" to arrest the entire union leadership at the Hawamadiya refinery for calling a strike in order to force 'Abbud to comply with the government's year-old (and ignored) cost-of-living decree. While the organizers languished in jail, 'Abbud was plied with further tax abatements to induce him to resolve the dispute.[12]

NATIONAL CAPITAL

Clearly, no investor benefited more from the Wafd's return to power and Sirag al-Din's dominance within the party than 'Abbud, who had arguably attained the height of his influence in the Egyptian political economy in 1950–1952. The 'Abbud group added new ventures and holdings to its bulging investment portfolio. They imported buses and trucks to supply the group's transport companies in Cairo, the Delta and Upper Egypt. 'Abbud expanded into textiles by buying the Nuzha Spinning and Weaving Company. He modernized the old Cozzika family distillery in Turah; took over as chairman of the board of the old Suarès-Cassel land-development enterprise in upper Egypt, the Kom Ombo Company (which produced sugar cane for the factory); and had himself named chairman and managing director of the Upper Egypt Hotels Company (owners of the Winter Palace and Cataract hotels), spreading his involvement in the southern region's economy still further. Newspaper articles at the time regularly referred to him as one of the richest men in the world (*Akhbar al-Yawm* 7 June 1947 and 31 August 1948; *Egyptian Gazette* 1 November 1950; *al-Musawwar* 2 March 1951 and 18 July 1952).

'Abbud promoted himself as the leading force in Egypt's national economic renaissance, working tirelessly to expand jobs in rural and urban Egypt, to create investment opportunities for the middle class, and to Egyptianize the country's economic institutions. The financially strapped *al-Akhbar* chain, among other presses, happily ran pages of these thinly (if at all) disguised self-advertisements, which are still on file in the paper's archives, even during the period when publishers Mustafa and 'Ali Amin were organizing against the 'Abbud-backed Wafd government, as I will detail below. Thus, when he was elected president of the Ahli (National) Club in November 1949, the club was framed symbolically against the vestige of colonialism next door, the Gazira Club, where Egyptians still constituted a minority and were second-class members. With the help of Sirri, Nahhas, and Sirag al-Din, as well as the British and French embassies, 'Abbud gained entry in 1950 to an equally exclusive foreign enclave: the board of directors of the Suez Canal Company, after the Paris-based administration tried for months to reject the government's new nominees. In his new hyperbolic nationalist style, 'Abbud declared his membership to the board of the canal company to be the harbinger of the renaissance of the Egyptian navy (*Egyptian Gazette* 23 October 1949, 8 August and 8 November 1950; *Akhbar al-Yawm* 15 and 29 October 1949, 14 January 1950; Picot 1978: 22–24).

But his $24 million chemical-factory complex, nearing completion ten miles southwest of Suez, was arguably the potentially more valuable contribution to the national economy. Delays in the delivery of machinery ordered in England and the switch from U.K. to U.S. and European suppliers pushed back the start of operations at the plant from 1950 to the summer of 1951. The plant was, however, plagued by a host of design flaws and shoddily built equipment, according to the main construction supervisor, and 'Abbud was forced to absorb the costs of an immediate, four-month-long overhaul. When production was finally resumed, late in 1951, operations would be disrupted by the political disturbances in the Canal Zone that followed the government's abrogation of the 1936 treaty with Great Britain.[13]

Even before the original plant was finished, 'Abbud had started to arrange with U.S. firms to expand the product line of the fertilizer complex and, with W. R. Grace and Company, to build his own paper mill near Cairo for packaging the fertilizers produced at Suez. He submitted an additional $5.2 million funding request to the ExIm Bank; bank personnel had reviewed the proposals favorably when, in the winter of 1951, the Truman administration blocked 'Abbud's loan together with the Wafd government's project proposals then before the World Bank. The Wafd leaders and their allies were unlikely to have missed the point. U.S. Ambassador Caffery had appealed to Nahhas not to cashier the fifteen-year-old canal-base treaty. And as the crisis quickly escalated into clashes between British troops and Egyptian volunteers, the Americans momentarily closed ranks with the Churchill government.[14]

There are thus two points to keep in mind about a period that is conventionally portrayed as one of profound social crisis—an *era* of violence and revolution. The first is that 'Abbud and allied investors seem to have assessed the situation somewhat differently from virtually all later historians and analysts if we use as an indicator 'Abbud's plans for new investments in this period. This is not to claim that politically powerful capitalists like 'Abbud or the Sirag al-Dins, who founded the new Banque du Caire in the spring of 1952, provided the more accurate or objective assessment, but, given their obvious investment stake, can we afford to ignore these apparently bullish views?[15]

The second and related point concerns the sudden and dramatic conversion of the U.S. and British embassies to the view of the Wafd as a party whose corruption and failure to move forcefully or far enough toward reform was the real problem facing Egypt at this juncture. Quite strikingly, it was during the summer of 1951, precisely as the Wafd escalated the stakes in the Anglo-Egyptian arena, that the embassies began radically to revise their view of Egyptian politics and society. For instance, as late as 28 April 1951, Caffery believed that "at no time in recent Egyptian history has the Party or Cabinet seemed more secure and in a better position to look to the future with confidence than can the present Egyptian Government."[16]

The Americans' assessment was hardly surprising. One month earlier, in March, Sirag al-Din had forced a powerful bloc of outraged landlords in parliament and his own party to back down on their threat to oppose the 100 percent increase in the tax rate on agricultural land that he had imposed as finance minister and made retroactive to 1949. The battle in the legislature is significant for a number of reasons, not least because it clearly contradicts the claim that Sirag al-Din and the landlord-dominated Wafd were unwilling or unable to undertake reforms in arenas like taxation. According to Caffery's account, Sirag al-Din marshaled support in the press and the streets for his position, which he turned into a vote "of personal confidence . . . in his policies as Minister of Finance," and scored a surprising victory. The outcome of this confrontation with the landlords had Caffery convinced anew of the Wafd's political strength and popularity and the Americans determined to press ahead with an aid program.[17]

Yet, together with other like-minded realists, within the space of months Caffery had turned upside down his appreciation of the domestic scene, until it was virtually indistinguishable from that of newspaper owners Mustafa and 'Ali Amin, whose stock, like that of other die-hard elite opponents of the 1950 Wafd government, began to climb at the U.S. embassy in the summer of 1951. The vague, authoritarian-leaning anticorruption and internal-reform plank put forward by these counterelites was the only possible alternative around which these businessmen might hope, however remotely, to build an opposition to a government—and here was the crux of the problem—that had simultaneously deflected the antiregime activities of groups like the Muslim Brothers and, arguably, augmented the ranks of supporters via a renewed campaign against the British occupation.[18]

There was thus a striking resemblance between the timing and form of the shift in the Americans' stance toward the Wafd in mid-1951 and the British state's own anti-Wafd turn in the summer of 1944. Quite logically, in both cases, specific and sharp policy disagreements preceded the discovery that the oligarchs were indeed too corrupt to undertake supposedly vital internal reforms. A comparison with Caffery's own judgments about King Faruq at this time is profitable.

Faruq was reportedly complaining to the Wafd cabinet about the problem of inflation. Caffery argued that "[e]ven though the cost of living is certainly a fundamental problem of primary importance, this emphasis on a perennial issue *at this particular time* when the Anglo-Egyptian question, the Army inquest, and the Opposition's campaign for a purging of the Palace entourage are all approaching an important climax *strongly suggests the presence of a* 'red herring.' "[19] And, of course, in this sphere Caffery was no less cynically imperial-minded than Lampson. More crucially, however, he was also generally no more clear than his British counterparts or those elite factions seeking to replace the government in defining these vital "reforms" or assessing the rate of progress toward them.

At the center of the "honest opposition" (Caffery's phrase) to the "Sirag al-Din–'Abbud Party" (to quote British ambassador Ronald Campbell) were a competing set of businessmen and technocrats, including the 'Amin brothers, who owned the *al-Akhbar* group; 'Afifi, the director who unsuccessfully opposed 'Abbud's membership on the board of Bank Misr and who in August 1951 attacked the Wafd's foreign policy in the pages of *al-Ahram*; Galil al-ʿImari, a rising star in the business community and a director of U.S. Anderson Clayton's cotton-exporting and cotton-seed-oil manufacturing subsidiary; landlord-turned-investor Sayyid Marʿi; the young, aristocratic social engineer Ahmad Husayn; and related members of the networks in which these elites were enmeshed (e.g., ʿAli Shamsi Pasha, Husayn Fahmi, Hilali Pasha).

Their motivations for opposing the Wafd government at this particular juncture were no doubt complex, but the factor that I want to draw attention to here, in part because it has not previously been discussed, is the obstacles they found in the way of their own ambitions. As we have seen, access to state-mediated resources (or a connection with those investor coalitions who had access to them) was the sine qua non for ambitious would-be capitalists. But the barriers to entry in the various oligopolistically structured sectors were formidable, and the oligarchs' grip on state power meant that the opportunities for private accumulation represented by the new round of big irrigation, electrification and manufacturing projects like the proposed Aswan iron and steel factory were effectively lost.

It was no accident, therefore, that the strategies of these new, would-be capitalists resembled the path followed by ʿAbbud in the late 1920s, when he first began to compete with the Suarès, Misr, Salvagos and Empain groups. They sought partnerships with foreign firms. More crucially, like ʿAbbud, who used his British political connections to good effect, elites like Husayn and the Amins (and those in their employ like Muhammad Haykal) turned to the American embassy and the CIA. Most important, though, these new investors dusted off and hoisted the same standards of progress and reform (together, of course, with the warnings of impending chaos) that frustrated competitors like ʿAbbud raised as justification for supporting the authoritarian project between 1928 and 1935.

The Twilight of Palace Pluralism and Business Oligarchy

The Wafd's audacious act of brinkmanship in October 1951 in canceling the Anglo-Egyptian treaty divided the national political arena and its constituent groups into two complex, sharply polarized, lopsided camps. On the one side was a "reactionary capitalist" Wafd party elite leading what is referred to in Egyptian historiography as the national movement (*al-haraka al-wataniyya*), including its own left-wing (the Wafdist Vanguard), Muslim Brothers, large parts of the organized workers' movement, and the dissident army officers who would later organize a coup against King Faruq. This alliance, though undoubtedly driven in part by the fear that a mobilized and armed movement might spiral out of control, gained the Wafd strong support at a critical moment, while producing some incongruous events—for example, Sirag al-Din helped the Free Officers smuggle a mine into the Canal Zone, and Egypt's leading industrialist, 'Abbud, ostensibly moved by the patriotism of workers who had left their jobs at the British bases, pledged one million Egyptian pounds of his own to the strike fund he was promoting![20]

Arrayed against this relatively broad bloc of Egyptians were those elements of the liberal establishment who had either been locked out of power by the Wafd or else were less confident than Sirag al-Din that a minor guerrilla war in the Canal Zone would not end in disaster for Egypt. It is plausible that these are the elites who are given the collective designation "industrial bourgeoisie" in some historical accounts, despite the label's poor fit with the actual investment portfolios and political preferences of leading anti-Wafd businessmen like the Amins or Sayyid Mar'i. Gravitating to their side were those parts of the left either unconvinced or else threatened by the Wafd's brand of anti-imperial struggle (Botman 1988: 93, 112–113). It is not surprising that the disparate set of minority-party politicians, landlords, businessmen, royalists and technocrats counterpoised and tried to rally supporters around a project of domestic social reform and anticorruption. After three decades, the basic formula for unseating a democratically elected government remained the same: join forces with the king and the imperial power.

The Truman administration's growing, active interest in Egyptian affairs and its emerging fixation with instability worldwide, which were hallmarks of post-Kennan global strategy, meant that the U.S. embassy loomed increasingly large as a site and focus of elite Egyptian political activity. Caffery dutifully recorded the appeals for U.S. support and the progress of various proposals: from the prospective purge of the party leadership or the creation of a nonparty salvation cabinet to the formation of a "New Wafd" party. Though the British embassy, primarily through the Amin brothers, encouraged the idea of overturning the Wafd, its own capacities were limited, and the Americans were extremely wary of taking sides in this lopsided domestic power struggle—at least officially. No wonder, therefore, that the situation seemed so bleak to certain opposition figures like the former minister Ahmad Husayn, even as he outlined plans for a palace-backed cabinet purge to the U.S. ambassador.[21]

Nebulous as it was, the basic plan—to dismiss the Wafd and install a government more genuinely committed to tackling the problems of corruption and social inequality—had little chance of winning the unqualified backing of the king or his more astute advisers. At no time was the palace more wary than in the months after October 1951 of the dangers in siding openly with the opposition (and the "imperialists") against a government leading such an obviously popular struggle. Nor is it clear that the question of corruption actually mattered very much to politically mobilizable opinion, with perhaps the single exception of the charge, which predated the Wafd's return to power, implicating various members of the king's family and his entourage in illicit profiting from arms sales during the Palestine War (Gordon 1989: 193). Clearly, though, as the conflict over the Suez-base policy deepened, elites like the Amin brothers and others seeking the government's fall recognized that the corruption theme was valued by their embassy contacts who were fed a steady diet of such charges.[22]

The well-worn accounts of Wafd malfeasance—drawn from the infamous (and misogynist) exposés of the prime minister's wife and her family in the Amin brothers' press (after all, they needed to sell newspapers) or the sensational charges against the Wafd leaders raised in the early "revolutionary tribunals"—have distracted us from the steady if less immediately accessible increase in conflicts over the government's economic policies through the latter part of 1951 and the growing opposition among sectors of the business community that fed the Amins' campaign against the Wafd. Parts of the banking and exporting sectors in particular were up in arms about the disastrous effects of the government's defensive interventions in a collapsing world cotton market. The pound suddenly began to drop faster than other currencies, exports failed to rise, the disturbances in the Canal Zone triggered an unprecedented flow of capital out of Egypt, and manufacturers faced at once sharply rising raw material prices and new taxes.[23]

In the changed economic circumstances, the extent of government collusion with big investors like 'Abbud and Yahya and the particular privileges these investors were thought to have, for instance, in escaping the costs associated with the government's policies were evaluated differently. Certainly, some were being encouraged even more positively than before to seek such a position for themselves. Until now, though, we have glossed over crucial details of these elite conflicts in the rush to narrate (rather too cataclysmically) the events leading up to the army coup in July 1952 or have considered them only insofar as they figure in the successive and now widely assimilated indictments of (circa 1952–1954) the *ancien régime* and of (circa 1955–1961) Egyptian "monopolists."

During the months of deepening crisis in late 1951, 'Abbud pursued the unenviable goal of trying to prevent the British and American embassies from counseling either for an escalation of repression inside the Canal Zone or for a change of government inside Egypt. Throughout the fall he served as one of the main channels through which the Egyptian antagonists in effect tried to contain the conflict. He of course would attest to the "moderation" of the Sirag al-Din faction (and his own influence over Sirag al-Din) and its alleged capacity to coopt the "extremists," while arguing that any other government in Egypt would in effect leave the British worse off. The Amins and others in the anti-Wafd camp, however, would portray Sirag al-Din as a power hungry, would-be demagogue who paid for the guerrillas that were terrorizing British personnel.

Once the Wafd government fell in January 1952, 'Abbud and his allies organized in order to stave off—successfully, if temporarily—a challenge by rival investors for greater access to (or redistribution of) parts of this formidable "private" economic empire. There were heavy costs involved in what turns out to have been the last elite economic conflict of the liberal era. Egyptian investors played a central role in the rise and fall of Egypt's three last and infamously short-lived governments. At the same time, the unfolding of these events strongly suggests that elites differed in their assessments of the nature, sources, extent and depth of the crisis triggered by the fighting in the Canal Zone and the end of the Korean War–driven cotton boom. Certainly, 'Abbud acted as if he had more to fear from his class rivals than his class enemies.

DECONSTRUCTING THE DISCOURSE OF REFORM

A lopsided, bloody battle in Isma'iliya between Egyptian police and British artillery led to a massive demonstration in Cairo the next morning, 26 January 1952 ("Black Saturday"); the demonstration turned into an uprising against the European presence in the city.

Shops, showrooms, hotels, cinemas, bars and nightclubs were burned, leaving millions of pounds in damage, twenty-six Egyptians and foreigners dead and the Nahhas government dismissed from office in the fire's wake. No wonder that labor-union militants, the Free Officers and other parts of the counter-establishment viewed the fire as an imperialist plot and the palace as now squarely in league with foreign powers. The imposition of martial law led to a new wave of arrests of the regime's enemies; the Americans approved the shipment of riot-control gear (including armored cars and sub-machine guns) to the police and encouraged the new 'Ali Mahir government in a strategy of purging communist leaders from the trade-union movement; and, most crucially, all anti-British activities in the Canal Zone were ended.

In the aftermath of the Cairo fire, royalists in the Misr group led the effort to shore up the monarchy. Elias Andraos, a Sudan-born investor whose rise from clerk at the Beida Dyers textile mill at Kafr al-Dawwar to managing director and a key decision maker had gained him a reputation as a financial genius, played a pivotal role. Andraos, who originally supported and profited from the Wafd's return to power, was following the path carved by 'Abbud himself between 1928 and 1935 by using the palace to assist his own lightning rise in the local political economy. He was appointed pasha, senator and Suez Canal Company director in 1950 as he prepared to move into the chemicals sector and expand his textile interests with a new project in the Sudan. Unsurprisingly, this aggressive press into the center of Egyptian business and political arenas was accompanied by the same kinds of contemptuous judgments that political enemies and business rivals in the 1930s offered about 'Abbud.[24]

In October 1951 Andraos was named "honorary economic adviser to the royal khassa" (that is, the king's treasury), where he steered the palace's last realignment, in alliance with the heads of the minority parties, the British embassy and ex-palace stalwarts like the Amins, whose newspaper empire, according to American embassy files, had originally been bankrolled by Faruq.[25] Andraos shared the chore with the eminently more "clubbable" Misr Bank board chairman, 'Afifi, who resigned his positions with the Misr group in December 1951 to became chief of the royal cabinet.[26] Once again, therefore, 'Afifi and, presumably, a pro-'Afifi faction within the Misr group of firms were aligned against his long-time personal and business rival 'Abbud, who was straining throughout the fall and winter of 1951–1952 to keep the Wafd in power.

Both the British and the Americans were naturally inclined at this juncture toward the elite opposition's appeal to address Egypt's "real" need for internal reform. The dilemma consisted in the utter lack of any practical political strategy for advancing this project in the face of the Wafd's immensely popular gamble of confronting the (much-weakened) British imperial state. While the Amins would insist in the weeks before the fire that "the first steps" in getting rid of the Wafd had already been taken, aside from some desultory contacts with CIA officer Kermit (Kim) Roosevelt, they offered nothing more concrete than a campaign in the pages of *Akhir Lahza* accusing the Sirag al-Din family of selling cotton to Israel. And Ahmad Husayn had no more practical plan to offer to the Americans than to wait for the Wafd to lose control of events—though he could hardly have known that the strategy would turn out to be the correct one.[27]

When the venerable politician and Misr group director 'Ali Mahir was named prime minister in January 1952, he showed himself willing to take the heat for the strong dose of austerity that bankers were demanding while trying to undo the damage of the Wafd government's disastrous cotton price-support policy. He refused, however, to carry out a vendetta against the Wafd itself, in effect, double-crossing the 'Amin-palace bloc that had put him in the prime minister's seat, and these tireless if not very skillful cabinet makers returned to the shop.

In less than a month Mahir had been cast aside and, with the help of the British embassy, replaced with an obviously embittered and tragically shortsighted Hilali, who had finally broken with the Wafd in November 1951 over the treaty-abrogation issue. CIA operative Roosevelt appears to have been involved, at least on the periphery, with these maneuvers (Gordon 1992: 34, 162; Sayed-Ahmad 1989: 41–42, 48). More important, for the next three months, Hilali did exactly what his sundry backers had wanted: burying the treaty issue and launching a full-scale attack on the Sirag al-Din–'Abbud party, which included the arrest of the Wafd's secretary general, the dissolution of parliament (where Sirag al-Din had demonstrated his dominance) and an attack on 'Abbud's business empire.

U.S. Ambassador Caffery heralded Hilali as an honest patriot, a corruption buster and essentially Egypt's last chance for reform, though a mere nine months earlier Hilali was leading the battle in parliament against "American imperialism" in the guise of the U.S. Point IV program.[28] Caffery's pragmatism is less interesting here than the unraveling of the main discursive thread in the American narrative about Egypt under the Wafd, which for one year posited reform as the real problem.

Thus, in the first days of the new Hilali administration, one of Caffery's key Egyptian contacts, Ahmad Husayn, revealed that he would not be joining the government of his "close friend and confidant" both because he ostensibly objected to the "engineering" of Mahir's dismissal by the Amin brothers and the palace, and, more importantly, because the government had zero public support. As Husayn put it, in the eyes of most Egyptians, Hilali's reform plank was simply a distraction from the real issue.[29]

Husayn was correct, of course. Relative to forcing Great Britain to end its military presence in the Canal Zone there was indeed little concern about this latest round between oligarchic factions that he had been dragged into and now appeared desperate to escape, though Husayn's depiction of the situation was more understated than that of some others. For example, in a broadside, the clandestine Free Officers condemned Hilali as the servant of "imperialists and Egyptian traitors" who had "forgotten that the source of the greatest corruption is imperialism," and they branded his war against the Wafd as "a new coup d'état" (Gordon 1992: 51).

For broadly the same reasons, the Truman administration found that its own modest effort to build a coalition inside the Hilali government in support of a land-reform program faced resistance from some officials, though Hilali's own position remains unclear. It should also be noted that American proposals for land reform in 1951–1952 centered on reclamation, the settling of landless peasants and the regulation of landlord-tenant relations.[30] In fact, proposals along these lines began to proliferate in the months after the Cairo fire, promoted most strongly by those who did not want to see the Wafd back in power or the campaign revived against the British bases.

Again, the issue of land reform is often presented as something that was objectively necessary for industrial development, and the fact that Egyptian investors failed to pursue such a course is viewed as a sign of their incapacity to act in their own best interests at a critical juncture. The premise is, minimally, a contestable one. Many argued the opposite, for instance, pointing to the disruptions in production that would accompany the redrawing of property lines, and we know that this argument eventually won the backing of the military in 1952, even as they carried out the confiscation of royal properties and other massive holdings.

There were additional rationales for land reform. The most basic— social justice—was for obvious reasons the one least likely to win the backing of property owners. A second rationale was that land reform would preempt the potential organization of a communist movement in the countryside. Again, it is hardly surprising that many Egyptians would be left unpersuaded, at least in the short run.

A third rationale was implicitly derided in the observation by Ahmad Husyan quoted above. A reform agenda centering on land redistribution had little direct connection with the discontent and demands of largely urban-based constituencies who backed, or more properly propelled, the Wafd's act of brinkmanship. Fourth was the possibility of building an alternative, relatively conservative, rural-based constituency as the base of support for a non-Wafd party or, more likely, an authoritarian (reform) regime. Though the military leaders would pursue this course, it hardly solved the Canal bases question.

For good reason, therefore, American policymakers themselves began to reconsider the relative weight of internal and external obstacles to stability in the spring of 1952. Caffery attempted to bring local representatives to the bargaining table, while Dean Acheson looked to Eden for new concessions to break the Anglo-Egyptian stalemate.

London conceded little, however, in part because with the Canal Zone calm, the Wafd out of power, and Hilali engaged in his vendetta against the Sirag al-Din–'Abbud party, Churchill's hard-line government concluded (not entirely unreasonably) that they had gained themselves some time and maneuvering room. Acheson and his staff pressed Eden more heavily in June, arguing that Hilali would eventually fall if the British continued to resist concessions. And though the Americans later wrote that they had also expected Hilali to hang on until October, he handed the king his resignation unexpectedly on 28 June.[31]

'ABBUD AND "HIS ILK"

The most notorious tale of the regime's last days is the rumored plot behind Hilali's resignation—the truth so explosive, warned the Cairo correspondent of the *Times*, as to be "unpublishable." The rumor mills were in truth running overtime during the last week in June, as stories started circulating about intense contacts between the king and Sirri Pasha, intrigues taking place behind Hilali's back and the king under intense pressure to change the government. One incontrovertible fact broke the rhythm momentarily: Hilali's unexpected resignation. The cause of his downfall followed quickly in his letter to the king, leaked by Hilali's foreign minister among others:

'Abbud had allegedly paid £E 1 million into one of the king's Swiss bank accounts in order to bring Sirri back as prime minister.

Two names were most often linked with 'Abbud's in this venture. The first was Karim Thabit, an ex-journalist, adviser to a host of major firms and groups (including ICI and Beida Dyers), and the king's personal friend, though he seems to have had little contact with Faruq at this juncture. The second was Andraos, the king's financial adviser, but others would occasionally add and subtract names from this basic list of "intriguers." [32] Since Thabit was regularly excoriated by the pashas then and historians now as an unqualified, unwise and corrupting influence on Faruq (e.g., see Gordon's (1992: 18) description of the "sycophants"), it is worth noting that Caffery described him as "one of the keenest political minds in Egypt" and relied on Thabit extensively for his own views of Egyptian power politics. For aristocrats like Sirri and 'Afifi, who resented and at times paid the price for Thabit's influence inside the palace, it was naturally soothing to criticize his relative lack of social standing (i.e., he was born in Khartoum, he did not come from an established "Egyptian family") and, of course, to condemn the zeal with which Thabit amassed his wealth. [33]

The way the 'Abbud-Thabit-Andraos bribery plot was fitted into various narratives tells us a great deal about the forces most intensely involved in the game for control of the Egyptian state and its policies on the eve of the coup, including the Americans, the British embassy and rival parts of the oligarchy. Needless to say, 'Abbud, Thabit and Andraos all vehemently denounced the bribery rumor as an outrageous lie. What could not be denied, however, is their having worked in loose cooperation for the past two months to weaken Hilali and, at least in 'Abbud's case, return the Wafd to power. The British embassy and its intelligence arm tried during the next weeks to confirm details of the alleged bribery, but could not, and once the army took power three weeks later the evidence no longer mattered.

The British seized upon the bribery story for two reasons, and then clung to it for a third. First, they were heavily invested in Hilali and his reform project, as we have seen, and they considered his resignation a setback in their strategy vis-à-vis both the Egyptians and the Americans. They feared the return of the Wafd and wanted Hilali reinstated, and the ostensible outrageousness of the alleged action justified and provided ammunition for pressuring the king on Hilali's behalf. A second reason for running with the story was so purely instrumental and logically convoluted that cynicism is the most reasonable interpretative strategy to employ in this case. Members of the Foreign Office saw the story as a "heaven sent opportunity" to force "Andraos and company" out of the king's orbit and to leave him more firmly under the influence of Hilali's main palace ally, 'Afifi. Whitehall concluded that it was the king's two disreputable advisers, Thabit and Andraos, who were preventing the Egyptian government from negotiating "realistically" with them.[34]

Third, there were formidable obstacles in the way of reversing the course set in motion by Hilali's resignation. As British officials admitted, his domestic support was now limited "practically to the Amin twins," and though his vendetta against the Wafd was a policy the British state encouraged, its officials had a remarkable capacity to absolve themselves of its unintended consequences—namely, that it tended to mobilize those who were most threatened. Thus in targeting figures like Sirag al-Din and 'Abbud, they concluded that Hilali had possibly been "tactless and ill-advised." The bigger problem, however, is that the Foreign Office wanted the Americans to line up behind them in support of a joint intervention on behalf of Hilali and 'Afifi against the "crooks," yet Caffery and the State Department refused, arguing that the British were in fact the main cause of Hilali's downfall.[35]

Since the bribery story had only limited value for the Americans, they were eager to downplay its significance. At best, it reinforced the view that Hilali represented a reasonable ("moderate") alternative to the Wafd and "vested interest[s]" such as those represented by the "venal trio" of 'Abbud, Thabit and Andraos. Yet, it also clearly allowed the British to escape recognizing that Hilali's (or any other non-Wafd led government's) best chances remained in winning concessions in the deadlocked bases talks. Instead, Eden's first, petulant response to these events was a vow to let Faruq and his new prime minister Sirri "stew." He could contemplate this plan because, as his foreign-policy staff made clear, they saw no threat to Egyptian security and stability from this newest turn of events, at least in the short term.

In their view, the long-run threat of the Wafd remained the most serious problem, and the Foreign Office continued to hold up the bribery claim in order to deflect the Americans' criticisms. Another threat was that the Americans would push harder for treaty concessions. The obsession with the Americans can be seen in the British embassy's theory that Caffery himself was at least indirectly to blame for Hilali's fall since his frequent and well-publicized contacts with 'Abbud made it appear as if the Americans were leaning toward the Wafd![36]

The game was an immensely complicated one but also one that key players hardly viewed as deadlocked in early July 1952, which explains both the cautious optimism of the 'Abbud–Sirag al-Din wing as well as the increasing frustration of the *al-Akhbar* circle, its British backers, the king and 'Afifi, who was probably Faruq's most influential adviser during the last month of rule. As various American and British officials acknowledged, the probability was high that a new round of elections would be held sometime in the fall, and many Egyptians viewed elections as the most likely route to resolving the national question.

All the relevant forces in the Egyptian scene had come to recognize the crucial importance of the United States in the outcome. There is no clearer evidence than 'Abbud's and Sirag al-Din's appeal to the Truman administration to back the Wafd's return to power. In exchange, they had proposed a "detailed secret agreement with the United States." The RCC would try to do the same six months later.[37] A U.S.-Wafd alliance was one of the chief fears of all those who, for various reasons, coalesced around Hilali's alternative reform project, the British state foremost among them.

As I have noted, the fear was palpable in the rather paranoid complaints about Caffery's meeting too frequently with 'Abbud or, of course, the idea that 'Abbud could simply buy the premiership for his ally Sirri. But the fear is equally palpable in the energy spent trying to sell the "venal trio" scenario to the Americans. Egypt's most famous journalist, Muhammad Haykal, then in the employ of the Amins, turned over to the Americans dubious proof of the conspiracy against Hilali—a private letter forwarded by the premier to the king.[38]

Perhaps the best evidence for this growing fear among elites that a new round of elections was in the offing and, thus, that a renewed mandate for the 'Abbud–Sirag al-Din party was probable is the sudden appearance of and frequent references specifically to land reform in records of conversations, other archival sources and the Egyptian press, especially by anti-Wafd elites in the late spring and early summer of 1952. The logic is simple, though this particular path to building a counter-electoral coalition (or, alternatively, to securing a degree of popular support for authoritarian rule) was fraught with its own dangers and uncertainties: could Hilali or some alternative set of elites run successfully against the Wafd on the basis of land-reform program? In any case, the situation in Egypt in mid-1952 was far from deadlocked— this was the real problem.

At the same time, the situation was hardly one of calm or of business as usual. No action is more symbolic of the errors in judgment during this prolonged crisis than the disastrous decision by the monarchy in mid-July to try to reassert its authority within the army, the step that prompted dissident officers to plan and mount a coup d'état on 23 July 1952 in order to protect themselves against arrest (Gordon 1992). Certainly, the size and scope of the January uprising had sobered many. But from mid-February until the military conspirators carried out their preemptive coup on 23 July, strikes, demonstrations and other usual indicators of political unrest had dropped effectively to zero.[39] Repression had proved effective.

On 24 June 1952, in a conversation with U.S. secretary of state Acheson, Britain's ambassador to Egypt, Ralph Stevenson, guessed that Hilali would hold on a few more months at best before a new caretaker government was brought in to oversee the next elections. Acheson naturally pressed the ambassador for his view of the next six months and, particularly, whether he anticipated a decline in stability. But Stevenson judged the situation positively, in part because of improved internal security and in part because, before elections, he expected the government to concentrate on the issue of "redistribution of land."[40]

Two weeks (and two governments) later, and literally on the eve of the coup, the king's top official and ex-Misr group head, 'Afifi Pasha, was even more upbeat than Stevenson. Specifically, 'Afifi had told another top British embassy official that his optimism was higher than at any time in the previous six months for two reasons. First, the attempt by 'Abbud and his allies to hijack the state had gone awry. Second, and what must in retrospect be the single most ironic commentary on the future of the *ancien régime* by one of its chief pillars, 'Afifi looked forward to a swift resolution of the "army problem."[41]

There were at least two broad and, in the eyes of the key players, viable solutions to the crisis. One of course was familiar from the past—namely, extending the boundaries of sovereign decision-making authority in arenas still contested by the ex-colonial power. The second solution entailed some kind of redistributive project in the countryside. The Wafd was probably in the stronger position. Certainly, those like the Amins or Thabit, who tried to imagine Faruq as head of a reformist-authoritarian regime, were no doubt discounting the future somewhat more heavily in July 1952 than was the Sirag al-Din–'Abbud party, who had placed Sirri back in power and had begun setting the stage for a new round of elections in the fall before leaving for their regular summer vacations in Europe.

The Americans enjoyed the luxury of hedging their bets. As I have argued, Caffery's superiors were moving the machinery of state in position to pressure London for concessions on the bases or Sudan or both. At the same time, by the spring of 1952, two land-reclamation experts had been seconded to Egypt under the auspices of the Technical Cooperation Administration (Point IV) and were working with a circle of policymakers and Hilali allies in advancing a land-reform project. The same mission was augmented in mid-August to facilitate the implementation of the army's highly publicized land-reform initiative, launched within weeks of the coup, though ambassador Caffery insisted that the American role was not to be publicized.[42]

The general logic of these two, competing approaches to resolving the Egyptian crisis was confirmed by events subsequent to the coup. With critical American support, the new revolutionary regime moved in both these directions simultaneously (Binder 1978; Waterbury 1983).

Before the Fall

Most discussions of business and politics in the post-1952 period (e.g., Abdel-Malek 1968, Waterbury 1983, Zaalouk 1989, Tignor 1992) start with the assumption that the turn to "Arab socialism" was neither foreseen nor pursued by the military officers who took power in July. O'Brien first developed this argument systematically in *The Revolution in Egypt's Economic System* (1966). His formulation of the Revolution's various phases in terms of the regime's general policy toward capital and, in particular, its first so-called free-enterprise phase between 1952 and 1956 underpins virtually all subsequent accounts until now. Thus, from varying ideological positions, both Beinin (1990: 87) and Tignor (1992: 274) emphasize the wide gulf dividing pre– and post–Suez War policies toward Egyptian and foreign investors. But the imperatives that once made it crucial to label Egypt's political economy as either capitalist or socialist have lost their force, and the terms now seem both somewhat crude and quaint. What others have insisted was a policy of encouraging private enterprise is analyzed here as a strategy of opposing the local business oligarchy and its privileged position within the political economy.

The analysis builds on a point that Waterbury (1983) usefully counterposes to the more structurally oriented and determinist conceptions of the military regime's taking power in order to fulfill the bourgeois project: namely, the regime's profound suspicions of, and antipathy toward, Egypt's leading capitalists. I argue that the key military leaders had an explicit, broad ideological orientation toward capital, articulated in terms of antimonopolism, which shaped the regime's policies, while the relatively feeble or ineffective regulatory capacities of the state agencies that the army officers inherited further encouraged the early (i.e., pre–Suez War) shift toward dismantling or taking over rather than regulating existing capitalist institutions and particularly those at the center of the business oligarchy, beginning with the 'Abbud group.[43]

THE "BLESSED MOVEMENT" AGAINST THE MONOPOLISTS

The idea that the army officers took power without clear or specific designs for economic reform and, crucially, "without an economic ideology" has been repeated so often over the years that it has ceased even to require a defense (e.g., Lacouture and Lacouture 1958; O'Brien 1966). Yet this kind of claim rests on an understanding of ideology as being more akin to "lofty theory" or a fully worked out philosophical system than to the kind of "common sense" view(s) of the world held by most men and women. (Augelli and Murphy 1988: 13–30). The ideologies of Nasser and his comrades were no more or less coherent, organized and contradictory than the "ideologies" of Eden, Acheson, Eisenhower and their representatives in Cairo, Stevenson and Caffery, among other key actors at this juncture.

The officers had collectively defined their project in terms of six underlying "principles," widely believed to have been written by marxist officers Ahmad Hamrush and Khalid Muhiy al-Din, including the commonly cited one about "ending feudalism." Though often disparaged, this formulation does not seem particularly vague when compared with contemporary discourses about strengthening the market, encouraging democracy or respecting difference. And, as is readily recognized, once in power the officers had little difficulty in mobilizing the necessary intellectual and technical resources for developing specific policies that reflected this principle, as attested to by the land-reform program developed by Egyptian civilians (with the input of Italian advisers and American technicians) and put into law six weeks after the coup. The other principles of the Revolution were no less important in shaping the military's approach to the political economy.

Probably the least discussed part of the officers' project was the commitment to "ending the monopoly system," a system which, as we have seen, was designed, built and nurtured by British colonial state officials, foreign and local investors and Egyptian national political elites. By 1952 large-scale production and distribution were no longer sectors monopolized by foreign capital and nonnationals; instead, control of these monopoly and oligopoly sectors was shifting to coalitions of Egyptian investors. The "monopoly system" was in essence a synonym for Egypt's business groups and their cross-sectoral holdings in textiles, shipping, transportation, chemicals, services, food processing, etc. Even more concretely, the essence of that system seemed to be represented by the country's single most powerful capitalist at mid-century, 'Abbud.

Opposition to monopoly was as much or more a part of the contemporary landscape as land reform and was made explicit in the work of Rashid al-Barrawi, the radical Egyptian economist who rose to prominence as a publicist for the Revolution on the left and adviser to the new regime on economic issues. According to Gordon (1992: 167), U.S. Ambassador Caffery blocked a cabinet post for Barrawi in the first post-coup government. The Americans then tried to coopt the increasingly influential left-technocrat, offering to bring him to the United States for an educational-study tour in 1954.[44] Together with a handful of other intellectuals on the left, Barrawi met regularly with the junta and was important in shaping its populist discourse and programs. Between 1953 and 1958, he directed the state's industrial-development bank and served with the marxist lawyer Ahmad Fu'ad, Nasser's closest economic adviser in the 1950s (Lacouture and Lacouture 1958), as the left wing of the government's advisory council on industrial policy.

Since the mid-1940s, Barrawi had been writing in favor of land reform and a government-directed industrialization drive, which was to include nationalization of basic industries in line with welfare-state development models then being adopted in Europe (Rashid al-Barrawi and Muhammad Maza 'Ulaysh 1945). In his 1952 "instant" account of the military coup, Barrawi had focused on the inordinate power exerted by "monopolists" like 'Abbud and the Misr group, both as an indictment of the old regime's reactionary social-political order and as part of an argument for the inevitability of the kind of progressive economic programs to be undertaken by the revolutionary leadership (Rashid al-Barrawi 1952; Meijer 1990).

The antimonopolist component in the new leaders' world views was evident to observers at the time in the form of the deep suspicions that were openly harbored toward 'Abbud and every other business oligarch, from Farghali to Yahya, even as an uneasy and relatively short-lived accommodation was negotiated with them. Yet, rather than reconciling themselves to business privilege, in a way that might have produced alternative discourses and practices (e.g., the inevitability or necessity of concentration; self-regulation by business interests; societal corporatism), the revolutionary leaders made antimonopolism the explicit rationale for successive encroachments by state agents during 1954–1955 into the factories and boardrooms of the business oligarchs.

'Abbud's relations with the new leaders and the institutions they sought to build illustrate the complex politics behind the regime's encounter with the country's leading capitalists. 'Abbud chose prudently to remain abroad for most of July through September. From Paris, where he was attending the September meeting of the Suez Canal Company board, he praised the government's brutal handling of the infamous strike at the Misr group's textile mills in Kafr al-Dawwar in August, applauding Nagib as head of a movement that "all Egyptians" had welcomed. 'Abbud assured reporters that life in Egypt was "back to normal." Four days later an extraordinary military tribunal executed two of the strikers by hanging (*al-Akhbar* 3 September 1952; Beinin and Lockman 1987: 421–426; Gordon 1992: 62–63, 94–95; Botman 1988: 125–131).

Once back in Cairo, 'Abbud reached instinctively to various parts of his decades-old repertoire in order to recover from the setback of the coup and the expropriation of his 5,000-faddan estate. For instance, by late December 1952, *Akhbar al-Yawm* had been enlisted in a new public-relations effort. The paper reported that the exiled King Faruq had once allegedly offered £E 1,000 to his royal guard to kill 'Abbud! As 'Abbud solemnly declared, "Faruq loathed every person who worked in his country." His new investments in "human capital" followed along these same lines, to judge from the emergence in the post-1952 period of new managers and directors in various of 'Abbud's ventures, such as Isma'il Sabri Baligh, the brother of a trusted, second-rank Free Officer, 'Ali Sabri.[45]

The basis of the new bargain between 'Abbud and the country's military leaders was, nonetheless, his institutional position as the country's leading owner-investor. The output of his nitrate factory was a vital raw material for ammunition as well as for fertilizers, and the military turned to him for help in developing a domestic weapons industry. Unfortunately, little is known about the origins and operations of the military sectors of the economy. Yet proregime papers began to promote 'Abbud's contribution to the country's renaissance, even as his allies in the Wafd were dragged off to jail. And, by the winter of 1952, U.S. Ambassador Caffery was describing relations between the businessman and the junta as "cooperative" though not "*cordial*" since the officers obviously needed capital and at the same time distrusted capitalists.[46] Little that the officers and their backers would do in the following months can be interpreted as allaying the equally deep and understandable suspicions of the oligarchs themselves.

The attack on the party system in 1952–1953 was a serious blow to 'Abbud, but the effort to contain his influence encompassed nonparty arenas as well. The best example is the creation of the various public economic authorities and quasi-planning agencies in 1952–1953, notably the Permanent Council for Development of National Production (hereafter the NPC). Here, as in other policymaking domains, investors like 'Imari, the regime's new minister of finance, battled with less reliably procapitalist counsel (e.g., Barrawi, Magdi Hasanayn, Ahmad Fu'ad, Khalid Muhiy al-Din). If anything, analysts have tended to underrepresent the force of etatist currents in these unfolding institutional arrangements.[47] But, just as crucially, 'Abbud and other leading business oligarchs had been kept out of them.

The representation of local capital in these new institutions tells us something about the Revolution's early impact on the business community, while at the same time reminding us of the limits that the Free Officers quickly ran up against after seizing control of the state. (See Table 5.) Given the highly concentrated, overlapping structure of ownership and control across key industries, it was virtually impossible to tap Egyptians who were not linked in one way or another to the 'Abbud, Yahya, Salvagos, etc., groups. At the same time, the opportunity appeared irresistible to an ambitious set of second-tier investors (or would be investors) seeking to advance their own fortunes in time-honored fashion: through preferential access to decision makers and a relatively more rather than less intense courting of foreign backers.

'Imari played the pivotal role in shaping what might be thought of as the Kom Ombo wing of the RCC, or so it seemed to American observers such as Caffery, who described him as a key figure in the RCC's ten-person "inner cabinet."[48] 'Imari's own protégé at the Finance Ministry, 'Ali al-Giritli, was appointed to the NPC. Other invest-

Table 5 *Membership in the Permanent Council for Development of National Production, January 1953*

Name	Position in the Political Economy
Husayn Fahmi (chair)	b/d, Salt and Soda Co. (Yahya), FEI
Yahya al-ʿAlayli	agricultural engineer; b/d, Kom Ombo Co. (ʿAbbud), FEI, LR
ʿAli Fathi	civil engineer
Ibrahim Biyumi Madkur	ex-minister, senator, investor?
Shalabi Sarufim	landowning engineer, investor
Rashid al-Barrawi (FT)	economist
Muhammad Ibrahim (FT)	geologist/engineer
ʿAbd al-Rahman Hamada	b/d, Misr Spinning and Weaving
Muhammad ʿAli Husayn	engineer-contractor (ʿAbbud's son-in-law)
ʿAli al-Giritli	economist, National Bank of Egypt
Fathi Rizq (Army)	engineer
Samir Hilmi (Army)	civil engineer
Gamal Salim (Army)	Free Officer; LR
ʿAbd al-Razzaq al-Sanhuri	President, Council of State; lawyer
Muhammad Salim (secretary general)	engineer

NOTE: LR = member, High Committee for Land Reform; FEI = Federation of Industries; FT = full-time member of committee

SOURCES: *Akhir Saʿa* 7 January 1953; *Who's Who in Egypt*, 1952. Cairo: Impre. française; USRG 59 files.

ors whose political fortunes were on the rise included Husayn Fahmi, chair of the NPC; Yahya al-ʿAlayli, the managing director of the Kom Ombo Company and member of the land-reform committee; Sayyid Marʿi and his family, another key businessman on the land-reform committee drawn from the board of directors of the Kom Ombo Company; and the Sarufim family, who, like ʿImari, were identified with the Anderson Clayton–owned oil mills and cotton-exporting complex in Minya and Alexandria.

As we have seen, many of these investors had actively opposed the Wafd-oligarch alliance and remained outspokenly critical of ʿAbbud and his methods, though their support of this new, foreign-backed authoritarian turn was almost identical to the course ʿAbbud had pursued so successfully in the 1930s.[49] The most successful Egyptian capitalists of the interwar years had now become an entrenched set of interests standing in the way of this new cohort, much in the way that Suarès, Cattaoui and other minority investors must have been viewed three and four decades earlier. At the same time, however, there are no credible grounds for describing these key supporters of the 'Ali Mahir and Nagib governments (1952–1954) as the core, finally, of an industrial bourgeoisie. Certainly, many of them had opposed land reform (or at least the confiscation of their own estates), and, under their influence, the NPC (and the government's investment policies generally) were still weighted toward support of agricultural production.

Unlike the situation in any other period in the twentieth century, though, these new and by all accounts politically ambitious investors had to contend with a regime in which local capitalists' prerogatives, preferences and property rights were openly challenged for the first time, not least via the expropriation of their estates. As early as 1953 individual members of the RCC began to press for "socialization of portions of the economy." 'Imari was described as eager to counter such pressure and reassure the business community. Yet, 'Imari was distrusted by currents within the junta who were keeping "a very close check on his activities," and, as I will discuss below, he and his allies fell victim to the regime's antimonopolist currents by 1954–1955.[50] In similar fashion, Nasser approved the creation of the cabinet-level national planning committee in 1955, which was a step intended to weaken still further the influence of capitalists in the fashioning of industrial policy. By 1956, and, importantly, prior to the sequestration of French- and British-owned enterprise, Nasser appointed 'Aziz Sidqi, a main architect of etatism in Egypt, to head the newly created Ministry of Industry.[51]

The influence of 'Imari and allied investors in various policy arenas (e.g., the regime's public investment priorities and their financing, the expanded U.S. contribution in land-reform and industrial-development policies, the revision of the mining law) was a bargain whose terms the RCC probably had relatively little capacity to shape, at least initially, though the military would gradually adopt a more openly clientelist policy toward capitalist factions. At the same time, the Americans seemed no less wary of the oligarchy than Egypt's new rulers, and they were no less implicated, finally, in promoting an alternative set of "weaker" Egyptian capitalist elites. Specifically, the U.S. State Department, like the British Foreign Office in the 1930s (see Chapter 3) launched a campaign of its own against 'Abbud.

Within months of the coup, representatives of W. R. Grace and Company informed the Bureau of Near Eastern Affairs of their interest in going forward with plans to build a paper mill in Egypt. 'Abbud was undoubtedly pressing his new U.S. partners on supplying the hard currency required, hoping among other things to demonstrate his continuing commitment and indispensability to Egypt's industrial development. The State Department was equally interested in assisting the industry-building efforts of Egypt's new military regime. It is especially noteworthy, therefore, that Assistant Secretary Henry Byroade and his advisers in this case pressed the U.S. multinational to abandon 'Abbud and find an alternate set of local investors before undertaking the project.[52]

PIPE DREAMS: THE MIRAGE OF FOREIGN INVESTMENT IN EGYPTIAN ISI

The Revolution's course was relatively open-ended, but we have tended to confuse the exigencies of regime consolidation and the extremely limited capacities of the junta with the officers' alleged ideological incoherence (or, alternatively, their pragmatism). In the case of the Aswan electrification project (Chapter 5), vast stretches of the policymaking terrain were effectively seized by, or conceded to, pre-existing elite networks who pursued their own agendas.

One of the more controversial and surprising policy initiatives of the Revolution, given the thrust of nationalist discourses before and since, was the reversal of many of the Egyptianization policies of the late 1940s—laws governing foreign investment, oil prospecting and company formation—for the purpose of attracting new flows of foreign capital to the country (O'Brien 1966: 71–72; Ministry of Commerce and Industry 1955: 144–165; Waterbury 1983: 60–63, 123–134). Authorship of this package rests chiefly with the Fu'ad I Society for Political Economy, Legislation and Statistics (roughly, Egypt's first economic-policy think tank), where much of it had been outlined as early as 1950–1951. It was implemented by Hilmi Bahgat Badawi, the society's assistant secretary general. Badawi, who became the first minister of commerce and industry after the coup, was one of the key voices in the summer 1951 debate over Point IV aid.[53]

Though virtually unrecognized until now, Point IV was the institution through which the Truman and Eisenhower administrations paid for the American business leaders, economists, engineers and other technical consultants who helped design and promote the Revolution's early industrial-development initiatives, which were associated, perhaps too exclusively, with Nasser, the military regime and technocrats in the

NPC.[54] The NPC was itself a reconfiguration of the business-dominated advisory council on economic policy created by the Wafd. More important, during the summer and fall of 1951, the Wafd government and the Fu'ad I Society were negotiating with the Americans in Cairo to cooperate in a comprehensive development plan for the political economy.

Within weeks of the coup, Ambassador Caffery and the Point IV office were pressing the new premier, Mahir (no doubt in conjunction with Egyptian currents), to revive the Wafd–Fu'ad I project in the form of a "national planning body" to survey Egypt's economic potential and establish priorities for investment.[55] Mahir quickly approved the plan, but it was his successor, Nagib, who would follow through with the initiative. Months before the NPC held its first meeting, the State Department contracted with the Cambridge, Massachusetts, consulting firm A. D. Little for an initial $30 thousand survey of the economy; this survey formed the basis for the subsequent, four-year-long $300–500 thousand A. D. Little mission to Egypt. And A. D. Little selected a high-profile U.S. executive to lead the mission and advise Nagib on industrial policy.[56] The line of continuity between the Wafd and post-Wafd era is clear in this case, though the Americans helped to ensure it.

Thomas Cabot, the former president of United Fruit who had helped organize the State Department's foreign-aid program, visited Egypt in the winter of 1952–1953, and his February 1953 report to the incoming Eisenhower administration urged support for industrial development in Egypt while laying out a virtual blueprint of subsequent government reforms in company law, mining law, taxes, tariffs and profits remittance.[57] Six months later, the NPC published its four-year public and private investment program, which was derived from the proposals of the Cambridge consulting firm for extending Egypt's road network and investing in tire assembly, food-processing industries, oil production, tourism, etc.[58] By 1954, the Americans had committed more than $40 million for an Egyptian development strategy that resembled other U.S.-backed ISI programs then being undertaken throughout the developing world (Nolt and Maxfield 1990; "The Future of Point Four," *New York Times Magazine* 26 September 1954).

Though Nagib and the RCC faced growing criticism for its increasingly open alliance with the Americans, Nasser himself defended the regime, for instance, before a hostile group of students in Alexandria protesting the Point IV program:

We cannot live in isolation, refusing any helping hand, because we think it has ulterior motives behind it. It may have happened before, but it was we who let it, because we were not alert. . . .

We should get rid of this complex and with it the policy of isolation and fear. We should accept any kind of assistance whether it be in the form of Point IV or any other; and we should proceed with all the projects that we have started, condemning once and for all this erroneous complex.[59]

The early emphasis on foreign capital and expertise, together with the growing prominence of aid as a key foreign-policy problem in 1954–1956, reflected some of the same underlying factors—the lack of hard-currency resources and administrative capacity—that hampered the Wafd's even more modest development efforts.[60] What is perhaps more remarkable about investment policy after 1952 is that the A. D. Little consultants and their clients may have actually believed the forecasts of £E 7 million annually in new direct foreign investment flowing to Egypt as a result of improvements in the ever elusive "investment climate" or of doubling employment in manufacturing industry between 1955 and 1965.[61]

Internal White House assessments diverged sharply from those of A. D. Little, Caffery and others of the Revolution's most avid boosters inside the American Embassy: "It is doubtful that the removal of all administrative impediments would produce a sizable inflow of foreign capital. This is because at the present time there appears to be a relatively small number of good investment opportunities in Egypt."[62]

This more pessimistic line of analysis can be traced back as early as the mid-1930s, in the assessments by senior executives of ICI, who, as discussed in Chapter 3, were at the time part of the pioneering wave of the world's leading chemical producers investing in overseas manufacturing.[63] And while ICI found long-term investment prospects uninviting, those multinational owners and managers who did risk expansion into niches of the Egyptian market in the 1930s and 1940s, such as Anderson Clayton, obviously did not find so-called administrative impediments particularly onerous or burdensome.

The ultimate targets of the new, liberal foreign-investment laws were international oil companies. In 1949, the two multinational subsidiaries that controlled 100 percent of domestic oil production and roughly 75 percent of all sales of refined products in Egypt had stopped all exploration operations, using as a well-publicized excuse the Nuqrashi government's Egyptianization campaign. Yet, it is clear from the companies' correspondence with American officials that the core of the dispute was the pre-1952 Egyptian state's audacious attempt (in the companies' view) to set the selling price for indigenous crude and to increase royalty rates for new production.

The new Nagib government granted additional generous concessions to U.S. independents such as Continental Oil (Conoco) and Cities Service in return for prospecting new fields, presumably with the view of pressuring the established producers, Anglo-Egyptian Oil (Royal Dutch Shell) and Mobil, but the agreement eventually reached with the larger firms in 1954 left both the old rate and the royalty structure intact.[64] This was arguably one of the most impressive displays of bargaining power by foreign firms in decades and ultimately was the source of most of the new private foreign capital invested in Egypt between 1953 and 1961. The oil was obviously vital to the new regime. Local investors gained some of the rents from trading the concession rights. But the U.S. embassy's attempt to hail the employment-creating benefits of this new investment activity (the oil industry is highly capital-intensive) rings especially hollow.

Adoption of a more systematic ISI investment strategy after 1952 may have been overdetermined, but it is important to recognize that American expertise and financial assistance were weighing in on one side of a debate. Though we have tended to see post-1952 industrial policy as a seamless continuation and extension of pre-1952 tendencies, and thus a policy undertaken on the behalf of national capital, it turns out that segments of the business community had begun to question the logic of ISI at this precise moment. In the case of the textile industry, the country's biggest industrial sector and employer, I found evidence of sharp disagreements over the best way to secure the industry's future prosperity, including calls for a more export-oriented industrial policy. As chairman of the sugar industry, 'Abbud supported the argument for deregulating prices and removing export controls. And though it is generally unrecognized, in late 1951 the Federation of Industries had come out in favor of a new, proexport regime.[65]

In a revealing interview with the A. D. Little consultants in early 1953, Robert Gasche, the managing director of Filature Nationale d'Egypte and the son of the person who had been the country's leading textile man for a generation, insisted that the future of the industry hinged on opening up new export markets. At the same time he vehemently rejected the argument that his spinning and weaving complex or the industry as a whole had been hurt by the exclusive use of Egyptian long and extra-long staple cotton as a raw material, marshaling figures to show why imports of so-called low-quality cottons would cost too much![66] Instead, he claimed that the single factor most responsible for increasing the costs of production was the existing labor regime and, in particular, the obstacles that the government had erected to reducing employment levels at the mills.[67]

THE EXPANSION OF THE PUBLIC SECTOR

Conservative economists of the era, such as Raymond Mikesell, attacked the precise kinds of development policies being promoted by U.S. agencies in Cairo and elsewhere for departing from cherished free-trade principles, encouraging "state ownership and control" and "their bias toward planning and against free enterprise."[68] If, indeed, preferred American designs for developing countries implied new forms of state intervention ("ownership and control") in Egypt, and this priority coincided with that of would-be Egyptian planners (e.g., 'Aziz Sidqi) and others who constituted the emerging antimonopolist current within the new ruling group, the business oligarchs were just as clearly opposed to the extension of a direct state role in the ownership and operation of their private industrial sinecures. Thus, as O'Brien notes, state agents involved themselves in the finance and management of these projects "[d]espite opposition from the Federation of Egyptian Industries" (1966: 84). Waterbury instead argues that public ownership was a belated response to longstanding "private sector appeals for greater state sponsorship" of industrial development (1983: 61).

Records from the time suggest that the specific distribution of local private and public investment shares in various industrial sectors after 1952 was the outcome of an ongoing contest, along the lines of the electric-power sector discussed in Chapter 5. Certainly, some investors actively resisted attempts by government agencies to claim an equity interest in new import-substitution enterprises. For instance, Sayyid Mar'i and local partners in the National Paper Company apparently had to divert the plans of Free Officer Magdi Hasanayn to build and run the proposed new paper mill as a state-owned enterprise.[69]

This tendency grew more pronounced over time. The local partners in a much-touted, 1954 automobile tire–making venture (a project originally proposed by A. D. Little) resisted pressures from public authorities to make the state a partner in the factory.[70] Yet in another case, despite the relatively small amount of capital involved (£E 200 thousand), the state emerged as the largest shareholder in the new Edfina food-processing company, registered officially in early 1956.[71] And though it is argued that the impetus for public ownership, at least until the watershed expropriations of British and French properties in 1956–1957, was a response to private sector failure, 'Abbud's proposal to take an equity share in the state's expanded petroleum-refining capacity was firmly rebuffed by the junta (*Akhbar al-Yawm* 11 April 1953).

The Revolution provided an expanded arena for etatist currents that had emerged after World War II, and the results were quickly apparent in various sectors, from fertilizers, construction, heavy industry and petroleum to the private press. The railways had of course never been privatized and were the real core of Egypt's contemporary state-owned enterprise sector. The decision to expand the capacity of the government petroleum refinery, another key party of the contemporary landscape, was taken late in the 1940s, and carried out with the heip of U.S. firms; this project was endorsed and extended by the military regime. The model of an independent hydropower commission devised in the early postwar years was adopted for overseeing the construction of the new government-owned power stations at the old and (proposed) new Aswan dams (Ayubi 1980: 218–220; Issawi 1963: 54; Waterbury 1992).

The new regime showed no particular inclination to divest itself of the diverse industrial portfolio gained as a result of the expropriation of the property of the king and his family in 1952, along with the property of emerging enemies of the state, such as the Abu al-Faths, investors whose properties were confiscated in 1954 following the March Crisis. Thus, the Nagib and Nasser governments emerged as probably the single largest domestic shareholder in the National Bottling Company, which produced and distributed Pepsi Cola, and a major shareholder in the Empain's old power-supply company.[72] Yet since capitalists like 'Abbud had opposed the extension of state ownership in sectors like power and chemicals, precisely because they envisioned them as new and lucrative investment sites, it seems safe to assume that the oligarchs viewed the increasing support for public or mixed ownership of new industries inside the regime, correctly, as the most ominous of the threats directed against them.

Though analysts have described the new regime's industrial policy as a simple extension of the previous, private-enterprise-oriented economy, with the most unique element being the numerous new incentives designed "to encourage domestic capital investment," this generalization is misleading (Issawi 1963: 52; Dekmejian 1971: 122–123; Zaalouk 1989: 24–27). So, too, are the various explanations for the ostensible lack of positive response by Egypt's biggest investors. The problem lies in the failure to see how for over seventy years virtually all domestic industrial investments had rested on privileged access to public resources, subsidies and other incentives. Once we factor in the increasingly restrictive regulatory environment, which was what public ownership ultimately meant, the government's terms after 1952 are better understood as disincentives to cooperate, and we can see how coercion came to play the dominant role in the regime's unfolding relations with capitalists like 'Abbud.

THE END OF THE BUSINESS OLIGARCHY

In a series of bold and unprecedented actions between 1954 and 1956, Nasser and his comrades turned on its head the seventy-year-long regime that had governed capital in Egypt and brought to an end the era in which investors governed the economy. The military rulers were explicit about this project, conceived of terms of ridding Egypt of "monopolistic capitalism" and elevated as a chief objective of the Revolution by 1955. Nasser's allies in the expanding American community in Cairo, top-heavy with businessmen, bankers, aid specialists and spies, generally gave this project their continued support.

The stages of this project are easily discerned, beginning with the March Crisis of 1954, when Nasser triumphed over Nagib and the Nasser-dominated RCC crushed the movement to return the country to parliamentary rule.[73] Realistically or not, late in March, the Wafd's cadres were anticipating Sirag al-Din's triumphant return as prime minister and "man of the year."[74] Days later, the American embassy weighed in on the side of police-organized crowds and regime-sanctioned strikers chanting, "No political parties and no democracy," "Long live the Revolution." For instance, on March 30, Caffery stressed the Peronist "undertones" in Nasser's strategy, noting how "[o]rganized labor has been deliberately and effectively used for political purposes on nation-wide scale for first time in Egyptian history and must henceforth be expected to make its voice increasingly heard." The ambassador concluded "that the results from our point of view can be called satisfactory."[75]

Investors who sided openly with Nagib, including the staunchly pro-American finance minister, 'Imari, were among the first to pay the price for opposing the consolidation of a "military dictatorship" (Caffery's term). 'Imari and other technocrats-turned-businessmen who had joined the regime in 1952, such as 'Ali al-Giritli, were forced from office. U.S. embassy observers correctly gauged the broader implications of the purge, arguing that it was the effect of Nasser's turn to labor leaders at a critical point and marked, minimally, a shift in the regime's social coalition. 'Imari's brand of fiscal conservatism was being sacrificed.[76] More ominously, the owners of *al-Misri* and prominent Wafd party funders, the Abu al-Fath brothers, were tried and convicted for treason, and lost their printing press, while a score of *ancien régime* party elites were stripped of all political rights.[77] In the following months, the Americans rewarded the Nasser regime with a new, $40 million aid package as the RCC went on to sign the Canal Base agreement with Great Britain.

The second stage in the project began in early 1955, coinciding with the military leaders' increasing preoccupation with economic development issues such as the Aswan Dam. This stage involved the expansion of state authority to the remaining, non-party-based institutions from which business oligarchs still acted to shape basic contours of the political economy. As the newly appointed minister of state for production affairs, Hassan Ibrahim, a member of the RCC, took over supervision of the NPC from its nominal head, businessman Husayn Fahmi, and Sidqi Sulayman, one of the original Free Officers, was named as its replacement secretary general.[78] Along these same lines, the RCC engineered its purge at the Ministry of Commerce (businessman Hassan Mar'i resigned) and its landmark corporatist reorganization of the Chambers of Commerce, reserving for itself the right to appoint one-half their directors and then further centralizing control through the creation of a new umbrella confederation (Bianchi 1989: 165–166, 168–169). "Reform" of the old Federation of Industries soon followed.

More crucially, though, the regime struck at the heart of the business oligarchy and a key institution of Egyptian capitalism—namely, the pattern of centrally controlled, cross-sectoral holdings and interlocking directorates that comprised the country's various business groups. By amending the basic company law in 1955, the regime limited the numbers of firms for which individuals could serve as directors (six) or managing directors (two); at the same time it forced company directors to retire after reaching the age of sixty. The decrees affected some 200 businessmen from families who had steered the economy for over two generations—including Mahmud Shukri, Jules Klat, Atta 'Afifi, Husayn

Sirri, Alexandre Benaki, Wahib Duss, Aslan Cattaoui, Akhnoukh Fa-
nous, Albert Cicurel, Ahmad Rushdi, Rene Ismalum and Joseph
Kfoury.[79] O'Brien claimed that this measure was designed to
strengthen the rights of shareholders, repeating the old canard that
company directors (and interlocking directorates) played no useful role
in company policymaking (1966: 73–74). But, as the list above attests,
those affected were pioneering investors and dominant figures in the
business community.

The regime went on to engineer the retirement of the leading lights
at the pinnacle of local finance, including Shamsi, the long-time director of the National Bank of Egypt; 'Imari, who had only recently been
named managing director of Bank Misr; the Misr group's chairman,
'Abd al-Maksud Ahmad; and its largest shareholder, 'Abbud.[80] Though
it is generally not discussed in the standard economic histories, both
firms were declared public utilities in the spring of 1955. Other firms
in the finance sector reported intense pressure to accept government-
sanctioned appointees under threat of being declared public utilities as
well. The new minister of finance and one of the architects of the
emerging etatist political economy, 'Abd al-Munim al-Qaysuni, presided over this partial reconfiguration ("deprivatization") of the finance
sector, which was driven at least in part by concern for mobilizing the
enormous resources necessary for the high dam project.[81]

Nasser provided a blunter defense of these interventions, according
to internal U.S. embassy documents, having reminded Ambassador Byroade that one of the objectives of the Revolution was to rid Egypt of
"monopolistic capitalism" and the "big capitalists" whom the regime
had lumped together with its other foes in the March Crisis.[82] At the
same time, a more explicitly populist Nasser brought the same theme
to the fore in his public appearances, including a well-publicized April
1955 address to military officers, where he stressed the government's
objective of ending "monopoly and capitalist dominance of government." Importantly, and again according to American reports, Nasser
advocated nationalization of the country's big industries.[83] O'Brien's
(1966: 68–69) discussion of *widespread* support for the government's
policies from the Chambers of Commerce, and the chairmen of Bank
Misr and the National Bank of Egypt must be evaluated in light of the
direct interventions by the regime *at this precise moment*, U.S. accounts
speak in the same period of growing unease among big investors.

The third phase or component of the renewed campaign against the
oligarchs, therefore, is marked by Nasser's following through on his

proposal and sanctioning the takeover of the country's oldest existing monopoly, the sugar industry, in August 1955, an action directed specifically against the country's single biggest capitalist, 'Abbud. The pretext for the sequestration was a ten-year-old dispute over the state's share of the monopoly rents, but more was involved, including 'Abbud's suspect political loyalties and reluctance to subordinate his firms and their resources to the state-building projects of technocrats like Qaysuni. As the U.S. embassy analysts argued, the regime was both frustrated by the organization of 'Abbud's group and "would like to break his power but . . . has been afraid to do so because of the effect on his industrial enterprises, which are so important to the country's economy."[84]

The recourse to expropriation was, manifestly, a sign of the regime's inability to enforce its own policy preferences in a critical economic sector (Chaudhry 1993). At the same time, it represented an escalation of the regime's campaign to subordinate the major centers of power in the domestic political economy—the local families who constituted the core of the various investor coalitions and their firms—via an increasingly coercive alternative to regulation. Thus, by the end of 1955, 'Abbud had been forced from the board of Bank Misr, while the sequestrator of his sugar mills and distillery joined the board of the massive bank-holding company, together with Nasser's confidant and ex-DMNL (communist party) member, Ahmad Fu'ad, as the bank became a quasi-government agency (Ahmad Hamrush 1984: 51–54).

The partial nationalization of the 'Abbud group in 1955–1956 is conventionally described as a departure from the main tendency in the government's vaunted policy of "encouraging the private sector" until the October 1956 Suez War, and the sequestration of French-, British- and Jewish-owned firms that followed (the Egyptianization of the economy) is usually described as marking a policy shift determined first and foremost by "external" factors. This line of analysis necessarily de-emphasizes the remarkably explicit intensification of the etatist-oriented, antimonopolist discourse of the regime after the March Crisis, including the branding of the business oligarchy as political hangers-on from another era who obstructed the return to democracy. And as O'Brien correctly notes, the new June 1956 constitution reflected and extended this ideological and programmatic shift (1966: 85).

Crucially, I have found the first clear evidence that the regime was preparing plans to take over other industries. Specifically, American records report numerous meetings between Egyptian officials and foreign consultants in 1955 to prepare for the formal nationalization of the power sector. The state was already a minority holder (40 percent), again mainly through expropriation of the king's holdings in large ventures like the old Empain group's power-generation companies (by 1955 the Empain group was being represented by a French state agency acting as trustee). According to U.S. embassy documents, Nasser was planning to nationalize the remaining privately owned shares, following his new, populist orientation.[85]

Along these same lines, on 21 July 1956 the government formally absorbed the sugar company, declaring it a state-owned enterprise, though this passed relatively unnoticed in light of the more dramatic takeover of the French- and British-owned Suez Canal Company five days later. After July 26, though, the regime found it more useful to promote the fiction that 'Abbud's sugar company was another tentacle of the foreign octopus that had the national economy in its grip.[86] No wonder that Americans in Cairo described the canal-company takeover and related expropriations as the outcome of trends "already clearly evident before the [July-November 1956 Suez] crisis."[87]

'Abbud's actions in the wake of the earlier and, for the local oligarchs, more decisive March Crisis reveal an investor desperately maneuvering to survive the regime's escalating assault on business privilege. As we have seen, like virtually all other Egyptian elites, he had at least a decade earlier recognized the growing involvement of the U.S. embassy and U.S. capital in Egypt and attempted to shape this evolving relationship to his own advantage. But this bargain had always been one piece of a complex strategy, its terms reflecting the strategic position occupied by 'Abbud and other local investors in post-1922 Egyptian politics, economy and society. With the collapse (or the defeat) of the liberal project between 1950 and 1954, the Americans were 'Abbud's last hope, yet most of them were betting on the state.

As the March Crisis unfolded, 'Abbud was once again abroad, where, according to the boiler plate that was the Amin brothers' specialty, the "king of Egyptian industry" was busy planning new joint ventures, including an oil-prospecting company, a paper mill, the expansion of his chemical complex, and other deals whose details could not be revealed (*Akhbar al-Yawm* 7 March 1954; *al-Akhbar* 14 July 1954). The projects grew more expansive a year later, as he traveled in London, Paris, New York, Washington, Miami and San Francisco. The Cairo dailies reported a final agreement on a new national airlines, meetings with the petroleum firms that would be "cooperating with him" in the Western Desert, and the signing of a new $6 million loan agreement with the ExIm Bank, along with an account of a recent interview with the *Miami Daily News*. 'Abbud had assured readers in Florida that Nasser was "building the government on a strong democratic basis," a claim that was no more true than any of these alleged new business triumphs (*al-Ahram* 12 May 1955; *al-Akhbar* 15 May 1955).

'Abbud had little success after 1952 in completing the projects that had been planned before the Revolution, and his group's three decades of expansion came slowly to an end. The expropriation of the sugar mills and distillery, which followed closely on the heels of the false ExIm Bank loan story, may have been connected to this disappointing investment record, though the takeover effectively ended 'Abbud's plans with W. R. Grace and the ExIm Bank for the paper mill.

Other reports from the period were wild exaggerations at best. For instance, he had, in fact, begun to develop a business relationship with W. Alton Jones, the investor who owned the large U.S. independent oil firm, Cities Service, and was a partner in concessions for the Western Desert and other parts of Egypt. Though 'Abbud liked to claim he was busy developing the country's oil resources, the reality is that an offer by Jones for a 10 percent share in Cities Service's part of the consortium had never been taken up. More important, Jones was contemplating taking a large stake in 'Abbud's Suez factory but Cities Service instead abandoned the Egyptian concession by 1957.[88]

In other words, 'Abbud was agreeing voluntarily to cede part of his empire to outside investors, reversing a pattern of protecting and expanding the extent of personal ownership and control that had marked all his investment activity over three decades. The only exception to this pattern had been the defeat at the hands of the Empain group in the war between the bus and tram line interests in the mid-1930s. This unprecedented move was no doubt related in part to the difficulties in financing the hard-currency costs of expansion. At the same time, there was a more explicitly political logic involved, in that expanded American participation in his chemical-manufacturing venture just might serve to protect him against the threat of creeping nationalization of the oligarchs' holdings.

The expansion of the Suez plant did take place in stages after 1952, though it is difficult to be precise about this development or to determine the extent of 'Abbud's personal investment. A plant to manufacture nitric acid was built at the site, for use by the military in the budding munitions sector. This plant was completed and preproduction final testing was underway by March 1957. When Jones declined to invest in the Suez plant, 'Abbud reopened negotiations with the ExIm

Bank to complete the original, pre-Revolution expansion plans, and the Eisenhower administration agreed to fund the project late in 1958 in conjunction with the Cairo subsidiary of First National City Bank, the first U.S. branch bank to open in the Middle East.[89]

By the time the new plant was finished, it was no longer 'Abbud's. His holdings in Bank Misr were finally nationalized in 1960, and his own group's core firms were taken over in 1961. On 22 October 1961, the government sequestered his family's personal property and the properties of 167 other "reactionary capitalists" and put him on trial the following month. The charges were eventually dropped on the grounds of his service to Egyptian industry. Ironically, the first company he founded, his contracting and dredging firm, was the last to be taken over, in April 1963. He died in London, eight months later (*al-Ahram* 11–13 February 1960, 21 December 1961, 31 January 1962, and 29 December 1963; *al-Akhbar* 25 December 1961; *Egyptian Gazette* 22 October 1961; *al-Jarida al-Misriyya* 8 April 1963: 512).

Summary: The Origins of Egypt's Comprador Bourgeoisie

In a manner reminiscent of Tal'at Harb and his allies at the end of World War I, Ahmad 'Abbud and his rivals rode the crest of a new, post–World War II nationalist wave through what turns out to have been a long last summer for Egyptian oligarchic capitalism. Thus, despite the exceptional expansion of national administrative capacity during the war, etatism remained at best a subordinate current in the postwar political economy, while between 1950 and 1952, the 'Abbud–Sirag al-Din party pursued the most audacious governing strategy deployed in Egypt since the Sidqi dictatorship of 1930–1933.

Against the Wafd's continuing powerful claim over the nation (and its business wing's ever tighter grip over public resources), opposition elites were reduced to protesting corruption and, even more elusively, promoting reform. As a means for mobilizing votes, particularly in the cities where the Sa'dist party did its worst at the polls (despite the standard identification of the party as "representative" of the country's national bourgeoisie), the strategy proved useless.

We saw this corruption/reform counter-discourse deployed time and again against the Wafd or Wafd-led coalitions: in the late 1920s and the mid-1930s (Chapter 3) and again in the 1940s (Chapters 4 and 5). It may have been marginally more useful by 1951–1952 in securing the acquiescence of random intellectuals, investors and like-minded elites to another round of palace-based minority rule. But as we have also seen, it seemed absolutely essential to the interwar and wartime interventionist narratives composed by British embassy officials. In the 1950s, U.S. Ambassador Caffery and kindred souls came to rely on the same story. We can date its origins precisely: August 1951, the month that the Wafd's foreign minister first threatened to overturn the Suez Canal bases treaty with Great Britain.

By the fall of 1951, as the Egyptian leadership made good on its threat and volunteers began a campaign of armed assaults on British personnel and property, the Americans denounced the turn of events as an act of desperation by a corrupt elite trying to stave off its downfall. That this is one of the rare moments when the views of the Truman administration coincide perfectly with contemporary marxist historiography would seem noteworthy in and of itself, but I believe it points to the same fundamental dilemma facing Egyptian communists and crusading American anti-communists at the time. Whether or not they were desperate, the Wafd's business wing nonetheless fashioned a strategy that coopted broad sections of the polity, reinforced its own cross-class coalition and undercut its rivals. The task of promoting an alternative to the 'Abbud–Sirag al-Din party appeared more daunting to those in 'Abdin, Qasr al-Dubbara and Whitehall after October 1951 than at any other point in the Wafd's history. Unfortunately for the Wafd, the concessions it demanded from the British were delivered in 1954, not 1951, to a U.S.-backed military authoritarian regime.

The process of undermining the business oligarchy and its dominant position in the political economy followed the extraordinary coup d'état in July 1952. The mechanisms that the new regime employed are well known, at least in their broad outline, and included the dismantling of parliament and the parties, expropriation and redistribution, new forms of economic regulation or, in place of regulation, nationalization by degree of key firms and sectors. As we have seen, the RCC's antimonopoly project, to use its own term, unfolded in stages—first, with the support of what I called antioligarchic (or would-be oligarchic) capitalists, among others, and after March 1954 turning in a more populist direction (i.e., appealing more directly to sections of organized labor).

As was the case with every other extraconstitutional, dictatorial government since that of Muhammad Mahmud in 1928, the RCC obtained material and symbolic support from the dominant foreign power in the country, which in 1952 was the United States. I took special note of the Americans' contribution to the key phases of this unfolding antimonopoly project and, in particular, their investment in an expanded public sector.

The reinvention of nationalist discourses was one of many practices which undermined the power of the business oligarchy. Thus, perhaps the most remarkable and heretofore enduring myth of the Revolution is that in 1956 foreigners rather than Egyptians controlled the country's economy, or that after the "Suez invasion" the regime reversed its policies toward foreign capital generally. The reality is that in sector after sector of the economy, power had shifted steadily in past decades from shareholders in Paris, Brussels and London to owners and managers in Cairo and Alexandria—that is, to local capital. Within this local set, the 1919 generation of Egyptian investors such as ʿAbbud, Yahya, ʿAfifi, Farghali, Andraos, the Abu al-Faths, and post–World War II rising stars such the Mariʿs and ʿImari came to displace the positions once occupied by minority resident owners and managers. We have dissected this process at length and, in particular, the political bases of the Egyptian business oligarchs' rise. The general thrust of this argument is simply reinforced if one looks carefully at the impact of the 1956 sequestration of British-, French- and Jewish-owned firms.

Most of the firms were old, locally founded enterprises in sectors where private Egyptian investment groups and their joint-venture partners had since come to dominate the market—for instance, in building materials, textile production and cotton trading—with the result that government agencies now owned additional instruments with which to try to alter the preferences of Egyptian capitalists.[90] At the same time, the single largest sequestered British asset, the £E 56 million refinery and distribution network of Shell Oil, was quickly returned to its legal owners. Thus, after 1956, the Nasser regime continued its policy of courting the transnational oil companies (and playing the independents off of them).

Other foreign firms, such as the Anderson Clayton subsidiary, the Nile Ginning Company, remained on extremely good terms with the Egyptian authorities and, as late as February 1961, had plans for increasing their investment in Egypt.[91] If we think in terms of sectors, foreign capital probably showed no markedly greater propensity to invest in Egypt in the decade or two before 1956 than after, and the same kinds of firms—oil, pharmaceuticals, engineering, automobile companies—remained actively interested in the Egyptian market through the so-called socialist era (Handoussa 1974, Ahmed 1984, Tignor 1990). I agree with Tignor that the government showed a propensity to strike more advantageous bargains with foreign capital over this period, but disagree that the multinational corporations were "given little encouragement" or that his characterization of Ford's experience holds for companies generally in the 1950s and 1960s.

The most important impact of the Suez sequestration for the economy's "commanding heights" was probably in advancing the nationalization of the finance sector, including both branches of foreign banks (what we have since come to refer to as transnational banks), such as Barclays or Crédit Lyonnais, and smaller, local enterprises owned by "foreignized" Egyptian Jews such as the Commercial Bank of Egypt.[92] The government's misleadingly named Egyptianization program for the banking sector was designed to overcome the ineffective regulation of the money supply and credit flows by turning the main lending institutions into parastatals.[93] Numerous other industrializing political economies pursued similar policies in the finance sector, including Mexico and South Korea. In fact, in 1963, Korean President Park Chung Hee claimed Nasser as an inspiration for Korea's own authoritarian industrialization drive.[94]

As Amsden (1989) and Jung-en Woo (1991) make clear, in the South Korean case, control of the finance sector was the means to discipline private capital while encouraging the country's own business oligarchs—the Korean *chaebol*—to build up their vast private holdings. South Korean capitalists pursued an explicit strategy of privileged access to resources in the 1950s and 1960s to create the Samsung, Hyundai and other industrial empires (Mason et al. 1980). As I have tried to show, in Egypt under Nasser, business-state relations moved in the precise opposite direction.

The legacy of this unfolding confrontation with Egypt's own oligopolists is found in places such as the entryway to the gothamesque Immobilia Building off Sharif Street, where the nameplates of 'Abbud's group of firms are still fixed to the wall; in Zamalak, where 'Abbud's twin villas house Helwan University's fine arts faculty; in the Belgravia section of London, where 'Abbud's family now resides; and in key texts of the Revolution, where Egypt's comprador bourgeoisie was invented.

Conclusion

Relatively little is known about the politics of investment in Egypt in the decades before the July 1952 Revolution, the period under study here. This point seems important to restate at the outset, and not only because it serves as a kind of reassurance for the time spent reading (not to mention writing) a book on an Egyptian capitalist and his role in promoting an electrification project and building a fertilizer industry. It is an argument for skepticism about the status of the conventional wisdom (whether about interest-group activity or the textile industry's use of domestic cotton), for undertaking new work in these areas, but also for examining more rigorously than is common the assumptions that underpin the conventional wisdom. In other words, analysts need to reconsider the overarching narrative that has served since the 1950s as a template for constructing accounts of the "historical process" (Dawley 1991) in Egypt and that has been "made to stand in place of the sort of knowledge of political processes and struggle which academics do not have" (Kitching 1985: 31).

I called this approach colonial exceptionalism. As in other exceptionalist cases, the explanation of the emergence and consolidation of the capitalist mode of production (or of capitalist property relations or of production for the world market) in Egypt relies on comparison with a highly stylized account of the putative development trajectory of Great Britain and France. The starting point is the relatively abrupt imposition of capitalist relations on the Egyptian social formation "from the outside" via the country's incorporation into the world market between

1820 and 1860, the great influx of foreign capital and immigrant capitalists between 1850 and 1880 and the formal colonial regime that emerged between 1875 and 1915—hence, "colonial." What makes this process "exceptionalist" is an underlying similarity in logic and method such that the most basic explanation for German exceptionalism (whatever the character of its particular "pathology") is the same as for Egypt and all other cases.

Exceptionalist accounts are generally not a celebration of difference but a way within the historical materialist tradition of accounting for some failure of the political-economic-moral order, which in Egypt's case would be the apparent inability of capitalism or of the bourgeoisie to engender thoroughgoing transformations of state, society and economy, to support a nation-building project, to deepen the process of industrialization, to sustain the process of accumulation, etc. Central to this mode of thinking and writing about Egyptian history is a set of theses about the nature of capitalists and of capitalist-class formation.

The hallmark of Egyptian radical texts of the 1940s and 1950s is a fairly rigid application of Marx's framework of forces/relations of production to Egyptian society. Thus, the class of rural private property owners that had emerged between 1840 and 1880 has been portrayed as a feudal order, against which stood a nascent, rising national bourgeoisie. But whatever potential might have existed for a bourgeois-led revolution was precluded by the continuing dominance of the colonial power and foreign capital. A new round of materialist-oriented historical analysis in the 1960s and 1970s argued, in contrast, for viewing Egyptian landowners as an agrarian bourgeoisie pursuing a kind of backward colonial capitalism (again, in comparison to "the West") in alliance with foreign capital. As I noted in Chapter 1, analysts were at pains to concede that a measure of industrial investment had in fact taken place in Egypt and that British colonial officials had not opposed its development.

To level a blunt objection at these ostensibly less-mechanistic accounts of nation and class formation: the trajectory of the economy is seen to parallel precisely the fortunes of the national independence movement, which has long been condemned for having fatefully compromised with British power in 1936. Thereafter, a neocolonial coalition steers Egypt erratically yet inexorably toward the crisis of 1951–1952, and though the disparate strata that constitute the industrial bourgeoisie are portrayed as realizing what needs to be done in order to avert disaster and allow capitalism to develop, they are unable to act in their objective class interests.

Labor historians Joel Beinin and Zachary Lockman offer a succinct synthesis of the state of the art of these post-1950 Egyptian debates on capitalist development and class structure, one which provides as clear a statement as any of the essence of colonial exceptionalism:

> By the end of the Palestine war it was becoming increasingly apparent that the coalition of class forces that had ruled Egypt since the end of the First World War *was incapable of* offering a solution to the political and economic crisis of Egyptian society. The large landowners who dominated both the Wafd and the opposition political parties clung tenaciously to their privileges, and were unwilling to concede even minimal reforms in the vital areas of land tenure, ground rent, and the taxation of agricultural property. . . .
>
> The Egyptian industrial bourgeoisie and its representatives in Parliament, often identified with the Sa'dist party, acknowledged the need for agrarian reform, a more equitable distribution of wealth, and accelerated industrial development, though in practice, *because the industrialists were closely linked to large landowning interests* by family and social ties and derived much of their capital from agrarian interests, they shared the same social conservatism and fear of unleashing the anger of the impoverished rural and urban masses. Many proposals for economic and social reform were blocked by this fear.
>
> The industrialists did not comprise an independent and self-confident class prepared to challenge the hegemony of the agrarian bourgeoisie. Egyptian industry did not, *and still has not,* transcended the limitations created by its original formation under the domination of European capital. In order to survive, Egyptian industrialists had to conciliate and ally with both the large landowners and the West to obtain capital and political support. (Beinin and Lockman 1987: 395–396, emphasis mine)

In its basic outline the more general story told here about Egypt is the story told countless times in the 1960s, 1970s and 1980s about many different countries, and it is the "original" German variant that is the central point of criticism in the book-length essays by Blackbourn and Eley in *The Peculiarities of German History*. As they wrote in their joint introduction:

> One of our intentions was to probe the normative assumptions which proponents of the *Sonderweg* necessarily made about what a proper historical development looked like. And here, sometimes explicitly and often implicitly, it was "western" and most particularly Anglo-American and French developments that were taken as a yardstick against which German history was measured. There are, however, problems with this kind of approach. It can easily come to rest on a misleading and idealized picture of historical developments in those countries that are taken as models. . . .

A second series of points in our argument follows from the first. What was it, in terms of content, that was said to mark an aberration in German history when judged by western norms? It was, above all, the failure of a proper bourgeois revolution. Bourgeoisies are supposed to rise, but the German bourgeoisie was commonly depicted as moving disastrously through modern history in the opposite direction. . . . Each of our contributions also questioned a different part of the widespread idea of a "feudalized" bourgeoisie. . . . There was, of course, undoubtedly a form of social *rapprochement* between bourgeoisie and landowning class in Germany from around the 1870s. *But we wondered how far this was exceptional in European terms and what it actually signified.* (1984, pp. 10–13, emphasis mine)

Much of this book is concerned with the effects of a similar if not the same misleading and "idealized picture of historical developments" on the understanding of capitalists and politics during the first decades of Egyptian independence. Is there a remarkable underlying regularity in the unfolding of the historical process, despite otherwise profound cultural, spatial and temporal differences, or have analysts told a story about the course of the Egyptian political economy that is as rigidly scripted as any classical marxist stages-of-history model, however much they believed that they were arguing against such teleologies?

When Capitalists Collide combined a revisionist view of Egyptian investors with an alternative narrative about and trajectory for the early decades of capitalist development. In Part II, which forms the core of the study, I challenged the pivotal idea that a nascent national industrial project was somehow undermined during the course of the 1920s and 1930s. While I supplied both empirical and conceptual arguments for an alternative model of capitalist organization, collective action and conflict, at the same time, what is ultimately at stake is a collective interpretation of Egypt's political economy that is rooted in the anticapitalist and third worldist discourses of the 1970s. From my vantage point, the cumulative impact of postdependency writings in Latin American and African studies, the critiques of nationalist industrialization strategies (rent-seeking states, state-owned enterprises, export-led industrialization) and, above all, the disillusion with and disappearance of non-market-based economic systems creates a different context for assessing Egypt's past. The overall result is to see the process of capitalist development propelled by estate-dominated export production and the transition to import-substitution manufacturing in both a relatively more nuanced and a less exalted light. This is particularly so if the implicit comparison with Egypt circa 1945 is not the United States, Great

Britain, Japan or France, but a more plausible range of cases such as Turkey, Syria, East and West Africa, Korea or the Philippines.

I do not mean to suggest that this process of capitalist development was uncontested; it was, and much of the exceptionalist historiography is itself testimony to the discursive dimensions of this challenge. But neither was its "failure" assured merely by the existence of well-documented British neocolonial ambitions or Egyptian joint ventures with embattled Manchester textile firms and London insurance agencies. By the end of World War II, the neocolonialist project itself had collapsed, opening up new possibilities for the national political class to consolidate power. At the same time, if one adopts the terms in which these issues are customarily posed, the balance of power between foreign and local capital in Egypt appears to have been shifting in favor of the local capital and, within this category, in favor of Egyptian nationals. Such a view is consistent with the kind of revisionist argument that Colin Leys, Nicole Swainson and others were advancing circa 1978–1981 in the debate on neocolonialism in Kenya.

My thesis is, however, based on an implicit aggregation of outcomes across discrete cases of competitive conflict—for instance, the 'Abbud group's bargaining power with the EEC in 1942–1944—and of the shifts in locus of control inside particular firms or sectors, as in the case of Beida Dyers and the textile industry more generally. I have drawn a sharp distinction between this model of competing investors and the more familiar model of capitalist class- or class fraction–based action via their putative representative associations. Such an outcome-by-aggregation or investment-conflict approach requires no prior assumption about collective consciousness (not to mention authenticity).

The various institutional arrangements for regulation of the economy that became sedimentized over the course of the late nineteenth and early twentieth centuries—oligopolistic markets, the central role of bank-holding companies associated with small numbers of wealthy urban and rural-based families, cross-sectoral investment patterns, etc.— produced much of what has since come to be identified as the emergence of an Egyptian national industrial bourgeoisie, which was composed, nonetheless, primarily of settlers, noncitizens, representatives of foreign firms, landowners, bankers and cotton exporters!

The significance of the feudalization argument in the Egyptian case—the idea that capitalists were unable to pursue their objective class interests because of their dependence on and social interconnections with landlords—is the role it plays in filling in the account of bourgeois failure and its ready availability to stand in as the alternative internal explanation either for fewer industries on the margin or, more incredulously, for Egypt's not having become an advanced industrial power once the so-called cruder claims about imperialism and dependency (the external factors) have been partially displaced in various texts.

The origins of accumulation in large landownership and the specific forms of production instituted there are clearly important, but the implications for the history of Egyptian industry building are more often asserted than developed systematically, beginning with the implicit counterfactual.[1] If the assumption is an alternate development trajectory in the 1870s and 1880s underpinned by a social coalition that did not include a class of large landowners, say, along the lines of a more autonomous peasantry and state bureaucracy, then, as the Turkish case suggests, a distinctly possible outcome could have been fewer large fortunes, less rapid accumulation and less private manufacturing industry.[2]

Alternatively, if the thrust of the feudalization argument is, as it often seems, that over the 1920s, 1930s and 1940s the dominance of large landowning interests checked the growth of the manufacturing sector, then there are competing explanations, beginning with the oligopolistic structure of the sector itself. The point is that until now the claims about the effects of landlord dominance or feudalization tend toward the metaphysical, assuming that some force or set of forces must have prevented the bourgeoisie from playing its normal role as history maker.

In Chapter 2 I reinterpreted the existing research on how basic elements of Egypt's capitalist market system—(1) the institutionalization of private property rights in the Egyptian countryside, (2) the formation of a class of large estate owners, and (3) the development of new urban businesses, professions and manufacturing enterprises in the interstices of the booming, foreign-funded, large-estate-based cotton-export economy—were forged in the mid-1800s and then extended in the aftermath of the British occupation in 1882. A key point in that chapter is that Egypt's laissez-faire-era economy was not some spontaneously emerging process (though also not something purposely constructed in all its dimensions by political authorities either). At the same time, its organization did not remotely resemble the ideal of a perfectly competitive market. The ensemble of practices from the mid-1800s that we refer to as state formation and that is most often traced through an evolving system of bureaucratic institutions (the Finance Ministry, public works, the Ministry of the Interior, the hydraulic regime) also entailed the institutionalization of a system of private oligopoly in land-ownership, commerce and industry.

The processes of state and class formation were bound up with one another in ways that to me do not seem to be usefully captured in the idea that "the state" was "creating" classes in Egypt, particularly when that idea tends to connote a willed or intended objective (Waterbury 1983, Anderson 1987, Richards and Waterbury 1990). Such a view rests once again on a highly idealized view of capitalism's emergence in "the West."

Accepting for the moment conventional ways of defining the two classes in Egypt, the emergence of the bourgeoisie and of the landowning class not only happened at roughly the same time but rested on the same kind of privileged access to the resources of the khedival state in formation. As Owen (1981a: 535–536) notes about the creation of landed estates,

> [This process] had its origin not in the development of local market forces but in an exercise of state power. It was Egypt's rulers who handed over a large part of the Delta to government officials and Egypt's administrative system that allowed others to seize land for themselves. . . . The first tentative move toward the establishment of private property in land was entirely the work of the country's rulers, for reasons of their own, and they were always prepared to disregard what some have taken as the spirit of their policy in the interest of building up their own holdings or confiscating the assets of an official . . . who had fallen from grace.

I have tried to document the parallel process at work in the formation of Egypt's "modern" industrial and commercial sectors.

Yet I would argue that the kind of arbitrary exercise of absolutist-like authority that Owen and others see as constitutive of this mode of class formation was rapidly checked by the occupation, the capitulatory regime and the gradual institutionalization of the private market economy. Certainly, the British administrators found the Capitulations and Mixed Courts impeding their own absolutist-like ambitions, while the business community, Britain's foreign rivals and leaders in the Egyptian national movement came to see the Mixed Court system more favorably, for the same reasons (Brown 1993). Put another way, one effect of state formation—that is, the Debt Administration's and later Cromer's pursuit of fiscal reform—was the creation and consolidation of institutions and practices that rapidly empowered investors.

Whatever the conceptual value of maintaining the distinction between landowners and bourgeoisie, particularly industrial bourgeoisie, the distinction is not easily made at the sociological level, where, if any-thing, we run the risk of underestimating the degree of indivisibility between landowning and capitalist families. There is probably little ground for ever seeing large landowners and bourgeoisie as two distinct class cores in Egypt that at some point start to merge, but certainly there was nothing gradual about this process.

For instance, to adopt a familiar if not very convincing model of class formation, did "class consciousness" proceed qualitatively faster and further than feudalization? If we use the standard marker of "class-for-itself" type development in the Egyptian case—namely, the formation of organized interest groups (e.g., the Cotton Growers Association)—the answer would be no, given that such associations emerged around the first decade of the twentieth century.

Thus, if "[b]y the Second World War there was . . . no sharp distinc-tion between the agrarian and industrial sections of the bourgeoisie" (Beinin and Lockman 1987: 11), then this was equally true at least a generation earlier, at the time of the First World War, and back even further. The same family sets or individuals, beginning with Tal'at Harb, avatar of the national bourgeoisie, helped to found and served as heads of virtually all the country's business associations, including the Federation of Industries, the Property Owners Association, the Cotton Growers Association, the Cotton Exporters Association, the Egyptian General Agricultural Syndicate. This is unsurprising. A small number of family-based or similarly closely linked investor coalitions (e.g., the Su-arès, Yahya, Misr, Salvago, Rabbath groups) all had cross-sectoral hold-ings in banking, trade, urban real estate, cotton export, manufacturing and rural land-reclamation companies, not to mention their many indi-vidually owned estates.

As is often noted about this kind of multisectorally oriented local business oligarchy, circa the Second World War, "There were divisions and conflicts among landed, financial, commercial, and industrial inter-ests as well as among foreign, *mutamassir* (quasi-Egyptian) and Egyp-tian capital before 1952, but there was also considerable overlap and a fair degree of common interest" (Beinin and Lockman 1987: 11). The point is roughly correct, though it hardly exhausts the matrix of conflict and cooperation within the political economy, and it is just as true for earlier decades. Ignoring, as I do in this book, conflict between capital/ landlords and peasants/workers as a constitutive part of the narrative of the development of capitalism in Egypt, there were "divisions and conflicts" between regions, between large and small firms, across industries or sectors (e.g., shipping, road and rail transport) and, as I have shown in some detail, among competitors.[3]

There are understandable, theoretically grounded, historically plausible and politically compelling reasons why analysts privileged two type of divisions rather than others during the formative phase of theorizing about peripheral political economies. In any particular account, the underlying logic is that the degree or extent of industrial development attained in Egypt was a function of the bourgeoisie's autonomy vis-à-vis foreign capital and the landlord class. What I have tried to show in this book, however, is that the argument is wrong in the Egyptian case. All I can do here is note that the kinds of evidence—in terms of definition of interest, how interests acted, and how policy outcomes emerged—used to illustrate the alleged political effects of feudalization in the Egyptian case are generally similar to the kinds of evidence that allegedly demonstrate how foreign capital and its comprador allies sapped the strength of the bourgeois project.

In the third and final part of this book, I pursued the logical implications of this critique of colonial-exceptionalist accounts: questioning the grounds for continuing to see inscribed in the complex and causally overdetermined events of 1950–1952 the overarching logic of an aberrant capitalist development path and investors collectively incapable of taking even minimal steps to resolve the country's deepening dilemmas in their own interests, though the solution has been made to appear so obvious.

> Structural changes—land reform to help the peasantry and free capital for industrial development, a state-sponsored development program, a commitment to improving the standard of living of the workers and peasants, complete sovereignty in both the political and economic spheres—*were essential to removing the barriers to further economic development*. . . . While the industrial interests would have benefited from such measures as land reform, they were generally too closely tied to conservative agrarian interests to take the initiative (Beinin and Lockman 1987: 12, emphasis mine).

Again, Beinin and Lockman provide a cogent synthesis of the prevailing wisdom traceable from Issawi's (1954) study of the Revolution to Zaalouk's (1989) rehearsal of its betrayal, while their own approach to issues of working-class formation and identity politics in *Workers on the Nile* goes far in challenging many of the conventions of colonial exceptionalism. But the inclusion of ideas such as "complete sovereignty in both the political and economic spheres" in a checklist of development prerequisites is a potent reminder of the strong strand of romanticism that is woven through such views (Phillips 1977).

In this first detailed account of the role played by the country's leading capitalists in the events that led up to the July 1952 army takeover, it was both inevitable and overdue that a discussion revise the relatively more sweeping judgments about class and politics—such as Wafd = landlords, Sa'dist = bourgeoisie—that were first put forward in Egyptian marxist texts in the 1950s and 1960s. Chapters 5 and 6 show that investors were certainly divided about what the future portended and what was the best strategy for dealing with it. The benefit of my approach is that the investors are actually identified. But there is ultimately little that distinguished them save that some had captured the resources that others coveted. Of course, such forms of instrumentalism are hardly unique in the annals of postcolonial politics (e.g., Strachan 1976, Robison 1986, Hawes 1987).

The rent seeking that British consuls never ceased championing on the part of their own national captains of industry and that underpinned the creation of much of Egypt's "modern" economy, was just as routinely read as a sign of the hopeless venality of the Egyptian elite when practiced by 'Abbud and his rivals. The archives of both the British and the American governments are bulging with the records of interest conflicts over rent seeking and industry building in Egypt. And these texts evince a clear pattern of escalating protestations of corruption and demands for reform by their authors at those precise points when investment conflicts were perceived to be threatening British or, increasingly after World War II, U.S. interests.

More important than what the declassified records predictably reveal about the cynicism of a host of actors from the past, like U.S. Ambassador Caffery, and those who are still the occasional subject of U.S. embassy reporting today, like Sirag al-Din, Mustafa Amin and Muhammad Haykal, is the surprising and powerful support they lend to critics of the idea of the capitalist class as a corporate political agent with a collective class interest. The notion that the Egyptian industrial bourgeoisie in particular believed in and pursued some collective interest in the redistribution of private estates has long been taken for granted. Perhaps some individual investors had come to champion this particular strand of post-1945 development doctrine, though I found little evidence of this in the actions of Egypt's biggest industrialists. I did, however, uncover a great deal of evidence that investors and investment groups were powerful actors who were involved in virtually every facet of governance of the state and economy.

The post–World War II years were hardly auspicious for the efforts by the political class to consolidate power over the postcolonial state. The resurgence of urban labor and student protest in 1945–1946, the mounting of a sporadic if still ominous campaign of political assassinations and bombings of European and Jewish institutions, the agitation over the Palestine crisis, etc., all can be read as signs that relatively broad strata of Egyptians were intent on reshaping the political agenda, even if toward different ends. Certainly, the institutions that buttressed the oligarchs' influence would not go unchallenged. The Canal Zone crisis of 1951–1952 epitomizes this process of contestation from below, though my own reading was intended as a caution against a too close-ended and mechanistic account of class, politics and history at this juncture.

The premise that the treaty-abrogation issue, the fighting in the Canal Zone and the Cairo fire of January 1952 were all reflections, fundamentally, of the deeper structural crisis of Egyptian society rooted in a backward form of colonial capitalism and in a feudalized bourgeoisie that was incapable of offering a solution is no longer convincing. After all, with the single exception of land reform, the specific economic policies followed during the early years of the army regime were developed by and were underway in the late 1940s and early 1950s—under the Wafd. The new military leaders (and their U.S. backers) likewise were no less compelled to pursue the canal bases issue. And though a great deal of theoretical weight is attached to the army's land-reform project, in reality, its purposes, execution and consequences had little to do with deepening capitalist development in Egypt. Richards, convinced that it could have mattered, concludes that the failure to pursue "the kind of far-reaching land reform carried out in South Korea" is "one of the many tragedies of modern Egyptian economic history" (1992: 44). Still, there is no need for a complicated sociological analysis to understand industrial investors' lack of enthusiasm.

The confiscation of the assets of the royal family and two hundred or so other powerful families may have been popular, just and useful to the officers in engineering the transition to populist authoritarianism, but it did little for capitalists or capitalism in Egypt. The counterfactual—a July 1952 government pursuing Mahir's alternative strategy—is worthwhile positing, even though one may well prefer the course ultimately followed by Nagib and Nasser. Among other cases in Latin

America, the Brazilian experience is a reminder that a type of capitalist development similar to Egypt's continued to unfold and deepen in the absence of land redistribution. And although the national bourgeoisie, land reform's putative champion, is now said to have extended its dominance in Egypt and across the postcolonial third world (Ahmad 1992), land reform itself has virtually disappeared as an international norm.

At the same time, a moment's reflection on the post–World War II history of Asia, Central and Latin America can serve as a reminder of the tolls exacted by and on those who in the past, and no doubt with less certainty than historians, identified other revolutionary moments in countries such as Vietnam (Kolko 1985), El Salvador (Dunkerley 1982) or the Philippines. In the Philippine case, there were scathing critiques inside the New Peoples' Army of their leaders' past errors in acting on predictions of a revolutionary situation in Manila in the mid-1940s (Lachica 1971: 125–126, 302–316). And recall that this was in a country where armed revolutionary cadres already formed a highly disciplined fighting force opposing the state. The Egyptian countryside was a placid sea in comparison, while the country's small and splintered communist leadership(s) had little success in mobilizing the cities. Historians do not have to pay for errors in judgment. Still, there is no avoiding the need to revisit the historical-structural account of the origins and unfolding of the July 1952 Revolution, which is what colonial exceptionalism ultimately purports to explain.

Regarding the ideas about the bourgeoisie that are a legacy of this particular approach to historical-comparative political economy, it is no longer convincing to view and speak of a capitalist class as a potential or partially realized collective agent or agency. Rather than narrating (heroically or tragically) the process of evolution of that agency, researchers should think of class or classlike effects that are institutionalized in different ways and in different degrees through various practices, many of which have nothing to do with the willed objectives of vast numbers of capitalists or the representative associations of those who own the means of production. Blackbourn and Eley (1984) make a similar point more elegantly and using alternate language; more important still, they begin to develop the analysis systematically as does, from another direction, Mitchell in *Colonizing Egypt*. (1988). I looked at a different set of Egyptian institutions, practices and class effects in this book, employing the concept of business privilege.

Though I paid relatively little attention to the discursive dimensions of this process, Owen's (1981b) argument, that the versions of economic nationalism promoted in the 1920s and 1930s were important mainly as a strategy to preserve and extend private market-based, oligopolistic privilege, is undoubtedly correct. Egyptian capitalists pressed their claims for more power, wealth and industry on the basis of protecting Egypt against foreign domination. In the 1940s and 1950s, economic nationalism was being reinscribed with a radical, indeed anticapitalist content and deployed in a struggle with the oligarchs.

The invention of Tal'at Harb as a direct ancestor of etatism in Egypt and of Ahmad 'Abbud as the avatar of neocolonial domination marks a moment of successful resistance to the expansion of capitalism and of private market privilege, a moment that many Egyptians have not yet ceased defending.

Notes

Preface

1. Hansen insists that "[r]adical stereotypes of class struggle, neocolonialism, and dependency were not useful for understanding developments" in Egypt's economy in the years after 1922 (1991: xiii). But, surely, this is far too sweeping a judgment. Given his preference for the "new" political economy, it is surprising to find him unconcerned with the historical origins and consequences of the particular configuration of property rights and other institutions that shaped the inefficient investment strategies and "failed" development path of the 1920s–1950s.

1. Divided Rule

1. This argument is now standard in the literature on the Egyptian political economy. See, for example, Hussein (1977), Deeb (1979), Davis (1983) and Bianchi (1989).

2. Particularly useful overviews are found in 'Abd al-'Azim Ramadan (1971), Gran (1978) and 'Asim al-Disuqi (1981).

3. See for instance Zachary Lockman's review of Tignor (1984) in the *Middle East Journal*, 39 (1985). Though Tignor was publishing extensively on the same topic in the late 1970s, Davis (1983) fails to discuss or even cite any of this work.

4. For this reading, see Tignor (1984: 2–5, 251–252). Following the quote about Egyptian leaders trying to "create a vibrant and autonomous Egyptian

capitalism" (2), he argues that it "had never been the intention of the Egyptian elite to detach themselves from metropolitan capital" (12). I agree with the latter statement, but it is then hard to understand what is meant by "autonomous Egyptian capitalism." The overstatement itself is a hallmark of exceptionalist narratives.

5. Contrast with Waterbury (1983) and Richards and Waterbury (1990).

6. Przeworski defines hegemony as popular "consent to exploitation" resting on a widespread understanding and acceptance of the "development and expansion of the particular group . . . as being the motor force of a universal expansion, of a development of all the 'national' energies" (1980: 24).

7. As framed, the Egyptian case would thus seem to pose a challenge to a central thrust of the revisionist, dependent-development literature and its critique of the idea of monolithic and unalterable structures of metropolitan economic domination. My alternative reading draws heavily on the dependent-development canon. See Cardoso and Faletto (1979) and, for a retrospective account, Evans and Stephens (1988).

8. To make the point another way, in terms of understanding capitalists and politics in Egypt, distinguishing between foreign and indigenous "wings" is akin to distinguishing between left- and right-handed wings. There were presumably many more of one type of capitalist than another. What is crucial is specifying how, why and for whom it matters.

9. To be fair, Robison is clear about the limitations to an analysis focused narrowly on clientelist arrangements. It tells us little about the social coalitions underpinned by this particular mode of domination. Both Boone and Robison argue for a broader focus on class formation. See as well Fatton (1988).

10. In the Egyptian case, this kind of bargaining perspective vis-à-vis foreign capital or states is more often applied to public agencies seen to be acting in the national interest.

11. I have drawn extensively on Strachan (1976) and Leff (1978, 1979a and 1979b). Leff's work provides numerous references to studies of groups in Pakistan, India, Nigeria, El Salvador, Mexico, Brazil, Venezuela, Colombia and elsewhere. I am indebted to John Waterbury for first bringing this literature to my attention.

12. Strachan (1976: 2) and Leff (1978: 663–664). Note, however, that Strachan, who mapped the basic contours of the business community in late-Somoza Nicaragua, stressed the difficulty in defining the group precisely enough to identify it (and distinguish it from other organizational arrangements) and generally enough to permit comparison. See his Chapter 2, "Definition and Description."

13. Documentation on Egyptian business groups can be found in Issa (1970), Kalkas (1979), Davis (1983) and Krämer (1989).

14. These particular features are repeatedly highlighted in a range of studies on this form of capitalist organization. Useful sources include Strachan (1976), Leff (1978), Evans (1979), Markovits (1985), Robison (1986), Zeitlin and Ratcliff (1988) and Saragoza (1988).

15. For example, the Federation of Industries and other multisector associations tend to be described as pressure groups, with little if any consideration

given to other more common logics underpinning these capitalist institutions—
e.g., organizing markets, exchanging information. In general the whole area
of discussion is undertheorized, while the existing historical accounts rest on
exceedingly thin empirical evidence. The basic sources are reviewed in the two
best studies on this subject, by Mustafa Kamil al-Sayyid (1983) and Bianchi
(1989). The far richer literature on the history of labor unions and workers'
federations makes my point that much more obvious. See, in particular, Goldberg (1986), Beinin and Lockman (1987) and Posusney (1991).

16. As described in another context: "What then is the political task which
confronts the major indigenous capitalist? Primarily it is to secure a guaranteed
position in the conglomerate of capitalist factions operating in Indonesia. Given
the increasing internationalization of capital . . . its future is as a more or less
developed component of complex international corporate and financial structures" (Robison 1986: 364).

17. I am grateful to Ellis Goldberg for pressing me on the concept of rent
and for suggesting its particular relevance to the sectoral conflicts that are detailed here. His close reading of this chapter was instrumental in developing the
arguments in this section and the one that follows.

18. While this is how the broad dynamics of the liberal regime are conventionally interpreted, and I don't challenge this framework here, there is good
reason to believe that this convention will require revision once subjected to
the kind of critical scrutiny that I have given to the organization of business
interests. And our understanding of many aspects of the liberal regime (e.g.,
legislative practices) is exceedingly thin.

2. The Origins of the 'Abbud Group and Its Rivals

1. The history of this period and especially the impact of capitalist integra-
tion has been extensively analyzed. Begin with Landes ([1958] 1979), Issawi
(1961), Owen (1969), Berque (1972), 'Ali Barakat (1977), Clawson (1981),
Richards (1982) and Marsot (1984).

2. Crouchley (1936) made sure to distinguish the roles of "foreign" and
"local" capital in the economy. Tignor (1984) has helped to revive this distinction. At the same time, his work challenges Crouchley's overly broad general-
izations about the locus of "control" in firms operating in Egypt, based on
aggregate statistics on shares held locally and abroad. See Tignor (1989).

3. I have adopted the Europeanized spellings used in Krämer (1989), which
is by far the most valuable source on the Egyptian Jewish community. See in
particular her discussion of the "Cattaoui–Suarès–de Menasce–Rolo group"
(41–43). In addition see De Guerville (1905), Wright and Cartwright (1909:
321–322, 362, 448–450, 464), Landau (1969: 10–11, 14, 53, 137–148), Kalkas (1979), Anis Mustafa Kamil (1981) and Shamir (1987).

4. I have used the spellings found in Kitroeff (1989). Kalkas (1979: 186–187) graphs the marriage links among these families as well as some of their early financial ventures. These established merchant families arrived from various Mediterranean ports, beginning in the early 1800s, though they were all originally from the island of Chios. The following additional sources have useful information on Greek businessmen: Wright and Cartwright (1909), Landes ([1958] 1979) and Owen (1969).

5. Remarkably little has been written about Cassel, generally, and with regard to his role in the post-1882 Egyptian political economy. For Cassel's business activities in Egypt and elsewhere in the Middle East, see Thane (1986), the best general account of Cassel available. On Cassel's involvement in the original Aswan project see Middlemas (1963: 144–146); Tignor (1966: 222); and Thane (1984: 604–614). For Cassel's relations with Baring Brothers, see Ziegler (1988: 276, 289).

6. Ahmad Yahya (b. 1840) took over his father's cotton-exporting business, served as both an elected and appointed official of the Alexandria Municipal Council and by the early 1900s was one of the biggest landowners in the Alexandria area. He was prominent in the early gradualist wing of the national movement. His son, Amin Yahya (1866–1936), built a business group around the cotton-export house which he incorporated under the name the Egyptian Produce and Trading Company (1919). Amin's brother, 'Abd al-Fattah Yahya, served as prime minister in 1934. On Amin's death, the business group was taken over by his son, 'Ali Amin Yahya. Wright and Cartwright (1909: 439); Berque (1972: 356); Tignor (1976: 51). Also see Kalkas (1979: 195–196) for hints of an early conflict between Amin Yahya and the Salvagos. By the 1930s, Yahya had joined descendants of the Salvagos and Suarès groups on the boards of major industrial firms.

7. The Suarès group hired Harb away from the state in 1905 and employed him in the management of the Kom Ombo company. He moved to another Suarès group venture, the Société Foncière d'Egypte, as managing director in 1908. He remained a close ally until the end of his career in 1939. By the early 1920s, he had joined the board of directors of Crédit Foncier, as well as other Suarès group–foreign capital joint ventures. In the years prior to his founding Bank Misr, he was also a publicist for the foreign-dominated land companies and large Egyptian landowners, as well as the emerging wing of the nationalist movement associated with the *Jarida* group. Davis (1983); Tignor (1976 and 1977a); Deeb (1976).

8. Harb managed the private estate of 'Umar Sultan, son of a powerful Egyptian notable and a financial force in the nationalist movement. Sultan has also been described as a protégé of the British administration. The Siyufi family were Egyptian merchants and business partners of Belgian-allied capitalists like Eid. Lutfi 'Umar had business links with Eid as well. His chief claim to fame, however, was his role in organizing labor and farmers (cooperatives) on behalf of the nationalist movement. Davis (1983: 97–98, 104); Wright and Cartwright (1909: 375); Tignor (1966: 304 and 1976: 55); Berque (1972: 243).

9. The report was first presented in November 1917. I am referencing it

here according to its official publication date. See Commission du Commerce et de l'Industrie (1918). For summaries, see Issawi ([1967] 1975: 453–460); Tignor (1984: 55–58); and Kalkas (1979: 43–56). For samples of then-current economic critiques see Tignor (1976); Deeb (1976); and Owen (1969).

10. See FO 141/680, file on the "Aswan Power Scheme."

11. Tignor (1977a: 181). For instance, Tignor explains the empirical puzzles in terms of Harb's "enigmatic and complex" character, a mixture "of the old and the new" (1976: 54), colored originally by a "simplistic" and "naive sentimentality and boundless optimism" which gradually gave way to a more realistic attitude toward foreign capital as the bank "evolved and matured" (1977a: 161, 166, 180). Davis relies on a structural explanation to show why the "nationalist elements in the Misr group" were forced "to come to terms during the 1930s with foreign capital" and with the "Europhile segment of the Egyptian bourgeoisie" (1983: 9).

12. In contrast to the standardized mass production associated with modern (Fordist) manufacturing industry, the construction industry specializes in customized products assembled on-site rather than in a central location. The typical product is large and expensive; and for all but the largest firms, costs and other variables associated with production engender significant risks. It is a particularly labor-intensive industry that has only had limited success in rationalizing the production process. For details, see Hillebrandt (1974); Bowley (1966); and Haber (1931).

13. As Landes ([1958] 1979) and numerous other sources make clear, the market for contracts and concessions under Khedive Isma'il was relatively free-wheeling. When the British occupied and colonized strategic parts of the state, they exercised a monopoly over the state's resources tighter than that of any Ottoman sultan, creating in effect a protected trough for feeding British enterprise (and their local allies). U.K. firms recognized this advantage explicitly, hence their fanciful demands after 1922 that the Egyptians be pressured to guarantee that a fixed percentage of the public-works budget would be turned over as contracts to British manufacturers and engineering firms. See the letter dated 3 March 1924 from Hannon, secretary of the "industrial group" within the House of Commons, to the Prime Minister, contained in FO371/10060, E2003/2003/16.

14. FO371/11588, J95/41/16, minute by Murray reporting conversation with Sir Edmund Wyldbore Smith, 8 January 1926.

15. I am indebted to Texas New Dealer Creekmore Fath whose understanding of the relations between the Brown Brothers and Lyndon Johnson helped me in thinking about what businessmen and politicians offer one another.

16. FO371/11588, J95/41/16, minute by Murray, 8 January 1926.

17. "[G]roups began to organize and to articulate views of a changed Egyptian economy. . . . The new economic ideas represented a vague strategy of economic development . . . Even the founders of Bank Misr realized that their vision of an industrialized and more autonomous Egyptian economy depended on projecting their message into the far corners of the country" (Tignor 1984: 54–55).

3. Shifting Lines of Power

1. See FO141/680/45, reporting conversation between Hartopp and 'Abbud; and FO141/680/54, "Outline of events which have led up to the present examination by the Egyptian government of schemes for the utilization of the Assuan Dam for power purposes."

2. The quotation is from the British high commissioner. See FO141/498, 218/5/34, draft telegram from Lampson to Simon, 18 March 1934.

3. The description and account of 'Abbud's role are found in FO371/12359, J2345/8/16, Selby to Murray, 22 August 1927.

4. See FO371/13127, J194/18/16, Lloyd to FO, 5 January 1928, memorandum on the Egyptian press during the period 22 December 1927–4 January 1928; for 'Abbud's pessimistic view of the post-Zaghlul political scene and early evidence of his intentions to work toward changing it, see FO371/13115, J336/4/16, FO minute (Steward), 25 January 1928, enclosing letter from 'Abbud to Grant; for a retrospective view of these events, colored by the renewal of 'Abbud's ties to the party in the 1940s, see *Akhbar al-Yawm* 5 November 1949.

5. FO371/13140, J1424/240/16, Lloyd to FO, 21 April 1928. FO371/13120, J1575/4/16, Patrick Hannon to Austen Chamberlain, 10 May 1928.

6. Details on 'Abbud's offer are found in FO371/13140, J578/240/16, FO minute (Murray), 13 February 1928. The British government's position on the sale is found in J487/240/16, FO minute (Tyrrell), 3 February 1928, which includes the reference to "native" control. For details on the syndicate which Docker organized, see files J487/J578/240/16, as well as Davenport-Hines (1984b: 208). The author's assumption that Docker finally acquired control of the *Gazette* is incorrect however. The newspaper eventually passed into the hands of Oswald Finney, the cotton merchant, investor, and owner of the *Gazette's* main competitor, the *Egyptian Mail*. The Foreign Office records of the ongoing negotiations for the paper are included in FO371/13864, J75/J560/J771/J3542/75/16.

7. FO141/577, Embassy Cairo File 529 (pp. 382–end), Assuan Dam, 1915–1929, 529/452, Resumé of Assuan Heightening Commission 1928.

8. The basic evidence on the attempted bribe is found in a letter from Watlington of the EEC to Dawson, which at one point mentions "practical suggestions which might be to our mutual advantage." See FO371/13877, J1076/1056/16, Lloyd to FO, 20 April 1929; J1391/1056/16, Lloyd to FO, 5 May 1929; Davenport-Hines 1984: 210. Officials of the EEC told the head of the Department of Overseas Trade (DOT) that the document was a forgery. Another explanation may be that EEC was seeking a way to inform the consultant, Dawson, that the American-owned utilities trust on whose board he sat was in the midst of secretly organizing the bailout of EEC.

9. Harb was registered as a founding shareholder in the newly formed Egyptian branch of Siemens. See *al-Waqa'i' al-Misriya* 19 January 1928.

Harb's ties to the Deutsche Orient Bank dated back to the prewar years, and he had facilitated the re-establishment of the Deutsche Orient bank branch in Cairo in the mid-1920s. Davis 1983: 70–71, 75–76. British sources noted a "co-relation of interests" between the two German firms' Egyptian operations. J2382/297/16. FO371/10029, E3341/122/16, Allenby to FO, 4 April 1924, and Mulock to DOT, 5 April 1924.

10. See FO371/13877, J1129/J1167/J1174/1056/16. As the latter file records, the British prime minister, foreign minister, and president of the Board of Trade met to discuss the question on the night of 1 May 1929. The next day the chairman of Metrovick, Sir Philip Nash, was shown a proposed dispatch to Lloyd to pressure the Egyptian government on their behalf.

11. See FO371/13877, J1391/1056/16, Lloyd to FO, 5 May 1929; J1476/1056/16, Lloyd to FO, 15 May 1929, and FO371/13870, J2382/297/16, enclosing memo by Larkins, 8 August 1929.

12. J1448/1056/16, Lloyd to FO, 23 May 1929; and J1603/1056/16, Turner to DOT, 24 May 1929.

13. FO371/14646, J1978/752/16, enclosing letter from 'Abbud to Turner, 27 May 1930, and documents entitled "notes from Egypt" and "Société Egyptienne de Electricité," both dated 25 March 1930; Clement Levy, *The Stock Exchange Year-Book of Egypt,* 1943 edition, p. 695; minutes of Misr Bank board meetings show the bank had agreed in principle as early as 1928 to cooperate with the Empain group in industrial ventures. This information was supplied by Helmut Fischer, a German researcher in a personal communication, undated but written in 1987.

14. For 'Abbud's role in negotiating the overturn of the constitution, see FO 371/14616, J2235/4/16, Cairo Chancery to Egyptian Department, 29 June 1930; J2360/4/16, 'Abbud to Selby, 10 July 1930; J2371/4/16, FO minute (Selby), 15 July 1930; and J3167/4/16, telegram from Mr. Hoare (Cairo), 22 September 1930.

15. FO 371/14633, J3323/93/16, Hoare, 27 September 1930; J3291/93/16, Hoare, 4 October 1930; J3459/93/16, Hoare, 11 October 1930; J3558/93/16, FO minute (Mack) 29 October 1930. For 'Abbud's position generally, see FO141/766 801/5/31, minute by Miller to the High Commissioner, 11 November 1931.

16. The first evidence I found of this development within government circles to run the power plant as a public enterprise dates to the 1930 Wafd government, which, according to Belgian investors, had refused "on principal to grant concessions for the utilization of the dams to private interests." See FO371/J1978/752/16, "notes from Egypt" and "Société Egyptienne de Electricité," both dated 25 March 1930; and J752/752/16, DOT, 3 March 1930. On the hydraulic administration generally, see Tignor (1966). For Sidqi's pragmatic antimonopolism, see FO 371/15420, J1606/357/16, Loraine to FO, 7 May 1931; FO 141/769, 512/1/31 'Abbud to Turner, 5 May 1931, enclosing letters exchanged with Sidqi. For early sources of this antimonopolist attitude, see Tignor (1984).

17. FO371/16116, J128/128/16, Turner to DOT, 13 January 1932;

J1457/128/16, Turner to Farrer, 6 May 1932; and RG59, 1930–1939, 883.6113/59, Jardine to State, 9 February 1932.

18. On the elections and London's efforts to damage 'Abbud's influence with his ally, Sidqi, see FO141/766, 801/3/31, Vansittart to Loraine, 30 May 1931; 801/2/31, Turner to Murray (FO), 21 May 1931; 801/5/31, minute, Miller to the high commissioner, 11 November 1931; for an account of the intervention on 'Abbud's behalf by Lord Balfour, the British steel maker, including London's derogatory and harmful response, see FO141/766, 801/5/31, Peterson to Loraine, 27 November 1931.

19. On 'Abbud and his "increased influence with palace circles," see FO371/20916, J1989/815/16, Lampson to FO, 16 April 1937, Egyptian Personalities Report, entry for 'Abbud.

20. Details on 'Abbud and Korayyim appeared in 1934, in the course of a libel suit, which was itself a by-product of these ongoing commercial and political conflicts. See *La Réforme* 15 March 1934; *al-Ahram* 13 March 1934; FO371/18014, J3219/660/16, Peterson to FO, 22 December 1934, reporting on proceedings of the Cairo assize court in libel action brought by 'Abbud against *al-Siyasa* on 15 December 1934; also see the discussion of the libel suit brought by Korayyim against the *Times* in J2831/660/16, Peterson to FO, 22 November 1934. Details on Muharram's activities with the EEC representative emerged much later, beginning with a series of purloined letters published by opponents of the Wafd. See, for instance, Hochstein to Grey, 1 August 1932, reproduced in *al-Balagh* 7 September 1937; and Hochstein to Grey, 5 August 1932, in *al-Balagh* 8 September 1937.

21. On the impact of the *Daily Telegraph* issue, see FO141/759, 254/1/33, "Minutes of First Meeting Held at the Residency, 6:30 pm, 10 January 1933." The high commissioner, Percy Loraine, doubted the claim that 'Abbud was bribing correspondents, but the Foreign Office insisted on its accuracy. See FO371/17019, J127/127/16, FO minute, 16 January 1933, and J303/127/16, Loraine to Peterson, 28 January 1933, and, especially, note by Mack. For 'Afifi's view and his role in discrediting 'Abbud, see FO371/16110, J3362/14/16, Loraine to FO, 10 December 1932. On the origins of this highly personal antagonism, see, for instance, "Une Curieuse Polémique," *La Réforme* 15 March 1934; and FO141/766, 801/5/31, minute (Miller), 11 November 1931. The two remained implacable foes for decades. Mona 'Abbud-Husayn confirmed the life-long rivalry between her father and 'Afifi, interview, London, August 1986.

22. For details on Sidqi's maneuvers, see FO371/16116, J3398/128/16, enclosing a letter from Larkins (no. 1108), 17 November 1932; and J3317/128/16, Larkins to DOT, 23 November 1932. For the Jabal Auliya' dispute in particular, see USRG 59, 1930–39, 883.6113/72, Jardine to Secretary of State, 19 November 1932; FO371/17002, J2651/10/16, Loraine to FO, 1 November 1933; FO371/16977, E7412/10/16, enclosing DOT minute 25222/31/S/174, dated 6 December 1933; and FO141/498, 218/3/34, Larkins to Selous, 14 March 1934.

23. FO371/16116, J3398/128/16, Larkins to DOT, 7 December 1932;

FO371/17003, J15/15/16, Selous to DOT, 11 February 1932; J507/15/16, 'Abbud to Larkins, 22 January 1933; and J2344/15/16, memo by Larkins, "Hydroelectric Scheme for Generation of Power by Means of the Aswan Dam."

24. FO141/759 [Residency file 254 on 'Abbud for 1933], 254/2/33, Keown-Boyd to Smart, 1 April 1933; FO371/17002, J1561/10/16, Campbell to FO, 26 June 1933; USRG 59, 1930–39, 883.6113/Gebel Awlia1, Jardine to State, 15 June 1933.

25. St. Antony's College, Oxford, Middle East Archives, Diaries of Sir Miles Lampson, Lord Killearn [hereafter *Killearn Diaries*], 13 April 1934; FO141/498, 218/5/34, draft telegram from Lampson to Simon, 18 March 1934; 218/4/34, minute sheet by Selous, "Abboud and Company versus Dentamaro and Company," 13 March 1934; FO371/17009, J2329/25/16, Campbell to FO, 25 September 1933; J2343/25/16, Campbell to FO, 27 September 1933; 17996, J667/71/16, Lampson to FO, 9 March 1934; 17978, J1228/9/16, Heathcote-Smith to Cairo, 7 May 1934; and 18019, J1772/1772/16, memo by Thompson; USRG 59, 1930–39, 883.00/777, Rives Childs to State, 23 September 1933.

26. See FO371/17003, J507/15/16, Farrer to Cairo, 23 February 1932.

27. FO371/19086, J348/348/16, enclosing letter from Simpson to Nasim Pasha, 31 December 1935.

28. FO371/19086, J1484/348/16, Lampson to FO, 5 April 1935, reporting interview between Selous and Horsfall, 3 April 1935.

29. FO371/19086, J602/348/16, DOT, record of interview with Nelson and Rice, 14 February 1935.

30. See FO371/19086, J1495/348/16, Kelly to FO, 11 April 1935; J1598/348/16, record of interview with Nelson, Rice, Crowe and Farrer, 17 April 1935; and J978/348/16, DOT, 12 March 1935 (Grey quote). Also see J1229/348/16, DOT, 27 March 1935, which includes copies of cables between the firms and their Cairo representatives.

31. ICI's partners included Chase National Bank (New York) and U.S. Westinghouse. For ICI's links to the EEC, see FO371/17984, J2984/31/16, Selous to DOT, 13 November 1934; the "syndicate" quote is found in FO371/19086, J1598/348/16, record of interview with Nelson, Rice, Crowe and Farrer, 17 April 1935; the "diversion" quote is found in J1484/348/16, Lampson to FO, 5 April 1935, reporting interview between Selous and Horsefall, the EEC director, 3 April 1935.

32. FO371/19086, J2290/348/16, enclosing letter from 'Abd al-Wahhab to EEC, 5 June 1935; J9171/348/16, Lampson to FO, 29 November 1935, and J8889/348/16, DOT, 5 December 1935; USRG 59, 1930–39, 883.659 Fertilizers/1, Merriam to State, 5 September 1935.

33. FO371/23358, J343/285/16, enclosing letter from Jacob Maller [the British investor in the iron-ore deposits] to Sir Ernest Roney [Maller's attorney], 24 January 1939.

34. On the delays and dissent in the EEC scheme, see Chamber of Deputies (1948: 5–6); FO371/20139, J3628/445/16, enclosing letter from Grey [EEC, Cairo] to Nelson [EEC, London], 17 April 1936; J3491/445/16,

Lampson to FO, 26 April 1936; J3559/445/16, Lampson to FO, 22 April 1936; and J3619/445/16, Lampson to FO, 28 April 1936; *Killearn Diaries* 23 April 1936. For the EEC's attempt to disguise a long-running connection to 'Uthman Muharram, see FO371/20144, J4104/1553/16, Lampson to FO, 8 May 1936; FO371/20139, J4845/445/16, enclosing Selous to DOT, 12 May 1936; and J4261/445/16, Farrer to Pink, 12 May 1936.

35. FO371/20139, J7414/445/16, memorandum by Lampson, 1 September 1936.

36. For 'Abbud's opposition to Wafd, see FO371/20119, J7708/2/16, FO minute (Pink), 17 September 1936; for the composition of the opposition bloc, see FO371/20120, J8211/2/16, Kelly to Houston-Boswell, 13 October 1936; and for an example of British assumptions about 'Abbud's political activities, see FO371/20915, J811/623/16, Lampson to Eden, 15 February 1937.

37. See, for instance, FO371/20915, J811/623/16, Lampson to Eden, 15 February 1937.

38. For 'Ali Mahir's rejection of the EEC's claims to some exclusive right under the June 1935 letter, see FO371/20139, J3559/445/16, Lampson to FO, 22 April 1936. Makram also misled the Egyptian public on the matter of concessions. While the terms of the original proposal envisioned a 51 percent (Egyptian private and public)–49 percent (foreign) split in share capital, the initiative for a change came from the foreign bankers, before the Wafd took office. See J4035/445/16, enclosing memorandum by Watson (financial adviser to the Egyptian government), 25 April 1936. And, despite the government's public claim, foreigners were expected to hold shares in the venture as well as finance the debenture. See FO371/20915, J1186/623/16, memo from Selous, 5 March 1937, recounting conversation with Nelson (EEC chairman) on his negotiations with Makram. Compare with Egyptian government document excerpted in *al-Ahram* 15 August 1937, titled "Memorandum from the Minister of Public Works to Cabinet" (n.d.).

39. *al-Balagh* 6 September 1937; *Majalla ghurfa al-Iskandariya* 9, April 1937; Chamber of Deputies (1948: 6); FO371/20915, J623/623/16, draft telegram to Lampson, 11 February 1937; J811/623/16, Lampson to Eden, 15 February 1937; J1645/623/16, Lampson to FO, 5 April 1937 and including letter from Makram 'Ubayd, 1 April 1937.

40. For details see FO371/20915, J1891/623/16, Lampson to DOT, 7 April 1937. The embassy and companies also concerted on the organization of the new advisory committees. For details of the process, see J1965/J2332/623/16.

41. On the entreaties to Mahmud in 1938, see FO371/21993, J400/78/16, enclosing record of conversations between Lampson and Mahmud, 15 January 1938; J559/78/16, letter from Grey to Selous, 31 January 1938; *Killearn Diaries* 17, 24 and 25 March 1938. For the 1939 round, see, for example, FO371/23358, J1433/285/16, Lampson to FO, 5 April 1939; J2675/285/16, Lampson to FO, 26 June 1939; and the *Killearn Diaries* 26 and 30 May, 24 and 26 June, and 3 and 22 July 1939.

4. War within "the War"

1. See FO371/23355, J2676/234/16, Lampson to FO, 26 June 1939.

2. On Mahir's business connection with 'Abbud, see FO371/23355, J3126/234/16, enclosing letter from Kelly (FO) to Sir Julian Foley, Board of Trade, 10 August 1939. As Killearn would later write, "Abboud was of course a particular friend and confidant of [Ahmad Mahir] with whom he had for years past the closest ties." See FO371/45919, J974/3/16, Lampson to FO, 6 March 1945. These ties were confirmed by 'Abbud's daughter, Mrs. Mona 'Abbud-Husayn, interview, London, August 1986.

3. 'Abbud had been discovered the previous summer in a Paris hotel room with the wife of a Syrian from Alexandria. According to Lampson, the aggrieved husband possessed a number of letters from 'Abbud to his mistress, which, "while containing compromising expressions of affection, also included accounts of 'Abbud's daily business activities." Eager for revenge, the husband turned some of the letters over to the Wafd, and the party published them in *al-Wafd al-Misri*. The most compromising bragged of Mahir's value in helping 'Abbud with his subsidy. The paper promised that more revelations would follow. FO371/23355, J2676/234/16, Lampson to FO, 26 June 1939; 'Abd al-'Azim Ramadan (1978: 236–239); Davis (1983: 155–156). These latter sources accept at face value the opposition's claim that 'Abbud served as a front man for British capitalists.

4. For the negotiations between 'Abbud and the British government, see FO371/23355, J3126/234/16, *et seq.*; FO371/27458, J579/201/16, Lampson to FO, 26 February 1940. Amin 'Uthman served as the businessman's intermediary. For the account of the "lobbying amongst deputies and other subterranean work" in the Aswan scheme, see FO371/23359, J4875/285/16, Lampson to FO, 27 November 1939.

5. FO371/24622, J67/67/16, Somerville-Smith to Cook, 2 January 1940.

6. FO371/J2701/285/16, Nelson (EEC) to Cavendish-Bentinck (FO), 7 July 1939, and enclosures; J2713/285/16, Lampson to FO, 7 July 1939; J3022/285/16, Nelson to Kelly (FO), 1 August 1939; J3148/285/16, Rice (EEC) to Kelly, 10 August 1939.

7. For the "fallah" quote, see FO371/23359, JJ4875/285/16, Lampson to FO, 27 November 1930; on the effort to block the Yahya group, see FO371/23359, J2356/285/16, Cavendish-Bentinck to Bennett (Alexandria), 8 July 1939; also FO371/24622, Cook (Treasury) to Jopson (Department of Overseas Trade—DOT), 13 February 1940; and FO371/23359, J5071/285/16, Somerville-Smith (Export Credits Guarantee Department—ECGD) to Waley (Treasury), 28 December 1939.

8. Killearn, quoting a company representative, in his *Diaries* 20 October 1939. See as well the entry for 6 November 1939, for the ambassador's contribution to mapping out the EEC's lobbying strategy.

9. For the EEC's new terms, see FO371/23359, J4224/285/16, Lampson to FO, 18 October 1939. For a contemporary perception of the structural pressures impinging on Mahir, see FO371/24622, J67/67/16, Somerville-Smith (ECGD) to Cook (Treasury), 2 January 1940.

10. FO371/23359, J5040/285/16, Lampson to FO, 21 December 1939.

11. For this remarkably swift turn around, see FO371/23359, J4993/285/16, Waley (Treasury) to Mullins (DOT), 14 December 1939, and enclosures; J5050/285/16, Waley to Thomson (FO), 21 December 1939; and J5071/285/16, Somerville-Smith (ECGD) to Waley, 28 December 1939. Parts of the economic bureaucracy tried to distance themselves from the past history of exclusive support for the EEC and laid the blame for the policy on the Foreign Office. The Board of Trade appears to have continued to support the EEC. As one participant recalled, "In the meantime, another group in this country with large American participation [i.e., BTH and American Cyanamid] entered the field in full knowledge that their action was contrary to the wishes of HMG. The President of the BOT [Board of Trade] asked them to withdraw and was refused." See BT11/1151 1941, "The Spears Mission" file, letter from H. Somerville-Smith to Ronald Overton (BT), 1 March 1941.

12. FO371/24622, J648/67/16, Lampson to FO, 24 February 1940; and J857/67/16, Lampson to FO, 17 March 1940.

13. See *Killearn Diaries* 8 and 9 April 1940; FO371/24622, J1221/67/16, Lampson to FO, 12 April 1940; FO371/24625, J1500/92/16 [Green File], Lampson to FO, 20 May 1940; and BT11/1511 1941, "The Spears Mission" file, letter from Somerville-Smith to Overton (BT), 1 March 1941.

14. See FO371/27396, J1846/3/16, FO Minute, 3 June 1941; J1852/3/16, Ministry of Supply, 10 June 1941; and FO371/27407, J737/9/16, FO Minute (Bateman), 26 March 1941.

15. See BT11/1511 1941, "The Spears Mission" file, Somerville-Smith, Egypt, correspondence regarding the proposed Aswan Dam and nitrate scheme, minute sheet, 27 November 1941. This does not preclude the possibility that the Egyptians were lobbying for the scheme. The MESC request might have been in response, but I did not find documentation on this.

16. See BT11/1151 1941, "The Spears Mission" file, letter from Somerville-Smith to Overton (BT), 1 March 1941.

17. See FO371/31583, J289/289/16, Nixon (United Kingdom Commercial Corporation) to Scrivener (FO), 17 January 1942, and enclosures.

18. FO371/35586, J3432/844/16, minute by E. Chapman-Andrews.

19. FO371/35586, J4559/844/16, Cairo Chancery to Egyptian Department, 27 October 1943; FO371/35534, J2119/2/16.

20. This is a paraphrase of the explanation for the Wafd's tolerance of corruption. See FO371/35536, Kellar to Scrivener, 7 June 1943, "The Black Book and Its Moral," cited in Warburg (1985: 155, n. 98) (file number omitted in citation); also FO371/80348, J1016/25, Labor Counsellor, Cairo, to FO, 7 January 1950. For a description of 'Abbud as the money behind the Wafd, given by the French ambassador to the chairman of the Suez Canal Company, see FO371/80521, JE1016/71, Sir Francis Wyle to Allan, 22 August 1950.

21. The basic files on this case are found in FO371/31556, 31557 and 35563. For Makram 'Ubayd's attack on 'Abbud, see FO371/31557, J2475/7/16, enclosing Lampson to FO, 26 May 1942; for the "thief's bargain" quote, see J5081/7/16, Ministry of War Transport [UK], 26 November 1942, and enclosures; for the terms of the agreement finally concluded with the help of 'Abbud's friend, Lord Woolton, see FO371/35563, J2324/10/16, Killearn to FO, 23 May 1943, J2352/10/16, Ministry of War Transport to FO, 21 May 1943, and J2382/10/16, Killearn to FO, 31 May 1943; for evidence that 'Abbud was negotiating behind the government's backs see *Killearn Diaries* 17 June 1943, which notes both 'Abbud's concern to keep the details from the authorities and Lampson's acquiescence to 'Abbud's scheme. Makram 'Ubayd later attacked the government for its role in this deal. See Killearn's account of the "sequel" to the *Black Book*, FO371/41326, J526/31/16, Killearn to FO, 30 January 1944. Finally, the account in Woolton (1959), while colorful, should not be read without consulting the FO documents.

22. On the contract, see FO371/35586, J4559/844/16, Cairo Chancery to Egyptian Department, 27 October 1943.

23. FO371/35530, J1409/2/16, Lampson to FO, 26 March 1943.

24. FO371/35586, J4445/844/16, Shone to FO, 24 October 1943; FO371/41305, J972/3/16, Killearn to FO, 8 March 1943, including note by Empson, "Holdings of Abboud Pasha in Bank Misr," 15 November 1943.

25. The quote is from FO371/41305, J972/3/16, Killearn to FO, 8 March 1944, emphasis mine. This file contains details of the plan. For Amin's original approach to Lampson, see *Killearn Diaries* 11 February 1944. Lampson noted that "Amin . . . obviously had his knife deep into Hafiz Afifi."

26. See FO371/41305, J3/3/16, Killearn to Cadogan, 17 December 1943, and enclosures.

27. For Amin's attack in parliament in July and the king's visit a short time later, see FO371/41331, J2953/31/16, Lampson to FO, 8 August 1944. The ambassador's account is straightforward: "There can be no doubt that these two royal visits were designed as a demonstration against the recent attacks made by Amin Osman," and "it has been evident that the Palace was in sympathy with Hafiz Afifi as against Abboud and Amin Osman." 'Abbud later recalled this as one of the two failures of his life. See *Akhbar al-Yawm* 4 January 1947.

28. *Killearn Diaries* 26 November 1943; FO141/875, the embassy's internal file on 'Abbud, enclosing a dispatch from Killearn to FO, 28 November 1943.

29. For Makram's appeal, see FO371/31556, J865/7/16, Lampson to FO, 21 February 1942; other interventions by the minister of public works and the prime minister are found in J844/844/16, Lampson to FO, 18 February 1943; and FO371/35586, J2165/844/16, Lampson to FO, 12 May 1943.

30. See, for instance, the minute attached to FO371/31583, J3202/289/16, Lampson to FO, 16 July 1942.

31. See FO371/41305, J3/3/16, Killearn to Cadogan, 17 December 1943, and enclosures, which documents Lampson's strong support. The quote is found in a minute to this file. In addition, see J972/3/16, enclosing note by

financial counselor, 6 March 1944; and J1194/3/16, Leach (DOT) to Scrivener, 30 March 1944.

32. See FO371/35586, J5100/844/16, enclosing Dalton to Lyttelton [minister of state for middle east affairs, Cairo], 17 December 1943, and Eden to Lyttelton, 31 December 1943; FO371/41305, J149/3/16, Lyttelton to Eden, 8 January 1944. For the policy debates themselves, see, for example, BT11/1151, "The Spears Mission" file, correspondence of H. Somerville-Smith, minute sheet, 6 December 1943; FO371/35586, J4233/844/16, O'Neill (Ministry of War Transport) to Scrivener, 8 October 1943. J4445/844/16, enclosing Peterson to Cairo, 16 November 1943.

33. Peterson, another FO official, showed that he had not forgotten his department's attitude to the Egyptian businessman before the war: "He is a rascal but I agree that we cannot ignore and must have him." Both quotes found in FO371/35586, J5100/844/16, BOT, 20 December 1943, and enclosures.

34. See the revealing series of minutes and dispatches contained in FO371/41397, J756/756/16, including Killearn to Peterson, 18 February 1944.

35. FO371/35586, J4852/844/16, Kennedy to Roberts, November 1943, for reports of the misgivings of Nelson, the EEC chairman; J4925/844/16, Lampson to FO, 5 December 1943; J5240/844/16, enclosing Grey to 'Abbud, 13 December 1943, and 'Abbud to Grey, 14 December 1943.

36. FO371/41305, J376/3/16, FO to Cairo, 3 February 1944, repeated to Washington; FO371/35586, J5240/844/16, Grey to 'Abbud, 13 December 1943, and 'Abbud to Grey, 14 December 1943.

37. USRG 59, 1940–44, Box 5158, 883.6463/32, memos by Parker, 18 and 20 March 1944; 883.6463/20, Kirk to State, 21 March 1944; 883.6463/26, enclosing memorandum by Warfield, 10 March 1944; and 883.6463/30, Tuck (Landis) to State, 20 June 1944; FO371/41305, J1058/3/16, Lampson to FO, 23 March 1944, and J1083/3/16, Killearn to FO, 24 March 1944; FO371/41306, J1606/3/16, Lyal (DOT) to Scrivener, 1 May 1944, and J1620/3/16, Lyal to FO, 4 May 1944; BT11/1151, Somerville-Smith correspondence, memo 218, 26 April 1944, and brief 217 by Mullins, 27 April 1944.

38. For evidence of Badrawi 'Ashur's involvement in the Delta Scheme, see FO371/41305, J1739/3/16, enclosing Campbell to Empson, 27 April 1944.

39. See FO371/41305, J1083/3/16, Lampson to FO, 24 March 1944; FO371/41306, J1896/3/16, Lampson to FO, 22 May 1944; J2061/3/16, enclosing telegram from EEC to Grey (in letter to Scrivener), 13 June 1944; and J2213/3/16, Lampson to FO, 16 June 1944. These files confirm the EEC's involvement.

40. For details, see FO371/41307, J2778/3/16, enclosing message from ICI to ICI Cairo, 5 August 1944, and J3034/3/16, 'Abbud to Scrivener, 28 August 1944.

41. FO371/41307, J3166/3/16, DOT, 7 September 1944; USRG 59, 1940–44, Box 5158, 883.6463/9-1144, State to Cairo, 11 September 1944.

42. For evidence of 'Abbud's lobbying, see FO371/41305, J153/3/16,

Scrivener to Gilbert, 12 January 1944; FO371/41331, J2752/31/16, Lampson to Eden, 14 July 1944; and *Killearn Diaries* March 22, 1944. Warburg's discussion of "collaboration" in the 1942–1944 period leads him to mischaracterize 'Abbud as acting at Lampson's behest ("used . . . the good services of 'Abbud Pasha") (1985: 148).

43. FO371/41307, J2678/3/16, Scrivener to Leach, 14 August 1944; USRG 59, 1940–44, Box 5158, 883.6374/7-2044, State to London, 20 July 1944; 883.6374/7-2644, London to State, 26 July 1944; 883.6463/9-1144, State to Cairo, 11 September 1944; *Egyptian Gazette* 11 August 1944.

44. FO371/45980, J1836/142/16, Lampson to FO, 31 May 1945; FO371/53394, J435/435/16, Gilbert (DOT) to Scrivener, 28 January 1946; and J504/435/16, enclosing Empson to Gilbert, 30 January 1946.

45. See FO371/20898 J3270/61/16, enclosing memorandum from Lord McGowan to Sir R. Vansittart, 13 July 1937.

5. Power and the Postcolonial State

1. See Central Intelligence Agency, Situation Reports, SR-13, 27 September 1949, Truman Papers, President's Secretary's Files, Box 260, Truman Library. Similarly see the 11 April 1947 address by Mahmud Hassan, first Egyptian ambassador to the United States, stressing development of Egypt's water-power resources. Truman Papers, White House Central Files, Office File, OF 283, Box 913, Egypt, Truman Library.

2. USRG 59, 1940–44, Box 5158, 883.6463/11-1144, memorandum of conversation on the Aswan Dam project, 11 November 1944, and 883.6463/11-2444, Landis to State, 24 November 1944; RG 151, Box 4102, file marked "Construction and Development"; FO371/45979, J1006/142/16, Lampson to FO, 6 March 1945, and Campbell to Empson, 14 February 1945.

3. See the correspondence intercepted by the British censorship service and enclosed in FO371/41307, J3830/3/16, Shone to FO, 26 October 1944; and J4141/3/16, Pope to 'Abbud, 26 October 1944.

4. For details see USRG 59, 1945–49, Box 6914, 883.655/2745, Hudson to State, 27 July 1945; FO371/45979, J738/142/16, Killearn to FO, 19 February 1945; FO371/45943, J2296/19/16, Lampson to FO, 5 July 1945; FO371/53394, Empson to Gilbert, 30 January 1945; and *Killearn Diaries* 22 December 1945.

5. See FO371/45980, J1836/142/16, Lampson to FO, 31 May 1945; on the bargaining taking place at this time, see FO371/45979, J1226/J1285/142/16; FO371/45980, J1757/142/16; FO371/45921, J1755/3/16; and the *Killearn Diaries* 19 May 1945.

6. *Egyptian Gazette*, 3 and 15 June 1945; Chamber of Deputies (1948: 9; FO371/45980, J1829/142/16, Lampson to FO, 31 May 1945; FO371/45943, J2052/19/16, Lampson to FO, 21 June 1945.

7. See the *Killearn Diaries* 6 and 31 March, 5 July, 15 and 22 December 1945.

8. See Export Import Bank of the United States archives, Denison to Maffry, memorandum regarding "Ammonia Fertilizer Plant in Egypt," 26 June 1946, released through the Freedom of Information Act (FOIA) and in my possession.

9. See FO371/53394, J504/435/16, Empson to Gilbert, 30 January 1946; and J3900/435/16, Campbell to FO, 14 September 1946.

10. See the *Killearn Diaries* 19 May 1945; FO371/45980, J1972/142/16, Lampson to FO, 9 June 1945.

11. FO371/53394, J1325/435/16, memo by Bowker, 20 March 1946.

12. For details, see FO371/53394, J1196/435/16, Betts to Short [EEC], 2 March 1946; J5158/435/16, enclosing memorandum on the Aswan Dam Electrification Project, November 1946.

13. USRG 84, Box 243, 510.21, "Electrical Development Company," Cairo 1187, May 23 1950, and 1589, July 5, 1950; Shishini is sometimes described as a Westinghouse consultant. See Qaddah 1979; interview with Qaddah, Cairo, 24 April 1985.

14. See FO371/53394, J5158/435/16, Lyal to Scrivener, 5 December 1946; and FO371/63023, J4620/100/16, which includes a memo from Speyer, a director of ICI in London, to Mackay, the head of their Cairo office, 8 September 1947.

15. For 'Abbud's negotiations to secure the release of hard currency to finance the Delta deal, see FO371/53394, J4012/435/16, France to Riches, 25 September 1946; J4279/435/16, Bowker to FO, 12 October 1946; and J5158/435/16, Lyal to Scrivener, 5 December 1946. Completion of 'Abbud's Suez factory was delayed by continued supply bottlenecks in Great Britain, which required him to shift a larger part of the order to U.S. manufacturers.

16. FO371/53394, J4279/435/16, Bowker to FO, 12 October 1946.

17. The difficulties with finding dollars for the project and for Egyptian imports more generally can be traced in USRG 59, 1945–49, 883.51/12-3046, Tuck to State, 30 December 1946; 883.51/1-2247, Marshall to Embassy, 20 February 1947; 883.51/11-1047, Tuck to State, 10 November 1947; and 883.5151/10-747, memo by Polk, "Dollar Crisis," 26 September 1947. Details on Westinghouse's postbid maneuvers can be found in USRG 59, 1945–49, 883.4A/3-1047, Acheson to Embassy, 10 March 1947.

18. On the government's optimism after the signing of the Anglo Egyptian Financial Agreement (30 June 1947), see USRG 59, 1945–49, 883.5151/7-2147, Embassy to State, 21 July 1947; and 883.5151/9-347, Patterson to State, 3 September 1947, dispatched after the Atlee government suspended all of its convertibility agreements.

19. For the estimates of foreign exchange, see USRG 59, 1945–49, 883.5151/10-747, memo by Polk, 26 September 1947; and 883.5151/2-248, Doherty to State, 2 February 1948; for the impact of the exchange crisis and details of the negotiations, see FO371/63023, J5181/100/16, BT, 27 October 1947; and J5323/100/16, Cairo to FO, 27 October 1947; for the continuing political fall out from the exchange crisis, which included the dis-

missal of a key undersecretary and Nuqrashi's personally taking over the finance portfolio, see USRG 59, 1945–49, 883.51/11-1047, Tuck to State, 10 November 1947; and 883.51/11-2247, Tuck to State, 22 November 1947.

20. See FO371/63023, J3090/100/16, Lyttelton to McNeil, 27 June 1947. The quotations are drawn from correspondence between the Cairo embassy and the Board of Trade, found in J3314/100/16.

21. Information from Ahram Foundation Archives, Cairo, folder marked "khazan Aswan, kahraba khazan Aswan, no. 99"; and interview with Geoffrey Kennedy, Jr., August 9, 1986, Thetford, England.

22. FO371/14219, J5926/14219/16, Stephen [John Cochrane and Sons Ltd.] to Bevin, 15 July 1949; J6774/14219/16, Fitch [ECGD], 23 August 1949; and J9450/14219/16, Campbell to FO, 30 November 1949.

23. USRG 84, Box 238, 504.14, memorandum, "North Cairo Power Plant," 30 January 1950; FO371/80523, JE1423/16, Campbell to FO, 16 May 1950.

24. FO371/80523, JE1423/16, Campbell to FO, 16 May 1950.

25. See USRG 59, 1950–54, 774.13/11-2250, Cairo 1196, Caffery to State, 22 November 1950, "Significance of Cabinet Changes"; and 774.13/1-251, for the royal decree establishing the HAC in December 1950. These events are discussed further in Chapter 6.

26. These decisions, taken in the Ministry of Public Works in September, were approved by Nagib's cabinet in November 1952. I have based this paragraph on the following: al-Ahram 30 August 1953; 'Abd al-'Aziz Ahmad (1955: 66); FO 371/102782, JE1101/1, Monthly Economic Report 55, December 1952; and interview with Hamid al-Qaddah, 14 July 1985. In addition, see Waterbury (1983: 60) and Moore (1980: 156–157) for partially conflicting accounts.

6. Indigenous Roots of Egypt's Socialist Transformation

1. For background on the reform efforts of the late 1940s and 1950s, see Tignor (1982: 20–55) and Gordon (1989). On the antiregime opposition movement and the regime's response, see Beinin and Lockman (1987: 335–359, 369–376, 399–403, 412–417). On the views of businessmen, see for instance al-Ahram interview with Hafiz 'Afifi, 25 August 1951; and USRG 59, 1950–54, 774/3-2351, Caffery to State, reporting conversation with the Sa'adist party president Ibrahim 'Abd al-Hadi.

2. USRG 59, 774.00/3-1050, Caffery to State.

3. FO371/80348, JE1016/36, Creswell, 14 March 1950; USRG 59, 774.00/3-2351, desp. 2275, Caffery to State, 23 March 1951. My discussion is indebted to, draws heavily on, and respectfully dissents at key points from that of Gordon (1989: 196–197, 204–206).

4. For the resignation of Husayn, see USRG 59, 1950–54, 774.00/7-3151, desp. 223, "The Inner Story of Ahmed Hussein's Resignation"; and Gordon (1989: 205). My reading of the conflict as entailing a backlash against Husayn's overzealous accumulation of power at the expense of other ministerial agencies (rather than his ignoring party patronage lines) is buttressed by the post-1952 description of "muddled administration with all its irrationalities" that was partly the outgrowth of Husayn's tenure. Ayubi (1980: 188–189).

5. See USRG 59, Lot File S5D5, Box 3, folder labeled "Background Information 1950," document titled "Political Instability in Egypt," Secret Security Information IR 5782, Office GIR/IDR, n.d. Quotations in this paragraph taken from pp. 1, 5 and 14.

6. For Habashi's endorsement of the Wafd, see USRG 59, 1950–54, 774.00/1-1150, desp. 1232, Caffery to State.

7. See, for instance, USRG 59, 1950–54, 874.1521/1-2750, Cairo, no. 102; 874.152/5-1250 Cairo, no. 1061; 874.152/5-2750, incoming tel. 568; 874.152/6-1950 Cairo, no. 1414; 874.152/8-1451, desp. 263, Caffery to State; and 774.13/11-2250, Caffery to State, 22 November 1950.

8. See the account by Laszlo [Ladislas] Pathy [Polnauer], Hungarian Project, Interview 1077, Oral History Research Office, Columbia University, 1977, p. 34.

9. For the controversies surrounding the terms of and control over economic programs, see USRG 59, 1950–54, 774.13/7-1050; 774.13/7-2950; 774.13/11-2250, Cairo 1196; and 774.13/11-2550, Cairo 1222.

10. USRG 59, 1945–49, 883.659/7-549, Cairo Embassy to State; *Egyptian Gazette,* 19 April and 15 December 1950; USRG 84, Cairo Post Files, Box 236, Cairo 1430, Adams to State, 18 December 1950; Sirag al-din interview in *al-Ahram* 9 September 1951. I have been unable to trace the outcome of the Monsanto joint venture.

11. For subsidies awarded by the Wafd, see the *Egyptian Gazette,* 24 July, 3 and 4 November 1950. For Sirag al-din's role in resolving the oil-pricing dispute, see USRG 59, 1950–54, 874.2553/5-1051, Lager to State, "Petroleum Developments in Egypt," April 1951.

12. Beinin and Lockman (1987: 399–400); Mahmud Mutawalli (1985: 79–380). In addition, see Tignor (1989: 61) for evidence that the Misr group escaped the government's employment regulations. The "people's party" quote is found in the U.S. embassy's report of the opposition's attack on the Wafd-'Abbud connection. See USRG 59, 1950–54, 774.00/8-2450, Caffery to State, no. 467, "Propaganda of the Opposition."

13. ExIm Bank Archives, "Memorandum to the Board of Directors Re: Eximbank Mission to Egypt," 4 May 1950; 'Abbud to Arey [ExIm Bank], 27 November 1951; USRG 59, 1950–54, 874.3972/11-851, Caffery to State, 26 September 1951.

14. For 'Abbud's expansion plans and the course of the new loan applications, see USRG 59, Lot File 5SD5, folder "Aid and Loans," memo From Jones to Kopper, n.d (but probably early 1952); and Truman Library, Papers of Dean Acheson, Memoranda of Conversations, 1952, Box 67, 22 April 1952. For 'Abbud's role as a conduit between Caffery and Sirag al-din during the

unfolding crisis, see FO141/1451 [1951, "Egypt Change of Government"], 10121/18/51G, Wardle-Smith, 8 November 1951. The financial pressure has not previously been disclosed. On the diplomacy of the crisis, see Louis (1984: 686–700, 720–735), Hahn (1991: 93–139), Aronson (1986: 25–38), and Sayed-Ahmed (1989: 26–32).

15. On the founding of Banque du Caire, SAE, see USRG 59, 1950–54, Box 5375, Lardicos to State, 7 June 1952, reporting the royal decree published in [Official Journal], no. 82, 15 May 1952.

16. See USRG 59, 1950–54, 774.00/4-2851, Cairo no. 2566, "Current Internal Political Situation in Egypt." Compare with 774.00/9-1851, desp. 729, "'The Real Situation' in Egypt," forwarding Mustafa Amin's editorial in *Akhbar al-Yawm* September 8, 1951.

17. For details of the conflict over tax reform, see USRG 59, 1950–54, 774.13/3-2051, embassy desp. 1964, 16 February 1951, "Overwhelming Parliamentary Vote of Confidence for Egyptian Minister of Finance." For background on the tax question, see the (partially conflicting) accounts in Deeb (1984: 433–434) and Hansen (1991: 93).

18. See, for example, the assessment by Ahmad Husayn, the former minister of social affairs, who was being cultivated by the Amins and was involved by the fall in a plan to seek power in the name of what Caffery called an "honest opposition." USRG 59, 1950–54, 774.00/10-551, desp. 882, 5 October 1951, "Continued Activities of Former Minister of Social Affairs"; and Sayed-Ahmed (1989: 40–42). For the treaty-abrogation issue's relation to organized antiestablishment groups like labor, other parts of the left, the Muslim Brothers and the dissident army officers, see Beinin and Lockman (1987: 406–410), Botman (1988: 100–104), and Gordon (1992: 25–27, 49–51).

19. USRG 59, 1950–54, 774.11/11-350, Cairo 1050, 3 November 1950, "King's Return to Cairo," emphasis mine.

20. Elias Andraos, who recounted the story of 'Abbud in an interview at the British embassy, noted that he had immediately reneged on the pledge, while the strike fund was the excuse he used to obtain the cabinet's agreement to a rise in the price of sugar. See FO141/1451, 10121/4/51G, Conversation with Andraos, 29 October 1951; on Sirag al-din and the Free Officers, see Gordon (1992: 50).

21. See USRG 59, 774.00/10-551, desp. 882, Caffery to State, 5 October 1951, "Continued Activities of Former Minister of Social Affairs"; and Gordon (1989: 209). Caffery's studied noncommitment no doubt contributed to Husayn's view that conditions in Egypt would get worse before they got better and to his gradual disenchantment with the machinations of the Amin brothers. Also, see businessman and ex-finance ministry official Galil al-Imari's assessment that the Wafd had to be kept in power to resolve the crisis and that plans for a reform-oriented coalition no longer made sense. USRG 84, Box 236, memorandum of conversation between Caffery and Imari, 8 December 1951.

22. For example, see FO141/1451, 10121/17/51G, reporting Mustafa Amin's plan to depose the government, n.d. [but probably late October or early November 1951]. The public standard bearers of the 1950–1952 anticorruption campaign, newspaper owners Mustafa Amin and 'Ali Amin, eventu-

ally (and quietly) offered a U.S. multinational its own private feature column in their papers for a program of pro–oil company propaganda. See USRG 59, 1950–54, 874.2553/6-153, desp. 2620, June 1 1953, "Socony-Vacuum Plans for Press Relations in Egypt."

23. Details on the widening dissent to the government's fiscal, tariff and price-support policies are found in USRG 84, Box 238, desp. 2366, May 23 1952, "Transmittal of Annual Report for 1951 of Egyptian Federation of Industries"; Box 240, memorandum, Parker to Caffery, 26 November 1951, "Drop in Egyptian Pound Quotations in Relation to Egyptian Cotton Prices"; USRG 59, 1950–54, 874.152/8-1451, desp. 263, 4 August 1951, "Government Regulations on Cotton Sales"; and 874.152/9-1151, desp. 639, 11 September 1951, "Financial Aspects of Egyptian Government's Intervention in Cotton Market."

24. See USRG 59, 1950–54, 774.11/3-2951, Cairo, no. 2334, March 29, 1951, Relations between the King and Certain Court Personalities; 774.00/10-2051, desp. 997, Caffery to State, 20 October 1951, Appointment of Andraos Pasha as Honorary Economic Adviser to the Royal Khassa; Tignor (1989: 72–73).

25. See USRG 59, 774.521/4-2253, desp. 2217, Caffery to State, 22 April 1953, Confidential Biographical Data—Mustafa Amin. Caffery reported the credible rumors that the Amins were paid by a host of interested factions.

26. See USRG 59, 1950–54, 774.00/12-2551, tel. 945, 25 December 1951; and 74.00/1-1152, Caffery to State, 11 January 1952, Changes in Board of Directors of Bank Misr. If there is any doubt that 'Afifi and Andraos were cooperating at this point, it should be put to rest by the naming of Andraos as managing director of Bank Misr and his appointment to the board of several of the Misr-group subsidiaries simultaneously with 'Afifi's resignation.

27. FO141/1451, 10121/17/51G, Murray's Conversation with Mustafa Amin; USRG 59, 1950–54, 774.00/10-551, desp. 882, Caffery to State, 5 October 1951, Continued Activities of Former Minister of Social Affairs; Sayed-Ahmad (1989: 41).

28. See USRG 59, 874.00-TA/6-2751, Cairo desp. 3023, June 21, 1951, Chamber of Deputies Approves Point IV Agreement.

29. See USRG 59, 774.00/3-552 tel. 1491, 5 March 1952. There is simply not enough information at hand to construct a coherent explanation for Husayn's choice at this juncture, save to say that the reasons he gave to the ambassador are in and of themselves unconvincing. He was a prime architect of a plan in the fall of 1951 to have the palace engineer an overthrow of an elected government, when "the public" was no more concerned with corruption than in March 1952. Yet, when Caffery asked him what he and his group would do if it came into power, "Dr. Hussein replied that one of its first acts would be to try most of the members of the present government in regular Egyptian courts on criminal charges." See 774.00/10-551, desp. 882, 5 October 1951.

30. "We have these reclamation experts here from the United States on Point IV for the next two years. They are not telling us to break up the estates. That's what he [Mahmud Zaki Salam, under-secretary of state, ministry of national economy] thinks you want us to do but they have made it clear at Point

IV that they will not interfere. It is agreed that the Ministry of Social Affairs will pick propertyless peasant families and give the reclaimed land to them in farms no bigger than they can cultivate well. That's what we did at Kafr Saad where you [Caffery] and Mr. Swayzee [Cleon O. Swayzee, assistant to the assistant secretary of state for economic affairs] saw 600 families each with five acres of land to work." See USRG 59, 1950–54, 874.16/6-1652, [dispatch number unreadable], 16 June 1952, Attempt to Revive Land Reform committee.

31. For the American post-mortem on Hilali, see USRG 59, 1950–54, 774.00/7-352, memorandum from Byroade to Bruce, 3 July 1952, Change of Government in Egypt.

32. For instance, Mustafa Amin insisted Sirag al-din played a role. Others implicated Mahmud Abu al-Fath. See FO141/1453 (1952), JE1011/62/52G, record of interview with Mustafa Amin, 19 July 1952. For the message by the *Times* correspondent, see FO371/96876, JE1018/168, Creswell to FO, 1 July 1952. The Foreign Office took credit for keeping King Faruq's name out of the story. JE1018/169, minute attached to the file.

33. For Caffery's accounts of Thabit's background, power and fall, see USRG 59, 1950–54, 774.11/10-851, desp. 3065, Caffery to State, 26 June 1951, Resignation of Kerim Tabet Pasha as Press Counselor to the King; and 774.521/7-1852, desp. 89, Caffery to State, 18 July 1952, Confidential Biographical Data—Kerim Tabet Pasha; for the information on 'Abbud's payment to Thabit, see FO141/1453, JE1011/12/52G, Record of Conversation with Andraos, 24 January 1952.

34. See FO371/96876, JE1018/169, Creswell to FO, 1 July 1952, and enclosures.

35. See FO371/96876, JE1018/174, Franks [British embassy Washington] to FO, 2 July 1952; and JE1018/169, Creswell to FO, 1 July 1952.

36. The material in the last two paragraphs is based on USRG 59, 1950–54, 774.00/7-252, State to Caffery, 2 July 1952 ("venal trio" quote); FO371/96876, JE1018/174, Franks [British embassy, Washington] to FO, 2 July 1952, and enclosures (Allen's rejection of British responsibility in Hilali's downfall); JE1018/175, Creswell to FO, 2 July 1952 (rebuttal of Caffery, assessment of stability); JE1018/179, Creswell to FO, 2 July 1952 (Caffery's ill-advised contacts with 'Abbud); and Hahn (1991: 143–144), who misses these events in detailing Eden's sudden hardening of the line against the Egyptians.

37. See USRG 59, 1950–54, 774.00/4-1652, Further Wafd Maneuvers Against Hilali Government.

38. See USRG 59, 774.13/7-752, desp. no. 16, Caffery to State, 7 July 1952. As Caffery specified, it "is, of course, imperative that both the source of this note and the fact that the American Foreign Service possesses it be guarded most carefully." Ahmad Husayn, whom Haykal later criticizes as being too pro-American in the 1950s, explained his refusal to support Hilali as the result of Hilali's dependence on the British and the Amins. For Haykal's own peculiar recollections of this period, see his *Cutting the Lion's Tail* (1986). Undoubtedly, Haykal would not recognize himself as an agent of the British and the Amins at this key juncture, using the same logic that he employs when describing 'Abbud.

39. Objectively, then, it is difficult to support claims such as one in Hahn (1991: 139) that the Cairo fire "*inaugurated* a period of turmoil and instability in Egypt that *seemed to render the country vulnerable to communist revolution*" (emphasis mine). Unless qualified by the notation that this is how particular American observers saw the situation at particular junctures, and without explaining what constituted "turmoil and instability" in 1952, the argument is more easily made in the reverse—the fire allowed the regime once more to crush the antiestablishment opposition and render the country relatively less vulnerable to communist revolution. Hahn would be hardpressed to find any sign of revolutionary agitation during this period, according to historians of the left such as Botman (1988) and Beinin and Lockman (1987).

40. Papers of Dean Acheson, Memoranda of Conversation, 1952, Box 57, Ministerial Talks in London, June 1952, Summary Minutes, 24 June 1952 [dated 14 July 1952], Eisenhower Library. It should be noted that Stevenson's views followed closely the picture sketched by Thabit in May. See 774.00/5-1352, Caffery to State, 13 May 1952, The Political Past, Present and Future of Egypt According to Kerim Tabet Pasha.

41. See USRG 59, 774.00/7-2352, tel. 408, 23 July 1952, reporting conversation between Creswell and 'Afifi prior to coup. The potentially more important question this document raises is the extent to which (logically to my mind) the king's disastrous purge of the officers' club on 16 July and his strategy more generally toward the military at this juncture were not, as is often implied, the result of the king's own impetuousness or of his being closeted too long with his pimp and his butler.

42. See USRG 59, 874.16/8-2052, Caffery to State, tel. 409, 20 August 1952. "[N]othing [could] more jeopardize TCA in Egypt or elsewhere in Middle East if land reform program linked with Point Four publicity [should] backfire."

43. In developing these arguments about antimonopolism and regulation, I have drawn heavily on conversations with, and the work of, two particularly innovative analysts. See Ritter (1992) and Chaudhry (1989 and 1993).

44. See USRG 486, Records of Agency for International Development, Mission to Egypt, Executive Office, Subject Files (C. Files), 51–56, Box 1, folder 1.1, Numbered Letters, Stevens to Evans, 17 July 1954, letter 97.

45. See *al-Akhbar* archives, file on 'Abbud, no. 425 (article in *Akhbar al-Yawm* 27 December 1952); Gordon (1992: 155). Gordon (following the British at this juncture) emphasizes 'Abbud's attempt to "ingratiate himself" with the regime, but misses what was most important in bringing these two forces together. As Barrawi confirmed for me, 'Abbud was hated by the regime, but nonetheless they needed his resources and abilities as an industrialist. Interview, Cairo, 4 February 1985.

46. For Caffery's assessment, see USRG 84, Box 240, Caffery to State, 20 December 1952. For evidence of the overture from the junta to 'Abbud, see USRG 59, 1950–54, 874.3972/11-952, Williams [the embassy's economic-affairs counselor] to State, 19 November 1952; and FO371/102908, JE1461/3, Duke (Cairo) to Allen (FO), 27 January 1953. I am grateful to Joel Gordon for the latter reference. Also see *Akhbar al-Yawm*, 10 January 1953, which carries an advertisement for an 'Abbud-backed engineering workshop and ma-

chinery importer, Shirka Misr Lil-Handasa wa al-Sayarat, which was to be involved in ammunition and weapons production.

47. For a more recent example, see Zaalouk (1989: 24–27). She argues that the Free Officers failed to grasp that capitalists and landowners were part of the same class and, therefore, "holders of political power" as well. My account (and the officers' many statements) directly contradict this entire line of analysis.

48. USRG 59, 1950–54, 774.5/1-1253, Cairo to State, tel. 1625, 12 January 1953. For 'Imari's involvement in the appointments, see RG84, Cairo, Egypt, 1948–55, Box 238, folder "Egypt, 500, 1952," memorandum of conversation between Williams and Lt. Col. Abd al-Munim Amin, 17 November 1952.

49. Others in this cohort would include Niazi Mustafa, an MIT-trained engineer identified in state department records of the early 1950s as a contractor with U.S. partners and a member of the board of directors of the Kom Ombo Company by 1955. He reemerged in the 1980s with his son as partners with U.S. firms in Egypt's burgeoning agroindustry sector. See USRG 59, 874.053/12-1854, Ellis to State, 18 December 1954. For evidence of Husayn Fahmi's opposition to 'Abbud, in terms much like those used by his British competitors in the 1940s, see Records of ExIm Bank, letter from Ghiardi to Polk, U.S. Treasury, 9 April 1953 [obtained through FOIA request and in my possession]. Note that the Kom Ombo's multi-thousand-acre holdings were exempt from the September 1952 land-reform legislation on the grounds that it was engaged actively in land reclamation.

50. See USRG 59, 1950–54, 774.521/8-2953, desp. 557, 29 August 1953, Confidential Biographical Data—Al Emari; and RG84, Cairo, Egypt, 1948–55, Box 238, folder "Egypt, 500, 1952," memorandum of conversation between Williams and Lt. Col. Abd al-Munim Amin, 17 November 1952.

51. The most reliable chronology of the founding of competing planning agencies is found in Ayubi (1980: 226–228); for the history of planning, see the extremely useful comparative account of Egyptian and Indian experiences by el-Ghazali (1971). On Sidqi, see Waterbury (1983: 69–71). Sidqi served on the short-lived (1952–1953) high committee for planning and coordination. See USRG 486, Box 33, folder 1031, A. D. Little Reports, 1953–54, Sweeney to Nicols, Weekly Report 3, 2 February 1953.

52. See USRG 84, Box 240, memorandum of conversation, Hill (president, W. R. Grace and Co.), Byroade and Stabler, 25 November 1952.

53. See, for example, USRG 59, 1950–54, 874.00 TA/2-951, Cairo 1905, 9 February 1951, Egyptian Papers on Point IV.

54. See, for instance, Foreign Relations of the United States (FRUS), 1952–54, volume IX, no. 1035, p. 1897, Caffery to State, 26 November 1952, where Caffery notes the delays in the new Egyptian regime's aid request. "This derives largely from econ ignorance and inability of young colonels to formulate a sensible program for econ development which cld be appropriately supported by US or UK"; and no. 1054, pp. 1917–1918, Secretary of State to Embassy, 24 December 1952, where proposals are made to expand the numbers of technicians on the Cabot mission.

55. See USRG 59, 1950–54, 874.00 TA/8-2152, Embassy to State, desp. 303, 21 August 1952, enclosing proposal "transmitted to PM by point iv staff 'Point IV Plan for Egypt.' "

56. See USRG 59, 1950–54, 874.00-TA/11-752, State to Embassy, Cairo 967, 7 November 1952; 874.00 TA/2-735, Cairo to State, desp, 1583, 7 February 1953; USRG 486, Mission to Egypt, Executive Office, Subject Files, Box 33, folder "1030, Industrial Survey—1952" and Box 33, folder "1031 A D Little April-December 1953."

57. See USRG 486, Mission to Egypt, Executive Office, Subject Files, Box 33, folder "1031, A.V.[sic] Little, Reports 1953–1954," Cabot to Nicols, 5 February 1953, enclosing draft report to Secretary of State, 5 February 1953, p. 6. On Cabot, see USRG 59, Box 4874, 874.2614/10-2455, 7 November 1955; and the *Christian Science Monitor* 15 April 1953.

58. See Ministry of Commerce and Industry (1955) [A. D. Little 1953, revised 1954]; Arthur D. Little, Inc. (1956); Meyer (1980: 44–45). For the funding of the larger, development effort, FRUS, 1952–54, no. 110, pp. 2005–2007, Andrews (Technical Cooperation Administration) to Ohly (Mutual Security Agency), 3 March 1953. Compare with Hansen and Marzouk (1965: 255), O'Brien (1966: 69–70), and Waterbury (1983: 61).

59. Quoted in *al-Balagh*, 19 April 1953, and translated in USRG 59, 1950–54, 874.00 TA/5-1253, Embassy to State, desp. 2404, Report of Point IV Activities from April 1 through April 30, 1953, 12 May 1953, p. 26.

60. For instance, see the frank admission by key officials that the government's showcase development budgets and timetables in 1953 and 1954 were not achievable. According to 'Ali al-Giritli, "The so-called capital budget merely reflects a schedule of expenditures on development projects which should be undertaken during the year if funds were available." Confirming and expanding on the claim, 'Abd al-Munim al-Qaysuni, who by 1954 was finance minister, admitted that "the limited availability of physical, technical, and administrative facilities" were additional factors hampering development. USRG 59, 1950–54, 774.5 MSP/9-2054, Embassy to State, desp. 505, U.S. Development Assistance, 20 September 1954; and 774.5-MSP/9-1354, Embassy to State, desp. 443, U.S. Development Assistance, 13 September 1954. Compare with Hansen (1991: 98–99).

61. Ministry of Commerce and Industry (1955: 39–41, 144–167). For an extended analysis of the (unrealistic) expectations embodied in the A. D. Little studies, see USRG 59, 1950–54, 774.00/6-154, desp. 2814, "Political Stability Through Economic Development," 1 June 1954. According to Waterbury (1983: 63), £E 8 million was the *total* new investment from abroad between 1953 and 1961.

62. U.S. Council on Economic Policy, Records 1954–1961, Reports Series, Box 3, folder on US Foreign Investments in Less Developed Countries, enclosing National Advisory Council, Staff Document no. 740, Attachment D, "Factors Affecting Private and Public Investment in Egypt," p. 4, Eisenhower Library.

63. See FO371/20898, J3272, McGowan to Vansittart, 13 July 1937, and enclosures. Twenty years later, A. D. Little emerged with essentially the same list of manufacturing ventures.

64. The archival documentation on this long and complicated sectoral conflict is enormous and has yet to be satisfactorily analyzed. For evidence in support of the interpretation advanced here, see USRG 59, 1945–49, 883.6363/8-748, Patterson to State, 7 August 1948; 883.6363/1-749, Patterson to State, 7 January 1949; 1950–54, 874.2553/1-2750, Acheson to State, 27 January 1950; 874.2553/8-2650, Lager to State, 26 August 1950; and USRG 469, Executive Office, Classified Subject Files, Egypt, 1951–54, Grove to Stevens, 28 December 1953. I find little grounds for the claim that the Egyptian government had "gained the upper hand" over these firms in the 1950s. Tignor (1989: 94–99).

65. "Discussing the local industries which must turn to export markets if they are to progress, the Federation stated that the spinning and weaving industry topped the list." See USRG 84, Box 238, folder labeled "500-Egyptian Federation of Industries," Cairo desp. 2366, Peters to State, "Transmittal of Annual Report for 1951 of Egyptian Federation of Industries," 23 May 1952, quoting from summary attached to the translation of the annual report. For conditions underlying this newfound interest in export markets, see Tignor (1989: 59–60).

66. He dismissed "emphatically" the argument used for twenty years to prove that the "interests" of the textile industry had been sacrificed to the needs of the cotton lords. Tignor (1989: 63–64) also discovered splits on the issue and links to a broader debate about reorienting the textile industry, but argues that "most expert opinion" was on the side of importing "cheap" raw cotton.

67. See USRG 486, Mission to Egypt, Executive Office, Subject Files, Box 33, folder "1031 A V [sic] Little," Reports 1953–54, memorandum by Alt, no. 58780, 31 March 1953, "Cotton Textiles." Tignor (1989: 61) suggests that the Filature's chief competitors, the Misr group, successfully avoided the increasing restrictions on firing workers. The Filature's position on the cotton-import question may thus have been designed to stop the Misr group from further expanding its own domestic market share (representatives of the Misr mills had wanted the import ban on cotton lifted).

68. Both quotes are from the original, unpublished version of Maxfield and Nolt (1990: 21). The first is drawn directly from Mikesell (1954); the second is their paraphrase of Mikesell.

69. See USRG 486, Mission to Egypt, Executive Office, Subject Files, Box 33, folder "1032 A. D. Little April-Dec 1953," memorandum, Sweeney to Nichols, "Progress Report Covering Period April 12–June 13, 1953," 15 June 1953, p. 3.

70. See USRG 59, 1955–59, 874.053/3-2957, "Further GOE Penetration Into Private Industry." The A. D. Little mission was not above exaggerating their effectiveness. In their final report, they took credit for the paper-mill venture that 'Abbud had begun to pursue in 1951. See Arthur D. Little, Inc. (1956: 7).

71. See USRG 59, 1955–59, 874.00/7-2156, Second Quarter Economic review, 1956; and 874.053/6-1956. The American partner in this Egyptian-Saudi joint venture was James Lawrence and Company, cotton exporters, whose senior partner sat on the board of G.E. As late as December 1959 Lawrence used the help of Paul Nitze to negotiate an ExIm Bank loan for factory

equipment. Samuel Waugh Papers, Box 3, Alpha Records of Callers 1958–1959, Eisenhower Library.

72. RG 84, Box 259, Cairo Embassy, General Records, Embassy to State, 8 June 1954.

73. For the most thorough account to date, see Gordon (1992: 127–155, 171–174). As he notes (128), the crisis "passed through three distinct phases": (1) February 23–March 1, when Nagib resigned and then returned to office; (2) March 5–25, "played out largely behind closed doors," when Nagib tried "to wrest greater powers from the officers"; and (3) March 25–31, when Nasser and his allies "mobilized loyal street forces to defeat Nagib supporters."

74. On March 25, Nasser promised a return to party political life, a new parliament and the dissolution of the RCC, and then, as the opposition grew bolder, the RCC organized a proauthoritarian alternative linking parts of the army, labor movement and traditional anti-Wafdists like the Amin brothers (and the American embassy). See Gordon (1992: 134–135), On the Wafd's ambitions, see USRG 59, 1950–54, 774.00/3-2754, desp. 2310, 27 March 1954.

75. See USRG 59, 1950–54, 774.00/3-3054, tel. 1213, Caffery to State; and 774.00/3-3154, tel. 1218; Gordon (1992: 135); and Beinin and Lockman (1987: 437–443). Gordon sees the mobilization of labor ("the use of the mob," 135) as a turning point; some opponents of the regime had denounced Nasser "as a pro-American dictator." In Washington, the State Department official, Parker Hart, who was openly critical of Nasser, complained about the CIA's close contacts with the RCC, arguing that this backchannel was not the way to conduct diplomacy.

76. See USRG 59, 1950–54, 874.00/4-2254, Carr [counselor for economic affairs] to State, "Possible Inflationary Turn in Egypt's Economic Policy," 22 April 1954; for a summary of these measures, which included new minimum-wage legislation, a new benefits package and tightened restrictions over capitalists' discretion to fire workers, see O'Brien (1966: 75–76). Both union leaders and the rank and file were, predictably, divided at this juncture. For the continuing debate on state-labor relations during this period, see Beinin (1989), Posusney (1991 and 1993), and Goldberg (1992).

77. USRG 59, 1950–54, 774.00/4-1254, desp. 2449, 12 April 1954; 774.00/4-1654, desp. 2485, 16 April 1954; 774.00/4-2954, desp. 2570, 29 April 1954; and 774.00/5-554 tel. 1396, 5 May 1954. Two proregime businessmen were pointedly excluded from the worst of the retributive wave: 'Ali al-Shamsi and Saba Habashi (the Aramco counselor), both of whom served as advisers to the regime's new party, the Liberation Rally. For the ambivalences underlying Shamsi's early support of the regime, see USRG 1950–54, 774.521/6-1753, desp. 2782, 17 June 1953, Confidential Biographical Data—Ali Al Shamsi.

78. For the important and usually undiscussed organizational shift at the NPC, see USRG 59, 1955–59, Box 4868, 874.00/4-2055, Cairo to State, 20 April 1955, "The Significance of Recent Government Actions in Field of Economics and Finance." On Sulayman, see Moore (1980: 49). He took over from Muhammad Ahmad Salim, a favorite of the embassy, and though he was

appointed full time to the high dam project, Salim described it as a demotion and a sign that he was in disfavor with the RCC.

79. See USRG 59, 1955–59, 874.053/6-155, desp. 2210, Carr to State, 1 June 1955, which includes a list of retired directors.

80. See USRG 59, 1955–59, Box 4868, 874.00/4-2055; Bank Misr, *Annual Report* (1955); and Tignor (1992: 278–279). Tignor notes that two-thirds of the National Bank of Egypt directors were retired, together with seven out of ten Bank Misr directors, but I have not seen a full list. Also, according to my data, 'Imari was only fifty-three, so we must assume that the measures against the two banks involved more than the mandatory-retirement-age provision. After all, 'Imari remained a director of the Nile Ginning Company (ex-Anderson Clayton).

81. See USRG 59, 1955–59, Box 4868, 874.00/4-2055; and Tignor (1992: 279). The government was at the time preparing the largest budget in its history. For Qaysuni and his role in organizing the financing of the dam, negotiations for which were ongoing through the second half of 1955, see Kunz (1991: 48–60).

82. See USRG 59, 1955–59, Box 4868, 874.00/4-2055, together with the original draft of this dispatch in RG 84, Cairo Embassy, General Records, 1955, Embassy to State, 20 April 1955.

83. See USRG 59, 1955–59, Box 4868, 874.00/4-155, Cairo to State, "Prime Minister Outlines Economic Principles of the Regime," 1 April 1955.

84. See USRG 59, 1955–59, 874.392/8-155, desp. 135, Embassy to Cairo, "Ahmad Abboud—Egyptian Paper Plant Project," 1 August 1955 (for quote); 874.053/8-2755, desp. 235, Embassy to State, "Egyptian Government Sequestration of Ahmed Abboud's Sugar Company," 27 August 1955; and 874.053/9-655, Embassy to State, enclosing memorandum of conversation between Carr and Ahmad Abu al-Ila, 28 August 1955; and for essential background, *Egyptian Gazette* 28 February 1953.

85. Nasser was reported as seeking to carry out a "program of nationalization of the industry, getting rid of the French interest in particular, and to place the entire industry in a State organization under the Minister of Commerce and Industry, at the same time carrying out large development projects and standardizing voltages, etc., throughout the country. Hurst [one of Britain's most renowned electrical engineers and a consultant to the ministry] indicated that Colonel Nasser is looking forward to elections to be held early in 1956 and believes that launching a program of nationalization of the industry, combined with an ambitious program for hydro-electric development and irrigation, will have strong popular appeal." Representatives of the Ministry of Commerce and Industry had been seeking advice and consultants to help in reorganizing the proposed nationalized sector. See USRG 59, 1955–59, 874.2614/10-2855, American Embassy, Pretoria to State, desp. 126, "Information on Egyptian Government's Electric Power Program," 28 October 1955.

86. See USRG 59, 1955–59, Box 4868, 874.00/10-956 and 874.00/10-2456. Tignor (1989: 88–89) makes clear that control of the company had shifted to local investors by the 1930s.

87. USRG 59, 1955–59, Box 4868, 874.00/12-3156, "Egypt—Current Economic Situation"; also see Kunz (1991: 73–74) for an extremely revealing description of the escalating conflict between the regime and the canal company during 1955 and 1956. Contrast with Tignor (1992: 289–290).

88. See USRG 59, 1955–59, Box 4873, 874.2553/11-555, Byroade to McGhee, 1 November 1955; and 874.2553/10-257, Cairo to State, no. 878, 2 October 1957; and Box 4876, 874.3972/6-955 CSBM, Memorandum of Conversation, "Interest of Cities Service Oil Co. in Fertilizer Plant in Egypt," 9 June 1955.

89. See *al-Akhbar,* 22 January 1959; Export-Import Bank of Washington, Minutes of Regular Meeting of the Board of Directors, 13 November 1958; and USRG 59, 1955–59, Box 4868, 874.00/7-1555, Cairo to State, Economic Summary, Egypt, Second Quarter, 1955.

90. See the list in Tignor (1992: 276) and the insightful discussion of the position of these particular foreign firms in Tignor (1989: 72–75).

91. During the Suez crisis, the Anderson-Clayton Company (ACCO) subsidiary had apparently been used by the Egyptian government in order to sell cotton to France. See USRG 59, 1955–59, Box 4876, State Department, memorandum of conversation, "Current Egyptian Cotton Situation," 20 December 1956. For ACCOs plans in 1961, see Will L. Clayton, "Memo on My Trip to Egypt With Impressions, Recommendations, etc., Regarding the Future of the Nile Ginning Company," ACCO, Clayton Papers, folder "ACCO, 1961, Egypt," Wadsworth Research Center.

92. USRG 59, 1955–59, Box 4873, 874.19/2-1757, Embassy to State, 21 February 1957; 874.00/1-2958, Embassy to State, Weekly Economic Review, 20 January 1958; Tignor (1989: 92–94).

93. For example, the Sirag al-Din–owned Banque du Caire absorbed Crédit Lyonnais and Comptoir National d'Escompte de Paris, but the government owned all the new shares of the consolidated enterprise, forced Hamid Sirag al-Din to resign as managing director, and named a government appointee to the post. See USRG 59, 1955–59, Box 4871, 874.14/1-2157, "Egyptian Government Acquires Interest in Banque du Caire," 21 January 1957; and O'Brien (1966: 93–96).

94. See Park Chung Hee (1963: 129–134); Jung-en Woo (1991); Amsden (1989); and Mason et al. (1980).

Conclusion

1. For a good discussion of contrasting arguments about the effects of large landownership on development and class structure within the left in Latin America and, particularly, in Chile, another case of semicapitalist production relations in the rural sector, a feudalized bourgeoisie but, unlike Egypt, no land reform, see Zeitlin and Ratcliff (1988: 146–155).

2. Keyder (1991). His reading of the cases is usefully contrasted with that of Keddie (1981) to illustrate the seismic shift in ideological orientation (and hence interpretation) between the 1970s and the 1980s.

3. Having written what is now the classic text on the formation of the Egyptian working class, Beinin and Lockman obviously do not ignore the importance of workers to Egyptian history, but what now strikes me as a problem is that labor is not integrated into their summary statement of how, precisely, capitalism developed in Egypt. What would happen if we introduced labor as a variable affecting the trajectory of industrialization, much as we now think about the landlord class or foreign capital? For one way to think about the issue, see Goldberg (1986: 181–185 and 1992: 152–154); also Beinin and Lockman (1987: 453).

References

Abbreviations

BT   Board of Trade, Public Records Office, London
FO   Foreign Office, Public Records Office, London
USRG   United States Record Group, National Archives, Washington D.C.

Archival Sources

al-Ahram Center, Cairo. Subject Files.
al-Akhbar Archives, Cairo. Subject Files.
American University in Cairo. University Archives.
Columbia University, Oral History Research Office, Hungarian Project.
        Interview 1077, Laszlo [Ladislas] Pathy [Polnauer], 1977.
Egyptian National Archives (Dar al-Watha'iq), Cairo.
        Papers of the Council of Ministers (Majlis al-Wizara'u).
Eisenhower Library, Abilene, Kansas.
        Papers of Dean Acheson.
        Papers of Dwight D. Eisenhower.
        Papers of Samuel Waugh.
        U.S. Council on Economic Policy, Records 1954–1961.

Export Import Bank of the United States, Washington D.C.
> Records on the Suez Fertilizer Factory Loan [(obtained through the Freedom of Information Act).

Library of Congress, Washington D.C.
> Papers of William S. Culbertson.
> Papers of James M. Landis.

Massachusetts Institute of Technology, Institute Archives and Special Collections.
> Gerard Swope Papers, 1893–1959.

National Archives, Washington D.C.
> USRG 59, General Records of the Department of State.
> USRG 84, Post Records of the U.S. Consulates.
> USRG 151, Records of the Department of Commerce.
> USRG 486, Records of the Agency for International Development.

Public Records Office, London.
> Records of the Board of Trade, BT 11.
> Records of the Foreign Office, FO 141 and FO 371.

St. Antony's College, Oxford. Middle East Centre.
> Diaries of Lord Killearn (Sir Miles Lampson) (*Killearn Diaries*).

Truman Library, Independence, Missouri.
> Papers of Dean Acheson.
> Papers of William L. Clayton.
> Papers of Harry S. Truman.

Wadsworth Research Center, Rice University, Houston, Texas.
> Papers of William L. Clayton.

Newspapers and Periodicals

al-Ahram
al-Akhbar
Akhbar al-Yawm
al-Asas
al-Balagh
British Chamber of Commerce in Egypt
Christian Science Monitor
Egyptian Gazette
Engineering
al-Jarida al-Misriyya
al-Kutla
La Réforme
Majalla al-Muhandisin

Majalla ghurfa al-Iskandariya
Misr Synaʿiya
al-Misri
al-Muqattam
al-Musawwar
New York Times
New York Times Magazine
Ruz al-Yusuf
al-Siyasa
Time
the *Times* (London)
al-Waqaʾiʿ al-Misriya

Books, Journals and Official Publications

ʿAbd al-ʿAzim Ramadan. 1971. "Al-Burjwaziyya al-misriyya qablu thawrat 23 yuliyu" (The Egyptian bourgeoisie before the July 23rd Revolution). *al-Katib*, no. 123, pp. 91–102.

———. 1978. *Siraʿ al-tabaqat fi Misr, 1837–1952* (Class conflict in Egypt, 1837–1952). Cairo: Muʾassasa al-ʿArabiyya lil Dirasat wa al-Nashr.

———. 1981. *Dirasat fi tarikh Misr al-muʿasir* (Studies in the contemporary history of Egypt). Cairo: al-Markaz al-ʿArabi lil Bahth wa al-Nashr.

———. 1983. *Tatawwur al-haraka al-wataniyya fi Misr min sana 1937 ila sana 1948* (The development of the national movement in Egypt from 1937 to 1948). Second edition. Cairo: Maktaba Madbuli.

ʿAbd al-ʿAziz Ahmad. 1955. *Kahraba Misr* (The electrification of Egypt). Cairo: Ministry of Public Works.

ʿAbd al-Muʿti ʿAbd al-Wahab ʿAmr. 1960. *Aswan Dam Hydroelectric Scheme: Notes on Its History, Description and Economics.* Cairo: Ministry of Public Works.

Abdel-Malek, Anouar. 1968. *Egypt: Military Society.* New York: Random House.

Addison, Herbert. 1959. *Sun and Shadow at Aswan.* London: Chapman and Hall.

Ahmad, Aijaz. 1992. *In Theory: Classes, Nations, Literatures.* London: Verso.

Ahmad Hamrush. 1984. *Qissa thawra 23 yuliyu* (The story of the July 23rd Revolution). Volume 4, *Shuhud thawra yuliyu* (Witnesses to the July Revolution). Cairo: Maktaba Madbuli.

Ahmed, Mahmoud Hussein. 1984. "The Automobile Industry in Egypt." Master's thesis, American University in Cairo.

ʿAli Barakat. 1977. *Tatawwur al-milkiyya al-ziraʿiyya fi Misr wa atharuha ʿala al-haraka al-siyasiyya, 1813–1914.* (The development of landownership in Egypt and its effects on the political movement, 1813–1914). Cairo: Dar al-Thaqafa al-Jadida.

Amsden, Alice H. 1989. *Asia's Next Giant: South Korea and Late Industrialization*. New York: Oxford University Press.

Anderson, Lisa. 1987. "The State in the Middle East and North Africa." *Comparative Politics* 20, pp. 1–18.

Anis Mustafa Kamil. 1981. "Tarikh al-ra'smaliyya al-yahudiyya fi Misr." (The history of Jewish capitalism in Egypt). *al-Ahram al-Iqtisadi*, nos. 636–642.

Aronson, Geoffrey. 1986. *From Sideshow to Center Stage: U.S. Policy toward Egypt 1946–1956*. Boulder: Lynne Rienner.

Arthur D. Little, Inc. 1956. *Summary of Egyptian Studies*. Final report to U.S. International Cooperation Administration, Contract TA62-102-4001 C59200. April 30.

'Asim al-Disuqi. 1976. *Misr fi al-harb al-'alamiyya al-thaniyya, 1939–1945* (Egypt in the Second World War, 1939–1945). Cairo: Ma'had al-Buhuth wa al-Dirasat al-'Arabiyya.

———. 1981. *Nahw fahm tarikh Misr al-iqtisadi al-ijtima'i* (Toward an understanding of Egypt's socioeconomic history). Cairo: Dar al-Kitab al-Jami'i.

Aubey, Robert. 1969. "Entrepreneurial Formation in El Salvador." *Explorations in Entrepreneurial History,* second series, 6, pp. 268–285.

Augelli, Enrico, and Craig Murphy. 1988. *America's Quest for Supremacy and the Third World: A Gramscian Analysis*. London: Pinter.

Ayubi, Nazih. 1980. *Bureaucracy and Politics in Contemporary Egypt*. London: Ithaca Press.

Baer, Gabriel. 1962. *A History of Landownership in Modern Egypt, 1880–1950*. London: Oxford University Press.

Baker, Raymond William. 1978. *Egypt's Uncertain Revolution under Nasser and Sadat*. Cambridge: Harvard University Press.

Bank Misr. 1929. *Taqrir insha' al-sina'at al-ahliyya fi Misr*. (Report on the creation of national industries in Egypt). Bureau of Economic Research. Cairo: Imprimerie Misr.

Baram, Philip J. 1978. *The Department of State in the Middle East, 1919–1945*. Philadelphia: University of Pennsylvania Press.

BEAMA [British Electrical and Allied Manufacturers' Association]. 1927. *Combines and Trusts in the Electrical Industry: The Position in Europe in 1927*. London.

Becker, David G. 1983. *The New Bourgeoisie and the Limits of Dependency: Mining, Class and Power in "Revolutionary" Peru*. Princeton, N.J.: Princeton University Press.

Becker, David G., et al. 1987. *Postimperialism: International Capitalism in the Late Twentieth Century*. Boulder, Colo.: Lynne Rienner.

Beinin, Joel. 1982. "Class Conflict and National Struggle: Labor and Politics in Egypt, 1936–1954." Ph.D. dissertation, Department of History, University of Michigan.

———. 1989. "Labor, Capital and the State in Nasserist Egypt, 1952–1961." *International Journal of Middle East Studies* 21, pp. 71–91.

———. 1990. *Was the Red Flag Flying There?: Marxist Politics and the Arab-*

Israeli Conflict in Egypt and Israel, 1948–1965. Berkeley: University of California Press.

Beinin, Joel and Zachary Lockman. 1987. *Workers on the Nile: Nationalism, Communism, Islam, and the Egyptian Working Class, 1882–1954.* Princeton, N.J.: Princeton University Press.

Berque, Jacques. 1972. *Egypt: Imperialism and Revolution.* Translated by Jean Stewart. New York: Praeger.

Bertramsen, René Bugge, Jens Peter Frølund Thomsen and Jacob Torfing. 1991. *State, Economy and Society.* London: Unwin Hyman.

Bianchi, Robert. 1985. "Businessmen's Associations in Egypt and Turkey." *Annals of the American Academy of Political and Social Science* 482, pp. 147–159.

———. 1986. "The Corporatization of the Egyptian Labor Movement." *Middle East Journal* 40, pp. 429–444.

———. 1989. *Unruly Corporatism: Associational Life in Twentieth-Century Egypt.* New York: Oxford University Press.

Binder, Leonard. 1978. *In a Moment of Enthusiasm: Political Power and the Second Stratum in Egypt.* Chicago: University of Chicago Press.

Blackbourn, David, and Geoff Eley. 1984. *The Peculiarities of German History: Bourgeois Society and Politics in Nineteenth-Century Germany.* Oxford: Oxford University Press.

Block, Fred. 1987. *Revising State Theory: Essays in Politics and Postindustrialism.* Philadelphia: Temple University Press.

Boone, Catherine. 1992. *Merchant Capital and the Roots of State Power in Senegal, 1930–1985.* Cambridge: Cambridge University Press.

———. 1994. "States and Ruling Classes in Sub-Saharan Africa: The Enduring Contradictions of Power." In *State Power and Social Forces: Domination and Transformation in the Third World,* edited by Joel Migdal, Atul Kholi and Vivienne Shue. New York: Cambridge University Press.

Botman, Selma. 1988. *The Rise of Egyptian Communism, 1939–1970.* Syracuse, N.Y.: Syracuse University Press.

Bowles, Samuel, and Herbert Gintis. 1990. "Contested Exchange: New Microfoundations for the Political Economy of Capitalism." *Politics and Society* 18, pp. 165–222.

Bowley, Marian. 1966. *The British Building Industry: Four Studies in Response and Resistance to Change.* Cambridge: Cambridge University Press.

Bowman, John R. 1989. *Capitalist Collective Action: Competition, Cooperation and Conflict in the Coal Industry.* Cambridge: Cambridge University Press.

British Chamber of Commerce of Egypt. 1905. *List of Companies Established in Egypt.* Fourth edition. Alexandria.

Brown, Nathan. 1993. "The Precarious Life and Slow Death of the Mixed Courts of Egypt." *International Journal of Middle East Studies* 25, pp. 33–52.

Bryson, Thomas. 1981. *Seeds of Mideast Crisis: The United States Diplomatic Role in the Middle East during World War II.* Jefferson, N.C.: McFarland.

Cain, P. J., and A. G. Hopkins. 1993. *British Imperialism: Crisis and Deconstruction, 1914–1990.* London: Longman.

Cammack, Paul. 1988. "Dependency and the Politics of Development." In *Perspectives on Development: Cross-Disciplinary Themes in Development Studies,* edited by P. F. Leeson and M. M. Minogue. Manchester: University of Manchester Press.

Canack, William L. 1984. "The Peripheral State Debate: State Capitalist and Bureaucratic Authoritarian Regimes in Latin America." *Latin America Research Review* 19, pp. 3–36.

Cardoso, Fernando Henrique, and Enzo Faletto. 1979. *Dependency and Development in Latin America.* Berkeley: University of California Press.

Chamber of Deputies, Committee on Financial Affairs [Majlis al-Nuwwab, Lajna al-Shu'un al-Maliyya]. 1948. *Taqrir al-lajna 'an mashru' kahraba khazan 'Aswan* (Report of the committee on the Aswan Dam electrification project). Report 111. Cairo: Royal Printing Office.

Chaudhry, Kiren. 1989. "The Price of Wealth: Business and State in Labor Remittance and Oil Economies." *International Organization* 43, pp. 101–145.

———. 1993. "The Myths of the Market and the Common History of Late Developers." *Politics and Society* 21, pp. 245–275.

Clawson, Patrick. 1981. "The Development of Capitalism in Egypt." *Khamsin* 9, pp. 77–116.

Colander, David C., ed. 1984. *Neoclassical Political Economy: The Analysis of Rent-Seeking and DUP Activities.* Cambridge, Mass.: Ballinger.

Colburn, Forrest D. 1986. *Post-revolutionary Nicaragua: State, Class, and the Dilemmas of Agrarian Policy.* Berkeley: University of California Press.

Collins, Jeffrey G. 1984. *The Egyptian Elite under Cromer, 1882–1907.* Berlin: Klaus Schwarz Verlag.

Commission du Commerce et de l'Industrie. 1918. *Rapport.* Cairo: Imprimerie Nationale.

Cooper, Marc. 1982. *Transformation of Egypt.* Baltimore, Md.: Johns Hopkins University Press.

Crouchley, A. E. 1936. *The Investment of Foreign Capital in Egyptian Companies and Public Debt.* Technical Paper 12, Egyptian Ministry of Finance. Cairo: Government Press.

Dahl, Robert. 1959. "Business and Politics: A Critical Appraisal of Political Science." In *Social Science Research on Business: Product and Potential,* edited by Robert Dahl, Mason Haire and Paul Lazarsfeld. New York: Columbia University Press.

Daninos, Adrian. 1922. *Mushkila al-'azut fi Misr wa 'ahmiyya al-quwa al-ma'iyya fi 'Aswan lil-zira'a al-masriyya* (The problem of fertilizers in Egypt and the importance of hydropower in Aswan for Egyptian agriculture). Cairo.

Davenport-Hines, R. P. T. 1984a. *Dictionary of Business Biography,* s.v. "Norton-Griffiths, John." London: Butterworths.

———. 1984b. *Dudley Docker: The Life and Times of a Trade Warrior.* Cambridge: Cambridge University Press.

Davis, Eric. 1977. "Bank Misr and the Political Economy of Industrialization in Egypt, 1920–1941." Ph.D. dissertation, University of Chicago.

———. 1983. *Challenging Colonialism: Bank Misr and Egyptian Industrialization, 1920–1941.* Princeton, N.J.: Princeton University Press.

Dawley, Alan. 1991. *Struggles for Justice: Social Responsibility and the Liberal State.* Cambridge: Harvard University Press.

Deeb, Marius. 1976. "Bank Misr and the Emergence of the Local Bourgeoisie in Egypt." *Middle Eastern Studies* 12, pp. 69–86.

———. 1978. "The Socioeconomic Role of the Local Foreign Minorities in Modern Egypt, 1805–1961." *International Journal of Middle East Studies* 9, pp. 11–22.

———. 1979. *Party Politics in Egypt: The Wafd and Its Rivals, 1919–1939.* London: Ithaca Press.

———. 1984. "Large Landowners and Social Transformation in Egypt 1940–1942." In *Land Tenure and Social Transformation in the Middle East,* edited by Tarif Khalidi. Beirut: American University of Beirut.

De Guerville, A. B. 1905. *New Egypt.* London: Heinemann.

Dekmejian, R. Hrair. 1971. *Egypt under Nasir: A Study in Political Dynamics.* Albany: State University of New York Press.

DeNovo, John. 1977. "The Culbertson Economic Mission and Anglo-American Tensions in the Middle East, 1944–1945." *Journal of American History* 63, pp. 913–936.

Department of Overseas Trade [U.K.]. 1928. *Report on the Economic and Financial Conditions in Egypt for 1927.* London.

de Soto, Hernando. 1989. *The Other Path: The Invisible Revolution in the Third World.* New York: Harper & Row.

Devereux, Eric August. 1988. "Economic Models of Interest Groups and the Investment Theory of Political Parties." Master's thesis, University of Texas at Austin.

Dummelow, John. 1949. *1899–1949* [Metrovic company history]. Manchester: Metropolitan Vickers Electrical Company Ltd.

Dunkerley, James. 1982. *The Long War: Dictatorship and Revolution in El Salvador.* London: Verso.

Durrah, 'Albir [Albert Dorra]. 1939. *Muhadara ʿan mashruʿ tawlid al-kahraba min khazan ʾAswan ka-hal li-mushkila tamwin al-sinaʿa al-masriyya bil-quwa al-haraka* (Lecture on the project for the generation of electricity from the Aswan Dam as the solution to the problem of supplying Egyptian industry with power). Publication 138. Cairo: Royal Society of Engineers.

Evans, Peter. 1979. *Dependent Development : The Alliance of Multinational, State and Local Capital in Brazil.* Princeton, N.J.: Princeton University Press.

Evans, Peter, and John D. Stephens. 1988. "Studying Development since the Sixties: The Emergence of a New Comparative Political Economy." *Theory and Society* 17, pp. 713–745.

Fatton, Robert, Jr. 1988. "Bringing the Ruling Class Back In: Class, State, and Hegemony in Africa." *Comparative Politics* 20, pp. 253–264.

Ferguson, Thomas. 1983. "Party Realignment and American Industrial Structure: The Investment Theory of Political Parties in Historical Perspective." In *Research in Political Economy*, edited by Paul Zarembka, volume 6. Greenwich, Conn.: JAI Press.

el-Ghazali, Abd el-Hamid. 1971. *Planning for Economic Development: Methodology, Strategy, and Effectiveness*. Cairo: Modern Cairo Bookshop.

Godfried, Nathan. 1987. *Bridging the Gap between Rich and Poor: American Economic Development Policy toward the Arab East, 1942–1949*. New York: Greenwood Press.

Goldberg, Ellis. 1986. *Tinker, Tailor and Textile Worker: Class and Politics in Egypt, 1930–1954*. Berkeley: University of California Press.

———. 1992. "The Foundations of State-Labor Relations in Contemporary Egypt." *Comparative Politics* 24, pp. 147–162.

Gordon, Joel. 1989. "The False Hopes of 1950: The Wafd's Last Hurrah and the Demise of Egypt's Old Order." *International Journal of Middle East Studies* 21, pp. 193–214.

———. 1992. *Nasser's Blessed Movement: Egypt's Free Officers and the July Revolution*. New York: Oxford University Press.

Gran, Peter. 1978. "Modern Trends in Egyptian Historiography: A Review Article." *International Journal of Middle Eastern Studies* 9, pp. 367–371.

el-Gritly, A. A. I. 1947. "The Structure of Modern Industry in Egypt." *L'Egypte contemporaine* 38, pp. 241–242.

Haber, William. 1931. *Encyclopedia of the Social Sciences* (London), s.v. "construction industry."

Haggard, Stephan. 1986. "The Newly Industrializing Countries in the International System." *World Politics* 38, pp. 343–370.

———. 1989. "The Political Economy of Foreign Direct Investment in Latin America." *Latin America Research Review* 24, pp. 184–208.

Hahn, Peter. 1991. *The United States, Great Britain and Egypt, 1945–1956: Strategy and Diplomacy in the Early Cold War*. Chapel Hill: University of North Carolina Press.

Hamilton, Nora. 1982. *The Limits of State Autonomy: Post-revolutionary Mexico*. Princeton, N.J.: Princeton University Press.

Handoussa, Heba. 1974. "The Pharmaceutical Industry in Egypt." Ph.D. dissertation, School of Oriental and African Studies, University of London.

Hanna, Nelly. 1984. *Construction Work in Ottoman Cairo (1517–1798)*. Supplément aux Annales Islamogiques, book 4. Cairo: Institut Français d'Archéologie Orientale.

Hannah, Leslie. 1978. *Electricity before Nationalization: A Study of the Development of the Electricity Supply Industry in Britain to 1948*. Baltimore, Md.: Johns Hopkins University Press.

Hansen, Bent. 1991. *The Political Economy of Poverty, Equity, and Growth: Egypt and Turkey*. Oxford: Oxford University Press.

Hansen, Bent, and Girgis A. Marzouk. 1965. *Development and Economic Policy in the UAR (Egypt)*. Amsterdam: North-Holland Publishing.

Harris, Nigel. 1987. *The End of the Third World: Newly Industrializing Countries And the Decline of an Ideology*. London: Penguin.

Hawes, Gary. 1987. *The Philippine State and the Marcos Regime: The Politics of Export*. Ithaca, N.Y.: Cornell University Press.

Hawes, Gary, and Hong Liu. 1993. "Explaining the Dynamics of the Southeast Asian Political Economy: State, Society and the Search for Economic Growth." *World Politics* 45, pp. 629–660.

Haykal, Muhammad Husayn. 1986. *Cutting the Lion's Tail: Suez through Egyptian Eyes*. London: A. Deutsch.

Held, David. 1992. "Democracy: From City-States to a Cosmopolitan Order?" *Political Studies* 40, pp. 10–39.

Hillebrandt, Patricia M. 1974. *Economic Theory and the Construction Industry*. London: Macmillan.

Hinnebusch, Raymond A. 1985. *Egyptian Politics under Sadat: The Post-Populist Development of an Authoritarian-Modernizing State*. New York: Cambridge University Press.

Hubbard, G. E. 1935. *Eastern Industrialization and Its Effects on the West*. Oxford: Oxford University Press.

Hughes, Thomas P. 1983. *Networks of Power: Electrification in Western Society 1880–1930*. Baltimore, Md.: Johns Hopkins University Press.

Hussein, Mahmud. 1977. *Class Conflict in Egypt, 1945–1970*. Second edition. New York: Monthly Review Press.

Issa, Hossam M. 1970. *Capitalisme et sociétés anonymes en Égypte: Essai sur la rapport entre structure sociale et droit*. Paris. Librairie Générale de Droit et de Jurisprudence.

Issawi, Charles. 1954. *Egypt at Mid-Century: An Economic Analysis*. London: Oxford University Press.

———. 1961. "Egypt since 1800: A Study of Lop-Sided Development." *Journal of Economic History* 21, pp. 1–25.

———. 1963. *Egypt in Revolution: An Economic Analysis*. London: Oxford University Press.

———. [1967] 1975. *The Economic History of the Middle East 1800–1914: A Book of Readings*. Chicago: University of Chicago Press, Midway.

Jones, Robert, and Oliver Marriott. 1970. *Anatomy of a Merger*. London: Jonathan Cape.

Jung-en Woo. 1991. *Race to the Swift: State and Finance in Korean Industrialization*. New York: Columbia University Press.

Kalkas, Barbara Ellen. 1979. "Aborted Economic and Social Development in Egypt: New Leaders in an Old System." Ph.D. dissertation, Northwestern University.

Kasaba, Resat. 1988. *The Ottoman Empire and the World Economy*. Albany: State University of New York Press.

Keddie, Nikki R. 1981. "Socioeconomic Change in the Middle East since 1800: A Comparative Analysis." In *The Islamic Middle East, 700–1900: Studies in Economic and Social History*, edited by A. L. Udovitch. Princeton, N.J.: Darwin Press.

Keyder, Caglar. 1987. *State and Class in Turkey: A Study in Capitalist Development*. London: Verso.

———. 1988. "Introduction." *Review* 11, pp. 119–126.

————. 1991. "The Turkish Bourgeoisie: Its Genesis and Evolution in Comparative Perspective." Unpublished paper.

Khadr, Hassan, and Amin Hassoun. 1954. *Egypt's Republic in Its First Year.* Cairo: Department of Public Relations of the Egyptian Armed Forces.

el-Kholy, M. A. 1957. "Hydro-electric Schemes of Modern Egypt with Particular Reference to the High Dam Project South of Aswan." Section H, Paper 233 H/41. *5th World Power Conference,* volume 13. Vienna.

Kitching, Gaven. 1985. "Politics, Method, and Evidence in the 'Kenya Debate.'" In *Contradictions of Accumulation in Africa,* edited by Henry Bernstein and Bonnie K. Campbell. Beverly Hills, Calif.: Sage.

Kitroeff, Alexander. 1989. *The Greeks in Egypt, 1919–1937: Ethnicity and Class.* London: Ithaca Press.

Kolko, Gabriel. 1985. *Anatomy of a War: Vietnam, the United States and the Modern Historical Experience.* New York: Pantheon.

Krämer, Gudrun. 1983. "'Radical' Nationalists, Fundamentalists, and the Jews in Egypt or, Who Is a Real Egyptian?" In *Islam, Nationalism, and Radicalism in Egypt and the Sudan,* edited by Gabriel R. Warburg and Uri M. Kupferschmidt. New York: Praeger.

————. 1989. *The Jews in Modern Egypt, 1914–1952.* Publications on the Near East, University of Washington, no. 4. Seattle: University of Washington Press.

Kunz, Diane B. 1991. *The Economic Diplomacy of the Suez Crisis.* Chapel Hill: University of North Carolina Press.

Lachica, Eduardo. 1971. *The Huk: Philippine Agrarian Society in Revolt.* Manila: Solidaridad Publishing House.

Lacouture, Jean, and Simonne Lacouture. 1958. *Egypt in Transition.* Translated by Francis Scarfe. New York: Criterion Books.

Landau, Jacob. 1969. *Jews in Nineteenth-Century Egypt.* New York: New York University Press.

Landes, David. [1958] 1979. *Bankers and Pashas: International Finance and Economic Imperialism in Egypt.* Revised edition. Cambridge: Harvard University Press.

Leff, Nathaniel. 1978. "Industrial Organization and Entrepreneurship in the Developing Countries: The Economic Groups." *Economic Development and Cultural Change* 26, pp. 661–675.

————. 1979a. "Entrepreneurship and Economic Development: The Problem Revisited." *Journal of Economic Literature* 17, pp. 46–64.

————. 1979b. "'Monopoly Capitalism' and Public Policy in Developing Countries." *Kyklos* 32, pp. 718–738.

Lemonias, Hermes. 1954. "Monopoly, Oligopoly and Monopolistic Competition in the Egyptian Manufacturing Industries." Bachelor's thesis, American University in Cairo.

Levi, Clement, ed. 1952. *The Stock Exchange Year Book of Egypt.* 1950–1951 edition. Alexandria: Société des Publications Egyptiennes.

Lindblom, Charles. 1977. *Politics and Markets: The World's Political-Economic Systems.* New York: Basic Books.

Lloyd, E. M. H. 1956. *Food and Inflation in the Middle East, 1940–1945.* Stanford, Calif.: Stanford University Press.

Louis, Wm. Roger. 1984. *The British Empire in the Middle East 1945–1951: Arab Nationalism, the United States, and Postwar Imperialism.* Oxford: Oxford University Press.

Lubeck, Paul M., ed. 1987. *The African Bourgeoisie: Capitalist Development in Nigeria, Kenya, and the Ivory Coast.* Boulder, Colo.: Lynne Rienner.

Maghraoui, Abdeslam. 1991. "Dilemmas of Liberalism in the Middle East: A Reading of the Liberal Experiment in Egypt, 1920s-1930s." Ph.D. dissertation, Department of Politics, Princeton University.

Mahmud Mutawalli. 1985. *Dirasat fi tarikh Misr al-siyasi wa al-iqtisadi wa al-ijtima'i* (Studies in Egypt's political, economic and social history). Cairo: Dar al-Thaqafa lil-Taba'at wa al-Nashr.

Makram 'Ubayd. [1943] 1984. *Al-Kitab al-aswad* (The black book). Cairo: al-Markaz al-'Arabiyya lil Buhuth wa al-Nashr.

Markovits, Claude. 1985. *Indian Business and Nationalist Politics 1931–1939.* London: Cambridge University Press.

Marsot, Afaf Lutfi al-Sayyid. 1977. *Egypt's Liberal Experiment 1922–1936.* Berkeley: University of California Press.

———. 1984. *Egypt in the Reign of Muhammad Ali.* Cambridge: Cambridge University Press.

Marx, Karl, and Friedrich Engels. 1888. *Manifesto of the Communist Party.* English edition, edited by Friedrich Engels. (Reprinted in Robert C. Tucker, ed., *The Marx-Engels Reader,* second edition. New York: Norton, 1978.)

Mason, Edward S., et al. 1980. *The Economic and Social Modernization of the Republic of Korea.* Cambridge: Harvard University Press.

Maxfield, Sylvia. 1990. *Governing Capital: International Finance and Mexican Politics.* Ithaca, N.Y.: Cornell University Press.

Maxfield, Sylvia, and James H. Nolt. 1990. "Protectionism and the Internationalization of Capital: U.S. Sponsorship of Import Substitution Industrialization in the Philippines, Turkey and Argentina." *International Studies Quarterly* 34, pp. 49–81.

Meijer, Roel. 1990. "Rashid al-Barrawi and the Ideology of Reform in Egypt, 1945–1955." Unpublished paper.

Meyer, Gail E. 1980. *Egypt and the United States: The Formative Years.* Cranbury, N.J.: Associated University Presses.

Middlemas, Robert Keith. 1963. *The Master Builders.* London: Hutchinson.

Mikesell, Raymond. 1954. "Economic Doctrines Implied in the Reports of the United Nations and the International Bank for Reconstruction." *American Economic Review* 44, pp. 570–582.

Ministry of Commerce and Industry. 1955. *Opportunities for Industrial Development in Egypt.* Cairo: Government Press. (A. D. Little, Report to U.S. Government Foreign Operations Administration under Contract SCC-21504 C-58780. Cambridge, Mass., 1954.)

Mitchell, Timothy. 1988. *Colonizing Egypt.* London: Cambridge University Press.

Monteón, Michael. 1982. *Chile in the Nitrate Era: The Evolution of Economic Dependence, 1880–1930.* Madison: University of Wisconsin Press.

Moore, Clement Henry. 1980. *Images of Development: Egyptian Engineers in Search of Industry.* Cambridge: MIT Press.

Morsy, Laila Amin. 1989. "Britain's Wartime Policy in Egypt, 1940–42." *Middle Eastern Studies* 25, pp. 64–94.

Mustafa Kamil al-Sayyid. 1983. *Al-Mujtama' wa al-siyasa fil Misr: Dawr jama'at al-masalah fi al-nizam al-siyasi al-misri, 1952–1981* (Associations and politics in Egypt: The role of interest groups in the Egyptian political system, 1952–1981). Cairo: Dar al-Mustaqbal al-'Arabi.

Newfarmer, Richard. 1980. *Transnational Conglomerates and the Economics of Dependent Development: A Case Study of the International Electrical Oligopoly and Brazil's Electrical Industry.* Greenwich, Conn.: JAI Press.

O'Brien, Patrick. 1966. *The Revolution in Egypt's Economic System: From Private Enterprise to Socialism, 1952–1965.* London: Oxford University Press.

O'Brien, Thomas F. 1989. " 'Rich beyond the Dreams of Avarice': The Guggenheims in Chile." *Business History Review* 63, pp. 122–159.

Olson, Mancur. 1971. *The Logic of Collective Action.* Cambridge: Harvard University Press.

Owen, E. R. J. 1966. "Lord Cromer and the Development of Egyptian Industry, 1883–1907." *Middle Eastern Studies* 2, pp. 282–301.

———. 1969. *Cotton and the Egyptian Economy.* London: Oxford University Press.

———. 1972. "The Cairo Building Industry and the Building Boom of 1897–1907." In *Colloque international sur l'histoire du Caire,* edited by the Ministry of Culture, Arab Republic of Egypt. Cairo: General Book Organization.

———. 1981a. "The Development of Agricultural Production in Nineteenth Century Egypt: Capitalism of What Type?" In *The Islamic Middle East, 700–1900: Studies in Economic and Social History,* edited by Avram Udovitch. Princeton, N.J.: Darwin Press.

———. 1981b. "The Ideology of Economic Nationalism in Its Egyptian Context: 1919–1939." In *Intellectual Life in the Arab East, 1890–1939,* edited by Marwan R. Buheiry. Beirut: American University in Beirut.

Pamuk, Sevket. 1988. "The Ottoman Empire in Comparative Perspective." *Review* 11, pp. 127–150.

Papasian, Ed. 1926. *L'Egypte économique et financière.* Cairo: Imprimerie Misr.

Park Chung Hee. 1963. *The Country, the Revolution and I.* Seoul: n.p.

Philipp, Thomas. 1985. *The Syrians in Egypt, 1725–1975.* Stuttgart: Franze Steiner Verlag Weisbaden GMBH.

Phillips, Anne. 1977. "The Concept of Development." *Review of African Political Economy* 8, pp. 8–20.

———. 1989. *The Enigma of Colonialism: British Policy in West Africa.* Bloomington: Indiana University Press.

Picot, Jacques-George. 1978. *The Real Suez Crisis: The End of a Great Nineteenth Century Work.* Translated by G. Rogers. New York: Harcourt Brace Jovanovich.

Pilavachi, George. 1932. *Cotton Year Book for 1931–1932*. Cairo: Société des Publications Egyptiennes.

Platt, Raye R., and Mohammed Bahy Hefny. 1958. *Egypt: A Compendium*. New York: American Geographical Society.

Plotke, David. 1992. "The Political Mobilization of Business." In *The Politics of Interests*, edited by Mark Petracca. Boulder, Colo.: Westview Press.

Polk, Judd. 1956. *Sterling: Its Meaning in World Finance*. New York: Harper Brothers.

Posusney, Marsha Pripstein. 1991. "Workers against the State: Actors, Issues and Outcomes in Egyptian Labor/State Relations, 1952–1987." Ph.D. dissertation, Department of Political Science, University of Pennsylvania.

———. 1993. "Irrational Workers: The Moral Economy of Labor Protest in Egypt." *World Politics* 46, pp. 83–121.

Przeworski, Adam. 1980. "Material Bases of Consent: Economics and Politics in a Hegemonic System." In *Political Power and Social Theory*, edited by Paul Zarembka, volume 1. Greenwich, Conn: JAI Press.

al-Qaddah, Hamid. 1979. "Min amjad al-muhandisin" (The Most Illustrious Engineers). *Majallah al-Muhandisin*, October, pp. 155–163.

Rashid al-Barrawi. 1952. *Haqiqa al-inqilab al-akhir fi Misr* (The truth about the last coup in Egypt). Cairo: Maktaba al-Nahda al-Misriyya.

Rashid al-Barrawi and Muhammad Maza 'Ulaysh. 1945. *Al-Tatawwur al-iqtisadi fi Misr fi al-ʿasr al-hadith* (The economic development of Egypt in the modern era). Second edition. Cairo: Maktaba al-Nahda al-Misriyya.

Reader, William J. 1970. *Imperial Chemical Industries: A History*. 2 vols. London: Oxford University Press.

Richards, Alan. 1980. "Agricultural Technology and Rural Social Classes in Egypt, 1920–1939." In *Modern Egypt*, edited by Elie Kedourie and Sylvia G. Haim. London: Frank Cass.

———. 1982. *Egypt's Agricultural Development, 1800–1980*. Boulder, Colo.: Westview Press.

———. 1992. " 'America's Egypt': A Flawed Critique." *Middle East Report*. no. 174, pp. 2, 43–44.

Richards, Alan, and John Waterbury. 1990. *A Political Economy of the Middle East: State, Class and Economic Development*. Boulder, Colo.: Westview Press.

Ritchie, Donald M. 1980. *James M. Landis: Dean of the Regulators*. Cambridge: Harvard University Press.

Ritter, Gretchen. 1992. "Parties and the Politics of Money: The Antimonopoly Tradition and American Political Development." Ph.D. dissertation, Department of Political Science, Massachusetts Institute of Technology.

Robison, Richard. 1986. *Indonesia: The Rise of Capital*. Southeast Asia Publications Series, no. 13, Asian Studies Association of Australia. North Sydney: Allen and Unwin.

———. 1988. "Authoritarian States, Capital-Owning Classes, and the Politics of Newly Industrializing Countries: The Case of Indonesia." *World Politics* 41, pp. 52–74.

el Saaty, Hassan, and Gordon Hirabayashi. 1959. *Industrialization in Alexandria: Some Ecological and Social Aspects.* Cairo: Dar al-Maaref.

Sadowski, Yahya. 1991. *Political Vegetables? Businessmen and Bureaucrat in the Development of Egyptian Agriculture.* Washington, D.C.: Brookings Institution.

Samuels, Warren J., and Nicholas Mercuro. 1984. "A Critique of Rent-Seeking Theory." In *Neoclassical Political Economy: The Analysis of Rent-Seeking and DUP Activities,* edited by David C. Colander. Cambridge, Mass.: Ballinger.

Saragoza, Alex M. 1988. *The Monterrey Elite and the Mexican State, 1880–1940.* Austin: University of Texas Press.

Sayed-Ahmed, Muhammad Abd el-Wahab. 1989. *Nasser and American Foreign Policy 1952–1956.* London: LAAM.

Schmitter, Philippe, and Wolfgang Streeck. n.d. "Research Design to Study the Associative Action of Business in the Advanced Industrial Societies of Western Europe." Unpublished paper.

Shamir, Shimon. 1987. "The Evolution of the Egyptian Nationality Laws and Their Application to the Jews in the Monarchy Period." In *The Jews of Egypt: A Mediterranean Society in Modern Times,* edited by Shimon Shamir. Boulder, Colo.: Westview Press.

Shimizu, Hiroshi. 1986. *Anglo-Japanese Trade Rivalry in the Middle East in the Inter-war Period.* London: Ithaca Press.

Shudi 'Atiya al-Shafi'i. 1957. *Tatawwur al-haraka al-wataniyya al-misriyya, 1882–1956 (The Development of the Egyptian National Movement, 1882–1956).* Cairo: Dar al-Misri.

Smith, Charles D. 1979. "4 February 1942: Its Causes and Its Influence on Egyptian Politics and on the Future of Anglo-Egyptian Relations, 1937–1945." *International Journal of Middle East Studies* 10, pp. 453–479.

Springborg, Robert. 1989. *Mubarak's Egypt: Fragmentation of the Political Order.* Boulder, Colo.: Westview Press.

———. 1993. "The Arab Bourgeoisie: A Revisionist Interpretation." *Arab Studies Quarterly* 15, pp. 13–40.

Stigler, George J. 1986. "The Theory of Economic Regulation." In *The Essence of Stigler,* edited by Kurt R. Leube and Thomas Gale Moore. Stanford, Calif.: Hoover Institution Press. Reprinted from the *Bell Journal of Economics and Management Science* 2 (1971).

Stocking, George, and Myron W. Watkins. 1946. *Cartels in Action: Case Studies in International Business Diplomacy.* New York: Twentieth Century Fund.

Strachan, Harry. 1976. *Family and Other Business Groups in Economic Development: The Case of Nicaragua.* New York: Praeger.

Swainson, Nicola. 1980. *The Development of Corporate Capitalism in Kenya, 1918–1977.* Los Angeles: University of California Press.

Tariq al-Bishri. 1983. *Al-Haraka al-siyasiyya fi Misr, 1945–1952* (The political movement in Egypt, 1945–1952). Second edition. Beirut: Dar al-Shuruq.

Taylor, Graham D., and Patricia Sudnik. 1984. *DuPont and the International Chemical Industry.* Boston: Hall.

Thane, Pat. 1984. *Dictionary of Business Biography,* s.v. "Cassel, Sir Ernest Joseph." London: Butterworths.

———. 1986. "Financiers and the British State: The Case of Sir Ernest Cassel." *Business History* 28, pp. 80–99.

Tignor, Robert L. 1966. *Modernization and British Colonial Rule in Egypt, 1882–1914.* Princeton, N.J.: Princeton University Press.

———. 1976. "The Egyptian Revolution of 1919: New Directions in the Egyptian Economy." *Middle Eastern Studies* 12, pp. 41–67.

———. 1977a. "Bank Misr and Foreign Capitalism." *International Journal of Middle East Studies* 8, pp. 161–181.

———. 1977b. "Nationalism, Economic Planning and Development Projects in Interwar Egypt." *International Journal of African Historical Studies* 10, pp. 185–208.

———. 1980a. "Dependency Theory and Egyptian Capitalism, 1920–1950." *African Economic History* 9, pp. 101–118.

———. 1980b. "The Economic Activities of Foreigners in Egypt, 1920–1950: From Millet to Haute Bourgeoisie." *Comparative Studies in Society and History* 22, pp. 416–449.

———. 1982. "Equity in Egypt's Recent Past: 1945–1952." In *The Political Economy of Income Distribution in Egypt,* edited by Gouda Abdel-Khaleq and Robert Tignor. New York: Holmes and Meier.

———. 1984. *State, Private Enterprise, and Economic Change in Egypt, 1918–1952.* Princeton, N.J.: Princeton University Press.

———. 1989. *Egyptian Textiles and British Capital 1930–1956.* Cairo: American University of Cairo Press.

———. 1990. "In the Grip of Politics: The Ford Motor Company of Egypt, 1945–1960." *Middle East Journal* 44, pp. 383–398.

———. 1992. "The Suez Crisis of 1956 and Egypt's Foreign Private Sector." *Journal of Imperial and Commonwealth History* 20, pp. 274–297.

Tollison, Robert D. 1982. "Rent Seeking: A Survey." *Kyklos* 35, pp. 575–602.

Topik, Steven. 1987. *The Political Economy of the Brazilian State, 1889–1930.* Latin American Monographs 71, Institute of Latin American Studies, University of Texas at Austin. Austin: University of Texas Press.

Trimberger, Ellen Kay. 1977. *Revolution from Above.* New Brunswick, N.J.: Transaction Books.

U.S. Office of Strategic Services, Research and Analysis Branch. 1945. *Political Parties and Personalities in Egypt.* R&A 2519. Washington, D.C., September 15.

U.S. Tariff Commission. 1937. *Chemical Nitrogen.* Report 114, second series. Washington, D.C.: Government Printing Office.

Vatikiotis, Paniyotis. [1969] 1991. *The History of Egypt.* Fourth edition. London: Weidenfeld and Nicolson.

Vilas, Carlos. 1986. *The Sandinista Revolution: National Liberation and Social Transformation in Central America.* New York: Monthly Review Press.

Vitalis, Robert. 1990. "On the Theory and Practice of Compradors: The Role of 'Abbud Pasha in the Egyptian Political Economy." *International Journal of Middle East Studies* 22, pp. 291–315.

————. 1994. "Business Conflict, Collaboration and Privilege in Interwar Egypt." In *State Power and Social Forces: Domination and Transformation in the Third World,* edited by Joel Migdal, Atul Kholi and Vivienne Shue. New York: Cambridge University Press.

Wallerstein, Immanuel. 1988. "The Bourgois(ie) as Concept and Reality." *New Left Review* 167, pp. 91–106.

Warburg, Gabriel. 1985. *Egypt and the Sudan: Studies in History and Politics.* London: Frank Cass.

Waterbury, John. 1979. *Hydropolitics of the Nile Valley.* Syracuse, N.Y.: Syracuse University Press.

————. 1983. *The Egypt of Nasser and Sadat: The Political Economy of Two Regimes.* Princeton, N.J.: Princeton University Press.

————. 1992. "The Heart of the Matter? Public Enterprise and the Adjustment Process." In *The Politics of Economic Adjustment: International Constraints, Distributive Conflicts, and the State,* edited by Stephan Haggard and Robert R. Kaufman. Princeton, N.J.: Princeton University Press.

Woolton, Frederick James (Lord). 1959. *Memoirs.* London: Cassell.

Wright, Arnold, and H. Cartwright, eds. 1909. *Twentieth Century Impressions of Egypt: Its History, People, Commerce, Industries and Resources.* London: Lloyds.

Zaalouk, Malak. 1989. *Power, Class and Foreign Capital in Egypt: The Rise of the New Bourgeoisie.* London: Zed Press.

Zeitlin, Maurice, and Richard Earl Ratcliff. 1988. *Landlords and Capitalists: The Dominant Class of Chile.* Princeton, N.J.: Princeton University Press.

Ziegler, Philip. 1988. *The Sixth Great Power: Barings, 1762–1929.* London: Collins.

Index

'Abbud, Muhammad Ahmad: and the American embassy, 178, 186, 192–93, 202, 212; appointed to Suez Canal Company, 50, 180; and Aswan project, 66, 68, 126–28, 137; and Bank Misr, 107, 122–24, 178; and Canal Zone crisis, 186–87, 249n20; depiction of, xii, 31, 51, 55, 137; and foreign capital, 53–54, 72, 135, 137, 146; and Hilali's resignation, 190–91; and the monarchy, 83, 85, 101, 122; and politics, 52, 83, 125; relations with military, 198–99, 212–14; renewed Wafd ties, 105, 119–21, 137, 178–79, 242n20; and the residency, 54, 79, 85–86, 101, 122, 125, 127; and Sidqi regime, 76–79; and Sirag al-Din, 159, 172; split with Sidqi, 78, 80; split with Wafd, 55, 71–72; and Suez factory, 135, 142, 148, 156, 180–81, 213–14; support for authoritarianism, 55, 72, 75, 85–86, 94; support for Tharwat, 54, 71; support for Zaghlul, 50, 52, 71

'Abbud group: expansion of, 55–56, 101, 125, 179–81; nationalization of, 211, 214; origins of, 30, 49–51; in transport sector, 78, 146. See also al-Kashaf; Khedival Mail Line; Mahir, Ahmad

'Abd al-Mut'al, Zaki, 159, 175–77
'Abd al-Nasir, Gamal. See Nasser, Gamal
'Abd al-Qaddus, 'Ihsan, 169
'Abd al-Wahhab, Ahmad: as finance minister, 91–92; ties to Misr group, 92–93
Abu al-Fath brothers (Husayn and Mahmud), 151, 172, 174, 209
'Afifi, Hafiz: and Misr group, 86, 108, 111, 131; opposition to 'Abbud, 81, 123–24; and post-fire governments, 187, 194
Ahmad, 'Abd al-'Aziz, 146–47, 157, 163
al-Akhbar group, 182. See also Amin brothers
El Alamein, 118
al-'Alayli, Yahya, 200
Alexandria: commercial activities in, 33, 36; harbor expansion, 82, 84
Alexandria Cotton Futures Market, 176–77
American capital: in Aswan project, 129–31, 135; British fears of, 90, 119, 125, 130, 137; in Egyptian development, 143, 204–5, 207, 212, 255n71; in Suez factory, 148, 201–2, 213–14
American Cyanamid Corporation, 90, 115, 129, 132
Amin brothers ('Ali and Mustafa): opposition to Wafd, 182, 184, 187
Anderson Clayton Company, 183, 200

Compositor: Maple-Vail Book Mfg. Group
Text: 10/13 Galliard
Display: Galliard